MUSIC IN THE COLLECTIVE EXPERIENCE IN SIXTEENTH-CENTURY MILAN

Music in the Collective Experience in Sixteenth-Century Milan

CHRISTINE SUZANNE GETZ
University of Iowa, USA

ASHGATE

Published by
Ashgate Publishing Limited
Gower House
Croft Road
Aldershot
Hants GU11 3HR
England

Ashgate Publishing Company
Suite 420
101 Cherry Street
Burlington, VT 05401-4405
USA

Ashgate website: http://www.ashgate.com

British Library Cataloguing in Publication Data
Getz, Christine Suzanne, 1957
    Music in the collective experience in sixteenth-century Milan
    1.Music—Italy—Milan—16th century—History and criticism 2.Milan
    (Italy)—Social life and customs—16th century
    I.Title
    780.9'4521'09031

Library of Congress Cataloging-in-Publication Data
Getz, Christine Suzanne, 1957-
  Music in the collective experience in sixteenth-century Milan / Christine Getz.
    p. cm.
  Includes bibliographical references (p.   ) and index.
  ISBN 0-7546-5121-5 (alk. paper)
  1. Music—Italy—Milan—16th century—History and criticism. 2. Milan (Italy)—
Social life and customs—16th century. I. Title.

  ML290.8.M4G47 2005
  780'.945'2109031—dc22

2005005941

ISBN-10: 0 7546 5121 5

Printed and bound in Great Britain by MPG Books Ltd. Bodmin, Cornwall.

Contents

List of Tables

List of Figures

List of Musical Examples

Preface

The fall of Milan in 1499 not only heralded the end of an era marked by dazzling artistic and musical display, but also stimulated a series of adjustments to the existing political and social structure of Milanese society. A new aristocracy of diplomats and merchants emerged amidst the old nobility, forcing a shift in the traditional power base that yielded a burgeoning patrician class of decidedly international character. When it arose from the ashes at the end of the sixteenth century, Milan had forged a modern civic identity largely free of the trappings of its medieval feudal heritage. This modern identity achieved artistic expression in every aspect of public life. Music, an art traditionally associated with the court and cathedral, came to be appropriated by the old nobility and the new aristocracy alike as a means of demonstrating social primacy and newly acquired wealth. Yet Milan's social metamorphosis was slow, and the artistic manifestations of it initially were controlled by those very institutions already established via the traditional medieval hierarchy. As these institutions reached out to embrace the expanding middle classes during the sixteenth century, however, they imbued the public with a social and cultural self-consciousness that solidified the city's blossoming new identity. Many collective bodies in sixteenth-century Italy were dominated by the local church and court, and Milanese society was not, in that respect, entirely unlike them. But as class mobility assumed greater significance in Milan and the size of the city expanded beyond its medieval borders, music-making became ever more closely associated with public life.

The collective experience in Renaissance Milan was perhaps most outwardly expressed in the city's ongoing urban renewal. In addition to the continued construction of its Gothic cathedral, Renaissance Milan saw the evolution of several monumental structures of differing character, including the Castello Sforzesco, the church of Santa Maria delle Grazie, and the church of Santa Maria presso San Celso. The city's new architectural splendors were interspersed among its numerous pre-existing medieval edifices, such as San Lorenzo, Sant'Eustorgio, and Santa Maria della Scala. Thus, sixteenth-century Milan was comprised of a series of divergent architectural spaces. These diverse spaces were intertwined by a web of canals, narrow streets, and wide avenues that converged at the Duomo, a central structure that epitomized the city's continuous spatial and social transformation through its own ongoing construction. With its novel structures and diverse urban spaces, sixteenth-century Milan offered an unlimited variety of public performance arenas. The city's political and ecclesiastical authorities used these dissimilar venues to great advantage, staging grand processions, worship services, entertainments, and entries aimed at the propagation of both church and state. Yet the private citizen utilized them as well, creating his own miniature spectacle in a visual and an aural imitation of the ecclesiastical and political panoply of the age.

Systems of musical patronage in sixteenth-century Milan were defined primarily by the shared governmental and ecclesiastical supervision of the city's principal urban institutions. As a result, music was conceived largely through its role in the theatrical, be it an entertainment at court, a ducal ceremonial at the chapel of Santa Maria della Scala, a state service in the cathedral, a Hapsburg entry on the city's streets, a dance in a local residence, or an aristocratic Vespers service sponsored by the noble confraternity at Santa Maria presso San Celso. Rather than competing with the state for public attention, the Milanese church assisted in the propagation of state aims while maintaining its own spiritual programs. Even with the advent of post-Tridentine reforms under Carlo Borromeo during the 1560s, Milanese ecclesiastical institutions, although increasingly devoted to the promotion of public piety, continued to serve the state and civic ceremonial. Conversely, the state provided ongoing financial and political support for many of the city's ecclesiastical institutions and spiritual programs through its intricate ducal benefice system and burgeoning confraternities.

Using both archival sources and extant printed books, this monograph examines the musical culture of sixteenth-century Milan via its life within the city's most influential social institutions. It examines the manner in which fifteenth-century courtly traditions were adapted to the public arena by considering the relationship of the *cappelle musicali* at the Duomo of Milan, the court of Milan, Santa Maria della Scala, and Santa Maria presso San Celso to the sixteenth-century institutions that housed them. In addition, it investigates the sixteenth-century musician's role as an actor and a functionary in the political, religious, and social spectacles produced by the Milanese church, state, and aristocracy within the city's diverse urban spaces. Furthermore, it establishes a context for the numerous motets, madrigals, and lute intabulations composed and printed in sixteenth-century Milan by examining their function within the urban milieu in which they were first performed. Finally, it musically documents Milan's transformation from a ducal state dominated by provincial traditions into a mercantile center of international acclaim.

The archival research for this project was generously supported by a 1993 NEH Summer Stipend, a 1993 Baylor University Research Grant, a 1998 Fulbright Junior Research Fellowship, a 1998 Baylor University Summer Sabbatical, and two Summer Fellowships (2001 and 2004) from International Programs at the University of Iowa. In addition, the Obermann Center for Advanced Studies supplied much appreciated office space, computer technology, and research assistance during the 2000-2001 academic year, and the School of Music at the University of Iowa kindly provided a Research Assistant for the final work on the manuscript. I am especially grateful to the archivists and staff of the Archivio di Stato di Milano, the Archivio di Stato di Parma, the Biblioteca Trivulziana ed Archivio Civico di Milano, the Biblioteca Ambrosiana, the Archivio Storico Diocesano Milano, the Biblioteca Nazionale Braidense, the Biblioteca del Conservatorio Giuseppe Verdi, and the Raccolta Bertorelli, without whom this project could not have been completed. I am equally indebted to Roberto Fighetti at the Archivio della Veneranda Fabbrica del Duomo di Milano and Monsignor Bernardo Bosatra of the Archivio Storico Diocesano Milano for their generous assistance in making extensive documentary material available for my use. I also wish to thank Robert Kendrick and James Haar, who read preliminary drafts of several chapters and made thought-provoking suggestions that affected the overall trajectory of the book, Rob Ketterer, who helped me to sort out several problematic Latin phrases, Francesco dalla Vecchia, who edited the Italian translations, and Leofranc Holford-Strevens, who greatly improved several of my Latin translations. Last, but certainly not least, I wish to acknowledge the painstaking work of my Research Assistant, Fred Kiser, who corrected the musical examples and formatted the final manuscript.

Chapter 1

Forging a Modern Civic Identity: Music for the Battle of Pavia

Milan after the Fall of Ludovico il Moro

Following the fall of Ludovico Sforza in 1499, jurisdiction over the Duchy of Milan passed to Louis XII of France. For the next thirty years, Milan, formerly the most influential northern city of the Italian peninsula, remained in a state of constant political disarray. Besieged by the French and coveted by the Hapsburg empire, Milan was quickly reduced to the ignominious role of a chief pawn in continental negotiations. Although the recapture of the city and the subsequent restoration of the Sforza under Ludovico's son Massimiliano I in 1512 promised the reinstatement of an autonomous government, the respite from foreign interference was cut short by another incursion of the French. In 1515 the North Italian forces clashed with Louis XII of France at Marignano and suffered a disastrous defeat. With the fall of Marignano, the French again penetrated Milan's porous borders, and the dispirited duchy resigned itself to continued occupation. On 22 April 1521, however, Francis I of France declared war on Emperor Charles V of Spain and invaded Navarre, thus drawing Spain into the conflict. The invasion of Navarre may have been Francis I's greatest strategical error, for in challenging the Hapsburg crown he may well have hastened the loss of the Italian city-states then under his control, which included not only Milan, but also Naples and Sicily.[1]

Charles V's interest in an Italian campaign was stimulated by the political philosophy of his Grand Chancellor Mercurino Gattinara, who argued that expulsion of the French from Italy would facilitate an alliance with the papacy, thus ultimately insuring Spanish control over much of Europe. Because Milan was a chief communications link between Spain and other territories of the Empire and was easily accessed via the port of Genoa, it quickly became viewed as the lynchpin of Gattinara's Italian plan. In November 1521, Charles, confident that a Milan-centered strategy was sound, drove the French from the city, and claimed the Duchy of Milan as a vassal state of the Spanish Empire.[2] Thereafter, he permitted Francesco II Sforza, the second son of Ludovico il Moro, to assume the title of Duke of Milan. Yet initially the young Duke's title was only nominal. Moreover, the Duchy itself, which boasted as many French sympathizers as it did Spanish ones, was fraught with political instability and perched on the brink of financial ruin. As a result, Francesco II's relationship with Charles V, who had come to Milan's aid with the intent of eventually incorporating the Duchy into his own dominion, was riddled with paranoia and mistrust on all sides. The continuous political and financial discord may well have aided in preserving the city's autonomy during its initial incorporation into the Hapsburg Empire, for common sense dictated that Francesco II be granted full jurisdiction in order that Charles maintain his tenuous foothold.

Although Francesco II Sforza was not formally invested by Charles V as Duke of Milan until 1529, the Duchy actually was promised him at the conclusion of the Peace of Noyon in 1516. The accord specified, however, that Francesco's succession be effected only after the city had been properly stabilized. Thus, the successful Spanish initiative of 1521 marked only the first step of the restoration process. The real turning point in Francesco's fortunes occurred on 27 April 1522, when he, aided by Prospero Colonna, Ferdinand d'Avalos (the Marchese di Pescara), and Georg von Frundesburg, led Imperial, Italian, and Swiss mercenary troops to victory at Bicocca. The Milanese had found a champion of sorts in the young Francesco who, despite his legislative inexperience, demonstrated the persistence and precocity long associated with his father. His impending reinstatement promised a reprieve from the constant turmoil imposed by the turning kaleidoscope of European alliances.

Even after the victory at Bicocca, however, Milanese enthusiasm for its young duke remained somewhat subdued because heavy taxes were continually levied in order to replenish the coffers of the Imperial war machine. Moreover, the French, still encamped along the Ticino river, posed a constant threat to the city's stability. With the election of Charles V's' former tutor Pope Adrian VI in January 1522, a papal alliance that also included Venice and England was cemented, and a decisive defeat of the French seemed imminent. Unfortunately, however, Adrian VI passed on before the allies were able to act. Adrian's successor Clement VII proved reluctant to ally himself with either Charles V or Francis I, and equivocated to such a degree that the French had again entrenched themselves in Milanese territories by the fall of 1524. Indeed, Charles' Italian campaign seemed doomed to failure, for Venice and the papacy realigned themselves with France soon thereafter.

The extant documentary evidence indicates that the Milanese populace was fairly evenly divided by the conflict. While some citizens enthusiastically awaited liberation by the Spanish, others preferred to deal with French. According to the Milanese merchant Gianmarco Burigozzi, frequent rallies were held in the Piazza del Duomo between 1522 and 1524 by anti-French demonstrators who hoped to incite the lethargic populace against the French. As can be seen from his description of an altercation that occurred between a well-known anti-French protestor and the members of the Duomo choir, however, these demonstrations were not always viewed favorably by Milanese citizens. The incident in question was provoked by a political sermon given by a friar who frequently spoke out against the French during demonstrations, ceremonies, and other public events held at the Duomo:

> And it happened that one Sunday during the Advent of 1523 the Ordinaries of the Duomo were waiting for this Friar of San Marco della Barbossa to finish his sermon so that they might celebrate high mass, and he, lacking respect for his superiors, made it very long. For this reason, the clergy, seeing that the friar was without respect,

took its place in the choir and began singing the mass at the high altar. And the friar, seeing that the priest had begun to sing the Introit of the mass, took leave of the pulpit in fury. And a few of his followers who were in the audience began to condemn the ordinaries and other sacerdotes loudly, shouting a thousand curses. And there was the group of sacerdotes at the altar. But when they realized that these admirers were angry beyond restraint and extremely vociferous in their protestations, the ordinaries and sacerdotes fled from the choir in great fear. They went into the sacristy with difficulty. I will not speak to you of the uproar that took place in this blessed church. And this friar returned to the pulpit, comforting his satellites and sissies, who thought him blessed because he was able to speak badly of these venerable sacerdotes, our patriots. And when he was ready, he finished. And he made a point of his importance by speaking as long as he wished, so that he would be regarded as an admirable man. Because they were patriots and did not wish to neglect their duties, these ordinaries and sacerdotes sang the mass after the confusion had ceased, praying to God for their health and the health of the country.[3]

Despite the shifting sympathies, the political instability, and the heavy tax burdens, however, a sense of relief enveloped the city following the Imperial victories of 1522 and 1523. Charles, seizing the moment to engender Milanese favor, dispatched a representative to a victory mass held in the Duomo during January 1524:

At the close of December 1523, the Viceroy arrived in this city of Milan in the name of the Emperor. And on the first day of the year 1524, he went to a mass in the Duomo. There were a number of important dignitaries in his company, the most important of which was the Ambassador of Venice, who was the Duke of Urbino.[4]

Unfortunately, however, any lingering civic euphoria over the recent turn of events was eclipsed by one of the most devastating plagues that the city had ever experienced. The plague's effects can be seen in the rosters of the cathedral choir for the years 1523 through 1525, which demonstrate that approximately one-third of the adult membership was replaced during the year 1524.[5] In fact, Gianmarco Burigozzi reports that so many of the Duomo personnel fell ill that by July 1524 'there were usually neither ordinaries nor officials, but rather two or three priests who sang as well as they were able'[6] conducting the daily services. The ravages of the plague were turned to an advantage by the French army, and by September 1524 Francesco II was forced to retreat from Milan to Pizzighettone. However, the succeeding Imperial initiative yielded more lasting results. On 24 February 1525 the Milanese, aided by the Imperial forces of Charles V, soundly defeated the French army at Pavia and captured Francis I, thus effecting the surrender of the French forces then occupying much of the Italian peninsula. Francis I subsequently offered Carlo V his Italian territories, Burgundy, and Flanders in exchange for freedom. For Francesco II Sforza, the battle at Pavia proved to be the final hurdle in acquiring control of the Duchy. At the insistence of Clement VII, the Duchy of Milan was restored to the Sforza, and the young Duke triumphantly entered the embattled city.

Music for the Battle at Pavia

Following the victory at Pavia in 1525, Francesco II's first task as prospective Duke was to infuse the city with a cohesive civic identity. This was no simple endeavor, for the Sforza dynasty had not been overwhelmingly popular among those aristocratic families who, allied with the French, continued to thrive financially during the years of occupation. The tension which marked relations between the Sforza and the established nobility had hastened the financial and political fracture of the state under il Moro. Moreover, it continued to manifest itself in the widespread acceptance of foreign domination as a necessary means of political and financial survival. Although the general malaise of Milan's upwardly mobile classes with regard to local sovereignty gradually effected the formation of a cohesive governing structure, it had the immediate potential to diffuse Francesco II's power base.[7] Thus, Francesco was forced to embrace Milan's burgeoning artisan classes, setting before them a convincing portrait of princely authority. To that end, he relied greatly upon musical and visual effects for the creation of his ducal image. This is evident as early as the victory at Bicocca in 1522, which was marked by an impromptu entrance in the style of a grand condottiere that was reminiscent of his grandfather Francesco I. Charles V's historian Alfonso Ulloa described Francesco's entry as follows:

> ... and riding by night through the treacherous streets, he arrived in Milan, where he was received with great acclamation by all. The infantry of archibugeri fired formal salutes in celebration, and he was proclaimed him Prince and Duke by all of the soldiers and captains.[8]

Bugati's more detailed description echoes Ulloa's account:

> ... how all the people cheered during the entry of Francesco Sforza into Milan. And they accepted him as Duke with many honors even though he arrived at night with 6,000 Germans that he led from Trent by way of Verona and Mantova. And he passed the Pò at Piacenza and the Pavese accompanied by the Duke of Mantova with 300 horses in the name of the church that same year.[9]

Francesco II Sforza's visceral acuity in stylizing his ducal image after that of his grandfather was a direct reflection of his early diplomatic training. The youngest son of Ludovico il Moro and Beatrice D'Este, Francesco spent approximately nineteen of the first twenty-six years of his life in exile at the glittering Imperial court of Maximilian I. There he was exposed to the continent's most influential philosophical, artistic, and musical talent. Because Maximilian essentially had inherited the musical chapels of Burgundy through his first marriage to Mary of Burgundy in 1477 and those of the Tyrol from Archduke Sigismund in 1490, he had assembled an impressive array of well-known vocal and instrumental musicians by the 1490s. Many of these musicians, who included such luminaries as Paul Hofhaimer, Ludvig Senfl, Heinrich Isaac, Pierre de la Rue, and possibly even Josquin des Prez, accompanied him as he traveled from one location to another. Maximilian's spouse Bianca Maria Sforza (d.1510), accustomed to the elaborate musical forces that had been supported by her father Galeazzo Maria in Milan, encouraged and supervised the establishment of an Imperial Hofkapelle in the cathedral at Halle near Innsbruck, which she made her permanent home in 1497. Upon Vienna's designation as the new capital city of the Empire in 1496, moreover, Maximilian sent a group of musicians to Vienna, where the Hofkappelle was not only enlarged and remodeled, but also expanded to include a choir school.[10] Francesco evidently inherited a love for secular instrumental music, a preference for plainchant and organ alternatim settings in sacred worship, and a chapel management style modeled upon that commonly used by the Burgundians from Maximilian and Bianca Maria, and, as will be discussed below, these aspects of his Imperial experience were incorporated into the Milanese traditions of his parents through the establishment of an instrumental ensemble at the Milanese court and two new ducal cappelle at Sant'Ambrogio in Vigevano (1530) and Santa Maria della Scala in Milan (1531).

When the Duchy of Milan was briefly returned to Francesco's older brother Massimiliano Sforza (1493-1530) through the intervention of the Swiss in 1512, Francesco traveled to Italy to serve the new Sforza regime. During the brief three-year restoration that followed, Francesco spent part of his time in Rome as an emissary of the Milanese court. The letters that he sent to his brother from Rome, which primarily report on official issues of state, occasionally reveal the continued fascination with music and ceremony that had developed during his extended stay at the Imperial court. For example, in a dispatch dated 27 October 1513 Francesco noted that he and his party entered Rome earlier that day 'with the greatest triumph, jubilation, and celebration'[11] accompanied by the papal legate Cardinal de Grassis, the guard, and various important citizens 'to the sound of music, cheers of joyful approval, and artillery fire.'[12] Francesco's passing comments further indicate that he was frequently in attendance at performances of the papal choir and papal court musicians, at least one of which was given at his own residence in Rome:

> The Holy Father demonstrated that he had received charming news, and afterwards the Cardinals, Prelates, and other individuals, of which there are many very affectionate towards your Excellency and your state. And this evening in many locations of this city great fireworks displays accompanied by artillery fire and loud proclamations were held in honor of your Excellency with such universal joy of the inhabitants and foreigners that never again will something so joyful and festive as this be witnessed. And the Swiss Guard of His Holiness, along with all of his musicians and many other individuals remained for the greater part of the night to honor my lodgings in the chancery.[13]

Francesco's recognition that the collective spirit might be captured through visual and aural stimuli is never more evident than in the art and literature emanating from the monumental victory at Pavia. Four extant musical compositions are closely associated with the victory, and were likely commissioned with celebration and frequent commemoration of the event specifically in mind. One of these, *La bataglia tagliana*, has received extensive attention in modern scholarly sources, perhaps because it was reprinted and intabulated frequently during the sixteenth century. A three-section villotta for four voices that was composed by the Duomo's recently elected maestro di cappella Hermann Matthias Werrecore, *La bataglia tagliana* functions as an actual chronicle of the1525 battle. In fact, the preface to a 1544 German publication of the work entitled 'Die Schlacht vor Pavia' notes that the composer claimed to have been present on the battlefield.[14] However, certain extant copies of Werrecore's *La bataglia tagliana* are actually revisions of an earlier piece of the same title describing the Italian victory at Bicocca in 1522.[15] Recent studies demonstrate, in fact, that two different versions of the work circulated during the sixteenth century. The first version, which contains a text making direct references to events surrounding the Battle of Bicocca, exists in three manuscript sources and the aforementioned German print from 1544. The second, which features emendations rendering the text appropriate to the Battle of Pavia, is found in the editions of Gardane and Scotto printed between 1549 and 1552.[16] If, therefore, Werrecore's claims were not a mere marketing ploy, it seems likely that he actually witnessed the Battle of Bicocca, rather than the Battle of Pavia. Recognizing the comparatively greater significance of the latter battle to both Milanese history and the collective cultural memory, Werrecore later recast his account of the Battle of Bicocca for the victory at Pavia.

Werrecore's aural re-enactment of the battle is complemented by numerous tapestries, paintings, and woodcuts that were also commissioned in commemoration of the victory at Pavia. The most famous of these is a series of Flemish tapestries designed by Pietro de Pannemaker of the house of Van Orley for Alfonso d'Avalos, Marchese del Vasto, who participated in the battle as a general in the Italian forces. The tapestries, which have been dated 1531, sequentially record the important events of the battle, including the capture and surrender of Francis I.[17] Woodcuts of the battle also abound. Among the best known are the woodcut by Jorg Breü the Elder[18] and an anonymous woodcut housed in the Museo Civico in Pavia. The woodcuts appear to depend upon earlier fifteenth or sixteenth-century models featuring battle scenes, including those dedicated to the Battle of Marignano, for they are characterized by uncannily similar depictions of the battle in full swing. However, written descriptions of the battle are also known to have circulated,[19] so a common textual source may account, in part, for the striking similarities among the woodcuts.

Like the woodcuts, Werrecore's *La bataglia* depends upon a number of earlier works that describe military battles. For example, its modal orientation, frequent shifts in mensuration, and division into three parts suggests a familiarity with Heinrich Isaac's *A la battaglia*. However, Werrecore's villotta is modeled primarily upon Clement Jannequin's famous *La Guerre*, a programmatic chanson composed in honor of the French victory at Marignano in 1515 and printed by Attaingnant in 1528.[20] Jannequin's battle piece was evidently well known in Italian musical circles, for in the preface to the 1549 publication of Werrecore's *La bataglia*, Gardane mentions having heard it performed with a group of French chansons sung by Messer Sebastiano and company at the home of Alessandro Zamberti.[21] In fact, Werrecore's choice of mode and shifts of mensuration have as much in common with Jannequin's chanson as they do with Isaac's instrumental piece. Further, Werrecore borrowed motivic, harmonic, and textural aspects of Jannequin's chanson, but rearranged the order in which these materials are presented (Example 1.1).

Example 1.1 Werrecore, *La bataglia tagliana*, measures 1-25

The motivic materials of both Jannequin's chanson and Werrecore's villotta were partially derived from well-known soldiers' songs,[22] so a familiarity with these songs may have influenced Werrecore's selection of the borrowed material. Nonetheless, Werrecore's *La bataglia* is a textual paraphrase of Jannequin's chanson, particularly with respect to onomatopoeic devices. In addition, however, Werrecore illustrated the various national origins of the Imperial forces through mixed language and dialect. The polytextuality of Werrecore's villotta, in fact, parallels the careful pictorial detail found in the commemorative woodcuts, which sometimes even include written labels for each armed division present. The two-fold purpose of Werrecore's piece, consequently, is clear. First, it functions as an aural depiction of the battle that rivals the contemporary pictorial representations. Secondly, it provides an Italian musical response to Jannequin's celebratory piece. This musical response clearly indicates that the Italians viewed the victory at Pavia as a direct retaliation for the defeat they had suffered at the hands of the French at Marignano only ten years before.

Several professional issues may have provided the impulse for Werrecore's original composition, as well as its revision following the victory at Pavia. If Werrecore did witness the Battle of Bicocca, then he must have been working in the city prior to his appointment as maestro di cappella at the Cathedral of Milan on 3 July 1522. At the time of the appointment itself, Werrecore, indeed, was living in Milan, as both the cathedral and the state records consistently identify him as the son of one Elegio and resident of Milan.[23] However, he appears to have been relatively unknown in musical circles, and, as a result, it is not clear when he arrived in the city. A number of biographers have attempted to determine the composer's birthplace by exploring the etymology of his surname, and have proposed Sardinia, the Valle d'Aosta, Flanders, and Bohemia as possibilities.[24] Yet he is identified in numerous Milanese archival sources as 'Matthias fiammingo' and 'Matthias flandrensis,' thus suggesting that he hailed from Flanders. Since Werrecore's name has not yet surfaced in any Milanese documents prior to his appointment at the Duomo, it is very possible that he accompanied either Massimiliano or Francesco II to Milan from the court of

Maximilian I sometime between 1512 and 1521. Perhaps he was even dependent upon Francesco II's patronage and thus obligated to provide a commemorative work following the victory at Bicocca. In fact approximately two years after the victory at Bicocca, Werrecore was awarded a large ducal benefice at St. Michele of Busto in Gallerate via the patronage of the Sforza family.[25] In any case, the original version of *La bataglia tagliana* may well have earned him the attention necessary to assist in securing either the position at the Cathedral in 1522 or the benefice in 1524, if not both. The revised version celebrating the victory at Pavia probably arose from the expectation that the highest ranking musician in the city would of necessity provide a work to commemorate such a momentous occasion, particularly if that musician was himself a Milanese resident and held a benefice sponsored by the Sforza family.

Although Werrecore's *La bataglia tagliana* was originally composed in honor of the victory at Bicocca in 1522, it is highly unlikely that the work was heard during the celebration of that event, since the sources reporting on the triumphal entry of Francesco II following the victory at Bicocca indicate that the celebrations were impromptu. Nonetheless, Werrecore's villotta is the most occasionally flexible of the four occasional works associated with Francesco II's restoration. As a general chronicle of a decisive Italian and Imperial victory, it might have been performed as the banquet entertainment during any number of secular events held at the Sforza court during the succeeding years, including Charles V and Philip II's triumphal progressions through Milan in 1533, 1541, and 1548.

Two motets by Adrian Willaert are also associated with the victory at Pavia. The first of them, *Victor io salve/Quis curare neget*, features a long-note cantus firmus on the text 'Hail to the Sforza, the greatest Duke and Ruler.'[26] It makes specific references to the victory over the French at Pavia and the capture of the French monarch. The second, *Inclite Sfortiadum princeps*, is organized around a similarly derived cantus firmus on the text 'Long live the fortunate Duke Francesco Sforza.'[27] It also mentions the victory at Pavia, but celebrates the resulting restoration of the Duchy of Milan to the Sforza. The motets were first published by Scotto in 1539 as numbers 15 and 18 of Willaert's first book of five-voice motets.[28] Yet they appear to have originally functioned as a pair, since both not only are dedicated to Francesco II Sforza, but also are modeled upon Josquin's *Missa Hercules Dux Ferrariae*. Like the *Missa Hercules Dux Ferrariae*, both motets feature dedicatory cantus firmi derived through *soggetto cavato* technique. These cantus firmi follow the design of the *soggetti* used in the *Missa Hercules Dux Ferrariae* in that they are presented in uniform long notes in alternating natural hexachord and hard hexachord positions (Example 1.2a, b). Further, the successive statements of the cantus firmi, like those of the *Missa Hercules Dux Ferrariae*, are marked off by periods of rest rhythmically equal in length to the cantus firmi themselves. Finally, the cantus firmi of both motets are treated to uniform proportional diminution similar to that found in the Credo and Sanctus of the *Missa Hercules Dux Ferrariae*.

Josquin's *Missa Hercules Dux Ferrariae* continued to be of symbolic significance in Ferrara, where Willaert was employed from between 1514 and 1527,[29] long after Ercole's death in 1505. A number of other works utilizing similar *soggetto cavato* techniques were composed during the first half of the century by individuals connected to the Ferrarese court, including Cipriano da Rore and Lupus. Although they are related by their common debt to the Missa *Hercules Dux Ferrariae*, most of them depart more radically from the model than do Willaert's motets. Milanese singers were certainly equally familiar with the mass,

Example 1.2a Cantus firmus of *Victor io salve/Quis curare neget*

Example 1.2b Cantus firmus of *Inclite Sfortiadum princes*

as three of its movements are copied in the third of the four Milan Choirbooks (or *Gaffurius Codices*) belonging to the Duomo.[30] The close acquaintance with the *Hercules* mass shared by Ferrarese and Milanese audiences, in fact, may account for its use as a model for Willaert's motets.

Through their strict adherence to the structural perimeters of the *Hercules* model, the Willaert motets acknowledge Francesco II's Este heritage via his mother Beatrice d'Este. Moreover, they allude to the historical parallel between Francesco II's restoration and his grandfather's ascendancy following the Venetian wars. The role of the *Missa Hercules Dux Ferrariae* in underscoring the link between the two regimes is, in fact, indirectly suggested by Lewis Lockwood, who noted that the only place in the mass in which material from the cantus firmus appears simultaneously in another voice occurs in the Gloria on the text 'et in terra,' at which point the fragment of the cantus firmus spelling the word 'Ferrariae' appears in the cantus and altus voices. Lockwood interprets this as a special reference to Ercole I, the Ferrarese prince 'on earth' ('et in terra') and man among men to whom the mass is dedicated. Even in Lockwood's own transcription, however, the fragment of the cantus firmus that musically spells the word 'Ferrariae' actually falls on the text 'and on earth peace.'[31] The coupling of the musical motive 'Ferrariae' with the text 'and on earth peace,' likely refers to the peace with Venice negotiated by Ercole I in 1484. Ercole's treaty with Venice effected the restoration of many Ferrarese civic institutions that had been closed or suspended during the Venetian wars. Like the mass upon which they are based, Willaert's motets celebrate the restoration of civic continuity via the intercession of an Este. In the case of the motets, however, Francesco II replaces Ercole I as the 'prince on earth' to whom civic gratitude is owed.

Willaert's contributions to the canon of works commemorating the victory at Pavia remain somewhat puzzling from the standpoint of his relationship with Francesco II. Between 1525 and 1527 Willaert was in the service of Ippolito II d'Este, Archbishop of Milan.[32] However, the correspondence surviving in the Milanese archives from the 1520s and early 1530s not only confirms that Ippolito spent little to no time in Milan, but also reveals that affairs between Francesco II and Ippolito II were somewhat strained. Unless Willaert acted on his own in writing the two motets for Francesco II, their existence is likely owed to Ippolito II's concern over the eroding diplomatic relations between his native Ferrara and Milan, the seat of his episcopate.

Very little correspondence between Milan and Ferrara survives in the Milanese archives for the years 1520-1525. After 1525, as might be expected, the diplomatic exchanges appear to have become more frequent. The first hint of underlying discord is found in a rather cryptic letter written by Ippolito II from Ferrara to his cousin Francesco II in Milan on 4 November 1526:

> My most renowned and excellent Sir: My illustrious father [is] sending the famous ambassador Marco di Pij to your Excellency. I have asked him to convey my respects to you and remind you that I will persevere in your service as I am supposed to do. [I have also asked] him to say a few words on my behalf. And that is why I ask that you lend credence to that which he will explain in my name. And I entrust myself to your kind mercy. From Ferrara on the Fourth of November, 1526. From your most illustrious and excellent servant Ippolito d'Este.[33]

Some of the tension in diplomatic relations between the two courts may have resulted from the Estense's well-known reputation as Francophiles, but two other issues of contention emerge through further study of the archival documentation. First, Francesco II was irritated with Ippolito II because he had continually avoided taking residence Milan, choosing instead to remain in Ferrara for financial reasons despite Francesco's urging. The difficulty is discussed in passing throughout the diplomatic correspondence from the years 1531-1532, at which time Ippolito promised to make a trip to Milan as soon as is possible. Francesco, then occupied with the impending expansion of the ducal chapel at Santa Maria della Scala through the addition of musical benefices, likely was eager to engage Ippolito's ecclesiastical influence and expertise in expediting the matter. Nonetheless, Ippolito's father, Duke Alfonso I d'Este, continually discouraged discussion of the trip by remarking that it would be too costly. Although a letter dated 18 June 1566 from Ippolito II to Cardinal Carlo Borromeo implies that he never set foot in the Duomo of Milan during his tenure as archbishop,[34] other documentary evidence suggests that either Ippolito or one of his agents traveled to Milan in August 1532 for the official installation of the new benefices at the ducal chapel of Santa Maria della Scala.[35] Further, it indicates that Ippolito II hosted Christina of Denmark, Francesco II's new consort, in Ferrara during late 1534 at Francesco's expense. Apparently, the financial excuses proffered by the Estense eventually wore Francesco II down, for Christina's trip was arranged shortly after they had again refused him a visit to Milan, claiming, as usual, that the expenses would be too great a burden. In a letter of 8 December 1534, Ippolito II thanked Francesco II for sponsoring Christina's visit, making the usual promises to serve Francesco as faithfully as possible.[36]

Perhaps more significant than the postponed visits of Ippolito II was the Ferrarese expectation that Francesco II award Ippolito the episcopate at Modena, a benefice which was temporarily under Sforza control. Francesco II apparently had refused the request because the benefice was already occupied, but the Estense pressed the matter further, arguing that the current Bishop of Modena no longer actually resided on the property. There is extensive correspondence regarding this matter from the year 1531, at which time the impasse was finally broken. However, it is clear that by June 1531 Francesco was already weary of hearing about the matter and, further, that Ippolito was concerned by the furor that had erupted over it.[37]   Although Francesco II considered the issue closed, the Estense continually attempted to reopen negotiations. Thus, Ippolito's concern over Francesco's potential annoyance was well founded, and he was soon given the opportunity to assuage any ill feelings between the two courts. Upon Francesco II's express request, Ippolito undertook the transfer of the Convent of San Vincenzo from his episcopal authority.[38]   On 17 June 1531 Ferrante Gargano, Francesco's ambassador to Ferrara, sent a diplomatic brief communicating Ippolito's willingness to expedite the transfer. As a further demonstration of affection, he enclosed several songs by Jhan, maestro di cappella at the court of Ferrara:

> Finally, he wrote me that I send Your Excellency certain songs that were sent to me by Maistre Jhan, which were forgotten by the last messenger, and these I enclose for Your Excellency at his request.[39]

Arriving as they did with the update on the transfer, the songs promised to placate Francesco by appealing to his appetite for the sort of musical entertainment that he had witnessed in Austria and Rome. On 26 June 1531 Francesco responded, gratefully acknowledging Ippolito's efforts on behalf of the transfer of the authority of San Vincenzo. In the course of his reply, he also mentioned receiving the songs.[40]   In addition, he acknowledged the gift of songs more fully in a brief sent to Ambassador Gargano two days later:

> The songs that you have sent with the information in this letter were most graceful and we convey to you that you must persevere in keeping us advised . . .[41]

On 2 July 1531 Ambassador Gargano reported that no further progress had been made on the transfer of San Vincenzo, and noted that the Estense were still pressing the matter of the episcopate at Modena:

> . . .I have also spoken to the Most Reverend Archbishop regarding the situation of the venerable sisters of Santo Vincenzo, in order to have the instrument of agreement of His Most Reverend Lordship. He responded that he has still not received an answer from his agents in Milan, and that as soon as it arrives he will let me know.
> I informed His Most Reverend Lordship that I know that your Excellency is not able to serve His Lordship in the issue of the Episcopate of Modena, given that Morono will not surrender the title, and that your Excellency is resolute in not interfering in such a disagreement.[42]

Despite Francesco II's apparent resolve regarding the Episcopate, the Estense gained the upper hand. After the city of Modena was restored to Ferrara in September 1531, the Duke and Duchess of Ferrara pressured the current Bishop of Modena to resign his post.[43]   In order to protect his own appointment, the Bishop finally agreed to allow the Duke of Ferrara to appoint Ippolito as his assistant, and proposed a stipend of 250 lire per year.[44] Official negotiations regarding the benefice were concluded in February 1532.[45] In the end, Ippolito was appointed vicar of Modena, with a salary of 400 lire.[46] Nevertheless, Ippolito undoubtedly found himself in a precarious position over this matter, particularly given his reluctance to appear in Milan despite his responsibility to the city as its archbishop. He clearly was concerned by the tension in Milanese–Ferrarese relations felt between 1526 and 1532, and continually sought to placate Francesco II. Since he offered Francesco II the songs of Maistre Jhan as a conciliatory gesture during the final negotiations over the episcopate at Modena in 1531, it is likely that he asked Willaert to honor Francesco II with two motets when the disagreements between the two families first escalated around 1526.

There is no archival documentation that explicitly confirms such a theory, and, as a result, the possibility that Willaert was acting alone cannot be ruled out. The same theory might also be postulated for Maistre Jahn. What then might have attracted Ferrarese composers, and in particular Willaert, to Milan? First, he may have been interested in the position of maestro di cappella at the Duomo of Milan. By 1532 Matthias Werrecore, the current maestro di cappella, had alienated so many of the singers that the Milan cathedral chapter had become concerned about his inability to retain control over them. The first suggestion of discord is found in the archival sources as early as 1525, at which time Werrecore was called in front of the chapter to respond to unspecified accusations that had been leveled against him. No documentation outlining the particulars of the meeting has been discovered, but it is clear that the situation worsened between 1525 and 1532. In fact, Werrecore appears to have lost all control over the choir by early 1532. On 18 January 1532, he was required to explain his administrative objectives in a formal inquiry before the chapter officers, and was further directed to do the same for the singers in a separately scheduled meeting. The meetings culminated in a major reorganization of the cappella musicale that included the enactment of a number of rules governing the behavior of the singers.[47] Since a number of Milanese trumpeters traveled frequently from Milan to Ferrara with wartime communiqués and diplomatic documents during the 1520s,[48] Willaert had ample sources from which to hear about the incidents. Thus, he may well have hoped to be appointed in Werrecore's place. Secondly, Willaert may have desired an appointment at one of the ducal chapels found in the other major churches of Milan and its vicinity, including Santa Maria della Scala, Santa Maria presso San Celso, and Sant'Ambrogio in Vigevano. As will be seen below, the documentation indicates that the founding, renovation and expansion of some of these chapels was a chief concern during the early days of Francesco II's tenure. Finally, Willaert may have hoped to secure one of the other numerous benefices sponsored by the Sforza family. Since at least three Milanese singers were awarded such benefices between the years 1523 and 1527,[49] Willaert's candidacy was not out of the realm of possibility, given both his emerging reputation as a composer and his membership in Archbishop Ippolito's chapel. It, however, is not at all clear that Willaert was personally acquainted with Francesco II Sforza. The two may have met as early as 1518, at which time the composer accompanied Ippolito I d'Este to Krakow for the wedding of Bona Sforza and Sigismund I of Poland.[50] The records indicate that Bona's retinue alone included 287 Italians, thus strengthening the likelihood of Francesco's presence at the event as well.[51] Yet no existing documentation confirms a meeting between the two.

Although the Willaert motets, like Werrecore's villotta, rely upon modeling procedures, their reception among sixteenth-century audiences followed an entirely different path. *La bataglia taliana* allowed for the collective appreciation of coded musical symbols on multiple levels through its quotation of easily recognized soldier songs, as well as its more specialized references to works preserved in the written repertoire, including, of course, Jannequin's *La guerre*. Moreover, the performance of *La bataglia tagliana*, with its mixed languages and dialects and its onomatopoeic devices, posed an enticing challenge to amateur musicians and academy members who engaged regularly with the Italian madrigal. Thus, the work's success was not entirely dependent upon the recognition of references to pre-existing literature. The musical message of *Victor io salve/Quis curare neget* and *Inclite Sfortiadum princeps* required decoding by an audience thoroughly familiar with the organization and structure of the *Missa Hercules Dux Ferrariae*. Such a community of readers would have been, by definition, much smaller, for it would have comprised professionals and collectors who grasped the technical and historical context in which the motets were conceived. It, consequently, is not surprising that while *La bataglia tagliana* was reprinted numerous times during the sixteenth century, *Victor io salve/Quis curare neget* and *Inclite Sfortiadum princeps* survive in only two printed sources, both of which are dedicated to Willaert's five-voice motets.

Perhaps the most enigmatic of the four pieces associated with the victory at Pavia is the eight-voice motet *Vocem iocunditatis/Ecce Ducem nostrum*. The text of the motet is a gloss of the Roman introit for the fifth Sunday after Easter, which refers to the liberation of Israel, as well as of Psalms 46, 150, and 91.[52] In addition, the motet features a canonic cantus firmus on the text 'Francesco Sforza, Duke of Milan, will multiply just as the cedar. Rejoice Italy.'[53] The cantus firmus itself appears to be derived from a popular song, though the melody remains unidentified to date. It is stated in canon at the fifth between the Tenor 2 and Contratenor 2 voices. The two supporting bass voices, which feature close imitations at the unison and fifth, provide the added aural impression of moving in canon as well. Similar imitative entries in the other non-canonic voices are closely spaced, thus contributing to the overall effect of a sound mass driven by incessant imitation (Example 1.3). Here the nation of Israel, delivered by the Lord from the hands of its enemies, functions as a temporary impresa for the rejoicing Milanese. Within this allegorical context, Francesco II is heralded as the Messianic cedar that is planted 'in the mountain of the height of Israel.'[54]

Vocem iocunditatis/Ecce Ducem nostrum is found in two extant German sources, namely the manuscript *München, Bayerische Staatsbibliothek* 1536, where it is attributed to Gregor Peschin, and the print *Thesaurus musicus continens . . . tomo primi* (RISM 1564[1]), where it stands without attribution. No direct connection between Gregor Peschin and the city of Milan currently can be documented, and, consequently, a number of scholars have suggested that the work may have been composed by Hermann Matthias Werrecore.[55] Werrecore, who, as noted above, served at the Duomo of Milan at the time of the victory and during subsequent restoration of the Sforza, is represented with at least nine motets in the *Thesaurus musicus* series, while Peschin is not known to have contributed to the series at all.

Moreover, an attribution to Werrecore is arguable upon stylistic grounds. The canonic cantus firmi and dense texture that distinguish *Vocem iocunditatis* are characteristic of several motets found in Werrecore's *Cantuum quinque vocum* of 1555, which contains pieces with canonic cantus firmi for as many as seven voices. Despite its massive wall of sound, furthermore, *Vocem iocunditatis* features gracefully constructed imitations of the sort commonly found in the motets of Werrecore's 1555 book. Nonetheless, Gregor Peschin composed a number of ceremonial motets, and the treatment of the canonic cantus firmus of *Vocem iocunditatis* is reminiscent of that found in his extant German lied settings. The list of German lieder attributed to Peschin in *Heidelberg, Codex Pal. Germ.* 318 reveals that his experience in setting popular tunes was far more extensive than that of Werrecore, who apparently composed only a handful of Italian villanesche.[56] If, indeed, the cantus firmus is derived from a popular song, Peschin's experimentation with popular genres may lend further weight to the attribution in the Munich manuscript.

Peschin may be associated to Francesco II Sforza via the court of Sigismund I of Poland, and this connection, in turn, may shed further light on the two motets contributed by Willaert. Sigismund I was an avid patron of music, art and architecture, and the documentation amassed to date reveals that from 1501 to 1540 he traveled frequently to Buda to acquire instruments and other musical services, and sent to Silesia and Germany for musicians as well. When Sigismund married Bona Sforza, in 1518, moreover, his musical contacts were further extended to include Italy.[57] Gregor Peschin was educated and subsequently served in the court chapel in Budapest until 1526, and then transferred to Salzburg to accept a position as organist there in 1527.[58] It, therefore, is quite possible that Peschin had some contact with Sigismund I and Bona Sforza while residing in Budapest. If the attribution to Peschin in the Munich manuscript is correct, *Vocem iocunditatis* may represent a commission from Sigismund I and Bona Sforza. Interestingly enough, Willaert not only accompanied Ippolito I d'Este to the wedding of Sigismund I in 1518, but also spent the preceding year in Budapest.[59] Thus, it is quite possible that Willaert's *Victor io salve/Quis curare neget* and *Inclite Sfortiadum princeps* originated via Sigismund I and Bona Sforza as well.

Example 1.3 Werrecore, *Vocem iocunditatis,* measures 19-41

In any case, the eight-voice texture of *Vocem iocunditatis* suggests that the composition may have been conceived with the ducal choir at the collegiate church of Santa Maria della Scala in mind. Its chapter, which was founded in 1384-1385 by Barnabò Visconti for the purpose of preserving the Ambrosian liturgy, originally consisted of twenty canons, four clerics, two custodians and a provost. In 1531-1532, however, Francesco II Sforza augmented its size through the addition of eight choral appointments. The archival documentation reveals that the ducal choir at Santa Maria della Scala subsequently played a major role in ducal and royal ceremony in Milan. Although the names of the original eight choral singers are preserved in the documents, their voice types are nowhere specified. However, the balanced division of the eight singers into groups of 2 mansionari, 4 chaplains, and 2 deacons, each of

which had specific responsibilities during the performance of a given service, carries with it the probability that the voice types were similarly distributed, particularly since the choir was known to have sung polyphony.[60] Nonetheless, it is equally possible that the motet was intended for use in the Duomo, which boasted a choir of approximately sixteen members and traditionally hosted most formal celebrations of state.

The four musical works commemorating the victory at Pavia and the subsequent restoration of the Sforza were originally conceived, like most ceremonial works of the period, as the aural embellishment of a celebration at a public gathering. Yet none of the Milanese chronicles or accounts surviving from the period mentions a formal Milanese celebration immediately following the victory at Pavia. Thus, it appears likely that the four commemorative works associated with the victory were performed at later celebrations held after the

restoration of the duchy to Francesco II Sforza had been assured. The archival and
early printed sources record several such celebrations, but none of them takes place
before December 1529, just shortly after the formal restoration. The earliest Milanese
celebrations of the restoration mentioned in the sources occurred in December 1529,
and, interestingly enough, were Imperially generated. A proclamation was sent to the
Duchy of Milan from Bologna in which the general terms of the accord were outlined
and a mass of celebration in every city of the affected territories was mandated. The
mass was to be performed as follows:

> . . .you along with the Magnificent President, Senators, Magistrate, and our other
> officials and citizens celebrate a sung Mass of the Holy Spirit in order to give immortal
> thanks to God the Father for this wonderful gift. In the case that the hour is already late

fulfill our order the morning immediately following. [We are] advising all the officials of our land to do the same.[61]

A brief description of the other Milanese ceremonies held in honor of the aforementioned accord is provided by sixteenth-century historian Gaspare Bugati.

> When this good news arrived in Milan, the city celebrated with the greatest ceremony through fireworks, processions of the clergy and populace, ringing of all the bells, and decoration of the sacred churches. All [were] thanking God, who had liberated the Sforza from the Spanish.[62]

According Gianmarco Burigozzi, a merchant working in Milan between 1500 and 1544, two additional ceremonies were held in 1531. The first of these took place on 1 February 1531, at which time the Castello Sforzesco was officially turned over to the Sforza.

> The evening of the same day that the ducal castellano entered the castle, they held fireworks and artillery displays, accompanied by the ringing of the bells for all the city. And this lasted three days. And on Tuesday morning all of the gentlemen and governors processed to the mass in the Duomo of Milano, praising God for his mercy.[63]

The second marked Francesco II Sforza's official return to the city of Milan as its Duke, which occurred on 18 April 1531. The celebrations culminated with a mass in the Duomo held on 20 April 1531.

> On April 20th (which was the following Tuesday) a chair decorated in gold brocade was placed, as was customary, before the main altar in the Duomo of Milan, where the high mass was to be held. Then early in the morning on the aforementioned day our Duke arrived in the Duomo, accompanied by a few members of the company. Upon arrival at the church he approached the main altar of the Madonna dell'Albero, where he was to hear the mass. After the mass, he came [closer]; he did not enter within, but remained standing there, invoking the name of God. He then departed for the Castello, and did not remain instead for the high mass that the ordinaries had prepared. Nevertheless, the ordinaries celebrated the mass, praying for the health of our Duke and the prosperity of the republic of Milan.[64]

Burigozzi's description of the Duomo mass is especially interesting for two reasons. First, it demonstrates that the ducal ceremony under Francesco II continued to be patterned upon that established by Francesco, Gian Galeazzo, and Ludovico Maria Sforza, all of whom placed the Duomo mass at the center of state festivities.[65] Moreover, it contains some uncommon detail in specifying that Francesco II's party approached the altar of the Madonna dell'Albero for the performance of the mass. This altar had been the principal altar in the ancient cathedral of Santa Tecla, and was transferred during the fourteenth century to the Duomo, where it served as the primary Marian altar. Its name was derived from the fact that it was adorned with a wooden sculpture of the Madonna and Child springing from the Tree of Jesse, and its role in Milanese devotional practice was to be redefined several times throughout the sixteenth century.[66] Burigozzi appears to call attention to the altar of the Madonna dell'Albero in his narrative because it was historically central to the ducal ceremonial of the Sforza. His description of the choir singing as Francesco II approached the altar evokes images of *Vocem iocunditatis*, with its allegorical references to the preservation of Israel and the thriving cedar, sounding in the background.

In any case, the four commemorative works composed in honor of the victory at Pavia would have been equally appropriate for the December 1529, the February 1531, or the April 1531 ceremonies. Further, all of them would have functioned well as post-banquet entertainment during the general festivities. While Werrecore's villotta would have been entirely inappropriate for performance during the mass, the three motets were suitable to both the 1529 and the 1531 masses celebrating the restoration of the Sforza. In fact, the Willaert motets may even have functioned in the same manner as did their model. Polyphony usually was sung during the *Ingressa* (roughly corresponding to the Roman Introit), *Transitorium* (Roman Communion), and *Confractorium* (Roman Agnus Dei) of the Ambrosian Mass at the Duomo during the latter half of the fifteenth century.[67] Several notations found in the fourth Milan Choirbook, which bears a completion date of 22 June 1527, demonstrate that the practice of singing polyphony during the *Transitorium* and *Confractorium* was retained there at the outset of the sixteenth century.[68] Moreover, the notations further reveal that motets were sometimes assigned to the *Offertorium* as well.[69] If this early sixteenth-century practice was applied to Willaert's motets, then they likely functioned as a pair to be inserted into at least two of the three prescribed sections. Additionally, division of the motet *Victor io salve/Quis curare neget* into its two partes results in a total of three sections that might be distributed across the three liturgical items for which polyphony was frequently prescribed. The two-section motet *Vocem iocunditatis/Ecce Ducem nostrum* might have been distributed across the *Transitorium* and *Confractorium* in a similar manner.

The archival documentation suggests one other possible political arena for performance of the two motets composed by Willaert. In the Fall of 1530 a Milanese delegation traveled to Venice, where Willaert was serving as maestro di cappella at the basilica of San Marco, to participate in diplomatic negotiations intended to strengthen Milanese ties with the Venetian state. In addition to a number of Milanese statesmen, the delegation included the Provost of Santa Maria della Scala and several musicians.[70] The surviving diplomatic correspondence between Milan and Venice dating from October and November of 1530 describes a number of elaborate ceremonies held in Venice. According to Francesco II's secretary Gian Angelo Rizzo, the Milanese delegation made its formal entrata via the water on 12 October 1530, and was enthusiastically received by the Venetian populace:

> . . .We were received by the Most Serene Prince and all of this Illustrious Signoria with all of the signs of happiness, triumph, and festivity, and as soon as we and the major part were boarded in their bucintoro, we were accompanied by countless people in boats, gondolas, and masks, and music with an abundance of joy that one has not witnessed, according to public opinion, in many years in many celebrations and universal amusement of this glorious city. We disembarked at San Marco, and were conducted to the rooms where the Procurators of San Marco, the principal ruling body of this city, usually live, and there we were directed to our optimal lodgings with royal decoration.[71]

During the succeeding month, moreover, the Milanese delegation attended at least two special masses in San Marco[72] and was treated to numerous balls, regattas, banquets and entertainments:

The festivals and ceremonies that were hosted by this Illustrious signoria on the bucintoro, including a regatta, balls, a combat at a castle on the seas, and a naumachia with lavish collations, as well as a universal demonstration of love and goodwill, were grand, as one is able to understand from the other groups. So that we remain infinitely obliged to them, we have been in the Collegio a total of three times, and before our departure we will go to it once or twice, after which we will depart for home with the blessing of the aforementioned Illustrious signoria.[73]

Since the two Willaert motets are known only through printed sources that were not issued until 1539, it is entirely possible that they were composed especially for the ceremonies held in Venice during the 1530 visit of the Milanese delegation. The entertainments prepared by the Venetians certainly provided ample opportunity for the performance of musical tributes to the newly restored Duke of Milan.

The four compositions commemorating the Battle of Pavia and the subsequent Sforza restoration comprise a core repertory aimed at glorifying a pivotal political and military event in which Francesco II Sforza played a significant role. They not only served to place the battle within the historical context of related occasions from the past, but also provided a musical reference point heralding the initiation of a new regime. Through their musical connections to earlier works, the works commemorating the victory at Pavia underscored the perpetuity of the Sforza dynasty. Yet by their very emphasis upon the events that marked the restoration of Francesco II Sforza, they also shaped and reinforced the collective cultural memory of an event that cemented the city's modern civic identity.

Notes

1   For modern summaries of the historical events that occurred between 1499 and 1525, see Gino Franceschini, 'La dominazioni francese e le resaurazioni Sforzesche,' *Storia di Milano* (Milano: Giovanni Treccani degli Alfieri, 1957a), VIII, 83-132, and Caterina Santoro, *Gli Sforza: La casata nobilare che resse il ducato di Milano dal 1450 al 1535* (Milano: Casa Editrice Corbaccio s.r.l., 1992), 344-387.

2   John Lynch, *Spain 1516-1598: From Nation State to World Empire* (Oxford and Cambridge: Basil Blackwell, 1991), 110-116.

3   'Et per questo accadette, che li Signori Ordinari del Domo, una Domenica dell'Advento 1523, che aspettavano che costui, cioè questo Frate de San Marco della barbassa, livrasse la sua predica per voler celebrare la sua messa grande; et costui, senza rispetto delli suoi superiori, la teneva longhissima: dondechè la gieresia, vendendo costui senza discrezione, se misero in coro comezando la messa all'altare grande. Et vedendo questo Frate che le preti comenzorono a cantare lo introito della messa, se partì dal pulpito in furia; et alcune de quella generazione che erano a quella udientia, se miseno a voce alta a improperare li Ordenarii et altri Sacerdoti, diandoglie mille ingiurie; et all'altare li era il sacerdoto apparato; donde vedendo loro la furia di questa generazione senza freno, et che glie boriano adosso, con paura grande fugiriano fora del coro, et andorono in sagrestia con gran fatica. E del strepito che fu in quella benedetta giexia, non te ne parlo; e questo Frate tornò sul pulpito, confortando li suoi satelliti e femenuze, che, infra loro, beato che poteva dir male de questi venerandi sacerdoti, nostri patrioti. Et quando volesse, la livrò

et volesse venzere la sua ostinazione de librare el suo cianciare quando lui volesse, per esser tenuto mirabile uomo. Passata questa furia, come amatori della patria, questi Ordinarii et sacerdoti non volseno restare per questo de non mancare del seco officio, et cantorono la sua messa, pregano Dio per la salute loro et della patria.' Marco Burigozzi, *Cronaca milanese di Gianmarco Burigozzi merzaro dal 1500 al 1544* (Milano: Francesco et Simone Tini, 1587; reprinted in *Archivio storico italiano serie I*, vol. III, 421-552), 443-444.

4   'Alla fine de Decembre 1523, rivò in questa Città de Milano el Vincerè a nome dell'Imperatore; et el primo giorno dall'anno 1524, andò alla messa nella ecclesia maggiore del Domo; et gli era in compagnia sua assai grandi, maggiori, maxime l'imbasciatore di Venezia, qual era il Duca di Urbino . . .' Burigozzi, *Cronaca*, 444.

5   See Appendix II.

6   Burigozzi, *Cronaca*, 446.

7   See Giorgio Chittolini, 'Di alcuni aspetti della crisi dello stato Sforzesco' in *Milano e Borgogna. Due stati principeschi tra Medioevo e Rinascimento*, edited by Jean-Marie Cauchies e Giorgio Chittolini (Roma: Bulzoni Editore, 1990), 21-34, and Giorgio Chittolini, 'La crisi dello stato milanese alla fine del Quattrocento' in *Città, communità e feudi negli stati dell'Italia centro-settentrionale XIV-XVI secolo* (Milano: Edizioni Unicopli, 1996), 167-180.

8   ' . . . et cavalcando di notte, per strade torte giunse a Milano, ove fu ricevuto con grande applauso di tutti, et dalle fantierie armate furono scaricate con bellissime ordine molti archibugi in segno di allegrezza et da tutti i soldati, et capitani fu chiamato Principe et Duca.' Alfonso Ulloa, *Vita e fatti dell'invitissimo Imperator Carlo Quinto* (Venezia: Vincenzo Valgrese, 1562), 70a.

9   ' . . .quanto che s'intese l'entrata di Milano di Francesco Sforza gridato da tutto il popolo, et accettato per Duca con molti honori, benche l'entrata sua fosse di notte con sei mila Tedeschi, che egli condusse da Trento pel Veronese nel Mantovano, e passato il Pò nel Piacentino, e nel Pavese, accompagnato dal Signor di Mantova con trecento cavalli à nome della Chiesa l'anno Sudetto.' Gaspare Bugati, *Histoire universale di M. Gaspare Bugati milanese* (Venetia: Gabriele Gioliti de Ferrari, 1571), 760.

10   See Louise Cuyler, *The Emperor Maximilian I and Music* (London: Oxford University Press, 1973), 29-61.

11   ' . . .con grandissime Triumpho, Jubilo, et festa.' *Sforzesco* 132 (Potenze estere: Roma 1513-1514), non numerati (hereafter n.n.), (27 octobre 1513), Archivio di Stato, Milano (hereafter ASM).

12   ' . . . di soni, cridi in segno, di Letitia, et strepite di Artegliarie.' *Sforzesco* 132 (Potenze estere: Roma 1513-1514), n.n. (27 octobre 1513), ASM.

13   'La Sanctità di *Nostro Signor* ha dimonstrato havere ricevuto gratissima nova, e dopoi, li Cardinali Prelati et altri particolari, che sono molti, affectionatissimi, ala Eccellentia vostra et stato suo et questa sera, in molti lochi, di questa Cita si sono facti grandissimi fochi, con strepiti de Artegliarie, et altissimi cridi, in honore di vostra Eccellentia con tanto et universale, piacere de questo Populo, et forestieri, che mai piu si trova per cosa particolar' como questa, essere facto, tanto Iubilo, et festa, et La Guarda di Suyceri, de la Sanctità di *Nostro Signor* Insieme con tutti li Musici di quella et molti altri particolari sono stati sino ad gran parte dela nocte, ad honorare Lo Alogiamento mio dela Cancelleria.' *Sforzesco* 132 (Potenze estere: Roma 1513-1514), n.n. (25 novembre 1513), ASM.

14   See F.X. Haberl, 'Matthais Hermann Werrecorensis. Eine bibliographisch-kritische Studie,' *Monatschefte für Musikgeschichte* III (1871), 201-204.

15   This hypothesis was first advanced by Michel Brenet, *Musique et musiciens del la vieille France* (Paris: Librairie Félix Alcan, 1911), 149.

16   Marco Brusa, 'Hermann Matthias Werrecoren "maestro di cappella del Domo di Milano" 1522-1550, Biografia. Bibliografia. Elenco delle opere,' *Rivista internazionale di musica sacra* XV/3-4 (1994), 186-192.

17   The tapestries are housed in the Museo Nazionale, Napoli. Photographs of them are found in Gino Franceschini, 'Milano nell'ultima difesa della libertà italiana,' *Storia di Milano* (Milano: Giovanni Treccani degli Alfieri, 1957b), VIII, 254-262.

18   See Max Geisberg, *The German Single-Leaf Woodcut 1500-1550*, rev. and ed. Walter L. Strauss (New York: Hacker Art Books, 1974), I, 326. Stuttgart, Geisberg catalog 356.

19   See for example, the *Cronaca d'anonimo Vallesano* in *Archivio Storico Lombardo* XVIII (1912), 587, which is also reproduced in Franceschini, 'Milano nell'ultima difesa,' 254-255.

20   See Clément Janequin, *Chansons polyphoniques*, ed. A. Tilman Meritt et François Lesure (Le Remparts, Monaco: Éditions de L'oiseau-Lyre, 1971), VI, 41-77.

21   Matthais Werrecore, *La bataglia tagliana* (Venetia: Antonio Gardane, 1549; reprinted in facsimile by Peer: Alamire, 1987), dedication.

22   Brenet, *Musique e musiciens*, 135-155.

23   See Christine Getz, 'The Milanese Cathedral Choir under Hermann Matthais Werrecore, maestro di cappella 1522-1550,' *Musica Disciplina* XLVI (1992), 172.

24   The best summary of this literature is found in Brusa, 'Hermann Matthias Werrecoren,' 176-179.

25   See Getz, 'The Milanese Cathedral Choir,' 173-174, and Chapter 3 below.

26   'Salve Sfortiarum maxime dux et imperator.'

27   'Vivat dux Franciscus Sfortia felix.'

28   The motets were reprinted by Scotto in 1550. See Adrian Willaert, *Opera Omnia 3: Motetti V Vocum* in *Corpus Mensurabilis Musicae* III, ed. Hermann Zenck (Rome: American Institute of Musicology, 1950), i-vi.

29   Lewis Lockwood, Giulio Ongaro, Michele Fromson, and Jessie Ann Owens 'Willaert, Adrian,' *The New Grove Dictionary of Music and Musicians*, 2nd edition (London: Macmillan Publishers, Ltd., 2001b), XXVII, 389-390.

30   Howard Mayer Brown, ed., *Milan, Archivio della Veneranda Fabbrica del Duomo, Sezione Musicale, Librone 3 (olim 2267)*, facsimile (New York and London: Garland, 1987), 144v-147r. Only the Gloria, Credo, and Sanctus are included here. A modern edition of the *Missa Hercules Dux Ferrariae* is found in Josquin des Prez, *Masses Based on Solmisation Themes* in *New Josquin Edition* 11, ed. James Haar and Lewis Lockwood. Utrecht: Koninklijke Vereniging voor Nederlandse Muziekgeschiedenis, 2002, 2-31.

31   Lewis Lockwood, *Music in Renaissance Ferrara 1400-1505*. (Oxford: Clarendon Press, 1984), 247-249.

32   Lockwood, Ongaro, Fromson, and Owens 'Willaert, Adrian,' *The New Grove*, XXVII, 389-390.

33   'Illustrissimo et excellentissimo Signor mio osservatissimo: Mandando lo Illustrissimo signor mio padre a vostra Excellentia lo exhibitor' de la presente che'e lo Illustro signor Marco di pij: L'ho pregato, che le facci Reverentia et la visiti, nome mio, et le recordi chio perservero, quella osservatia verso lei che me si conviene', Et le dica appresso alquate parole da parte mia. Peró la priego che li presti fedé: In quello che'esso per nome mio le exporra: Et In sua bona gratia sempre mi raccomando. Da Ferrara a quatro di novembre del MDXXVI. De vostra Illustrissima et Excellentissimo servitor Hippolyto Estense.' *Sforzesco* 934 (Potenze estere: Ferrara 1500-1527), Busta Ferrara 1526, ASM.

34   Enrico Cattaneo, 'Elezione degli arcivescovi' in *Storia di Milano* (Milano: Giovanni Treccani degli Alfieri, 1961a), IX, 532-533.

35   See Christine Getz, 'The Sforza Restoration and the Founding of the Ducal Chapels at Santa Maria della Scala in Milan and Sant'Ambrogio in Vigevano,' *Early Music History* 17 (1998b), 119.

36   'Il*lustriss*imo et ex*cellentiss*imo signor mio oss*ervatiss*imo: La visita che si è degnata *vostra* ex*cellentia* farmi per mezo del corte *nostro* di casa de la ex*cellentiss*ima *signo*ra Duchesa sua consorte et mia *signo*ra mi è stata sopra modo grata. E*t* altro *ta*nto quanto esso sotto *lett*ere credenziali di *vostra* ex*cellentia* mi ha exposto. De che le rendo infinite gratie, remettendomj nel resto a quanto in mio nome dira *à vostra* ex*cellentia*. Il pre*f*ato corte sopra il desiderio che tengo di far servitio, purche potessi, in qual si voglia cosa a *vostra* ex*cellentia*, alla quale bacio la man e*t* humilmente mi raccommando in sua buona *gra*tia.   Di Ferrara alli viij di Decembre MDXXXIIII.   Da *vostra* Il*lustriss*ima et Ex*cellentiss*ima *signo*r Serv*it*or et Cugino Hippolito Estense.' *Autografi* 19/2 (Ippolito d'Este), 7, ASM.

37   'Et che il Rev*erendiss*imo *signo*r Don Hippolito habbia il titulo si fosse possibile, et che tene certo, che se *vostra* Ex*cellenti*a non accomodi tal cosa, no*n* spera che altro lo faccia, per essere *vostra* Ex*cellenti*a patrono del pre*f*ato vescovo, et dil sua Il*lustriss*ima *signo*ra, et dil *signo*r Don Hippolito, et che al fine vedendo sua Ex*cellenti*a che per il mezo di *vostra* Il*lustriss*ima *signo*ra no*n* si puosi accomodar', *no*n ne vorra altro che la iustitia, et me ha comessa voglia scrivere *à vostra* Ex*cellenti*a che per cosa alcuna la non piglia le sue parole se non in bene et che gli recresce che *vostra* Ex*cellenti*a habbi pensato che sua Il*lustriss*ima *signo*ra si sia alterata, ma che sua Ex*cellenti*a ha pigliata piu recrescimento che *vostra* Ex*cellenti*a *signo*ra habbi preso indispiacere le parole di sua *signo*ra Il*lustriss*ima havendo inteso che *vostra* Ex*cellenti*a non ne vole piu parlarce. Ho resposta *à* sua *signo*ra como da me che me pare una dura cosa che il Rev*erendiss*imo Vescovo di Modena qual havendo havuto ditto vescovato di ____ et havendo posto li habbiti, che adesso si voglia accontentare senza il vescovato, Me ha resposta sua *signo*ra che pare anche sa sua Ex*cellenti*a che essendo quella terra parciale, quanto piu sua Il*lustriss*ima *signo*ra gli ha superiorita piu sarà al preposito di sua signora et che ogniuno cerca la comodità sua . . .' *Sforzesco* 935 (Potenze estere: Ferrara 1529-1531), Busta giugno 1531, 10-12, ASM.

38   *Autografi* 19/2 (Ippolito D'Este), 1, ASM.

39   'Per le ultime me scrisse che io mandava a vostra Ex*cellenti*a certi canti ad me sporti per Maestro Ian, qual per p*ass*ato di messo fur*o*no smenticati et quali mando qui alligati a *vostra* Ex*cellenti*a di sua parte.' *Sforzesco* 935 (Potenze estere: Ferrara 1529-1531), Busta giugno 1531, 17. A missive from the previous day also makes reference to the songs, stating 'The enclosed songs, which I send to Your Excellency on his behalf, were sent to me by Maistre Jhan.' *Sforzesco* 935 (Potenze estere: Ferrara 1529-1531), Busta giugno 1531, 16, ASM.

40   'Havemo recevuto le *vos*tre di 17 del *pres*ente, alle quale gli erano alligati certi canti, et le del molto R*everen*do et Il*lustriss*imo *signo*r Arcivescovo ad noi. Et con le *pres*enti faremo risposta a dette *vos*tre solo circa al particulare de le Ven*erabili* Donne de S*an*to Vincenzo . . . volemo et vi commettemo debbiate transferirvi dal pre*f*ato *sign*or Arcivescovo et in nomine *nos*tro li referireli le debite gratie del piacere in ha fatto . . .' *Sforzesco* 935 (Potenze estere: Ferrara 1529-1531), Busta giugno 1531, enclosure to document 17, ASM.

41   'Li canti che *à* havete mandati, et li avisi erano in esse *lett*ere sono stati grat*issi*mi et vi dicemo che debbiate perserverare in tenerci avisati . . .' Sforzesco 935 (Potenze estere:

Ferrara 1529-1531), Busta giugno 1531, n.n (28 giugno 1531), ASM.

42   'Ho anche parlato al R*everendissi*mo sig*n*or Arcivescovo circa il caso delle ven*erabili* Donne di Santo Vicenzi per havere l'Instromento del conscenso di sua R*everendissi*ma sig*n*ora. Me ha resposto anchor' non haver'havuto la risposta dalli Agenti suoi de Millano, et che subito venuta la resposta me lo fara sapere. Ho fatto intendere a sua signora R*everendissi*ma che conoscendo vostra Ex*cellentia* non potere servire sua sig*n*ora in la cosa del vescovato di Modena, per non esser'il Morono per cedere al titulo, et che vostra Ex*cellentia* e ressoluta de non intromettersi in tal differencia . . .' *Sforzesco* 935 (Potenze estere: Ferrara 1529-1531), Busta luglio 1531, n.n. (2 luglio 1531), ASM.

43   *Sforzesco* 935 (Potenze estere: Ferrara 1529-1531), Busta settembre, 11 settembre 1531 and 23 settembre 1531, ASM.

44   *Sforzesco* 935 (Potenze estere: Ferrara 1529-1531), Busta settembre 1531, s.d., ASM.

45   *Sforzesco* 936 (Potenze estere: Ferrara 1532-1533), 6 febbraio 1532 and 15 febbraio 1532, ASM.

46   *Sforzesco* 935 (Potenze estere: Ferrara 1529-1531), Busta novembre 1531, 12 novembre 1531, ASM.

47   See Chapter 3 below.

48   For example *Sforzesco* 934 (Potenze estere: Ferrara 1500-1527), Busta marzo 1527 and Busta giugno 1527, ASM, contain four documents referring to the movement of trumpeters between Ferrara and Milan. These are dated 29 March 1527, 30 March 1527, 31 March 1527, and 1 June 1527.

49   These included Hermann Matthias Werrecore, Andrea de Germanis, and Giovanni Antonio de Rapis de Busti. See Chapter 6 below.

50   Willaert was in the service of Ippolito I at the time of the wedding. See Lewis Lockwood, 'Adrian Willaert and Cardinal Ippolito I d'Este: New Light on Willaert's Early Career in Italy, 1515-1521,' *Early Music History* 5 (1985), 86-90.

51   Kenneth A. Lewalski, 'Sigismund I of Poland: Renaissance King and Patron,' *Studies in the Renaissance* XIV (1967), 49.

52   Brusa, 'Hermann Matthias Werrecoren,' 193-197, provides a compelling analysis of the textual sources for the motet.

53   'Franciscus Sforcia Dux Mediolani sicut cedrus multiplicabatur. Laetare Italia.'

54   Ezekiel 17:22-23.

55   See Albert Dunning, *Die Staatsmotette, 1480-1555* (Utrecht: A. Oostoek's Uitgeversmaatschappij N. V., 1970), 317-321, and Brusa, 'Hermann Matthias Werrecoren,' 193-197. Brusa seems to accept an attribution to Werrecore without much question.

56   Jutta Lambrecht, *Das 'Heidelberger Kapellinventar' von 1544 (Codex Pal. Germ. 318): Edition und Kommentar* (Heidelberg: Heidelberger Bibliothekschriften, 1987), II, 589-591.

57   Lewalski, 'Sigismund I of Poland,' 67-69.

58   Jutta Lambrecht, 'Peschin, Gregor,' *The New Grove Dictionary of Music and Musicians*, 2nd edn (London: Macmillan Publishers Ltd., 2001), XIX, 482.

59   Lockwood, 'Adrian Willaert and Cardinal Ippolito I d'Este,' 86-90.

60   See Chapter 2 below.

61   '. . . voi insieme col M*agnifi*co Presidente, Senatori, Mag*istr*ate, et altri n*ostr*i officiali, et cittadini fareti cantar'una messa de sp*irit*o s*an*to per render' immortali gratie al Summo Iddio di tanto dono concesso, quando anche l'hora fosse tarda exequiereti questo n*ostr*o ordine la mattina immediate seguente, Advisando tutti li officiali de le Terre n*ostr*e che facciano il mede*si*mo . . .' *Sforzesco* 1424 (Milano città 1527-1529), Busta 1529

novembre, n.n. (23 dicembre 1529), ASM.

62 'Arrivata questa buona nuova à Milano; la Città fece di tutto cio grandissima festa con fuochi, e con processioni del Clero, e del popolo, suonando tutte le campane, ed ornandosi i sacri Tempij; ringratiando tutti IDDIO, che gli havesse liberati da gli Spanguoli.' Bugati, *Histoire universale di M. Gaspare Bugati milanese* (Venetia: Gabrieli Gioliti de Ferrari, 1571), 808.

63 'La sera del ditti dì che intrò el castellano ducal in Castello, fezono trionfi di foco et de tirare arteglaria, con campane de feste per tutto il Milano, et questo durò tri giorni; et la Zobia mattina, tutti li signori e Gubernatori andorono a messa nella ecclesia maggior del Domo con trionfi ordinati, magnificando Dio della grazia avuta.' Burigozzi, *Cronaca milanese*, 505.

64 'A di 20 aprile (fu la Zobia sequente) fu parato la ecclesia maggiore del nostro Domo de Milano, zoè all'altare grande, con la sedia ornata de brocato d'oro, e missa all'alto apresso all'altare grande, dove è l'uxanza; donde che la mattina del soprascritto giorno a bon'ora, andò el ditto signor Duca nostro in Domo, e con poca compagnia per essere cosi a bon'ora; e rivato in la ecclesia, andò all'altare grande della Madonna dell'Alboro, e lì uditte messa. Dopo la messe venne, e rivato alla boca del coro, non intrò dentro, ma restò li, cosi e in piedi stetti, invocans nomen Domini: e poi si partì, e retornò in Castello et non stette altramente alla messa grande, qual dalli Ordenari era preparata. Non per questo li ditti signori Ordinarii non lassarono de celebrarla, invocando loro el nome grando de Dio per la salute sua et la repubblica nostra di Milano.' Burigozzi, *Cronaca milanese*, 507.

65 Paul A. Merkley and Lora L.M. Merkley, *Music and Patronage in the Sforza Court* (Amsterdam–Cremona: Brepols, 1999), 92-100, 317-319, and 321-357.

66 Enrico Cattaneo, *Maria santissima nella storia della spiritualità Milanese in Archvio Ambrosiano* VIII (Milano, 1955), 103-104. A bronze tree was constructed for the altar during the era 1550-1570 via a gift by Giovanbattista Trivultio. Under Carlo Borromeo the altar became the meeting place for the Confraternità del Rosario, and between 1582 and 1584 was renamed the altar of the Madonna del Rosario.

67 See William Prizer, 'Music at the Court of the Sforza: The Birth and Death of a Musical Center,' *Musica Disciplina* XLIII (1989), 150.

68 Ibid..

69 See Lynn Halpern Ward, 'The *Motetti Missales* Repertory Reconsidered,' *Journal of the American Musicological Society* XXXIX/3 (1986), 491-502.

70 *Sforzesco* 1471 (Potenze sovrane: Francesco II Sforza 1499-1535), 18 and 19, ASM.

71 '. . . fossemo con tutti li segni di alegreze, Triumphi, et Feste receputi dal *Serenissimo* Principe, et tutta *questa* Ill*ustrissi*ma *signor*ia et colsi montati Nui con la maggior parte de *nos*tri loro Buzintorro fossimo accompagnati da una Infinita de Populo in Barche, et gondule, et maschare, et soni con tanta copia et alegreza che al juditio commune non si è veduto in molti armi questa Inclita Città in tanta Festa, et universal solazzo Demontassimo a *Santo* Marco, et condutti in la stantia ove sogliono habitare li Procuratori di *Santo* Marco Principal dignita in questa Città et qua collocati in optimi alloggiamenti con regio apparato. . .' *Sforzesco* 1428 (Milano città e ducato: ottobre e novembre 1530), Busta ottobre, n.n. (12 ottobre 1530), ASM.

72 *Sforzesco* 1428 (Milano città e ducato: ottobre e novembre 1530), Busta ottobre, n.n. (12 ottobre and 14 ottobre 1530), ASM.

73 'Le feste et honori che ci sono stati fatti per questa Ill*ustrissi*ma *signor*ia sopra el Bucintoro, regata de Nave, balli, combattere de uno Castello in Mari et Naumachia con collatione lautissime' oltra una dimonstratione universale di amore, et bene volentia sono

stati gran' come d'altre bande si potra Intendere, Di modo che gli restiamo con Infinito obligo, siamo stati in tutto tre volti in Collegio, et nanzi el partire nostro gli andaremo una volta o, due,' dopo con bona licentia de la prefata Illustrissima signoria partiremo per ritornare a casa.' *Sforzesco* 1428 (Milano città e ducato: ottobre e novembre 1530), Busta ottobre, n.n. (24 ottobre 1530), ASM.

Chapter 2

From Ducal to Gubernatorial Ceremonial

Despite the comparatively large number of occasional works dedicated to Francesco II between 1522 and 1531, the ducal ceremonial does not appear to have occupied his energies until after his official investiture as Duke of Milan on 29 November 1529.[1] More pressing concerns, including the subjugation of factionalism among the nobility and the assertion of his ducal authority, initially competed for his attention. In order to ensure the necessary patrician support for his new regime, Francesco II first assumed control of the Duchy's republican governing bodies by designating himself as the sole party responsible for appointment to them. The sixty Secret Councilors and the Vicar of Provisions, which traditionally had been elected from the nobility, instead were appointed by the Duke. In addition, the thirty members of the Senate, which included fifteen cavaliers and gentlemen and fifteen doctors and prelates, were selected by the Duke from among those who had already demonstrated their loyalty and capability in lesser public offices. One of these, Giacomo Filippo Sacco, was designated as President. Although all criminal cases were ultimately heard by the Senate, a tribunal with the requisite peace-keeping officers was established in each major city to handle judicial processes at the local level.[2] With the wheels of his legislative machine greased and turning systematically, Francesco II then set his plans for revitalizing the ducal ceremonial into motion.

While Francesco II did not entirely abandon the patronage style of his ancestors, he clearly sought to place the ducal ceremonial more squarely in the public eye by moving it beyond the walls of the Castello Sforzesco. This is particularly noteworthy, since three chapels constructed by Galeazzo Maria Sforza for ceremonial worship were readily available to him there.[3] Motivated, in part, by a desire to refrain from the excessive spending that had characterized the musical patronage of his ancestors, Francesco installed ducal chapels at the cathedral of Sant'Ambrogio in Vigevano the collegiate church of Santa Maria della Scala in Milan through the addition of ducal benefices and the reassignment of existing ones. Each of these institutions was already generously staffed with a number of ducal appointments that had been established by Francesco's predecessors and received ongoing support from the ducal treasury. The enlargement of their respective chapels through the addition of singers and other necessary officers effectively freed the court of the direct responsibility of supervising and maintaining a standing choir, while at the same time allowing the Duke both jurisdiction over the chapel choirs and ready access to them. Installing ducal chapels within each church not only proved to be economically expedient, but also gradually transformed the ducal ceremonial from a largely private into a relatively public function. The court was required to travel from its residence to the designated chapel, and thereafter established a presence within the site itself. The direct result of such processional and ceremonial display was the vicarious participation of the general public in courtly activity.

The Ducal Chapels at Sant' Ambrogio in Vigevano and Santa Maria della Scala

Sant'Ambrogio in Vigevano adjoins the Palazzo Ducale Sforzesco in Vigevano to form the forth side of a large rectangular enclosure that encases the local palace's central piazza. Originally assigned to the Diocese of Novara, Sant'Ambrogio was elevated to the status of an independent episcopate in 1530, and became the seat of the Diocese of Vigevano with the subsequent introduction of additional parish churches throughout the region.[4] When Galeazzo Petra, the Diocese of Vigevano's first bishop, assumed the bishopric, Sant'Ambrogio's chapter consisted of a provost and seven canons. Francesco II expanded the existing benefices to include four dignitaries (an archpresbyter, an archdeacon, a deacon, a cantor), five canonries, sixteen choristers and choral assistants (two mansionarii, two deacons, two sacristans, two custodians, and eight juvenile clerics), and an organist. The negotiations for the first expansion, which included all of the appointments save that for the organist, were concluded in December 1530,[5] while those for the second, which included the addition of the organist and special provisions for support of the eight clerics, were not finalized until 24 June 1533.[6] Yet as early as 3 January 1531 a set of statutes governing the administration of the chapter and its activities were approved,[7] and these provide a window into the daily routine of the singers.

Sant'Ambrogio was devoted to the performance of the Roman rite. Its choral beneficiaries were required to be present at Matins, Prime, Terce, Sext, High Mass, Nones, Vespers, and Compline daily,[8] and each was held responsible for the performance of specific musical or liturgical duties during these services.[9] The cantor directed the choir by intoning the Introit, Gradual, Offertory, antiphons, and other items that were customarily intoned during the Mass. In addition, he alerted the dignitaries and canons of the order and placement of the antiphons used in the canonical hours, and sang those daily masses assigned to him on the rotational schedule.[10] In the event that the cantor was absent, one of the mansionarii assumed his duties. The mansionarii further intoned the psalms and hymns, the Gloria and Credo of the Mass, the first antiphon at Vespers, and the antiphons accompanying the Magnificat, Benedictus, and Nunc Dimittis. In addition they led all antiphons sung in unison by the full group, and alternated the responsibility of singing the Requiem Mass daily during the month of June.[11] One of the two deacons sang the Gospel of the Mass, while the other performed the Epistle. Additionally, both of them assisted the canon responsible for celebration of the High Mass. The clerics sang the Short Responsory, Versicles, and *Benedicamus domino* in alternation at all of the canonical hour except Matins, as well as the *Iube domine* at Compline.[12] The sacristans and custodians do not appear to have participated in the performance the liturgy itself, but rather supported the services by attending to technical details. The sacristans assisted with such matters as closing the doors of the choir at the beginning of the service, while the custodians maintained order by chasing rowdy boys, dogs, and other animals out of the church.[13]

The names of only three of the original singers at Sant'Ambrogio in Vigevano have surfaced to date, and these include the mansionarius Francesco Quintero,[14] the cleric Vincenzo de Vercelli,[15] and the cantor Francesco Rosarino. Francesco Rosarino, who is likely the Roserino who served as maestro di cappella at the Duomo of Modena from 1524 to 1526,[16] served as cantor at Vigevano from 1530 until his death in late 1548,[17] for which he received a salary of 200 lire per annum.[18] In addition to supervising the musical activities of the chapel, Rosarino appears to have been responsible for the recruitment of the juvenile singers. In 1531, for example, he made several trips to his native Vercelli to enlist boy sopranos for Sant'Ambrogio's choir.[19] Rosarino apparently also provided some of the earliest polyphonic repertoire heard in the chapel. In a letter to Francesco II Sforza dated 5 June 1531, Bishop Galeazzo Petra reported that Rosarino had composed 'certain new songs for the Trinity that are so sweet and pleasant to the ear.'[20] These compositions do not appear to have survived, but other sixteenth-century repertoire found in the cathedral archives by such composers as Michele Varotti, Giovanni Battista Savonese, and Orfeo Vecchi suggests that a rich polyphonic tradition flourished there. The extant repertoire includes motets and masses for a wide variety of Roman feasts, several ceremonial motets, an anonymous setting of the Lamentations of Jeremiah, and polyphony for the organ.[21]

The ducal chapel at Santa Maria della Scala had a longer and more illustrious history. It was founded in 1384-1385 by Barnabò Visconti in honor of his spouse Beatrice della Scala for the express purpose of preserving Milan's ancient Ambrosian plainchant and festal traditions.[22] The church itself stood at the present site of the well-known Teatro della Scala, and was easily accessed from the Duomo, Palazzo Reale (Corte d'Arengo), Castello Sforzesco, and other major churches and basilicas via the city's intricate street and canal system. Santa Maria della Scala's original collegiate chapter consisted of a provost, twenty canons, four clerics, and two custodians, and was primarily responsible for the daily performance of the Ambrosian office.[23] At the time of Francesco II's investiture, the chapter membership included a provost, two additional dignitaries, fourteen canons, four clerics, and two custodians, most of whom were neither in residence nor readily available for the daily singing of the office.[24] On 28 November 1530 Francesco ordered the canons into residence for the performance of the office,[25] and thereafter embarked upon a plan to enlarge the choir through the addition of two mansionarii, four chaplains and two deacons.[26] The funding for the eight benefices was secured through the suppression and transfer of benefices currently belonging to the church of San Giovanni al Vedra,[27] as well as through the transfer of properties in the ducal park at Pavia,[28] with the result that the mansionarii were supported with salaries of 200 lire per annum, the chaplains with salaries of 150 lire per annum, and the deacons with salaries of 100 lire per annum.[29] On 23 May 1532 the eight choral appointments and their respective stipends were officially approved by the dignitaries and canons of the chapter, and on 17 August 1532 the eight choral prebendaries were named 'in the presence' of Ippolito d'Este, Archbishop of Milan (Table 2.1).[30] Although most of the canons continued to participate in the singing of the liturgy at Santa Maria della Scala after the addition of these eight benefices, only the choral beneficiaries were assigned duties of musical importance.

Table 2.1 The first eight choral beneficiaries at Santa Maria della Scala

Michaele de Bechario, mansionarius

Bartolomeo de Herba, mansionarius

Augustino de Tonso (de Monte), cappellanus

Carlo de Castiglione, cappellanus

Brumanesio de Manzoni, cappellanus

Francisco de Pagano, cappellanus

Baptiste de Bossio, levitus

Stefano de Leynate, levitus

A set of choral statutes drawn up for Santa Maria della Scala in 1539 reveal that the Ambrosian services performed daily there included Matins, Prime, Terce, Sext, Nones, High Mass, Vespers, and Compline. The eight singers, as a rule, were expected to attend and received daily distributions for each.[31] However, a rather curious rotational system that may have been based upon that used in the Duomo of Milan until 1534 was implemented for Matins and Prime. One mansionarius, two chaplains, and one deacon sang for fifteen successive days, after which the remaining four singers sang for the following fifteen days. The order of the rotation was determined according to each respective singer's position in the choir, as one mansionarius, two chaplains, and one deacon were permanently assigned to the right choir, while the other masionarius, two chaplains, and deacon were assigned to the left choir. Those who sat on the right served together, as did those who sat on the left. However, singers who were currently free were permitted to substitute for those currently scheduled for duty, and, consequently, it was necessary that a scribe carefully monitor the attendance of the singers at each office. In addition to singing the Mass and the Office, the choral beneficiaries were required to perform at chapter funerals and in special processions. For each of these activities the choral beneficiaries received daily distributions, the largest of which were reserved for Matins, Mass, and Vespers, and Compline.[32]

The 1539 statutes indicate that the rotational schedule used at Santa Maria della Scala did not apply to the most important feasts of the Ambrosian calendar, at which time all eight singers were required to be present. The statutes further specify that the most important feasts included the Nativity, the feast of St Stephen, the feast of St John the Evangelist, the Circumcision, the Epiphany, Passion Week, Easter and its octave, the Ascension, Pentecost and the two days following, Trinity Sunday, Corpus

Christi and its octave, all the feasts of the Blessed Virgin, the feast of Saints Peter and Paul, All Saints Day, All Souls Day, and the feast of St Ambrose on 7 December.[33] A later document reveals that between 1539 and approximately 1660 the feasts of St Anthony Abbot (17 January), the Conversion of St Paul (25 January), St Thomas Aquinas (28 January), St Julius Sacerdote (31 January), St Veronica Matron (4 February), St Benedict (11 July), St Anne (26 July), the Transfiguration of Christ (6 August), St James Sacerdote (30 September), St Francis Confessor (4 October), St Catherine Virgin and Martyr (25 November), and St Bibiana (2 December) had been added as feasts celebrated in perpetuity.[34]

Each prebendary at Santa Maria della Scala was further characterized by responsibility for the performance of specific items within the Mass and Office. One or more of the chaplains intoned the first responsory, the second lesson of Matins, and the Gospel unless it was read, and also sang the Gloria Patri, the psalms, and the lesson of the chapter Mass. In addition, each chaplain celebrated mass in one of the side chapels at a prescribed hour during the day. The two deacons served at the altar, and sang the Gospel and Epistle during Mass, the Lucenarium at Vespers, and the Kyrie eleison in the various Offices. They further read the first lesson on days when the Gospel was read rather than sung. The mansionarii shared the role of director, a function that they would later yield to a *maestro di cappella*. In addition to intoning the psalms, antiphons, versicles, and responsories not already assigned to the chaplains, deacons, or canons, the mansionarii were expected to organize the singing of the office, monitor the quality of the singing, and celebrate mass in a side chapel at a designated hour each day.[35]

Despite the fact that Santa Maria della Scala was razed on 5 August 1776 in accordance with a decree by the Hapsburg Empress Maria Teresa,[36] the visual effect of the ceremonial during Francesco's tenure is easily imagined. Construction of Santa Maria della Scala's famous choir stalls, which are currently preserved in San Fedele, was not begun until approximately 1560.[37] Prior to that time, the architecture of the cruciform-shaped Romanesque church did not feature a true choir.[38] As a result, the singers, which included those canons assigned to the singing of plainchant, reportedly assembled in the central nave in front of the main altar.[39] Thus, the references to a left and right choir found in the 1539 statutes suggest that the singers and the canons flanked the main altar in such a manner that the view of the celebrants was not obscured.

Auditions for the eight beneficiaries at Santa Maria della Scala were quite thorough, and new singers were admitted by chapter vote only after a three-month trial period in which the candidate served without remuneration. A suitable voice, the ability to sight read well, and proficiency in singing Ambrosian plainchant were among the most important skills required:

> It was likewise ordered by the above officials than any mansionarius, chaplain, or deacon newly admitted to residence or to daily distributions from this church is expected to serve this church for three months continuously by observing the divine offices and canonical hours without receiving any distributions from the same church. And he cannot be admitted to the assembly of those admitted to daily distributions

unless he is able to sing plainchant acceptably and knows how to read books, especially of this church, to sing the Ambrosian rite, to be familiar with all of its psalm tones, and to intone them well, not only the psalms but also the Gospel, Epistles, Readings, Benediction of the Paschal Candle and all other [items] necessary and suitable to the aforementioned office. [He must] be recommended and approved as suitable and adequate by the Reverend Chapter of canons, as well as by the aforementioned mansionarii, chaplains, and deacons. He cannot be admitted unless he is suitable as [described] above and recommended as [described] above.[40]

Santa Maria della Scala adhered strictly to the policy of a three-month trial period culminating with a chapter vote throughout the entire sixteenth century. In 1566 Augostino Pelizono was subjected to the standard probationary term when he auditioned for and subsequently won a postiton as levitus.[41] Even the renowned Orfeo Vecchi, who was already serving as maestro di cappella at Santa Maria Scala when he applied for the position of mansionarius in 1591, was forced to undergo the trial in singing Ambrosian plainchant and pass a chapter vote.[42]

The Ambrosian liturgy observed in Milan during this period generally included the hours of Matins, Prime, Terce, Sext, Nones, Vespers, and Compline, as well a High Mass that followed Terce, Sext, or Nones. The most elaborate hours of the day were Matins and Vespers, so it is not surprising that these services were among those yielding the highest daily distributions at Santa Maria della Scala. Matins, perhaps the most structurally complex, was organized into three nocturns in which readings alternated with psalms, canti, antiphons, hymns, and verses with responsories. In addition, the opening section usually featured a so-called "hymn of the three boys," which may or may not have been sung by youths, depending upon the composition of a given institution's choir.

Vespers, the most publicly visible of the hours, and, therefore, the one into which polyphony was often inserted, featured from three to six psalms, as well as the Magnificat. As in the Roman liturgy, psalms 109 to 147 were spread across the week so that each was heard at least once within the course of seven days, but these were grouped slightly differently than in the Roman liturgy. Five psalms, numbers 109 through 113, were sung at Sunday Vespers, while two proper psalms, the "Ecce nunc" (Psalm 133) and the 'Laudate dominum' (Psalm 116) comprised the core psalm group for feasts of the saints. The Commons of the Saints, the Virgins, and the Martyrs, as well as the Vespers for Matrons, Sacerdotes, Abbots, and Doctors, featured two proper psalms and the 'Ecce nunc.' The particular psalm group sung, however, was not the only distinguishing structural feature of the Ambrosian Vespers hour, for other aspects of the service varied according to the festal calendar as well. Following the Our Father and Ave Maria, which were said in secret, a short verse with respond introduced the Lucernarium, or proper chant for the lighting of the candles. This was followed by an Antiphon 'in coro,' a Hymn, and a Responsory sung either 'in coro' (at Second Vespers on solemn feasts or Sundays and First Vespers on ferial days) or 'in infantibus' (at First Vespers on Solemn Feasts). The aforementioned psalms and Magnificat with their accompanying antiphons were introduced thereafter. A psallenda and two completoria commonly closed the Ambrosian Vespers on Sundays and high feasts and a responsory 'in Baptisterio' and one completorium served the same function on ferial days. In addition, two to three proper prayers were inserted in various prescribed places between the close of the psalm group, which was marked off by a Kyrie, and the final completoria or responsory. Certain feasts of the saints were further elaborated by the addition of readings from the respective saint's *vita* between the first three psalms, as well as the insertion of a Litany of the Saints after the psallenda. Although the structural points for the potential introduction of polyphony are numerous, it seems most likely that a motet would have been sung either before or during the Lucernarium, while a polyphonic Magnificat would have replaced the corresponding plainchant version.

Terce appears to have achieved particular significance within the Ambrosian liturgy because the hour often preceded important religious and civic processions. A typical Terce opened with the obligatory secret Our Father and Ave Maria, which was followed by a short verse with respond, five psalms with their antiphons, and the Gloria patri with Alleluia on festal occasions or the Laus tibi during Lent. An epistle was then read, and a capitulum and a Kyrie eleison sung. The hour closed with selected proper prayers and a responsory that often were borrowed from the Matins service for the same feast. Because processions were less numerous at Santa Maria della Scala, however, Terce never achieved the prominence there that it was afforded at the Duomo.[43]

The Ambrosian missals of the period indicate that five main items of the Ambrosian Mass Proper—the Ingressa (roughly corresponding to the Roman Introit), the Post-Evangelorum (Post-Gospel), the Offertory, the Confractorium (Roman Agnus Dei), and the Transitorium (Roman Communion)—formed the core of the plainchant repertoire associated with the service. In addition, a cantus was sometimes performed after the Epistle on high feasts. In the extant printed missals, the texts of these chants are provided in much smaller print than that used to record the remainder of the liturgy, thus suggesting that the celebrant using the book was not responsible for them, but, rather, entrusted them to the choir. Many of the texts of the Ambrosian Mass Proper were shared with the canonical hours, and also served multiple functions across the liturgical year. For example, the Vespers antiphon for Sts Philip and James, 'Tanto tempore vobiscum sum,' also functioned as an Ingressa for both the feast of Sts Philip and James and the Fifth Sunday after Easter.[44]

The liturgical calendar observed at Santa Maria della Scala in 1539 was quite conservative by mid-sixteenth-century standards. The liturgical calendars found in missals and breviaries dating from around the same time list a number of solemn feasts not mentioned in the royal ducal chapel's statutes, including the those of St Vincent, St Matthew Apostle, the deposition of St Ambrose, St George, St Mark the Evangelist, the Invention of the Cross, St Barnabas, Sts Protasius and Gervaise, St John the Baptist, Sts Nabor and Felicia, St James the Apostle, Sts Nazaro and Celso, the Tranfiguration, St Bartholomew, the Exultation of the Cross, St Matthew the Evangelist, St Jerome, Sts Simon and Jude, St Luke the Evangelist, St Martin Confessor, St Andrew the Apostle, St Thomas the Apostle, the Passion of the Innocents, the Ordination of St James, and St Sylvester. Although a number of other solemn feasts, mostly dedicated to saints, gradually were added to Santa Maria della

Scala's calendar throughout the sixteenth century, the same observation can be made about Scala's late sixteenth-century calendar. Thus, the church's festal calendar did not even begin to keep pace with the general calendar observed in other Ambrosian institutions such as the Duomo.

Shortly after the choral beneficiaries were installed at Santa Maria della Scala in 1532, the financial supervision of Francesco II's entire musical chapel, including the court instrumentalists apparently fell to Hieronymo de Matia, the Provost at Santa Maria della Scala. Although Monzino, the maestro of the court band, was distributing the payments to the instrumentalists as late as 1531,[45] De Matia clearly had assumed this task by 1533. On 21 May 1533, in fact, De Matia contacted Francesco II to inform him that the singers and instrumentalists in the chapel were complaining that their salaries had not yet been paid, and requested some direction in handling the sensitive matter:

> Sir, no one could disabuse the royal usher, singers, wind players, trumpeters, and custodians of the household of the notion that Your Excellency has given me money to pay them, and they pester me with accusations. For this reason I am requesting that your excellency condescend to advise me if you wish that they be paid. I would not pay any of it except for that appearance for which Your Excellency told the royal [usher] above you to subtract ten scudi. I would pay all these creatures, if I would do what appears better to Your Excellency. The Provost of La Scala.[46]

No response to De Matia's plea for assistance has been unearthed thus far, but the letter itself may explain, in part, the highly sporadic payments to the court musicians found in the documents, as well as the large lump sums frequently advanced to the Provost for unspecified expenses in the chapel.

The Ducal Ceremonial of Francesco II Sforza

The surviving documentation regarding Francesco II's association with the ducal chapels at Sant'Ambrogio in Vigevano and Santa Maria della Scala is confined largely to organizational and financial issues. As a result, very little is known about their participation in the ducal ceremonial itself. A sense of the roles of the two ducal chapels in the Milanese ceremonial, nonetheless, can be garnered from study of both the extant financial documents and the contemporary accounts of ceremonies held in Milan between 1532 and 1535. With the exception of such singers as Matthias Werrecore, who held a full-time appointment at the maestro di cappella at the Duomo of Milan, Francesco II's so-called court musicians, which included several additional singers, trumpeters, pifferi an organist, and a lutenist,[47] appear to have traveled with the court retinue. The retinue spent most of its time in Milan, Vigevano, and Pavia, the cities which housed the primary ducal residences. In these fortresses they provided both sight and sound to the Sforza ceremonial, which had traditionally relied primarily upon human activity within a confined space, rather than purely static architectural and pictorial effects for its visual impressions. Under Galeazzo Maria and Ludovico

Maria, for example, the reception and banquet rooms of the Castello Sforzesco were decorated with simple heraldic devices and initials instead of the extensive frescos often found elsewhere. There, the ducal ceremonial was conveyed through the presence of a *tableau vivant* that featured a veritable kaleidoscope of sensual stimuli, including persons, possessions, food, drink, speech, and music.[48]

A similar predilection for a ceremonial that emphasized the integration of the sensual stimuli (sight, sound, touch, taste, and smell) can be seen in two Imperial entries that were held during the reign of Francesco II. The first of these was the 1533 triumphal entry of Charles V en route from his meeting with Clement VII in Bologna, and the second was the 1534 entry of Charles' niece, Christina of Denmark, who married Francesco II Sforza that same year. The festivities in honor of Charles, which began on 10 March 1533, commenced with a procession from the Porta Ticinese to the Piazza Castello to the accompaniment of instrumental music and singing.[49] The processional route from the ancient Porta Ticinese, which stands directly in front of the paleo-Christian church of San Lorenzo, to either the Duomo or the Castello, had long been associated with royal ownership of the city through its allusion to Milan's Imperial Roman heritage. Considered within this context, the processors, which included Charles' personal retinue, selected Milanese dignitaries, and Milanese court musicians, symbolized the pact between Charles V and Francesco II that guaranteed Sforza domination even as it assured Hapsburg inheritance of the city in the event that the Sforza line dissolved. This segment of the entrata was designed, of course, to humble and impress the viewers, who hailed from every strata of Milanese society. Although many of them may not have been overly conscious of the symbolism suggested by the processional route, they certainly would have recognized its adherence to long-standing tradition. The same might be said of the music performed, which, unfortunately, is not identified specifically in any of the surviving accounts.

A royal banquet that featured musical entertainments[50] and a mass in the Duomo[51] followed the entry itself. These, in turn, were succeeded by four further days of festivities in which the court chapel figured prominently. Unlike the processional entry, the entertainments held at the court catered to an elite audience of aristocrats and statesmen who read, at the very least, the *volgare* and were educated in the social graces. Their purpose, therefore, was to build rapport through intellectual and physical amusement, rather than to merely impress and stupefy. Alessandro Verini Fiorentino's reflections on these four days betrays the significance attached to the sensual stimuli created by the diverse array of activities that were available to the aristocracy within the confines of the Castello walls:

> Then with great happiness, love, and infinite benevolence they remained four days playing and singing with the grand festivity of the court band. There were so many balls, tournaments, and games that never was seen or heard such a thing [by] who is here, who is there, who was, who traveled south, who dances or sings, and who ate happily.[52]

Christina's entry on 3 May 1534 similarly marked a processional route from the Porta Ticinese to the Duomo, where her retinue heard the Vespers service.

According to Gianmarco Burigozzi, a Milanese historian who witnessed the event, the route itself was decorated with banners and triumphal arches bearing the arms of both Francesco and Christina, as well as lifelike statues of Saints Ambrose, Protasius, and Gervaise. In addition, a fountain featuring many figures that sprayed water was constructed in the Piazza Cordusio.[53] Christina, accompanied by the Cardinal of Mantua and several doctors who carried her canopy, processed behind two grand majors on horseback dressed in black velvet, a company of Milanese dressed as Turks, an armed company of Milanese bearing green banners, six trumpeters 'who played at locations and times,'the Milanese gentlemen dressed in white accompanied by their drummers who were also dressed in white, and the guard of Signore Antonio de Leyva. She was attended by twelve counts in embroidered gold brocade, the President of the Senate, the bishops, the senators, and other selected Milanese gentlemen. This magnificent retinue paused at the Castello for an artillery display, then proceeded directly to the Duomo for the Vespers service. The services were followed by a banquet in the Castello that presumably included musical entertainments.[54]

The careful attention afforded the design of the processional route, the appearance of the decorations, and the order and attire of the processors betrays the significance attached to the human tableaux created within an urban space laden with architectural references to its historical past. Such tableaux were intended not only to stupefy through an overwhelming display of affluence and power, but also to propagate a specific political theme. Although the motifs of both entries underscored aspects of the alliance between Francesco II and his Imperial sponsor, those of Charles's entry, which included triumphal arches bearing his Imperial arms, Imperial impresa, personal impresa, and motto, conveyed a message of ownership and overlordship that was set aside in favor of the ducal partnership during the nuptials of Francesco II and Christina.[55] Music most certainly contributed to this distinction, and the ducal chapels must have played some role in providing that music. Yet the lack of documentation pertaining specifically to the participation of the ducal chapels in these and other events suggests that their contribution was largely to the private spheres of Francesco II's ceremonial.

The Gubernatorial Ceremonial

The desire for a more publicly visible ducal ceremonial may, in fact, account for the abject inattention afforded Sant'Ambrogio in Vigevano during the years following the death of Francesco II on 1 November 1535. Although the governors who succeeded Francesco II (Table 2.2) sometimes resided in Vigevano as much as

Table 2.2 Governors of Milan, 1535-1584

27 November 1535 - 15 September 1536	D. Antonio de Leyva, Principe d'Ascoli
5 September 1536 - February 1538	Cardinal Marino Ascanio Caracciolo
February 1538 - 31 March 1546	Alfonso d'Avalos, Marchese del Vasto
April 1546 - 1 October 1546	D. Alvaro de Luna, castellano di Milano (interim)
October 1546 - March 1555	D. Ferrante Gonzaga, Principe di Molfetta and Conte di Guastalla
12 June 1555 - 31 December 1556	D. Ferdinando-Alvarez de Toledo, Duca d'Alba (appointed in April 1555)
31 December 1556 - September 1557	Cardinal Cristoforo Madruzzo, Vescovo e Principe di Trento e di Brixen (interim)
7 August 1557 - July 1558	D. Giovanni Figueroa (interim)
20 July 1558 - early 1560	D. Consalvo-Fernando di Cordova, Duca di Sessa
February 1560 - March 1563	D. Francesco Ferdinando d'Avalos, Marchese di Pescara (interim)
March 1563 - April 1564	D. Consalvo-Fernando di Cordova, Duca di Sessa
16 April 1564 - 20 August 1571	D. Gabriele della Cuerva, Duca d'Albuquerque
21 August - c. 15 September 1571	D. Alfonso Pimentel, in conjunction with the Consiglio segreto (interim)
c. 15 September 1571 - April 1572	D. Alvaro de Sande, Marchese di Piovera e castellano di Milano (interim)
7 April 1572 - 8 October 1573	D. Luigi di Zuniga y Requesens
17 September 1573 - 20 April 1580	D. Antonio de Guzman y Zuniga, Marchese d'Ayamonte
July 1580 - 12 March 1583	D. Sancho de Guevara e Padilla, castellano di Milano (interim)
21 March 1583 - 18 November 1592	D. Carlo d'Aragona, Duca di Terranova

one-fourth of the year, Sant'Ambrogio, isolated in a satellite community almost thirty-five kilometers from Milan that comprised a self-contained episcopate, lacked the physical prominence and social pedigree of Santa Maria della Scala. As a result, Santa Maria della Scala quickly assumed the primary responsibility for the gubernatorial ceremonial and, in keeping with its newly acquired Imperial sponsorship, adopted the designation Royal Ducal Chapel. Sant'Ambrogio, albeit still recognized as a ducal chapel under the protection of Charles V, gradually adopted a peripheral role by continuing to serve the court when it was in residence in Vigevano. Sant'Ambrogio's rather immediate relegation to a secondary status under the Milanese governors is perhaps most clearly betrayed by the payment records extant from the chancery; between 1535 and 1560 the cantor of Sant'Ambrogio's salary was continually in arrears.[56]Although Milan's first two Imperial governors, Don Antonio de Leyva and Cardinal Marino Ascanio Caracciolo, drastically altered the structure of the trumpeters' corps, they appear to have exerted little influence over the daily operations of the chapels. Their respective terms were perhaps too brief, and their only motivations for tampering with the state musical organizations, if judged by their treatment of the trumpeters, financially driven. Caracciolo, in particular, appears to have viewed music as frivolity to be trimmed from the budget. Since the salaries of the singers at Santa Maria della Scala and Sant'Ambrogio in Vigevano were provided via an elaborate ducal benefice system, Caracciolo likely saw no need to introduce the sorts of cost-cutting measures that he imposed elsewhere. Nor would it have been possible for him to do so without the express permission of Charles V, the chapels' new protector.

Under Alfonso D'Avalos, Marchese del Vasto, who served as governor of Milan from 1538 to 1546, Santa Maria della Scala became the object of ceremonial reform. Shortly after D'Avalos took office, a detailed set of statutes outlining the responsibilities of the choral beneficiaries at Scala and stipulating the daily distributions awarded for the timely performance of the duties enumerated therein were drawn up. These were subsequently printed and remained in force throughout the remained of the chapel's history. The statutes, the contents of which were discussed briefly above, provided for the organized execution of the divine offices and a high mass daily. It remains unclear whether Alfonso was actually responsible for this nascent attention to the religious aspects of the gubernatorial ceremonial, particularly since his additional responsibilities as commander of the Imperial forces in Italy occupied much of his energy and required frequent absences from the gubernatorial court. Alfonso's spouse Maria d'Aragona was a well-known exponent of Catholic reform, and gathered around her such figures as Bernardino Ochino, Pietro Carnesecchi, and Galeazzo Florimonte. Thus, it seems, at least at first glance, more likely that she initiated measures to clarify and streamline the daily functions of the chapel. According to some accounts, however, Maria did not actually transfer from Naples to Milan until 1543, thereby establishing a presence at the gubernatorial court only during the latter years of her husband's tenure.[57]

Both Alfonso D'Avalos and Maria d'Aragona have long been associated with the contemporary literary movement in sixteenth-century Italy. Maria's virtue and beauty were the subject of several *ottave rime* and *sonnetti* by Bernardo Cappello, Bernardino Matirano, Ferrante Carafa, and Luigi Tansillo, and both Niccolò Franco and Pietro Aretino dedicated works to her. Moreover, Alfonso was himself a poet of modest reputation, and is perhaps best known today for the texts 'Corrette, o fiume' and 'Anchor che col partire.'[58] The archival sources indicate that at least three letterati, Luca Contile,[59] Pietro Aretino,[60] and Alberto Albicante,[61] were employed at the Milanese court during D'Avalos' governorship. Despite the family's literary proclivities, however, the madrigal appears to have received less attention in Milan during this period than did the motet. In fact, musical activity at the Milanese court under Alfonso D'Avalos was singularly focused upon the production of motet books, first in Venice under the skillful hands of Girolamo Scotto, and then in Milan at the press of Giovanni Antonio Castiglione. The gubernatorial court's sudden emphasis upon the production of sacred works, whether for use at Scala or elsewhere, undoubtedly arose from the overt expression of Catholic religiosity that marked the D'Avalos governorship. The D'Avalos family's interest in the current dialogue regarding Catholic reform is manifest in its friendship with the conservative Girolamo Muzio, as well as in its correspondence with Bernardino Ochino,[62] the capuchin monk whose controversial teachings came under fire by the Vatican during the 1540s. Its extreme Catholicism is further evidenced by Alfonso's presence at the Diet of Worms in 1545 and Maria d'Aragona's commission of the vitae of St Catherine and St Thomas from Pietro Aretino in 1541 and 1543 respectively.[63]

It is not clear from the 1539 statutes whether or not the eight choral beneficiaries at Santa Maria della Scala were responsible for the singing of polyphony as well as the Ambrosian plainchant for which the institution was so well known. However, at least four motet collections–*Gomberti excellentis simi* (1539), *Nicolai Gomberti musici excellentissimi pentaphthongos harmonia* (1541), *Il primo libro de motetti a cinque voci de l'egregio Vincenzo Ruffo* (1542), and the *Mutetarum divinitatis liber primus* (1543)–can be associated through dedication and content with D'Avalos's Milanese tenure, and as I have suggested elsewhere, the systematizing of the choral benefices at the royal ducal chapel of Santa Maria della Scala in 1539 may well have provided the primary impetus for their compilation.[64] While the two collections printed by Scotto in Venice, *Gomberti excellentis simi* (1539)[65] and *Nicolai Gomberti musici excellentissimi pentaphthongos harmonia* (1541),[66] are dedicated primarily to the works of Gombert and feature nothing particularly Milanese in character, the latter does contain six previously unpublished motets by Vincenzo Ruffo, who served at the D'Avalos court in 1542.[67] These six motets are reprinted or copied in a variety of later manuscript and printed sources where they are variously attributed to Ruffo, Gombert, Morales, and Jachet of Mantua,[68] but careful examination of the variants and the cautionary ficta reveals that either *Nicolai Gomberti musici excellentissimi pentaphthongos harmonia* (1541), where the motets stand without attribution to anyone, or Ruffo's own *Il primo libro de motetti a cinque voci* was invariably the original source for each of the later concordances.

Table 2.3 Festal and voicing analysis of the content of Vincenzo Ruffo's *Il primo libro de motetti* (1542)

Motet	Liturgical Text Source	Cleffing
Muro tuo inexpugnabili	Psallenda for Fer III in Adv6, Fer VI of the Samaritan, Fer IV of Lazarus, Day 2 of Litanies (Vespers ant. for Saturday after 24th Sunday after Pentecost in Roman rite)	$C_1C_3C_4C_4F_4$
Peccantem me quotidie	Matins Responsory, Office of the Dead (Roman)	$C_1C_3C_4C_4F_4$
Veni electa mea	B.V.M., Assumption and Common of Virgins (Roman)	$C_1C_3C_4C_4F_4$
Laudate Dominum	Psalm 116; Vespers Fer IV; Vespers of Saints	$C_1C_4C_4C_4F_4$
Nigra sum sed formosa	B.V.M., Assumption and Common of Virgins (Roman)	$G_2C_2C_3C_4F_3$
Ave ignea columna caeli	St Ambrose (hymn)	$C_1C_3C_4C_4F_4$
Convertimini ad me	Psallenda for Fer II of Adv6, Fer II and IV of Cap XL, Fer IV of Caeco, and Day 1 of Litanies	$C_1C_3C_4C_4F_4$
O lumen ecclesiae	Rhymed office for St Hugo (Roman)	$G_2C_2C_3C_3F_3$
Respice in me Deus	Tuesday after Quadregesima Sunday (Roman)	$G_2C_2C_3C_3F_3$
Antequam comedam (2pars. Ecce non est)	Summer Histories, from Job	$G_2C_2C_3C_3F_3$
Circumdederunt me (2 pars. Omnes videntes)	Palm Sunday (Roman)	$C_1C_3F_3F_4$
Tanto tempore	Magnificat ant.,Psallenda, Ingressa, Saints Philip and James	$C_1C_3C_3C_3F_3$
Spem in alium (2 pars. Domine Deus)	Summer Histories, from Esther; Day 3 Of Litanies	$G_2C_2C_3C_3F_3$
Specia tua	B.V.M., Common of Virgins (Roman)	$C_1C_3C_4C_4F_4$
Averte oculos meos	Psalm 118; Terce on Saturdays, Matins and Terce on Holy Saturday	$G_2C_2C_3C_3F_3$
Illumina oculos meos	Sundays during Eastertide (Roman)	$G_2C_2C_3C_3F_4$
Virgo sancta Barbara	St Barbara (Roman)	$C_1C_3C_4C_4F_3$

Uxor sicut tua vitis	Baptism of Hermes Visconti	$G_2C_2C_3C_3F_3$
Domine Jesu Christe	Offertory, Mass for the Dead (Roman)	$G_2C_2C_3C_3F_3$
Tribulationes meae	Psalm 24; Matins for the Dead, Vespers and Matins of the Innocents, Matins Fer II in Adv 6, Ant. in Office of the Dead	$G_2C_2C_3C_3F_3$
Sume dei fideles	St Aurelius (Roman)	$G_2C_2C_3C_3F_3$
O sacrum convivium	Corpus Christi (Roman)	$G_2C_2C_3C_3F_3$
Laudibus laudemus	In honor of Melchior Saavedra	$G_2C_2C_3C_3F_3$
Hodie Christus natus est	Nativity (Roman)	$G_2C_2C_3C_3F_3$
Ecce crucem Domini	Invention of the Cross (Roman)	$C_1C_4C_4C_4F_4$
Stetit angelus	Matins Cantus, St Michael (Vespers ant. for St Michael in Roman Rite)	$G_2C_2C_3C_3F_3$
Deduc me domine	Psalm 118; Terce on Saturdays, Matins and Terce on Holy Saturday	$G_2C_2C_3C_3F_3$
O doctor optime	Doctors of the Church (Roman)	$C_1C_3C_3C_3F_3$
O quam gloriosam	All Saints; Visitation (Roman)	$G_2C_2C_3C_3F_3$
O Rex gloriae	Ascension (Roman)	$G_2C_2C_3C_3F_3$
Puer natus est nobis (2 pars. Hic est enim propheta)	St John the Baptist (Roman)	$C_2C_4C_4C_4F_4$
Francorum Rex illustris	St Louis (Roman)	$G_2C_2C_3C_3F_3$
Inter vestibulum et altare	St Barbara (Roman)	$G_2C_2C_3C_3F_3$
O quam mira refulsit	St Faustinus (Roman)	$C_2C_4C_4C_4F_4$
Convertere Domine (2 pars. Laboravi in gemitu)	Matins ant, Office of the Dead (Roman)	$C_2C_4C_4C_4F_4$

Ruffo's *Il primo libro de motetti a cinque voci* (1542), which was printed by Giovanni Antonio Castiglione of Milan, features several motets for specific feasts of the Ambrosian calendar celebrated at Santa Maria della Scala, including Christmas, Palm Sunday, Easter, the Ascension, the Trinity, Corpus Christi, the Ascension, All Souls, All Saints, and St Ambrose, as well as two state motets possessing decidedly Milanese associations.[69] Most of these motets utilize Roman texts, a characteristic that is surprisingly common to Milanese polyphony of the period. The rather puzzling inclusion, however, of several motets devoted to saints insignificant to Santa Maria della Scala's festal calendar, including St Barbara, St Faustinus, St Louis, St Aurelius, and St John the Baptist, suggests that at least some of the works included may have been composed for use elsewhere in the city, if not during a previous appointment in Verona.[70] Although Lewis Lockwood and Alexandra Amati-Camperi recently suggested that Ruffo entered the service of D'Avalos as late as 1543 or 1544 and remained until the governor's death in 1546,[71] the musical and archival evidence actually confirms that the composer served D'Avalos for approximately one year immediately after he left Verona in 1541. The dedication of Ruffo's *Il primo libro de motetti* (1542), which is addressed to D'Avalos, describes the composer as 'an indefatigable musician and servant of your excellency.'[72] In addition, the application for privilege, which is dated 2 June 1542, identifies Ruffo as a 'musician and member of the household in the court of the most illustrious and excellent Marchese del Vasto, Caesar your sovereign in Italy.'[73] Ruffo, in fact, left Milan sometime before 27 October 1542, when he accepted an appointment as the maestro di cappella at the cathedral of Santa Maria di Castello in Savona.[74] Although Ruffo's presence in Savona can be verified only through 24 April 1543, by which time the cathedral had become damaged to the point of condemnation, he did not likely return to Milan. In late 1545 and early 1546, he is found serving as the maestro di cappella at the court of Andrea Doria in nearby Genova.[75]

Nineteen of the motets from Ruffo's book are set in high clefs, while the remaining sixteen are cast in low or mixed clefs (Table 2.3). Many of the motets that feature the higher cleffing are intended for major feasts of the festal calendar, but no single generalization regarding the relative importance of a given celebration can be applied to Ruffo's overall approach to the voicing. At best, it can be said that high cleffing was frequently used for ceremonial occasions and primary feasts, while low cleffing was preferred for secondary feasts and Requiem texts. Although the inclusion of so many compositions in high clefs initially renders the collection's use at Santa Maria della Scala, a church boasting a choir comprised of eight adult male voices, somewhat suspect with regard to voicing, the archival evidence demonstrates that the Milanese court borrowed boy sopranos from other Milanese churches on special occasions.[76] Moreover, it has been suggested that high cleffing implied transposition downward by as much as a third in post-Tridentine polyphony, a theory that has not yet been thoroughly considered and tested in pre-Tridentine literature.[77] In any case, the Ruffo motet book currently stands as the most reliable testimony to the polyphonic performance traditions at the royal ducal chapel during the early years of Charles V's patronage.

Among the distinctly Milanese motets included in *Il primo libro de motetti* is the setting of a hymn for the feast of St Ambrose entitled *Ave ignea columna caeli*. Each line of the hymn text is treated to its own point of imitation. These points of imitation are clearly delineated by cadences on the final, dominant, and tenor of the mode, and their voicing is nicely spaced so that crossings are limited primarily to long notes and cadences. Although the hymn is six lines in length, the entire first half of the motet is dedicated only to the first two lines, each of which is repeated in a point of imitation that functions as a variant of the preceding statement. In contrast, only the last of the succeeding four lines is afforded varied imitative repetition. This asymmetrical parsing of the text into two and four-line groups that receive equal temporal weight creates a rhetorical effect of acceleration to the repeated closing line 'tu pro nobis Deum implora' ('you implore God always for us'). Despite this careful rhetorical attention to the delineation of the poetic structure, however, the opening exordium is melodically rather unremarkable. Its presentation seems somewhat labored, perhaps because the rhythmic motion is erratic and given to 'fits and starts' (Example 2.1).

Ruffo's willingness to sacrifice local musical details to the large scale structure is equally evident in his setting of the responsory 'Puer qui natus est' for the feast of St John the Baptist. The standard abcb responsory format is underscored both by a clear cadential division into two parts at the opening of the c section and a fairly literal repetition of the 'b' material at the close of the second part. The cadential layout of the motet, however, belies the responsory format in that cadences at potentially important structural nodes are evaded through unexpected directional irresolution or the overlapping of pitches that interfere with the raising of leading tones. When structural cadences are introduced, moreover, the weaker plagal cadence on A is often preferred to the potentially stronger cadences on the dominant D and final G. This motet was attributed to Morales in a later source, and the same attribution is still repeated in the current literature. The misattribution is not surprising, given the thick, miry texture of the closely spaced inner voices and the graceful, rhythmically compelling exordium.

Example 2.1 Ruffo, *Ave ignea columna caeli*, measures 1-29

The first of the book's two occasional motets, *Laudibus Laudemus*, is dedicated to the 'invincible Duke' Melchior Saavedra. Saavedra who is identified via both the motet and the archival sources as a military captain in the service of Charles V, is only mentioned occasionally in the surviving documents, and, consequently, the scope of his activity in Milan is difficult to determine. A brief notice of 1548 indicates that he had been conceded some sort of pardon on behalf of the state,[78] and in 1552 he was paid 40 scudi for making a diplomatic journey to Asti.[79] The notice of 1548 may be associated with a formal request that Saavedra be assigned a new command. The request, which was forwarded by the Milanese chancery to the Senate on 1 December 1548, notes that Saavedra had been convicted and pardoned of a homicide during D'Avalos's tenure.[80] In any case, D'Avalos must have hosted some sort of event in Saavedra's honor while Ruffo was present. Despite its occasional nature, *Laudibus laudemus* features no cantus firmus or similar scaffolding device. Instead, it is constructed on successive points of imitation. Richard Sherr observes that the cantus part may have been composed first, thus providing an overall formal structure of aba c that Ruffo was unwilling to abandon despite the harmonic difficulties introduced by the subsequent introduction of imitation. Sherr further suggests that Ruffo may have chosen this rather awkward mode of composition because he was unaccustomed to composing with a score.[81] Whatever the method used to compose the piece, the compositional problems identified by Sherr accurately reflect Ruffo's compositions of the early 1540s, which might be characterized as occasionally lacking in the elegance and mastery found in his later masses. In fact, technical difficulties similar to those noted by Sherr, which include 'infelicitous' dissonances, suppressed or truncated imitative entries, and irresolvable ficta problems,[82] can be detected in differing guises throughout the 1542 collection, and often seem due to the greater attention afforded large scale design.

The other occasional motet of the 1542 book, *Uxor sicut tua vitis abundans*, is a bit more graceful, perhaps because it was conceived around a cantus firmus that is presented in long notes in the quintus voice. The text of the motet, which paraphrases Psalm 127, indicates that it was intended for a baptism, and the cantus firmus itself addresses one Hermes. Consequently, Lewis Lockwood has suggested that the motet was written for the baptism of Ermes Visconti, son of the prominent Milanese nobleman Giovanni Battista Visconti.[83] Giovanni Battista Visconti was elected to the Milanese Grand Council in 1535, and was among the dignitaries scheduled to participate in the 1541 entry of Charles V into Milan.[84] The baptism of his children likely took place at Santa Maria della Scala, which was originally founded by his great grandfather Barnabò Visconti as a family chapel. Ruffo may have been asked to contribute the motet as a gift on behalf of the gubernatorial court for use in the ceremonies.

A similar Milanese baptismal motet dating from the same period is found in Bernardino Calusco's *Mutetarum divinitatis liber primus* of 1543.[85] In this setting, which was contributed by Hermann Matthias Werrecore, the maestro di cappella at the Duomo, the baptismal plainchant 'Uxor tua sicut vitis abundans' is presented in the contratenor in long notes against an imitative setting of the antiphon 'Beati omnes' in the four outer voices (Example 2.2). The circumstantial evidence suggests that Werrecore's motet was composed for the baptism of Carlo D'Avalos, Alfonso and Maria's seventh child. Carlo was baptized during Charles V's nine-day royal entry into Milan in August 1541, and the emperor himself stood sponsor and conferred upon the child the Order of Alcántara.[86] The ceremony supposedly took place at the Duomo, which had been decorated with various apparati for the duration of the festivities.[87] Werrecore, as the current maestro at the Duomo and a beneficiary of the court, probably provided the necessary ceremonial music, which he then may have turned over to Calusco for inclusion in the *Mutetarum*. On 28 June 1535, in fact, Werrecore had been contracted as the editorial consultant to Giovanni Antonio Castiglione, the printer of the *Mutetarum*. In this capacity, Werrecore was obligated to select noteworthy compositions for voices and consign them directly into the hands of Rainaldo D'Adda, a local book vendor, who thereafter forwarded them to Castiglione for publication. The profits of this venture were to be divided equally among Pietro Paolo Borrono, an international spy turned local lutenist, D'Adda, and Werrecore. The contract endured for ten years, but it has not been possible to document substantively its outcome for the Castiglione press.[88]

Example 2.2 Werrecore, *Beati omnes*, measures 1-20

Dedicated to D'Avalos, who is painted as an humanistic prince of international distinction, the *Mutetarum* contains five-voice motets 'collected from the many of the most distinguished musical academies' by its editor Bernadino Calusco, a local paper vendor and calligrapher who likely also sold books.[89] The print's focus is decidedly upon the Franco-Flemish school of the post-Josquin generation, with an obvious bias toward French composers.   Among those represented are Tugdual, Johannes Lupi, Denis Brumen, Morales, Maistre Jhan, Claudin, Jean Courtois, Jean Richafort, Willaert, Hilaire Penet, Werrecore, and Dominique Phinot (Table 2.4).   Aside from Werrecore, who contributed three motets, only Lupi and Phinot are honored by more than one work. The inclusion of two motets by Lupi appears more circumstantial than it does significant, while the nod at Werrecore is expected, given his local prominence.   However, the introduction of nine motets by the virtually unknown Phinot is somewhat stunning, for his works occupy nearly half of the space allotted in the print. Of the nine motets contributed by Phinot, moreover, only the *Homo Quidam*, which was included in Scotto's *Nicolai Gomberti musici excellentissimi pentaphthongos harmonia* of 1541,[90] appears to have been published previously. Thus, the *Mutetarum* seems to have functioned, in part, as a premiere volume for Phinot's five-voice works. This view of the *Mutetarum* may explain why none of its motets are reused in the two books of Phinot's five-voice motets that were issued by Beringen of Lyon in 1547 and Cesano of Pesaro in 1554.[91]

The *Mutetarum* must have been partially responsible for the reputation that Phinot enjoyed in Milan during the succeeding years. In an epigram addressing the Milanese that was written in honor of Antonio della Paglia's appointment as the chair of rhetoric at the studio of Pavia on 15 October 1555, the humanist Publio Francesco Spinola implies that Phinot was regarded as one of the city's own sons. Spinola first compares Della Paglia's accomplishments to the recent innovations in arms construction, an industry in which Milan dominated the

Table 2.4 Content of Bernardino Calusco, ed., *Mutetarum divinitatis liber primus* **(1543)**

Composer	Motet
Tugdual	Adorna thalamum
J. Lupi	Angelus Domini
Phinot	Aspice Domine
Werrecore	Adsit nobis gratia
Phinot	Ave virgo gloriosa
Werrecore	Beati omnes qui timet Dominum
Phinot	Cecus sedebat
Phinot	Congregate sunt gentes
Phinot	Deus in nomine tuo
Phinot	Homo quidam
J. Lupi	Hodie Christus natus est nobis
Werrecore	In nomine Jesu
Phinot	Illuxit nobis dies
Brumen=Briant	In illo tempore cum venerit
Morales	Lamentabatur Iacob
Phinot	Non turbetur cor vestrum
Maistre Jhan	O sidus hispanie
Claudin	Regina coeli
Courtois	Veni Domine
Richafort	Veni sponsa Christi
Hilaire Penet	Virgo prudentissima
Willaert	Vado ad eum
Phinot	Videns Dominus

marketplace. Attributing Della Paglia's accomplishments, at least in part, to progress, Spinola then observes that the skills of the current masters, represented by Phinot, exceed those of the past via a linear stylistic development:

> Don't the contrapuntists now create melodies to sound?
> Josquin surpassed the singers and Phinot surpassed Josquin;
> another, however, will overtake both of them.[92]

Since the other local images chosen by Spinola were readily recognizable to Milanese audiences of the period, the reference to Phinot surely functioned in a similar manner. Phinot evidently was well known to the readership either through the nine motets published in the locally produced *Mutetarum* or by his very presence in Milan. In fact, Calusco's access in 1543 to such a large group of works by the then relatively unknown Phinot, when considered in light of Spinola's later tribute to him,[93] suggests that the young French composer may even have received nominal support from either D'Avalos or a Milanese ecclesiastical institution before accepting an appointment at the court of Urbino in 1544.

If Phinot was not in Lombardy at the time of the preparation of the *Mutetarum*, then Calusco likely acquired the composer's new five-voice motets through Girolamo Cardano rather than through Werrecore. A renowned professor of medicine and mathematics at the studio of Pavia,[94] Cardano traveled frequently to Paris[95] and Lyons to lecture, teach, and treat patients.[96] According to the Milanese historian Paolo Morigia, Cardano was one of the most famous scholars and lecturers of his day, and read Greek and Hebrew, as well as Latin.[97] He also produced a theoretical treatise entitled *De musica* that was published with his other works in 1563.[98] Cardano's *De Tranquillitate* of 1561 is the only contemporary source that reports the details of Phinot's gruesome punishment by death for copulation with young choirboys, and also contains important biographical information on Gombert and Carpentras.[99] Cardano apparently was acquainted not only with Phinot, but also with Calusco, for his *Practica arithmeticae* was edited and printed by the paper vendor through the house of Giovanni Antonio Castiglione in 1539.[100] Thus, Cardano may well have been the French contact through whom Calusco acquired the Phinot motets, as well as several of the other works by French composers found in the *Mutetarum*.

Despite Phinot's blossoming local notoriety, Werrecore, a well-known figure in Milanese circles by 1543, evidently was considered the city's master composer during the D'Avalos years. In 1546, in fact, he provided the polyphony for the obsequies of Alfonso D'Avalos. The centerpiece of the service was a funeral motet that portrayed D'Avalos as the fallen military commander of Charles V:

> Ah, the affliction!
> Therefore, does death so unpatriotically seize D'Avalos?
> Ah, Italy, at what cost?
> Ah, Charles, at what cost do you surrender military protection?
> Alas, has anything ever so greatly affected us?[101]

The slow, declamatory introduction of the lament features long rhythmic values moving largely by whole and half steps against the ponderous dotted rhythms of the quintus voice. Adherence to the poetic meter and a natural style of declamation are achieved via a carefully selected combination of rhythmic values and pitch inflections (Example 2.3). The composer's concern with the proper declamation of the text is underscored by the exacting text underlay and the frequent employment of ligatures to indicate melismas, characteristics that are found throughout the motets of Werrecore's 1555 collection. In Werrecore's 1555 print, *Proh dolor* is preceded by a five-voice setting of the antiphon 'Sana me domine' from the Mass for the Dead. *Sana me domine* features the plainchant cantus firmus associated with the original antiphon in its tenor voice, and further utilizes the same cleffing, system, and final as does 'Proh dolor.' Thus, it is likely that both motets were intended for the funeral services.

Regardless of whether it was performed alone or paired with the *Sana me domine*, Werrecore's *Proh dolor* most assuredly provided a fitting counterpoint to the themes of D'Avalos's Milanese funeral procession. At the close of a sixteenth-

Example 2.3 Werrecore, *Proh dolor*, measures 1-24

century manuscript containing an oration given on the death of D'Avalos, an unidentified hand recorded an account of the funeral found in a contemporary *libro di memorie*. The account reports that from 31 March until 12 April 1546 the body lay in state at San Cristoforo sopra il Naviglio in the Porta Ticinese. On 12 April the body was transported to the Duomo via a procession led by 500 monastic poor, the cavalry on horseback dressed in brown with their lances 'torn to the ground,' and the guard of the *landsknechten* draped in brown mantles. Other calvary divisions bearing lances, swords, rapiers, cudgels, and firearms, as well as two standards of the infantry and four standards of the cavalry, all of which were draped in brown and black, followed. The rear of the procession comprised the governor's riderless horse escorted by

footmen, the trumpets and drummers dressed in black and brown, and, finally, the cadaver of the governor himself, who, incidentally, was attired in the red robes of the ordinaries of the Duomo, rather than military garb. A candlelight requiem mass in the Duomo, which undoubtedly featured the traditional plainchant liturgy interspersed with Werrecore's motets, followed. For the duration of the mass, the cathedral was draped in brown cloth, and the body of the deceased surrounded by numerous crosses of wood and silver. The mass was attended by the officials and the nobility of the court, as well as by all the friars of the local monasteries. The friars were charged with the responsibility of bearing the many torches, which, along with the candles used, communicated the status of the deceased through the relative opulence of their number.[102]

Aside from the funeral and baptismal motets, there is little music surviving from the D'Avalos years that can be tied directly to the court ceremonial. Although it is tempting to interpret Calusco's reference to 'the most distinguished musical academies' as evidence that the governor either was acquainted with or even participated in an academy of some sort in Milan, there is little reliable evidence attesting to the presence of such a group before the end of the century. In fact, only two local academies have been documented for this period. The first is the professional society for lutenists, string players, keyboardists, and bagpipers,[103] and the second is the well-known Accademia dei Trasformati. The former organization was well established by 1548, while the latter, which was dedicated to the promotion of the sciences, was founded by Girolamo Cardano in 1546.[104] Neither of these seems likely to have expressed a particular interest in sacred repertoire.

D'Avalos's successor, Ferrante Gonzaga, brought to the Milanese governorship a long and illustrious career as an officer in the Imperial army. Yet Ferrante was also a son of Isabella d'Este and Francesco II Gonzaga, and his Mantuan musical heritage was never far beneath the surface. Ferrante's legacy as a patron reaches back to the 1520s, when, as captain general of the Imperial army in Naples, he employed singers David Grandsyre, Joachim de Mons, and Michel 'de Duchi,'[105] as well as several unnamed instrumentalists.[106] In 1539 Ferrante, then Viceroy of Sicily, corresponded extensively with Vincenzo Andriasio, a diplomat from the Gonzaga court in Mantua, regarding the expenses and logistics of outfitting a promising young musician who recently had entered Ferrante's service.[107] Unfortunately, the identity of the musician remains unknown. Although the renowned Orlando di Lasso reportedly served as a musician in Ferrante Gonzaga's retinue during the 1540s, it does not appear that he could possibly be the singer in question. According to Samuel Quickelberg, Lasso's earliest biographer, Ferrante brought Lasso to Italy in 1544. The following year Ferrante's retinue traveled to Paris, Mantua, and Sicily, arriving in Milan, where Ferrante had been named governor, in early 1546. Lasso, a young singer who may also have played the lute, presumably accompanied Ferrante as far as Milan, thereafter remaining at the court until late 1548 or early 1549.[108] Yet no archival or musical evidence aside from Quickelberg's biography has yet surfaced to confirm or elucidate Lasso's presence there. In a letter to Ferrante Gonzaga's secretary dated 26 December 1546, Mantuan secretary Alessandro Donesio noted that

> . . . I have nothing other to report except that tomorrow morning I will meet with messer Orlando regarding the issue of the money, and I will endeavor to have and to send it to him as soon as will be possible.[109]

Although this passage may be a reference to Orlando di Lasso, there is no clear indication that the Orlando mentioned is a musician. Moreover, other documents reveal that Ferrante's staff also included a gardener named Orlando. From the 1520s onward, in any case, Ferrante strove to maintain several instrumentalists, as well as at least one singer-composer of note. Just several years after Lasso's supposed departure from Milan in late 1548 or early 1549, in fact, the esteemed madrigalist Hoste da Reggio entered Ferrante's employ.[110]

The bulk of Hoste's compositional output for the Milanese court was secular, but his *Il primo libro de madrigali a tre voci* of 1554, which is dedicated to Ferrante's daughter Hippolita, does include five motets for important feasts falling between the Nativity and the Purification: *Sic praesans testatur* (Nativity), *Ego vero orationem mean* (Pro defunctis), *Pastores qui audierunt* (Epiphany), *Tua est potentia* (Circumcision), and *Scriptum est enim/Postquam autem* (Purification).[111] Only the Psallenda *Tua est potentia* for the feast of the Circumcision, however, textually conforms to the Ambrosian rite; the texts of the others are borrowed from the Roman tradition. Since the collection was compiled for the celebration of Hippolita's nuptials to Antonio Carafa de Mandragone, the motets may well have been intended for use in Hippolita's own private chapel, rather than at Santa Maria della Scala. While their spare three-voice texture is suited, in principle, to Scala's small forces, performance of the works by an ensemble of exclusively adult male singers would likely have required downward transposition.

Despite Ferrante's reputation as an esteemed patron of music, the surviving documentation betrays his rather cavalier attitude toward the quality of the singers employed at Santa Maria della Scala and Sant'Ambrogio. His chief legacy to the chapels appears, in fact, to have been a perversion of the intentionally arduous process by which singers were selected and approved for appointments. In December 1550 Ferrante nominated Cristoforo Toccho, a sacristan with no apparent musical qualifications, to the recently vacated office of mansionarius at Sant'Ambrogio.[112] The nomination obviously was politically motivated, for it is quite clear from the surviving documentation not only that Ferrante was personally acquainted with Toccho, but also that Toccho's musical illiteracy was at least tacitly acknowledged by all of the parties involved in the decision. Alarmed by the impending appointment of an ignorant, irresponsible, penniless, and, above all, musically unqualified individual to an office which essentially might be described as assistant to the chief cantor,[113] Bishop Galeazzo Petra suggested that Luciano Ardicio, a former choirboy who was considered more than adequately trained for such a position, be considered.[114] Ferrante, undaunted by the Bishop's strong objections, insisted upon pushing the nomination of Toccho.

If the lack of the documentary evidence for the years 1555 to 1570 at all reflects the activity of the gubernatorial chapels, then it can be said that the ceremonial slipped into obscurity during the years following Ferrante's tenure. In 1561, when Ferdinando D'Avalos was serving as interim governor, a dispute arose regarding the right of the choral beneficiaries at Santa Maria della Scala to accept other appointments. The controversy apparently had come to a head primarily because one of the chaplains, Brumanesio de Manzoni, had secured a second benefice elsewhere. While the chapter dignitaries maintained that the original founding documents prohibited such activity, the choral beneficiaries argued that they had been given to understand otherwise.[115] After carefully examining the founding documents, royal apostolic protonotary Paolo Pallavicino ruled that the choral beneficiaries indeed were permitted to hold other benefices, provided that the stipulations attached to them neither conflicted with royal prerogatives nor interfered with the singing of the canonical hours at Santa Maria della Scala.[116] The very existence of the dispute itself suggests that at least a few of the eight choral beneficiaries were either eager to serve elsewhere or less than adequately attentive to their duties at Santa Maria della Scala. It is possible, moreover, that the singers derived their supposed right to sing elsewhere from the mere existence of the rotational schedule used for ferial days.

Had it not been for the administrative zeal of Cardinal Carlo Borromeo, who was appointed Archbishop of Milan in 1560, Santa Maria della Scala may well have limped slowly into further musical decline during the final quarter of the sixteenth century. Shortly his arrival in Milan in September 1565, Borromeo embarked on the daunting task of standardizing the liturgy by enforcing universal adherence to the Ambrosian rite.[117] The goal of conformity via a standard Ambrosian practice was not as easily achieved as is often imagined. Despite its reputation as an Ambrosian center, Milan was, in actuality, a city of liturgical diversity. Its churches depended variously upon the Ambrosian rite, the Roman rite, and, in many cases, an individualized combination of the two. Thus, it comes as no surprise that Borromeo was eager to exercise his recently acquired authority at the royal ducal chapel of Santa Maria della Scala, a collegiate church historically dedicated to the preservation of the Ambrosian rite[118] and the official Milanese chapel of the Hapsburg state.

Santa Maria della Scala offered the new Archbishop a rigorous challenge on several levels. Following its golden era as the state chapel of Francesco II Sforza and Alfonso D'Avalos, the church was neglected, to a greater or lesser degree, by the governors installed by Carlo V and Philip II. Yet Santa Maria della Scala retained its official status as the royal ducal chapel. Although Francesco II Sforza had initially required that all of its canons be present for the singing of the offices,[119] he saw to it that they were exempted from daily obligations after its choral benefices were established. Matters were made even more complicated by the fact that the chapter itself was also granted an exemption from all regular diocesan jurisdiction, but was to consult the local Archbishop directly in all such matters. These exemptions were granted during the tenure of Ippolito II d'Este, who resigned his office in 1550.[120] At the time of their enactment, they served to benefit all parties concerned. The exemption from diocesan jurisdiction, for example, allowed Francesco II great latitude in administering the chapel, for Ippolito did not reside in the dioceses and demonstrated very little interest in its day-to-day operation. At the same time this exemption, with its protective clause requiring the Archbishop's express approval, insured Clement VII that Francesco II's power would be held in check, at least theoretically speaking.

When Borromeo, well within his rights as Archbishop, ordered a pastoral visit to the church in 1569, the dignitaries, including the eight choral beneficiaries, officially protested by claiming their right of exemption. The visit was made, but not before a number of the dignitaries, including several of the choral beneficiaries, had been arrested for failing to appear and the entire chapter publicly excommunicated for insubordination.[121] The episode was perhaps the most notable of Borromeo's tenure, and is among the civic calamities recorded by historian Gaspare Bugati for the year 1569.[122] The resulting relationship between Santa Maria della Scala and Borromeo was an uneasy one at best. Yet Borromeo's successive 1574 visit clearly initiated a series of musical reforms that were to catapult the chapel to an unprecedented level of musical excellence by the turn of the century. The extant notes from this visit specify that information regarding the various tasks associated with the benefices founded by Francesco II Sforza, which included the eight choral chaplaincies, be researched and documented in writing within three months. Furthermore, a system for determining the celebrant and his assistants was established for the singing of the high mass. In addition, the canons and choral beneficiaries assigned to the choir were no longer permitted to serve in another church during the singing of the canonical hours and mass at Santa Maria della Scala. If, on rare occasion, however, one of them received permission from the Provost to serve elsewhere, he was not to accept any remuneration. Finally, the epistle, gospel, and other similar items were to be rehearsed before a canon appointed by the Provost, and the chants were to be sung directly from the books in order to avoid transmitting the melodies incorrectly.[123] As might be expected, the plainchant books to which the transcripts of the visit refer comprised a rich manuscript collection that has since been dispersed. According to one sixteenth-century inventory, they included an antiphonary, a modern missale, two ancient missales, another missale in manuscript used by the archpriests, a modern breviary, an ancient breviary, and a psaltery containing the calendar for 1461, as well as certain other songbooks and psalteries used by the choir.[124]

It appears that the aforementioned pastoral orders accomplished little in the way of shoring up performance of the liturgy, and, as a result, Borromeo resorted to the creation of the position of maestro di cappella, thus placing the responsibility of leading the choir, which had formerly been assigned to the two mansionari, in the hands of a single professional ecclesiastical musician. In 1580 he nominated Orfeo Vecchi, a young Milanese cleric and composer, to the post,[125] and this is the first surviving reference to any such position at Santa Maria della Scala.[126] The choice of Vecchi clearly was a calculated one; he was still inexperienced enough to be malleable, yet was also well trained. Moreover, like many musicians who had served previously at Santa Maria della Scala, he had been educated at the Cathedral of Vercelli, where he received the tonsure.[127] Evidently intending to bring Vecchi's nomination into compliance with the 1565 provincial council's dictate that all sacred musicians be selected from among the trained clergy when possible, Borromeo conferred the composer with minor orders on 23 September 1581.[128] However, the issue of the appointment itself was likely quite thorny, as Santa Maria della Scala operated via an established number of benefices that included eight appointments for choral musicians, none of which appears to have been vacant. Moreover, appointment to a choral benefice was contingent upon the successful completion of a three-month trial period in the performance of Ambrosian chant that culminated in a chapter vote as to the candidate's suitability. The lack of an actual benefice to which the maestro could be appointed may explain Vecchi's decision to resign the post two years later in favor of the position of maestro di cappella at the Cathedral of Vercelli,[129] an appointment which, in turn, led to his accumulation of five benefices outside Milan between 1582 and 1585.[130] After serving in Vercelli for four years, Vecchi presumably returned to Santa Maria della Scala,[131] despite the fact that no benefice was yet available. He was nominated to a chaplaincy at the altar of San Giovanni in Santa Maria della Scala in 1590,[132] but it appears that the nomination was not approved. Vecchi finally was awarded the post of mansionarius at Santa Maria dell Scala when it was vacated in 1591 upon the death of Cristoforo Vergha.[133] Ironically enough, although Vecchi's subsequent tenure at Santa Maria della Scala marked both the resurrection of the chapel to its former stature as a leading musical institution of the city and its ascent as a Milanese center for the post-Tridentine style, Carlo Borromeo did not live long enough to witness the effects of Vecchi's presence. Vecchi's output alone, which hails primarily from the period of Federico Borromeo, is a testament to the role that Santa Maria della Scala would come to play in defining the sacred style of post-Tridentine Milan. It includes a volume of spiritual madrigals, masses conforming to the edicts of the Milanese Council (presumably those of 1565), and numerous motets, psalm settings, hymns, falsebordoni, and Magnificats for use at High Mass, Vespers, and Compline throughout the liturgical year.[134]

While certain elements of the ducal ceremonial were retained and transformed under the Milanese governors following the death of Francesco II Sforza, other new practices were gradually introduced across the century. Under Francesco II's successors, for example, all public appearances of the governor were preceded by a low mass held in San Gottardo in Corte, the official cappella of the Palazzo Ducale, where three ducal chaplains were available to preside. This arrangement allowed the governor to move quickly and efficiently from the private sphere of the court chapel to the adjacent public domain of the Piazza of the Duomo. On solemn feasts such as Christmas and Easter, however, the mass, which was sung, was often transferred to the Duomo or another appropriate ducal chapel in order to accommodate a larger group of attendees that generally included the ambassadors, the senate, the magistrates, the Captain of Justice, the Vicar of Provisions and his tribunal, the judges, and the college of lawyers. In many of these instances, however, the mass was sung by the musicians of the governor, presumably the eight serving at the royal ducal chapel of Santa Maria della Scala, rather than by the resident choir.[135] The only exceptions to this practice appear to have been made for royal entries and funerals, which were held in the Duomo, where the Archbishop presided with the assistance of the Duomo choir.[136]

By the early seventeenth century, the eight choral chaplains from Santa Maria della Scala not only performed the Ambrosian liturgy daily in the royal ducal chapel, but also sang frequently for private and semi-public courtly devotions sponsored by the governor of Milan and his family in various other ducal chapels of Milan, presumably at the Vespers hour. There they routinely were joined by four additional chaplains drawn from the host chapel:

> . . .for greater convenience, particularly when the signory is also present, twelve sacerdotes, of which eight are invited outside of the house from the royal cappella, perform [the service]. They sing the psalms in alternatim. The aforementioned eight sacerdotes are paid by the governor. The other four are cappellani from the cappella to which fall the bequests.[137]

In addition to providing for the court ceremonial, the royal ducal chapel at Santa Maria della Scala hosted the gubernatorial celebration of the Purification, which was marked by the annual blessing of the candles. The feast of the Purification itself, which was introduced into the Ambrosian liturgy around the ninth century,[138] was among the most important Milanese feasts devoted to the Blessed Virgin. At Santa Maria della Scala, it culminated in a sung mass, the blessing and lighting of the candles, and a candlelight procession through the church. Apparently, the liturgy of the Purification was performed there in the traditional Ambrosian manner, for the documents describe the intoning and recitation of the Gloria, Gospel, Credo, Sanctus, and Dona nobis pacem in a style reminiscent of the directives for the performance of Ambrosian plainchant items found in the chapel's 1539 statutes.[139]

Santa Maria della Scala was not however, the only place in which special services were heard on the feast of the Purification. While the governor's party was ensconced in Santa Maria della Scala, much of the local population evidently participated in a procession from the Duomo to Santa Maria Beltrade. Upon arriving at Santa Maria Beltrade, the processors witnessed the blessing of the candles and heard Terce sung. If the distribution of the candles consumed a great deal of time, they remained for the singing of Sext as well. In either case, the attendant population thereafter returned processionally to the Duomo for mass and the remaining canonical hours, thus concluding its exercises in a manner similar to that concurrently observed by the government officials at Santa Maria della Scala.[140]

At some point between 1538 and 1629 it became customary for the governor's retinue to attend Holy Week services at San Gottardo in Corte. These services included the singing of selected canonical hours beginning on Tuesday of Holy Week, as well as special services on Maundy Thursday, Good Friday, and Holy Saturday. Although the schedule for performance of the canonical hours is somewhat difficult to discern from the documents, it appears that at least one office was sung before the governor each day after the midday meal. It is particularly noteworthy that these offices sung before the governor were designated as semi-private functions, in contrast to the other Holy Week ceremonies sponsored by San Gottardo for the court. The latter included a high mass and a candlelight procession of the blessed sacrament on Maundy Thursday, a sung mass, a plainchant recitation of the Passion in alternatim, the singing of the Adoration of the Cross, and Vespers on Good Friday, and, finally, the blessing of the paschal candle and a high mass on Holy Saturday. The Saturday high mass was sung in the Roman rite, and the visitors washed their eyes during the Gloria. No services were designated for Easter Sunday, but during the seventeenth century the governor usually took communion with the Cavalgieri di Sant'Iago.[141]

The Good Friday services, and, in particular, the Adoration of the Cross and its accompanying Vespers, appear to have been the highlight of the Easter weekend at San Gottardo in Corte. Unfortunately, however, little is known regarding the musical details of the service. Nonetheless, Matthias Werrecore's five-voice motet *Popule meus*, which likely was composed for the concurrent ritual of the Adoration of the Cross in the Duomo, reveals not only the peculiar attention afforded the Adoration liturgy in Renaissance Milan, but also the inventive manner in which polyphony was incorporated into it. The motet, which is divided into four sections, opens with a free imitative setting of the verse 'Popule meus' for five voices. This free imitative section is followed by two successive sections in reduced scoring that correspond, in part, to verses that were often performed by two soloists in alternation (See Table 3.2). The motet closes with a setting of the verse 'Ego te pavi manna' for six voices that is woven around an ostinato cantus firmus 'Ego Deus salvator' in the added Tenor II voice. The ostinato is stated five times, and features alternating statements on G in the soft hexachord and D in the natural hexachord (Example 2.4).

Daily observances that were not directly attached to the gubernatorial ceremonial also abounded in sixteenth-century Milan, and many of these were supported, at least in part, by ducal benefices. At the collegiate church of San Giorgio al Palazzo, for example, the canonical hours and a High Mass were sung daily by the canons and chaplains. Vespers was clearly central to the service structure there, for it was performed by all of the chaplains and canons, whereas only the canons were held responsible for singing the other canonical hours. Moreover, the Provost presided at High Mass and Vespers on solemn feasts, but left such duties to the canons throughout

the remainder of the liturgical year.[142]   Matins and Lauds at San Giorgio, as at Santa
Maria della Scala, were conflated into a single service that was matched in musical
complexity only by the aforementioned High Mass and Vespers.[143] Approximately six
canons and twelve chaplains generally were in residence during the sixteenth
century,[144] and a prefect supervised the singing of the liturgy.[145]   Several of the
beneficiaries apparently were quite proficient, and, as a result, invited to sing
elsewhere. The surviving notes from the pastoral visit of 1569 repeatedly state that the
canons and chaplains were prohibited under threat of monetary fine from shirking their
duties at San Giorgio in order to accept engagements in other churches on special
feasts,[146] thus suggesting that the issue was an ongoing problem. In addition to singing
the High Mass and canonical hours, moreover, each beneficiary at San Giorgio was
expected to conduct his own daily mass in the chapel assigned to him.[147] Indeed, San
Giorgio was characterized by ceaseless liturgical activity, and a mass or service could
be found in progress there during any hour of the day. This phenomenon, of course,
was not atypical of most churches in Renaissance Milan.

Example 2.4 Werrecore, *Ego te pavi manna*, measures 1-34

Religious ceremony in sixteenth-century Milan, as in the Venetian Republic,[148] was intimately tied to public policy, international relations, and civic identity. Appearances of the governor, who not only represented the Emperor but also effectively replaced the recently defunct ducal family, were marked by liturgical observances in which the ducal ceremonial was transformed into a gubernatorial one.

Gubernatorial masses, Holy Week services, and the Blessing of the Candles on the feast of the Purification were variously assigned to the ducal chapels and churches in the city center that had formerly served the Sforza, including San Gottardo in Corte, Santa Maria della Scala, and, most importantly, the Duomo. Within this newly conceived gubernatorial context, both the royal ducal chapel of Santa Maria della Scala and the Duomo choir functioned as the principal musical ensembles. The former accompanied the governor as a part of his official retinue, while the latter, situated at epicenter of the city and host of the most lavish civic celebrations, officiated both within and without its walls.

Notes

1   On the events surrounding the investiture, see Gino Franceschini, 'Gli ultimi anni del ducato indipendente,' *Storia di Milano* (Milano: Giovanni Treccani degli Alfieri, 1961), VIII, 310-313; Santoro, *Gli Sforza*, 377-387; and Burigozzi, *Cronaca milanese*, 497-507.
2   Franceschini, 'Gli ultimi anni,' 316-317. Ludovico Maria Sforza apparently made similar attempts to contain some of these legislative bodies. See Evelyn Welch, *Art and Authority in Renaissance Milan* (New Haven and London: Yale University Press, 1995), 219.
3   See Welch, *Art and Authority*, 212-219, and Evelyn Welch, 'Sight, sound and ceremony in the chapel of Galeazzo Maria Sforza,' *Early Music History* 4 (1993), 151-190.
4   On the evolution of the episcopate and cathedral church in Vigevano, see Michele Ansani, 'Da chiesa della communitá a chiesa del Duca. Il vescovado sfortiana.' in *Metamorfosi di un borgo. Vigevano in etá visconteo-sforzesco* (Milano: , 1992), 117-144.
5   *Sezione* I R5 N5, fascicolo 1-3, Archivio Curia Vescovile, Vigevano (hereafter AVV). A much fuller treatment of the founding and early operation of the ducal chapels at Sant'Ambrogio and Santa Maria della Scala is found in Getz, 'The Sforza Restoration,' 109-159.
6   *Sezione* I R5 N5, fascicolo 5, numero 6 (Menso vescovile), AVV.
7   *Culto* p.a. 2218 (Vescovi e Vescovati: Vigevano A-Z), Statuti del Capitolo di Vigevano, ASM.
8   Ibid., Addenda, ASM.
9   Daily distributions were awarded each beneficiary for performance of his specified duties at each service.   *Culto* p.a. 2218 (Vescovi e Vescovati: Vigevano A-Z), Statuti del Capitolo di Vigevano, fols. 3r, 7r-v, and 10v.
10 *Culto* p.a. 2218 (Vescovi e Vescovati: Vigevano A-Z), Statuti del Capitolo di Vigevano, fol. 2v, ASM.
11 Ibid., ASM, and Autografi 12/2 (Galeazzo Petra, Vescovo di Vigevano, 1530-1552), fol. 65b, ASM.
12 On certain unspecified feasts, however, the singing of the *Benedicamus domino* and *Iube domine* might be assigned to the deacons. *Culto* p. a. 2218 (Vescovi e Vescovati: Vigevano A-Z), Statuti del Capitolo di Vigevano, fols. 8r and 10r, ASM.
13 *Culto* p.a. 2218 (Vescovi e Vescovati: Vigevano A-Z), Statuti del Capitolo di Vigevano, fols 2v and 10r, ASM.
14 Quintero died in 1550 and was replaced by Cristoforo Toccho. *Autografi* 12/1(Galeazzo Petra, Vescovo di Vigevano 1530-1552), fols 60, 64, and 65, ASM.

15   *Autografi* 52/2 (Augustino Gerrero, Vescovo di Vercelli 1511-1536), n.n. (5 gennaio 1532), ASM.

16   See G. Roncaglia, *La cappella musicale del Duomo di Modena* (Firenze: Leo S. Olschki, 1957), 22, 81, and 309. A setting of Sumens illud Ave that is attributed to 'Fran. Ros.' is found in Modena, Biblioteca et Archivio Capitolare del Duomo, MS Mus. III. The manuscript can be dated to Roserino's tenure there.

17   On 9 November 1548 Rosarino was honored with a long eulogy before the cathedral chapter. *Serie* II, numero 71 (Liber ordinationum Sancti Ambrogij 1543-1550) n.n., Archivio Capitolare, Vigevano (hereafter ACV).

18   *Cancelleria dello Stato di Milano* 32 (1541 gennaio), fol. 62, ASM notes that Rosarino's annual salary had been 200 lire since the reign of Francesco II. Rosarino wrote a number of letters to the Milanese chancery lamenting the declining quality of the choir after Francesco II's demise and requesting payment of his annual salary of 200 lire during the 1540s.

19   These recruiting ventures are mentioned in two letters from Galeazzo Petra, Bishop of Vigevano, to Francesco II Sforza dated 3 August 1531 and 7 August 1531, as well as in a letter from Augustino Gerrero, Bishop of Vercelli, to Francesco II Sforza dated 5 January 1532. *Autografi* 12/1 (Galeazzo Petra, Vescovo di Vigevano 1530-1552), fols. 27 and 28, ASM, *and Autografi* 52/2 (Augustino Gerrero, Vescovo di Vercelli 1511-1536), n.n., ASM. The soprano Vincenzo de Vercelli was acquired during Rosarino's recruiting trips to Vercelli.

20   ' . . . certi canti novi de Trinitate, tanti dolci et gratti al horechia.' *Autografi* 12/1 (Galeazzo Petra, Vescovo di Vigevano 1530-1552), fol. 22, ASM.

21   See Getz, 'The Sforza Restoration,' 143-145.

22   On Santa Maria della Scala's early institutional history, see Paola Meroni, 'Santa Maria della Scala: un aspetto della politica ecclesiatica dei duchi di Milano,' *Archivio Storico Lombardo* 115/6 (1989), 37-89.

23   A copy of the original ordinationes is preserved in *Culto* p. a. 1115 (Chiese-Communi, Milano: Santa Maria della Scala, Capitolo), n.n., ASM. Additionally, *Culto* p.a. 2126 (Patronati regi P.G.-1734), fasc. 3, fols 14-17, ASM, which comprises a manuscript history of the ducal benefices to 1561 by Agostino Bassanini, contains information of the early benefices at Santa Maria della Scala. A second copy of Bassanini's history is found in *Ms. 2F-1-18*, Biblioteca Capitolare, Milano (hereafter BCM).

24   *Culto* p.a. 2126 (Patronati regi P.G.-1734), fasc. 3, fol. 53, ASM.

25   *Sforzesco* 1428 (Milano città e ducato: 1530 ottobre e novembre), Busta novembre, n.n., ASM.

26   *Sforzesco* 1431 (Milano città e ducato: 1531 febbraio), n.n. (1 February 1531), ASM.

27   Ibid., (1 February 1531, 5 February 1531, and 10 February 1531), ASM. San Giovanni al Vedra, also known as San Giovanni ad Viperam, was located outside the Porta Vercellina. 'Al Vedra' and 'ad Viperam' may allude to the church's location near the Castello Sforzesco.

28   *Sforzesco* 1432 (Milano città e ducato: 1531 marzo), n.n. (4 March 1531), ASM.

29   *Sforzesco* 1431 (Milano città e ducato: 1531 febbraio), n.n. (1 February 1531), ASM.

30   *San Fedele* XXII-155 (Santa Maria della Scala: Visite pastorali e documenti aggiunti), q. 4 (D), Archivio Storico Diocesano, Milano (hereafter ASDM).

31   *San Fedele* XXII-155 (Visite pastorali e document aggiunti), q. 13 (Q), ASDM.

32   Ibid.

33   Ibid.

34   *San Fedele* XXVII-160 (Visite pastorali e documenti aggiunti), q. Q., ASDM. This list

also includes four feasts already listed in the 1539 statutes, including the Visitation BVM (2 July), the Nativity BVM (8 September), the feast of St Ambrose (7 December), and the feast of St John the Evangelist (28 December). The document itself is undated, but is found among a group of documents dating from 1539 to approximately 1660.

35 *San Fedele* XXII-155 (Visite pastorali e documenti aggiunti), q. 13 (Q), ASDM

36 Anna Maria Pedrocchi, 'Il coro della chiesa di San Fedele in Milano,' *Arte Lombarda* 65 (1983), 89-90.

37 Pedrocchi, 'Il coro della chiesa di San Fedele,' 89.

38 Ibid.

39 Ibid.

40 'Item ordinaverunt dicti officiales ut supra q*uod* quilibet tam mansionari*us* Cappellanus, qu*am* et levita de nova admittendus ad rescidentiam sive ad distributiones quottidianas ipsius eccle*sie* teneatur et debeat per tres menses continuos deservire ipsi ecclesiae in divinis offitijs et horis can*onic*is absque aliqua perceptione distributionum ipsius ecclesiae Et non possit admitti ad dietas distributiones nisi fuerit Idoneus in canto plano et optime, sciat legere libros max*ime* eisude*m* eccle*sie* et etia*m* cantare more ambrosiano cognoscere omnes tonos ac eos bene annuciare et no*n* solum psalmos sed etia*m* Evangelia Ep*isto*las ac lectiones Benedictione Cerei pascalis ac o*mn*ia alia circa dictu*m* offitiu*m* necessaria et opportuna, et laudatus et approbatus per R*evere*ndum Cap*itu*lum d*omino*rum Canonico*rum* et etia*m* per dictos d*om*inos Mansionarios Capellanos et levitas pro Idoneo et sufficienti nec aliter possit admitti nisi sit Idoneus ut s*upra* et laudatus ut s*upra*.' *San Fedele* XXII-155 (Santa Maria della Scala: Visite pastorali e documenti aggiunti), q. 13 (Q), ASDM. Also see Getz, 'The Sforza Restoration,' 126.

41 *San Fedele* XXV-158 (Santa Maria della Scala: Visite pastorali e documenti aggiunti), q. 1, ASDM. Giuseppi de Luca, '"Traiettorie" ecclesiatiche e strategie socio-economiche nella Milano di fine Cinquecento. Il capitolo di S. Maria della Scala dal 1570 al 1600,' *Nuova rivista storica* LXXVII/3 (1993), 531, gives 1565 as the date of Pelizono's appointment. De Luca's date appears to be based upon documents from the end of the century.

42 *Notarile* 22109 (Bartolomeo Fioreni q. Giovanni Battista 22/02/1590-06/09/1596), 24/07/1591, ASM. By the time of his appointment as mansionarius, however, Vecchi had been serving as maestro di cappella for several years. On the basis of information found in a Status personalis from a pastoral visit made to Santa Maria della Scala in 1596, Marina Toffetti, 'Nuovi documenti su Orfeo Vecchi,' *Nuova Rivista Musicale Italiana* 30/3-4 (1996), 454-455, has determined that Vecchi ascended to the post of maestro di cappella between June 1580 and September 1582.

43 Several printed Ambrosian breviaries of the period survive, including the *Breviarium iuxta istitutionem Sancti Ambrosij* (Venezia: Hieronymo Scotto, 1539); the *Breviarium mediolanense* (Mediolani: Nicolai Landriani, 1549), and the *Breviarium ambrosianum* (Milano: Matthaeus Besutius, 1574), all of which are preserved in the Biblioteca Nazionale, Braidense.

44 *Missale secundum morem . . . S. Ambrosij* (Mediolani: Giovanni Angelo Scinzenzeller, 1522. Milano, Biblioteca Nazionale Braidense H.XXII.125.

45 *Sforzesco* 1431 (Milano città e ducato 1531 febbraio), n.n., ASM. See Appendix I, document 1.

46 'Signor tutto el m*on*do non cazaria fora di fantasia a q*ue*sti regio bidello cantorij piferij trombetti custodi del domo che v*ost*ra Ex*cellen*tia no*n* mi habia facto dar dinarij p*er* pagarli di modo ch*e* mi son tanto fastidosi che me acuzano Dove sup*plico* v*ost*ra Eccellentia la si degni advisarmj se la vol ch*e* se pagano ma mj no*n* ne pagaria niuno

excepa quella cera che vostra Eccellentia disse al regio che sopra de Lej la tolesse dece scuti pagaria tutta questa generation se fara quello meglio pareva a vostra Eccellentia El prevosto da la Scalla.' *Sforzesco* 1444 (Milano città e ducato: 1533 marzo e aprile), 1533 marzo, n.n., ASM. An addendum to a letter dated 21 May 1533 from the Provost of La Scala to Francesco II Sforza. The letter is in the wrong cartella. Also see Getz, 'The Sforza Restoration,' 122.

47   See Chapter 5 below for further information regarding the instrumentalists.

48   Welch, *Art and Authority in Renaissance Milan*, 208-209.

49   'Che come giunse drento della porte . . . con festa suoni e canti tutta via.' Lessandro Verini Fiorentino, *La entrata che ha fatto il sacro Carlo Quinto Imperadore Romano nella inclita citta di Milano et la festa fatta* (Milano: Gottardo da Ponte, 1533), s.p.

50   'La cenna venne . . . e tutto in quella rocha suoni, canti, diletti, con vivande quanto puo cor pensare.' Fiorentino, *La entrata che ha fatto il sacro Carlo Quinto*, s.p.

51   ' . . .al Duomo andorono la Santa messa quivi per vedere e quella undita tutti in un drapello tornorono drento al pompelo castello.' Fiorentino, *La entrata che ha fatto il sacro Carlo Quinto*, s.p.

52   'Quivi con gran letitia tutti quanti// et con amore et carita infinita// stettono quattro di in suoni e canti e con gran festa di corte bandita// con balli e tornamenti, e giochi tanti// che mai tal cosa fu visto o sentita// chi qua, chi la, chi fu, chi giu andava, chi balla o canta, e chi lieto mangiava.' Fiorentino, *La entrata che ha fatto il sacro Carlo Quinto*, s.p.

53   Burigozzi, *Cronaca Milanese*, 517-518.

54   Burigozzi, *Cronaca milanese*, 519.

55   On the issues surrounding each entry, see Silvio Leydi, *Sub umbra imperialis aquilae: Immagine del potere e consenso politico nella Milano di Carlo V* (Firenze: Leo S. Olschki, 1999), 50-63. The Imperial impresa was an eagle. The eagle was often combined with the columns of Hercules and the motto 'Plus ultra,' which comprised Charles's personal impresa and motto, respectively.

56   Francesco Rosarino, who served as cantor from 1531 until 1550, submitted annual requests for the release of his unpaid stipend to the chancery. Upon his death in 1561, Rosarino's successor, Giovanni Maria Minolta, was owed salary from 1554 through 1561. *Culto* p.a. 1420 (Vigevano, sezione 1: Canonici cantori), n.n., ASM.

57   G. Alberigo, 'Aragona, Maria d'.' *Dizionario biografico degli italiani* (Roma: Società Grafica Romana, 1961), III, 701.

58   F. Fiorentino, 'Donna Maria d'Aragona, Marchesa del Vasto,' *Nuova Antologia* 43 (1884), 212-229. The religious works written expressly for Maria include Franco's *Dialoghi dove si ragiona della bellezza* (1542) and Aretino's *Vita di Caterina vergine e martire* (1541) and *Vita di San Tommaso beato* (1543). Lewis Lockwood, *The Counter-Reformation and the Masses of Vincenzo Ruffo* (Venezia: Fondazione Giorgio Cini, 1967), 23, also credits D'Avalos with 'Il bianco e dolce cigno,' but Antonfrancesco Doni identifies Luigi Cassola as the author of this text in his *Dialogo della musica* of 1544.

59   C. Mutini, 'Contile, Luca,' *Dizionario biografico degli italiani* (Roma: Società Grafica Romana, 1983), XXVIII, 497-498, notes that Contile claimed in a letter to have served D'Avalos in 1542, but is listed in the rosters of Cardinal Agostino Trivulzio that year as well. In 1545, however, Contile accompanied D'Avalos to the Diet of Worms.

60   Entries recording payments of Aretino's annual salary of 200 scudi are found in the *Registri della Cancelleria dello Stato* XXII/1 (Mandati 1536-1538), 40v-41r, *Registri della Cancelleria dello Stato* XXII/2 (Mandati 1538-1540), 128v-129r; and *Registri della Cancelleria dello Stato* XXII/3 (Mandati 1541), 8r; ASM. In addition, belated payments of his stipend are discussed in *Cancelleria dello Stato di Milano* 44 (1543 marzo), 162

and 181, and *Cancelleria dello Stato di Milano* 47 (1543 dicembre), 249, ASM. Aretino evidently had been on the payroll since the tenure of Francesco II Sforza, but resided in Venice rather than in Milan.

61   *Registri della Cancelleria dello Stato* XV/2 (Missive 1541-1543), 96r-v, ASM, records provisions made for Albicante's tax-free residence at the Castello in Abbiategrasso. According to A. Asor-Rosa, 'Albicante, Alberto Furibondo,' *Dizionario biografico degli italiani* (Roma: Società Grafica Romana, 1960), II, 1, Albicante was pronounced Milanese court poet with the publication of his *La notomia d'amore* of 1538. The text is dedicated to D'Avalos.

62   See Lockwood, *The Counter-Reformation and the Masses*, 24. In addition, Karl Benrath, *Bernardino Ochino of Siena*, trans. Helen Zimmern (New York: Robert Carter and Brothers, 1977), 93 and 141, reports two noteworthy pieces of extant correspondence. In the first, which is dated 10 February 1542, Ochino encourages D'Avalos to abandon his pursuit of worldly political and military fame. The second, which was penned by Bishop Matteo Giberti on 25 March 1542, suggests that Ochino was assisted by D'Avalos in his flight to the Swiss border following a summons to appear before the Inquisition.

63   Both are dedicated to Maria d'Aragona, Marchesa del Vasto. Fiorentino, 'Donna Maria d'Aragona,' 223.

64   See Getz, 'The Sforza Restoration,' 139-141. Also see Chapter 3 below.

65   The collection is dedicated to D'Avalos, and contains 22 motets by Gombert.

66   The print contains no dedication, but the inclusion of six previously unpublished motets that reappear in Ruffo's 1542 book the following year suggests a strong connection to D'Avalos. In addition to the six Ruffo motets, it features nine motets by Gombert, five by Jachet of Mantua, two by Morales, and one by Phinot. A further three motets are unattributed, though one has been ascribed to Grandsyre.

67   The motets include *O doctor optime, Inter vestibulum et altare, Puer qui natus est, Hodie Christus natus est, Convertimini ad me,* and *Spem in alium.*

68   These include RISM R3047, G1550, 155410, 15568, and 15644, as well as Stuttgart, Württemburgishe Landesbibliothek Chorbuch I/34 (c. 1548-1550), Treviso, Biblioteca Capitolare Ms. 4 (c. 1559-1575), Breslau, Universitätsbibliothek Ms. 6.114 (c. 1567), and Münster, Bischöflische Bibliothek, Santinischen Sammlung 2744 (19th century).

69   Vincenzo Ruffo, *Il primo libro de motetti a cinque voci* (Mediolani: Giovanni Antonio Castiglione, 1542). The collection contains thirty-five motets by Ruffo. Its partbooks are currently housed in London, British Museum, and Milano, Biblioteca del Conservatorio 'Giuseppe Verdi.' Both the application for privilege and the privilege itself survive in *Studi parte antica* 97, ff. 2-3, ASM. For a summary of the contents of the collection, see Table 2.3.

70   Lockwood, *The Counter-Reformation and the Masses*, 18-20, reports that the registers of the Scuola degli Accoliti at the Duomo of Verona record a payment of L10 s2 d6 upon his departure from the city in 1541. Here Lockwood also acknowledges the possibility that this was an isolated payment due Ruffo for some service performed earlier, as no payments appear in the registers for the years 1534-1541. However, no evidence to support an arrival in Milan before 1541 holds up to scrutiny.

71   Lockwood, Lewis and Amati-Camperi, Alexandra, 'Ruffo, Vincenzo' *in The New Grove Dictionary of Music and Musicians*, 2nd edn (New York and London: Macmillan Publishers, Ltd., 2001a), XXI, 874-875. Incidentally, the dates reported here do not correspond to those found in any of Lockwood's earlier work on the subject, and may result from an error in interpretation of the sources on the part of Amati-Camperi.

72   Vincenzo Ruffo, *Il primo libro de motetti*, dedication.

73   'musico, et familiare In curia Illustrissimo et Excellentissimo Marchionis del Vasto
      Caesareae Maiestatis Vestrae In Italia locumtenentis.' *Studi p.a.* 97, folio 3, ASM. Also
      see Mariangela Donà, *La stampa musicale a Milano fino all'anno 1700* (Firenze: Leo S.
      Olschki, 1961), 126, which contains a transcription of the entire document. The privilege
      itself, which is also dated 2 June 1542, survives as *Studi p.a.* 97, folio 2, ASM.

74   See Flavio Emilio Scogna, 'La musica nel Duomo di Savona dal XVI al XVII secolo,'
      Nuova rivista musicale italiana XVI (1981), 261-262, and Flavio Emilio Scogna, *Vita
      musicale a Savona dal XVI al XVII secolo* (Savona: Cassa di Risparmio di Savona, 1982),
      27-28.

75   Maurizio Tarrini, 'Contribuito alla biografia di Vincenzo Ruffo: l'attività a Savona e
      Genova (1542-1546, 1562),' *Note d'archivio per la storia musicale, nuova serie* IV
      (1986), 109-111, has documented the composer's presence at the Doria court on 14
      November 1545 and 12 January 1546, at which time he received remunerations of 10
      scudi for his salary as the maestro di cappella.

76   See Chapter 4 below. *Registri della Cancelleria dello Stato* XXII/4 (Mandati 1542-
      1545), fols. 44r and 47v, ASM.

77   See Jeffrey Kurtzman, 'Tones, modes, clefs and pitch in Roman cyclic Magnificats of the
      16th century,' *Early Music* 22/4 (1994), 641-664.

78   *Cancelleria dello Stato di Milano* 93 (1548 non datato), 426, ASM.

79   *Registri della Cancelleria dello Stato* XXII-10 (Mandati 1552-1555), 16r, ASM.

80   *Cancelleria dello Stato di Milano* 91 (1548 dicembre), 18, ASM. See Appendix I,
      Document 2.

81   Vincenzo Ruffo, *Il primo libro de motetti a cinque voci (Milan, 1542)* in *Sixteenth
      Century Motet* 19, ed. Richard Sherr (New York and London: Garland, 1988), xii-xiii.

82   Ruffo, *Il primo libro de motetti*, ed. Sherr, xii.

83   Lewis Lockwood, 'The Counter-Reformation and the Sacred Music of Vincenzo Ruffo'
      (Ph.D. dissertation, Princeton University, 1960), 295.

84   *Potenze sovrane* 1, n.n., ASM.

85   Bernadino Calusco, editor, *Mutetarum divinitatis liber primus* (Mediolani: Giovanni
      Antonio Castiglione, 1543). The collection is housed in Washington D.C., Library of
      Congress.

86   F. Fiorentino, 'Donna Maria d'Aragona,' 224, and Lockwood, *The Counter-Reformation
      and the Masses*, 20-21. Also see Gasparo de Caro, 'Avalos, Carlo D',' *Dizionario
      biografico degli italiani* (Roma: Società Grafica Romana, 1962b), IV, 619.

87   On the apparati see Giovanni Alberto Furibondo Albicante, *Trattato del'intrar in Milano
      di Carlo V* (Mediolani: A. Caluus, 1541), n.p.

88   Arnaldo Ganda, 'Giovanni Antonio Castiglione e la stampa musicale a Milano,' *La
      Bibliofilía* C/2-3 (1998), 304-305 and 319-320.

89   Numerous payments to Calusco for paper items are recorded in the *Registri della
      Cancelleria dello Stato di Milano* XXII (Mandati) of the Milanese court and the
      Vacchette of the Duomo. According to Ennio Sandàl, *Editori e tipograpfi a Milano nel
      cinquecento* (Baden-Baden: Valentin Koerner, 1977), Calusco, who published under the
      imprint 'al segno della croce d'oro' was granted a ten-year privilege in 1542 that gave
      him rights as an exclusive editor in Milan. In 1552, the privilege was renewed for an
      additional seven years. He was further granted a privilege by the Milanese senate on 4
      November 1541 for the printing of an unidentified work. The privilege identifies him as a
      calligrapher. *Studi p.a.* 97, folio 1, ASM.

90   =RISM 1541[3].

91   A modern edition of each is available in Dominici Phinot, *Opera Omnia* I in *Corpus*

mensurabilis musicae 59 (Rome: American Institute of Musicology, 1972) and Dominici Phinot, *Opera Omnia* II in *Corpus mensurabilis musicae* 59 (Rome: American Institute of Musicology, 1974).

92 'sonoros Organici melicos non peperere modo? Josquinus praestat cantoribus, atque Phinotus Josquino; olim alius vincet utrumque tamen.' Publio Francesco Spinola, *Epigrammi Liber* III in *P. Francisci Spinulae Mediolanensis Opera omnia* (Venetiis: I. Zileti, 1563), 85-86. I am grateful to the Brown University Library for access to this rare text.

93 Spinola's epigram, which is discussed in relation to Matthias Werrecore in Chapter 3 above, is reported in both Pio Paschini, 'Un umanista disgraziato nel Cinquecento. Publio Francesco Spinola,' *Nuovo archivio veneto, serie II*, XXXVII (1919), 78-79, and Raffaele Casimiri, 'Un accenno poetico a Giosquino e Finoto di Francesco Spinola (1520?-1567), *Note d'Archivio* VIII/1 (1931), 143.

94 On 21 January 1546 Cardano was paid his 1545 salary as a lecturer of mathematical theory at the studio. His salary of 400 lire was one of the highest awarded to studio members. *Registri della Cancelleria dello Stato di Milano* XXII-5 (Mandati 1545-1546), 13v, ASM. In the registers from the late 1540s and 1550s he is also identified as a professor of medicine. A short biographical study that relies primarily on both Cardano's own autobiography and the early printed sources containing his work is found in Hieronymus Cardanus, *Writings on Music* in *Musicological Studies and Documents* 32, trans. and ed. Clement A. Miller (Rome: American Institute of Musicology, 1973), 15-35.

95 Paolo Morigia, *La nobiltà di Milano* (Milano: Pacifico Pontio, 1595), 142-143.

96 On 5 February 1552, for example, Cardano petitioned the Milanese chancery for permission to travel to Lyons to treat the Monsignor de Sant'Andrea, governor of the city. The Milanese chancery appears to have been amenable to the request, once it had insured that Cardano was not colluding with the French. *Cancelleria dello Stato di Milano* 143 (1552 febbraio 1-15), 140, 217, and 227, ASM.

97 See Morigia, *La nobiltà di Milano*, 142-143. In his *Libro terzo dei grotteschi* (Milano: Paolo Gottardo Pontio, 1587), 156-157, moreover, Giovanni Paolo Lomazzo devoted two separate epigrams to Cardano's achievements in the arts and letters.

98 The treatise has been translated and edited by Clement A. Miller in Hieronymus Cardanus, *Writings on Music*.

99 According to Cardano, Phinot was beheaded and publicly burned. See Clement A. Miller, 'Jerome Cardan on Gombert, Phinot, and Carpentras,' *Musical Quarterly* LVIII/3 (1972), 412-419.

100 Ennio Sandàl, *L'arte della stampa a Milano nell'èta di Carlo V* (1526-1556) in *Bibliotheca Bibliographica Aureliana* CXIV (Baden-Baden: Valentin Koerner, 1988), 64.

101 'Proh dolor, ergo Avalum rapuit mors impia magnum? Ah quantum Ausonia, ah quantum tu Carole perdis praesidium; hei, nobis; quid tam grave contigit unquam?'

102 *Codice* N. 37 (Orazione per la morte di D. Alfonso D'Avalos, Marchese del Vasto, governatore di Milano, secolo XVI), fol. 12, Biblioteca Trivulziana ed Archivio Storico Civico, Milano (hereafter BTASCM). Although this manuscript is no longer available for consultation, segments of it have been transcribed in G. Porro, *Catalogo dei Codici Manoscritti della Trivulziana* (Torino, 1884), 320.

103 See Chapter 5 below.

104 Mario Bendiscioli, 'Vita sociale e cultura,' *Storia di Milano, prima edizione* (Milano: Giovanni Treccani degli Alfieri, 1957c), X, 465 and 480.

105 In a document dated 16 June 1522, Grandsyre, maestro di capella, and Mons and Michel,

singers, attested that they had been paid the salaries due them. The salaries themselves are not noted. *Gonzaga di Guastalla* 41/1, n.n., 16 June 1522, Archivio di Stato, Parma (hereafter ASP).

106   The instrumentalists included several trumpeters, a violist, and some unspecified 'sonatori.' *Gonzaga di Guastalla* 41/1, n.n., n.d., ASP.

107   *Gonzaga di Guastalla* 42/3, n.n., 23 aprile 1539, ASP, and Gonzaga di Guastalla 42/3, n.n., 2 maggio 1539, ASP.

108   James Haar, 'Lassus: (1) Orlande de Lassus,' *The New Grove Dictionary of Music and Musicians*, 2nd edn (London and New York: Macmillan Publishers, Ltd., 2001), XIV, 295. Also see Orlando di Lasso et al., *Canzoni villanesche and villanelle*, ed. Donna G. Cardamone, in *Recent Researches in Music of the Renaissance* 82-83 (Madison: A-R Editions, 1991), x. In early 1549 Lasso entered the service of Giovan Battista d'Azzia, Marchese della Terza in Naples. Lasso served D'Azzia, Ferrante Gonzaga's brother-in-law, from 1549 until 1551. Donna G. Cardamone, 'Orlando di Lasso and Pro-French Factions in Rome,' *Orlandus Lassus and his Time* (Peer: Alamire Foundation, 1995), 27-32, suggests that Lasso may have been placed in the Roman service of Archbishop Antonio Altoviti in 1551 by Ferrante for the purposes of spying.

109   '. . .non ho che dir altro excetto chio saro domattina con messer Orlando sopra el fatto della pecunia e procurero d'haverla e di mandargliela quanto piu presto sara possibile' *Gonzaga di Guastalla* 42/5, n.n. 22 maggio 1542, ASP.

110   After Ferrante's death in 1557, Hoste remained in the city and enjoyed a thriving career as a sacred musician at the Duomo and the church of San Calimero See Chapter 3 below.

111   Hoste da Reggio, *Il primo libro de madrigali a tre voci* (Milano: Francesco et Simone Moscheni, 1554b). Only the altus partbook, which is housed in the British Museum, is extant. However, the British Museum also owns the cantus and tenor partbooks of the 1562 reprint.

112   '. . .per amor mio favorir' dette prete Cristoforo persona catholica et di buona fama.' *Autografi* 12/1 (Galeazzo Petra 1530-1552), 66, ASM. An undated letter from governor Ferrante Gonzaga to Galeazzo Petra, Bishop of Vigevano.

113   '. . .non havrebbe pensato proveder' d'un' luogo di tanta importanza in questa chiesa di sua Maestà à costui, che non ha ne' musica ne' pur una lira al mondo, come per altre mie n'ho avisata vostra Eccellenza anzi semper è stato goicatore di mala vita et pessimi costumi come publicamente si sa.' *Autografi* 12/1 (Galeazzo Petra 1530-1552), 64a, ASM. A letter from Galeazzo Petra, Bishop of Vigevano, to governor Ferrante Gonzaga dated 28 December 1550.

114   *Autografi* 12/1 (Galeazzo Petra 1530-1552), 64b and 65b, ASM.

115   *San Fedele* XXII (Santa Maria della Scala: Visite Pastorali e documenti aggiunti), q. I and q. L, ASDM.

116   *San Fedele* XXII (Santa Maria della Scala: Visite Pastorali e documenti aggiunti), q. O., ASDM. See Appendix 1, Document 3.

117   Lockwood, *The Counter-Reformation and the Masses*, 106-108. Also see Mario Bendiscioli, 'I conflitti giurisdizionali tra l'arcivescovo card. Borromeo e le autorità pubbliche,' *Storia di Milano* (Milano: Giovanni Treccani degli Alfieri, 1957b), X, 200-255.

118   *Culto* p.a. 1115 (Chiese-Communi, Milano: Santa Maria della Scala in San Fedele traslocata), Capitolo, n.n., Archivio di Stato, Milano (hereafter ASM) contains a printed copy of the 1385 ordinationes that specify the church's role in promoting the Ambrosian rite. Modern studies of the early chapter and cappella musicale are found in Meroni, 'Santa Maria della Scala,' 37-89, and Getz, 'The Sforza Restoration,' 109-159, respectively.

119 *Sforzesco* 1428 (Milano città e ducato: 1530 ottobre e novembre), Busta novembre, n.n., ASM.
120 *Culto* p.a. 1115 (Chiese-Communi, Milano: Santa Maria della Scala in San Fedele translocata), n.n., ASM, contains a copy of the 1531 bulla of Clement VII that enumerates the exemptions. They are also discussed in *San Fedele* XXII-150 (Santa Maria della Scala : Visite pastorali e documenti aggiunti), q. 25, ASDM. Also see Meroni, 'Santa Maria della Scala,' 67-68.
121 *San Fedele* XXII-150 (Santa Maria della Scala: Visite pastorali e documenti aggiunti), q. 25, (ASDM). Also see Mario Bendiscioli, 'Carlo Borromeo cardinal nipote arcivescovo di Milano e la riforma della Chiesa Milanese,' *Storia di Milano* (Milano: Giovanni Treccani degli Alfieri, 1957a), X, 187-189.
122 Gaspare Bugati, L'aggiunta *dell'Historia universale et delle cose di Milano . . .dall 1566 fin'al 1581* (Milano: Francesco ed Heredi di Simon Tini, 1587), 66.
123 *Fondo di Religione* 364 (Capitolo Milano: S. Maria della Scala, Visite Arcivescovile), Busta Armario Primo: 1574, ASM. See Appendix I, Document 4.
124 *Metropolitana* LXXXII-456 (Visite pastorali e documenti aggiunti), q. 20, f. 3, ASDM.
125 *San Fedele* XIII-146 (Santa Maria della Scala: Visite pastorali e documenti aggiunti), q. 5-6, ASDM. Also see Laura Mauri Vigevani, 'Orfeo Vecchi, maestro di cappella at Santa Maria della Scala,' *Rivista internazionale di Musica Sacra* VII/4 (1986), 351. On the question of Vecchi's nationality, see Toffetti, 'Nuovi documenti,' 448-449.
126 The position was likely funded from the 500 lire set aside for music that are mentioned on fol. 56 of Agostino Bassanini's 'Libro economale di tutti li Iuspatronati fondati e donati dalli Signori Duchi di Milano.' Manuscript copies of the 'Libro economale' are preserved as *Culto* p.a. 2126 (Patronati regi P.G.-1734), fasc. 3, ASM, and *Ms. 2F-1-18*, Biblioteca Capitolare, Milano.
127 Toffetti, 'Nuovi documenti,' 450.
128 Toffetti, 'Nuovi documenti,' 454-455.
129 On the documents surviving from Vecchi's career at Vercelli see *Orfeo Vecchi, Missarum quatuor vocibus: Liber primus*, ed. Ottavio Beretta (Lucca: Libreria musicale italiana, 1991), XII-XVIII.
130 *San Fedele* LXVIII-201 (Santa Maria della Scala in San Fedele traslocata 1596-1636), q. 3, ASDM. Also see Toffetti, Nuovi documenti,' 464-465, which contains a complete transcription of the document. Vecchi subsequently resigned all five benefices.
131 Vecchi, *Missarum*, ed. Beretta, XVIII.
132 Toffetti, 'Nuovi documenti,' 455-457.
133 *Notarile* 22109 (Bartolomeo Fioreni q. Giovanni Battista 22/02/1590-06/09/1596), 24/07/1591, ASM. By the time of his appointment as mansionarius, however, Vecchi had been serving as maestro di cappella for several years. On the basis of information found in a Status personalis from a pastoral visit made to Santa Maria della Scala in 1596, Toffetti, 'Nuovi documenti,' 454-455, has determined that Vecchi ascended to the post of maestro di cappella between June 1580 and September 1582.
134 Vigevani, 'Orfeo Vecchi,' 355-364, includes a brief overview of the composer's musical contributions. Much work, however, remains to be done, as very little of the music has been edited and thoroughly studied.
135 *Codice* 1490 (Ceremoniale per i governatori di Milano, c. 1591), 1r-3r and 13r-14v, BTASCM, and Codice 1252 (Ceremoniale Spagnolo Milanese), 3r-4v, BTASCM.
136 *Codice* 1490 (Ceremoniale per i governatori di Milano, c. 1591), 6v, BTASCM. Also see Chapter 7 below.

137   '. . .per più commodità particolarmente quando vi è anco la S*ignoria* et questi si dicano da
        dodeci sacerdoti de quali otto s'invitano fuori da Casa, et la musica della cappella reale.
        Si cantano à vicenda li salmi. Li sod*detti* otto sacerdoti sono pagati dal Govenatore. Li
        altri quattro sono li cappellani della cappella a quali tocca à far le fontioni.' *Codice* 1252
        (Ceremoniale Spagnolo Milanese), 5r, BTASCM. Many chapels in Milan were supported
        by ducal benefices, but only a few Milanese churches, including San Gottardo in Corte,
        Santa Maria della Scala, Santa Maria presso San Celso, and the Duomo, were able to
        provide four ducal chaplains to assist in the services. *Culto* p.a. 2126 (Patronati Regi P.
        G. - 1734), fasc. 3, ASM, and *Ms. 2F-I-18*, BCM.
138   See Enrico Cattaneo, *Maria santissima*, 29-39.
139   *Codice* 1252 (Ceremoniale Spagnolo Milanese), 9r-12v, BTASCM.
140   'Processioni il giorno della Purificatione dal Duomo à Santa Maria Belta, ivi fatto la
        benediction' della cera, si canta *terce* tanto che si fa la distributione d'essa cera, et alcune
        volte, *sext*. Poi si ritorna in Domo, dove dopo messa si dice quelle hore restanta.'
        Metropolitana LXXX-456 (Visite pastorali e documenti aggiunti), q. 20, ASDM.
141   *Codice* 1252 (Ceremoniale Spagnolo Milanese), 5r-8v, BTASCM.
142   *San Giorgio al Palazzo* II (Visite pastorali e documenti aggiunti), q. 1, fasc. 5r-v, ASDM.
143   A list of the daily distributions assigned to the canons dating from 1569 indicates that
        they received 3 denari for singing Matins, Vespers, and High Mass, and 1 denaro for
        singing Prime, Terce, Sext, Nones, and Compline. *San Giorgio al Palazzo* II (Visite
        pastorali e documenti aggiunti), q. 1, fasc. 5r, ASDM.
144   *San Giorgio al Palazzo* II (Visite pastorali e documenti aggiunti), q. 9-10, ASDM. Q. 9,
        which is dated 1573, contains calculations for daily distributions for six canons. Q. 10
        contains documents relating to the chaplaincies dating from approximately 1535-1560.
        These indicate that only one of the chaplaincies, of which there were approximately a
        dozen, had ducal status.
145   *San Giorgio al Palazzo* II (Visite pastorali e documenti aggiunti), q. 1, fasc. 7v, ASDM.
146   Ibid., fasc. 5r-v.
147   Ibid., fasc. 5r-v.
148   See, for example, Iain Fenlon, 'Music, ceremony, and self-identity in Renaissance
        Venice' in *La cappella di San Marco nell'eta moderna* (Venezia, Fondazione Ugo e Olga
        Levi, 1998), 7-21, and Iain Fenlon, 'Music, liturgy, and identity in Renaissance Venice,'
        Revista de musicologia 16/1 (1993), 603-606.

Chapter 3

The Civic Ceremonial at the Duomo of Milan

In Medio Ecclesiae

In his *Di Lucio Vitruvio Pollione de architectura libri dece* of 1521, Cesare Cesariano identifies Milan as the model city. For Cesariano, the successful design of a republican seat was dependent, in part, upon the streamlined interaction of its principal architectural spaces. Milan was a city in which daily operations were centralized *in medio civitatis*, for the civic structures most frequently accessed by its dignitaries and officials, which included the gubernatorial palace, the cathedral, and the Archiepiscopal offices, were both centrally located and in close proximity to one another.[1]

The newly constructed Gothic Cathedral of Santa Maria Maggiore, more commonly known as the Duomo, stood at the epicenter of Cesariano's Milan. However, it was not surrounded by the spacious piazza that encircles it today. Santa Tecla, the old 'summer cathedral,' literally stood at its front doors,[2] and shops that had been erected in piazza space purchased from the *Fabbrica* of the Duomo encroached on all sides.[3] Flanked by the four churches devoted to the archangels and only a short walk from the gubernatorial palace and the Archiepiscopal offices, the Cathedral of Milan, nonetheless, virtually dominated the city center as the headquarters of a miniature city of God.[4]

The construction and the maintenance of the Duomo were matters of general civic interest and responsibility, and were under the auspices of the *Fabbrica* of the Duomo. Comprised of six deputies elected from among the various districts, a Vicar of Provisions, a representative from the Curia Vescovile, four doctors from the College of Notaries, and three Ordinaries from the Duomo, the *Fabbrica* of the Duomo was sixteenth-century Milan's largest corporation. It enlisted the assistance of the entire local population in raising funds to support the cathedral's construction, and drew from among the city's artisans to supply the necessary work force. After the completion of the *tiburio* under Giovanni Antonio Amadeo, who served as the Duomo architect from 1508 until 1522, work on the Duomo structure itself slowed considerably.[5] The gradual lull in attention to the edifice appears to have arisen from the financial constraints imposed by the French occupation, as well as from a dissipation of the sense of immediacy that understandably had motivated the earlier stages of its construction. In December 1537 a proposal for the Cathedral's unfinished *facciata* was presented to the *Fabbrica* by Vincenzo Seregni, but the project was shelved indefinitely. Instead, the *Fabbrica* turned to measures that might render the existing structure more functional. Five issues of serviceability were identified, and these received the *Fabbrica*'s attention until the arrival of Carlo Borromeo in 1565. They included the creation of a side door opening onto the Strada del Compito, the construction and decoration of the Antegnati organ, the repair of the campanile, the demolition of Santa Tecla and the incorporation of its functionaries into the cathedral chapter, and the acquisition of the Piazza del Verzaro.[6] The *Fabbrica* of the 1540s and 1550s thus focused its energies on those operations *in medio ecclesiae* that affected the Duomo's larger role *in medio civitatis*.

A number of side chapels and special altars ornamented the interior of the Duomo by the beginning of the sixteenth century. At least four of these, the main altar, the altar of San Gottardo, the altar of San Caterina di Siena, and the altar of Santa Maria del Pilone, were central to a distinctly Milanese ceremonial that was elaborated with music. The musical activities at the main altar included the daily performance of the Canonical Hours and a High Mass in both plainchant and polyphony, while those at the altars of San Gottardo, San Caterina di Siena, and Santa Maria del Pilone consisted of daily plainchant masses.[7] The music for the former was provided by the cappella musicale, while that of the latter was entrusted to clergy deemed competent in the performance of plainchant. By around 1522, the cappella musicale had evolved from its origins as a small vocal ensemble that served in conjunction with the organist and the Ordinaries assigned to the choir[8] into a professional ensemble of sixteen to twenty musicians. Assembled below the organ in the marble *cantorie* that overlooked the main altar, the cappella musicale's auditory and physical presence augmented a colorful ritual that had become a regular aspect of Milanese life *in medio civitatis*.

The maestri di cappella 1522-1582

As was common in most Italian cities of the period, the Milanese cappella musicale was supervised by a maestro who functioned as performer, teacher, composer and general supervisor of musical activities. Although a policy of hiring Italian singers was instituted under Franchinus Gaffurius,[9] this policy evidently was not extended to the position of maestro di cappella. The appointment of maestro di cappella was more frequently extended, in fact, to northern musicians who had already distinguished themselves as composers. Yet aside from Matthias Werrecore, the composers who served as maestri between 1522 and 1563 actually devoted very little energy to composing for the choir. Werrecore, who served as maestro di cappella from 1522 to 1550, composed a number of sacred compositions, and most of these were issued in printed collections only after he stepped down from the directorship. In contrast, Simon Boyleau, maestro di cappella from 1551 to 1557, and Hoste da Reggio, maestro di cappella 1558 to 1563, instead focused their compositional energies upon the highly popular Italian madrigal. This phenomenon probably stems from two issues that appear to characterize the position of maestro di cappella, namely a lack of time for much serious composition and the requirement that certain Duomo musicians participate in activities at the Milanese court. With the ascent of Carlo Borromeo to the seat of Archibishop of Milan in 1560, however, the more frivolous demands placed on the maestri by the court appear to have been set aside and serious attention turned to the activity of composing service music for the Duomo choir.

Hermann Matthias Werrecore, 1522-1550

Following the death of Gaffurius on 25 June 1522, the Flemish composer Hermann Matthias Werrecore was appointed maestro di cappella. Aside from the fact that he was residing in the city, nothing is known regarding Werrecore's activities in Milan or, for that matter, elsewhere, prior to his appointment.[10] Since a vacancy at the leading ecclesiastical institution in a city the size of Milan must have attracted a number of prominent candidates, the chapter's enthusiastic endorsement of Werrecore, a virtual neophyte at the time of the appointment, may reflect both the current insularity of Milanese society and an unwillingness among prominent foreign composers to ally themselves with the still politically unstable Sforza. It is, of course, quite possible that Werrecore's nomination was effected via the auspices of Francesco II Sforza, who awarded the composer a canonicate at the collegiate church of St Michael of Busto in Gallerate on 22 March 1524. In the ducal appointment letter, Werrecore is identified as 'our cantor.'[11] The ducal ownership implied by designation of 'our cantor' appears to have been sustained through the 1540s at the Milanese court, for a list of items heard in the chancery during February 1547 notes that 'Matthia, maestro di cappella at the Duomo, and Ottaviano, contrabasso, requested that they be released of extraordinary duties, as was done during the time of the signor Marchese [Del Vasto].'[12] Evidence that Werrecore, in fact, was serving Francesco II at the time of his appointment to the Duomo in 1522 can be inferred from his 'La bataglia tagliana,'a musical account of Francesco II's victory at the 1525 Battle of Pavia as witnessed by the composer. This well-known composition, which was discussed in Chapter 2 above, was originally composed to commemorate the Battle of Bicocca on 27 April 1522, but subsequently was amended through minor text alterations to accommodate the more decisive and famous Battle of Pavia.[13]

In any event, Werrecore's 3 July 1522 appointment notice specifies that he was to be responsible for directing the musical activities of the cappella, as well as for teaching the boys of the cathedral's choir school.[14] His teaching responsibilities were limited, however, to singing and counterpoint, for the records indicate that a Latin professor was hired especially to teach Latin grammar.[15] As compensation for both directing the choir and teaching the boys, Werrecore was paid a regular stipend of L12 per month, and was further provided chapter-subsidized housing adjacent to the Duomo.[16] Although this remuneration seems rather paltry by sixteenth-century standards, the proceeds from Werrecore's ducal benefice apparently provided enough income to support the purchase of additional properties, and the composer managed these as an accomplished businessman. On 11 April 1530 Werrecore's purchased a 'fifty measure' property in the territory of Caxorate from the cathedral chapter,[17] which held the title to the land.[18] Since he already had access to chapter-subsidized housing in the Campo Santo, Werrecore likely intended to lease the property. During the succeeding years he appears to have amassed a respectable income from it, for he later concluded numerous other property transactions related to this and other holdings in the local area.[19] Despite this seeming largesse, however, Werrecore attempted, albeit unsuccessfully, to secure a house from the chapter in 1542:

> 6 July 1542
> Convocation in the Audience Hall
> Then Magistrate Father Armano Werecore, also called Matthias Flamengas, director of the cappella musicale of the Cathedral of Milan, was heard. He desired that the Reverend and Magnificent Lords Prefects of the Fabbrica [either] award him–without obligation of any sort–another site which the Fabbrica has in Campo Sancto or beyond, or, in lieu of a house, increase in some way his yearly salary for the duration of his service.[20]

The officers of the *Fabbrica* denied Werrecore's request for a house and instead offered salary increase,[21] and their decision, when considered in light of other surviving archival documents, serves to elucidate his urgent, but seemingly irrational need for a second residence. Although the cathedral registers from the subsequent years report no actual increase in salary,[22] an annual payment of 16 lire commemorating the feast of St Michael was initiated around the year 1543. According to the register entries, this annual stipend served as reimbursement for the rent paid on a room that was used to audition singers and teach the choirboys.[23] It is thus possible that Werrecore envisioned a second house for this purpose. When Werrecore stepped down from the position of maestro di cappella in June 1550, moreover, he received an unprecedented allowance of 200 lire 6 soldi 9 denari for housing over the past eight months.[24] Unfortunately, the extant archival documentation fails to explain why the allowance appears for the first time so late in his career. Either the chapter finally fulfilled their 1542 promise of a higher salary by granting him a belated housing award, or Werrecore had already paid his own housing expenses, which were generally covered by the chapter, and was merely being reimbursed.

In June 1550 Olivero de Phalanis was appointed in Werrecore's stead, presumably because the eminent maestro had become either too feeble or too ill to continue.[25] Any infirmity that prompted his retirement was not fatal, however, for Werrecore continued to serve the musical chapel in various capacities for at least twenty-four more years. In fact, he is identified as the 'other director of the cappella musicale' in the cathedral records as late as 9 December 1574, on which date the *Fabbrica* awarded him three caskets of wine.[26] In 1559, moreover, Werrecore appears to have served as an extra singer, since he is listed among the tenors in the pay registers of late 1559.[27] However, a document dated 28 August 1559 notes his increasing inability to stand and sing with the other singers because of feebleness and extreme old age. Thus, it is likely that his activity as a performer ceased upon his own request in late 1559:

28 August 1559
Convocation in the Audience Hall

Master Matthias, the other director of the cappella musicale of the cathedral of Milan, was heard. He said that he had taken part in the cappella for over thirty years, serving it in accordance with his oaths of humility and obedience, as is the custom of the Fabbrica of the Cathedral of Milan. He is unable to stand and sing with the cantors of the cappella because of feebleness and old age, but he has served well, for which he is due half of his salary. And, therefore, because the master is considered unable to stand and sing, he is beseeching the deputy Lords Prefects to arrange an order that gives him the half of his salary due, as is usually given through the agency of the aforementioned Fabbrica.[28]

Werrecore was instrumental in the copying, purchase, and composition of polyphonic sacred works for the Milanese cappella musicale, and this activity may well have continued even after he officially stepped down from the post of maestro di cappella.[29] His *Cantuum quinque vocum quas motecta vocant*, which was published in Milan during the year 1555, provides a significant link between the Milanese musical traditions evidenced in the Milan choirbooks and the Post-Tridentine masses of Vincenzo Ruffo. The motets contained in the collection include not only one and two-part motets for various feasts of the liturgical year, but also ceremonial works, elevation motets, and motet cycles.

Werrecore's name appears quite frequently in Milanese notarial documents dating from the late 1550s and 1560s in connection with various property transactions. Although it is beyond the scope of this study, a thorough examination of Werrecore's extramusical affairs on the order of Davide Daolmi's recent study of Vicentino[30] promises to yield fascinating information regarding his commercial and perhaps even his editorial ventures. At the point of Werrecore's final documented appearance in the Milanese archival records, he had been serving the cappella musicale of the Duomo for almost fifty-two years.[31] He likely passed on during or shortly after the plague of 1576, for no notice of his death has been located and the Milanese *Registri mortuari* are incomplete for the years 1576, 1577, and 1579.

Olivero de Phalanis 1550-1551 and Simon Boyleau 1551-1557

Little is known about Werrecore's immediate successor Olivero de Phalanis, who held the appointment of maestro di cappella from June 1550 until June 1551. Phalanis's salary was equivalent to that which had been assigned Werrecore, and included the 16 lire annual housing allowance for a room in which to teach the boys of the choir. Since his appointment appears to have been for exactly one year, it is possible that Phalanis was hired as a one-year interim director until a suitable replacement for Werrecore could be found.[32] However, he may also have been the Oliverus de Preandis who 'died of an injury' in the parish of San Raffaele on 3 June 1551.[33] In any case, Simon Boyleau, a French composer active in northern Italy, succeeded Phalanis in July 1551, and was assigned a salary equivalent to that of his two predecessors.[34] By 1551 Boyleau had already established a reputation as a composer in northern Italy through the publication of both a collection of four-voice motets[35] and a book of four-voice madrigals.[36]   Although the provenance of these two prints suggests Venetian patronage,[37] the coincidence of Boyleau's appointment at the Duomo with the arrival of Ferrante Gonzaga, who served a governor of Milan between 1546 and 1554, points toward a potential connection to the Gonzaga family that is borne out by other documentary evidence. In February 1553 a madrigal by Boyleau was performed at the second of two *pompe* sponsored by the Milanese court during *carnevale*,[38] and his *Madrigali* of 1564 was dedicated to Ferrante's son Cesare.[39] Boyleau apparently also was a recognized musical figure outside of Italy at the time of his appointment, for a theoretical treatise attributed to him is discussed in Conrad Gesner's 1548 guide to theoretical writings.[40]

Aside from the entries recording payment of his salary and the 16 lire annual housing allowance for a room to teach the boys, Boyleau appears rather infrequently in the cathedral documents. In the latter half of 1552, he may have been fined for shirking his duties, as his six-month salary payment was recorded as 70 lire rather than the customary 72 lire.[41] In 1552 a vestment was given him for use during the services,[42] and between 1553 and 1556 he received an annual honorarium for performing on Christmas Eve,[43] a practice that appears to have been established the previous year when contrabasso Jo. Jacobo de Canibus received the same remuneration for singing at a Christmas Eve service.[44]

During the years 1556 and 1557 Boyleau evidently had difficulty managing the singers. On 16 July 1556 the chapter issued a revised version of the well-known 1534 statues governing the behavior of the singers,[45] and by 6 December 1557 it was rumored that some chapter ordinaries, presumably those from the choir itself, had voted to have Boyleau removed and replaced. His potential dismissal became a bone of contention between the ordinaries and the prefects, the latter of whom balked at such an intrusion upon their authority:

Whereas it has come to the attention of the aforementioned Lords Prefects, that Reverend Lords Ordinaries of the aforementioned Venerable Fabbrica of the principal church of Milan go about shouting that they mean to remove Master Simon Boyleau, maestro di cappella of the singers of aforementioned church without the consent of the Lords Prefects of said Fabbrica; and in order that the rights of the aforesaid Fabbrica shall not by chance suffer any loss, but be preserved unharmed and uninjured, the aforementioned Magnificent Lords Prefects, having collected their votes among themselves, ordered and order that if the said Master Simon shall be removed from the office of the said cappella by the aforementioned Reverend Lords Ordinaries without the consent of the aforementioned Lords Prefects present and for the time being, and another master of said cappella shall be elected without the consent of the venerable Chapter of the aforementioned Fabbrica, without observances of the things to be observed, he shall be neither admitted nor if admitted recognized as maestro of the said cappella by the Reverend and Magnificent Lord Prefects of the aforementioned Fabbrica, present and for the time being. Moreover, in the event that he is appointed as described above, he shall not receive compensation in the form of salary or income by persons acting in the name of the aforementioned Fabbrica, nor shall he be recognized as having been admitted for the purpose of having or receiving any salary or income from the aforementioned Fabbrica or agents on its behalf.[46]

Despite the apparent resolve of the prefects in maintaining the supremacy of their administrative authority, the wishes of the ordinaries prevailed, and Boyleau either quit or was dismissed shortly after the controversy began.[47] He evidently remained in the city of Milan, where his collection of five-voice madrigals was issued the following year.[48] Although it is not clear where he was employed, he apparently had some limited contact with Santa Maria dell' Annunciazione alla Vecchiabbia, the convent of which Carlo Borromeo's sister Suor Corona Isabella was a member, for in 1563 Conona Isabella suggested that her brother consider Boyleau for the position of maestro di cappella at the Duomo that had recently been awarded Vincenzo Ruffo.[49] The nomination of Boyleau seems not to have been taken seriously enough to have been mentioned to the *Fabbrica*. Instead, Boyleau served as maestro di cappella at Santa Maria presso San Celso in Milan from 1563-1564 and 1566-1568.[50] He was appointed, however, an interim maestro di cappella at the Duomo of Milan two additional times during Borromeo's tenure, the first between 25 June 1573 and July 1574, and the second between 29 november 1574 and early 1577.[51] Between 1577 and 1583, Boyleau relocated to Torino, where he enjoyed the patronage of Duchess Marguerite and Duke Emanuele Filiberto of Savoy.[52] From 1582 to 1585 he is listed on the rosters of the Duomo of Torino, where he served as maestro di cappella for approximately two years.[53] Boyleau presumably acquired the position in Torino through the auspices of the Savoyard court, and thereafter maintained a close relationship with his patrons there. The last extant archival reference to Boyleau, which is dated 28 June 1586, records a payment of 25 scudi made him by Duke Carlo Emanuele I for composing a piece and teaching a page named Putantino.[54]

Hoste da Reggio 1558-1563

Boyleau was succeeded at the Duomo in 1557 by Bartolomeo Torresani, a musician now known to be the composer Hoste da Reggio.[55] Hoste appears to have arrived in Milan around 1554, the year which marked the publication of four madrigal collections identifying the composer as a musician at the court of Milanese governor Ferrante Gonzaga.[56] By 4 September 1555, Hoste had acquired a benefice at the church of San Calimero in the Porta Romana district of Milan.[57] Although it is not clear exactly when the composer vacated his position at the Milanese court, it is possible that he left the post upon Ferrante's dismissal in 1555. In any case, he had accepted the appointment as maestro di cappella at the Duomo of Milan by late January 1558. Hoste's appointment notice, which is recorded in both the cathedral registers and an independent source of the curial archives, suggests not only that Boyleau had been grossly inattentive to his duties, but also that the behavior of the singers had spiraled totally out of control. The appointment notice spells out Hoste's obligations in very clear terms, a feature that is not characteristic of the other appointment notices of the period. First, Hoste was to teach the art of music to twelve boys at the house in Campo Santo, which was the residence commonly assigned the maestro di cappella, for nothing. Secondly, he was to select boys with the assistance of the deputies of the chapter and to ensure that they serve the choir until their voices mutate. Thirdly, he was to supervise the performance of the Duomo choir at the

Divine Offices of Solemn Feasts in other churches, all Vespers services on Solemn Vigils, the feast of the Commemoration of the Dead, and all masses commissioned by the Court of Milan. Fourth, he and the members of the choir were to attend all daily hours normally sung in the Duomo, which usually included the Offices and a High Mass. Fifth, he was to make certain that all of the singers were properly dressed for services. Sixth, he was to squelch the arguing, swearing, and otherwise inappropriate behavior of the singers while they were on the premises. Finally, he was neither to secure a substitute for himself nor to permit the substitution of other singers without the express permission of the chapter dignitaries.[58]

The issues addressed in Hoste's appointment notice not only shed further light on the use of polyphony at the Duomo during the mid-sixteenth century, but also reveal the operating conditions of the chapel during the same period. Vespers, the feast of the Commemoration of the Dead, and court masses clearly were still central to the services held there, and, thus, the repertoire of the Milan choirbooks probably was sung along with the motets of more recent Milanese collections such as Bernardino Calusco's *Mutetarum divinitatis liber primus* (1543)[59] and *Cantuum quinque vocum quos motetta vocant . . . liber primus* (1555).[60] Although Hoste does not appear to have composed repertoire for the choir, he did on occasion purchase new collections for its use.[61] Yet the rehearsals and services themselves must have been raucous, colorful, and not without incident, for the image of the angelic choir surrounding a beautifully copied choirbook or gathered together with individual partbooks is shattered by the documented reality of a poorly attired crowd of unruly singers jostling for attention. Hoste must have exercised at least adequate control over the situation, since his five years at the Duomo essentially appear to have been without incident. Initially, he was receiving the usual salary of 144 lire per annum, but petitioned for a raise on 30 June 1558. The dignitaries approved the raise,[62] which, though unspecified at the hearing, appears to have been 96 lire per annum.[63] In the summer of 1563 Hoste was granted a two-month leave to seek cure at the baths. When he failed to return on time, his appointment was terminated and Vincenzo Ruffo was hired in his place.[64]

Hoste evidently returned to Milan shortly after his dismissal from the Duomo, presumably to resume his duties as rector at San Calimero. In June 1567 he accepted, with the express approval and permission of Carlo Borromeo, the position of maestro di cappella at Santa Maria Maggiore in Bergamo. He held the position at Santa Maria Maggiore for only one year, and was back in Milan by November 1568.[65] He died on 5 October 1569 after suffering acute inflammation of the tonsils.[66]

Vincenzo Ruffo, 1563-1572

Vincenzo Ruffo was no stranger to Milanese circles, for in 1542 the young composer was found in the service of Alfonso D'Avalos, who served as the city's governor from 1538 to 1546. Although Ruffo's tenure at the D'Avalos court was short-lived, his legacy includes the first locally printed collection of five-voice motets.[67] When Ruffo left Milan in late 1542, he headed to Savona, rather than to his native Verona. There he accepted an appointment as the maestro di cappella at the cathedral of Santa Maria di Castello on 27 October 1542.[68] Ruffo did not likely remain at the cathedral itself beyond 24 April 1543, when the structure was condemned because of irreparable damage, but he seems to have resided in the general geographical area for at least three more years. Recently discovered archival records indicate that he was serving as the maestro di cappella at the court of Andrea Doria in nearby Genova in late 1545 and early 1546.[69]

By February 1547 Ruffo apparently had returned to Verona. At that time he was among three candidates nominated to the coveted position of maestro di musica of the Accademia Filharmonica di Verona, a post which was subsequently awarded to Giovanni Nasco.[70] Ruffo must have remained active in the Accademia thereafter, for upon Nasco's departure a mere four years later, Ruffo was elected by a sixteen to one vote.[71] Around the same time he was also appointed maestro di cappella at the Duomo of Verona, and a tug-of-war between Ruffo and the Accademia regarding his seeming inability to attend to the duties specified, which included teaching singing every afternoon to those members who were unskilled in the art and composing expressly for the academy, quickly ensued. Although the Accademia initially appears to have made several concessions by confining its demands on Ruffo's time to those hours in which he would have been free from obligations at the Duomo, it ultimately released him from responsibilities in October 1552.[72] Nonetheless, Ruffo appears to have remained active in the Accademia even after his dismissal. His compositions from the Verona period include not only a book of motets, but also numerous madrigals and a set of capricci that were published shortly after his return to Milan.[73] It is assumed that Ruffo remained at the Duomo of Verona until his appointment as maestro di cappella at the Duomo of Milan on 23 August 1563, but a document of 18 July 1562 indicates that he was in Genoa during the preceding summer, and guaranteed rent on part of a house with a cellar for his niece.[74]

Ruffo's role in implementing the liturgical and musical reforms promoted by the recently appointed Archbishop Carlo Borromeo is well known through the work of Lewis Lockwood.[75] Turning almost single-mindedly from the secular pursuits that occupied much of his compositional energy in Verona, Ruffo devoted himself to the production of intelligible settings of Magnificats, Masses, and Psalms that conformed to the directives set forth at Borromeo's first Provincial Council in Milan. Even after he left Milan for Pistoia in 1573, Ruffo continued to apply the techniques that he had developed in Milan to the composition of sacred music. The preface to his *Salmi suavissimi et devotissimi a cinque voci* of 1574, which is dedicated to Alessandro de Medici, states that the psalms feature a new manner of singing that grows out of his previous masses.[76]

Ruffo's directorship of the Milanese cathedral choir appears to have been largely without incident. The responsibilities associated with the position in 1573, which included directing and managing a choir of approximately sixteen singers, teaching the choirboys twice per day, and composing masses, Magnificats, and hymns as needed every month, were not inconsequential and the stipends of the musicians notoriously low in comparison to other institutions of similar stature, but the *Fabbrica* appears to have been relatively pleased with Ruffo's performance and management skills. It is not clear exactly why Ruffo chose to leave the Duomo of Milan for the Cathedral of Pistoia in 1573, but Boyleau's appointment as coadjutor on 10 March

1572 seems to suggest that he had been contemplating departure well before the chapter at Pistoia began considering his impending appointment. From 1573 to 1577 Ruffo served as maestro di cappella at the Cathedral of Pistoia, where he devoted his attentions to the composition of psalms and Passions.[77] In 1577 he returned to his native Verona, and little is known of his activities during the succeeding three years. In 1580 he was elected maestro di cappella at San Nicolo in Sacile, and there he spent the final years of his life. He passed on in Sacile on 9 February 1587, just one year after the publication of his *Soavissimi responsorii della Settimana Santa a cinque voci.*[78]

Pietro Pontio, 1577-1582

Pietro Pontio appears to have been the only maestro hired at the Duomo of Milan between 1522 and 1582 who had no relationship with the Milanese court during the first half of the century. Pontio was born on 25 March 1532 in Parma to a family of at least modest social standing. Little is known of his early career, but his imitation masses suggest a possible relationship with Jachet of Mantua. From 1567 to 1569, Pontio served as maestro di cappella at Santa Maria Maggiore in Bergamo, a position for which he was recommended by Cipriano da Rore.[79] Although Pontio was initially contracted for nine years of service, he, in fact, only served two before a processo was initiated against him for 'dereliction of duty, gambling, and association with prostitutes,'[80] as well as for encouraging the clerics under his supervision to rebel against new rules introduced by the chapter in connection with the 1566 reorganization of its academy for the training of the clerics.[81] The surviving documentation suggests that many of Pontio's difficulties actually arose from a pedagogical approach that differed markedly from that of his predecessors. In addition to saying a daily mass, singing the canonical hours, and supervising the performance of polyphony, Pontio was responsible for teaching ten of the most advanced clerics figured singing and counterpoint, and his performance in the latter responsibility engendered many of the complaints voiced during the proceedings. Pontio reportedly conducted singing lessons collectively rather than individually, reserving private lessons only for his favorite students, in contrast to his predecessor Baptista Mutio, who had heard each student alone and then all of them collectively. Had these been the only accusations lodged against the new maestro, he likely would have survived the processo unscathed, but compelling evidence of an imprudent lifestyle of gambling and frequenting prostitutes did not bode well for continuation of a career in Bergamo. On 13 January 1567, before the Consorzio had actually dismissed him, Ponzio accepted the position of maestro di cappella at Santa Maria della Steccata in Parma.[82]

Pontio's salary of 168 lire at the Steccata, appears, at least on the surface, to be a considerable reduction of his previous salary of 400 lire, but the new appointment did not include teaching responsibilities and additional income may have been available through a chaplaincy or other gifts. The Steccata observed an extensive musical calendar that included polyphonic Magnificats and Vespers hymns on specified feasts, Matins on Christmas, Masses on Holy Saturday, and the singing of a Marian Antiphon and two motets after Compline every Saturday.[83] The reputed quality of its choir and the many opportunities for polyphonic experimentation should have provided a stimulating atmosphere for the young composer, but two years later he inexplicably chose to return to Bergamo, this time as the maestro di capella at Sant'Alessandro in Colonna. Little is known about Sant'Alessandro during this period, but there Pontio served as a cappellano, directed the choir, and supervised twelve clerics in the singing of figured music and the study of counterpoint. His first book of four voice masses, which hails from his tenure at Sant'Alessandro, likely reflects the size and role of the choir under his direction. Pontio remained at Sant'Alessandro for five years, departing in September 1574 under another cloud of controversy.[84]

Pontio's activities over the next three years are shrouded in some mystery, but Russell Murray suggests that he may have been in Pavia under the patronage of Girolamo Cornazzano, the cavalier to the King of Portugal.[85] Two weeks after Simon Boyleau's dismissal from the Duomo of Milan on 5 March 1577, Pontio assumed the duties of maestro di cappella.[86] His annual salary of approximately 737 lire, a seventy-five percent increase over Boyleau's annual remuneration of 400 lire, suggests either great esteem or the ability to bargain shrewdly, for the position had incurred no new duties upon Pontio's arrival.[87] The increased sum may reflect the chapter's respect for Pontio's experience, but it also is somewhat surprising in light of his checkered history in Bergamo. It is possible that the authorities were unaware of the Pontio's disastrous tenure at Santa Maria Maggiore, but the fact that the issue never crossed Borromeo's radar screen seems unlikely, given that he himself released Hoste da Reggio from service in Milan during a period of personnel shortages to take the position at Santa Maria Maggiore in Bergamo on the heels of the Pontio debacle.

By 1579, in fact, Borromeo was seeking to replace Pontio with Costanzo Porta because his fitness to serve as maestro di cappella was being questioned by Archpriest Giovanni Fontana. Fontana had reported to Borromeo that the rector of the seminary objected vociferously to Pontio's 'fraternization with seculars,'and was threatening to resign in protest if Pontio were not removed immediately. Although some sort of accord was reached, the issue reared its head once more three years later, by which point Pontio had become quite dissatisfied with what he viewed as the chapter's intrusions upon his authority to hire adequate singers. At that point Borromeo resumed contact with Porta, and after considering several of his students, settled on Giulio Caesare Gabussi.[88] Pontio, already preoccupied with business affairs in Parma and eager to return to his native city, again accepted the position of maestro di cappella at Santa Maria della Steccata. He spent the remaining fourteen years of his life in Parma, serving ten successful years at the Steccata and then retiring to a benefice of the Consorzio dei Vive e dei Morti at the Cathedral of Parma. He is one of four native musicians honored with a monument there.[89] From the standpoint of compositional output, Pontio was among the most productive of Milan's sixteenth-century maestri. During his tenure at the Duomo, he produced a collection of four-voice psalms and Magnificats, two books of five-voice masses, and a collection of five-voice motets. Unlike Vincenzo Ruffo, however, he does not appear to have succumbed stylistically to Borromeo's liturgical influence.

The Cappella Musicale

General administration

Most of the singers hired at the Duomo of Milan during the sixteenth century were Italians rather than oltremontani, and this practice reflects the tacit adherence to a policy that had been introduced under Werrecore's predecessor, Franchinus Gaffurius.[90] When Werrecore was appointed maestro di cappella on 3 July 1522, the Duomo choir was comprised of eleven adult singers and seven boy sopranos.[91] During the decade that followed, the number of adult singers employed at any given time fluctuated between eleven and fourteen, and replacement was frequently necessary. In fact, only five adult singers were retained across the entire nine-year period extending from 1521 to 1530. The numerous changes in membership that characterize the choir of the 1520s appear to have resulted, at least in part, from a plague that swept through the city during the year 1524. The Milanese merchant Burigozzo remarked that the pestilence peaked during the July 1524, a month so difficult for the city that 'there were no ordinaries in the Duomo, nor the offices as usual, but rather two or three priests who sang as well as they were able.'[92] The instability of the roster between 1522 and 1530 may also have been a symptom of several managerial problems that were addressed at length by the cathedral chapter in 1534. A comparison of the rosters for 1522 through 1534 with those compiled for the years 1534 through 1559 reveals that changes in personnel occurred much less frequently during the twenty-five years following the reorganization that took place in 1534.[93]

Although the daily responsibilities of the Duomo singers included performance of both the offices and a high mass, the members of the chapel apparently were not required to sing all of the canonical hours every day until after the reorganization of 1534. Instead, they were assigned to different services each day according to a predetermined rotational system similar to that utilized at Santa Maria della Scala. Evidence that a rotational schedule of some sort had been implemented at the Duomo is found in the registers from 1522 through 1533, which record yearly payments of 6 lire to an individual responsible for 'listing the singers of the aforementioned cathedral assigned to celebration of the divine office.'[94] These payments ceased in 1534, at which time a roster of the current personnel was issued with an accompanying notice that 'The above listed cantors are expected to sing the daily hours that ordinaries generally sing, except when those [hours] are masses for the dead..'[95] Documents from later in the century suggest that the hours in question included only Terce, High Mass, and Vespers.[96] It is not clear whether the scribe responsible for these listings designed the schedule or merely recorded the names of those present, and no copies of a rotational schedule have survived, thus allowing for the possibility that all of the singers were expected to attend but did not commonly do so. Such a theory is, in fact, supported by the reappearance in 1560 of an individual responsible for notating attendance.[97] The use of a rotational system of some sort was not uncommon in Milanese choirs; as was noted above, a carefully designed plan for the rotation of singing duties at the offices and mass was put into place at the ducal chapel of Santa Maria della Scala in 1539.[98] And the cathedral of Sant'Ambrogio in

Vigevano used a similar system.[99] At Santa Maria della Scala, the choir elected a scribe who essentially took attendance at the mass and offices. The information that he provided was important to the determination of daily distributions of salary, which were based upon the singer's performance of all assigned duties.[100]

The distribution system at the Duomo, however, was apparently reserved only for ordinaries who participated in singing the hours, rather than for the 'professional' singers. Like the choirs of many sixteenth-century churches, the Duomo choir included not only the professionally trained singers who are listed in the registers as 'cantors,' but also a number of beneficiaries (maceconici, chaplains, and notaries) selected from among the ordinaries. The latter individuals were required to be present every day at Terce, High Mass, and Vespers, presumably to assist in the singing of plainchant. They were further expected to participate in specified services held on the principal feasts, and were remunerated for their contributions via a daily distribution system similar to that utilized by the choral beneficiaries at the Santa Maria della Scala in which each beneficiary received a predetermined sum for each service.[101] Although the documents do not elaborate upon the musical duties performed by the beneficiaries at the various services, it is likely that they assisted with the singing of plainchant items, leaving the performance of polyphony to the experienced singers.

The reorganization of 1534 appears to have been motivated primarily by general discipline problems in the cappella musicale, for several annotations in the surviving documents suggest that the chapter dignitaries had repeatedly taken Werrecore to task for ineffective management of the singers. The earliest of these, which is dated 9 February 1525, merely states that the chapter had requested an audience with Werrecore in order to discuss an accusation that had been leveled against him. Unfortunately, no specific charges are enumerated in the succeeding documents.[102] On 18 January 1532, however, Werrecore was requested to explain his methods of controlling the choir in a formal meeting before the *Fabbrica*. Although this entry, like the first, fails to elaborate upon the difficulties, it clearly reveals that the dissatisfaction of the dignitaries was shared in some measure by the singers themselves.[103] Werrecore's response to the *Fabbrica* must have provoked further investigation into the issues addressed, for by 5 June 1533 it had been determined that a complete overhaul of the cappella musicale was necessary. A committee was appointed to evaluate the conditions in the chapel,[104] and it made its recommendations to the chapter on 6 June 1534.[105] A list of ordinances governing the operation of the choir was drawn up thereafter, and higher monthly salaries were approved for each of the singers. The ordinances, which are dated 12 December 1534, imply that the singers were improperly dressed for services, blasphemed in church frequently, and quarreled amongst themselves regularly. They further suggest that Werrecore had been shirking his teaching duties at the choir school:

> The above listed cantors are expected to sing the daily hours that ordinaries generally
>   sing, except when those [hours] are masses for the dead.
> Furthermore, the cantors themselves are expected to appear reverent, dressed in long
>   vestments reaching completely to the ankles, white surplices, and the caps of the
>   sacerdotes. This is mandated from above, and if their dress appears altered in any

way, they will be sent away for the remainder of that week.

Also they [must] lay down quarrels that they have between themselves.

Likewise, they must neither speak vain words nor blaspheme in this church: if they behave to the contrary, they will be sent away for the remainder of that week in which such things have been uttered.

Furthermore, they cannot take leave through substitution.

Finally, Father Matthias is expected to teach the boys in the Fabbrica, and if he refuses to do so, he will be dismissed for the remainder of the month in which the offense occurs.[106]

Two days after the ordinances were recorded, an additional mandate granting the chapter dignitaries the power to levy monetary fines on any singer found to be in violation of them was appended, most certainly with the intention of further encouraging the singers towards more professional behavior.[107]

The 1534 episode reveals that the focus upon matters 'in medio ecclesiae' which had been adopted by the *Fabbrica* in its approach to the development of the Duomo's physical space was extended to its services as well. The *Fabbrica* clearly intended that the liturgical music which emanated from the cantorie that were to house the newly constructed organ be presented in an orderly and an edifying manner. Yet it appears that the *Fabbrica*'s every effort was resisted by the choir itself. In July 1556, when Simon Boyleau was maestro di cappella, a series of disagreements between the singers and their supervisors again erupted. The chapter prefects, clearly intending to avoid squabbles among the choral personnel, issued a revised version of the 1534 ordinances in response. The new statutes, which repeat the guidelines set forth in the 1534 document, contain an interesting addition that reflects both the penetrability of Milanese territorial borders and the lack of discipline that apparently characterized the choir during the years following the death of Francesco II Sforza:

The aforementioned singers may not leave the city of Milan temporarily without the written permission of the Reverend Deputy Fathers of the province of the aforementioned church . . .[108]

This new provision was likely motivated by the restrictions on travel that were enacted in Milan during the initial years of the Spanish occupation under Charles V, as well as by the potential staffing difficulties that might arise when singers were beyond the range of immediate contact with chapter officials. Limiting, documenting, and supervising the movement of its singers more carefully insured their legal and physical safety at a time when instrumental musicians had proven especially susceptible to entanglement in dangerous situations.[109] Even before the 1556 additions to the statutes, however, the Milanese chapter took a fairly dim view of granting singers extended leave. Only Gabriele Aliardis de Trivultio, a contrabassus who appears rather sporadically on the rolls between 1544 and 1549, seems to have been missing for more than one extended period.[110]

On 30 June 1572 the ordinances were issued yet again, but this time with a number of interesting additions that address the very concerns that emerged repeatedly during Carlo Borromeo's pastoral visits to various churches in the city. Order and decorum were of the utmost importance to him, and this is manifest in the amount of attention afforded proceeding to and leaving from the choir during the services, the placement of the boys upon the choir steps, the proper use of the choir itself, and the Christian character expected of prospective singers. Moreover, the singers were fined a day's payment for failing to bring the appropriate attire to services held in institutions other than the Duomo, and inattention to the the the maestro di cappella resulted in the loss of a day's salary for the first offense, punishment by the *Fabbrica* for the second offense, and dismissal upon the third offense. Yet the maestro's authority over the singers was limited to discipline, for he was not to hire or dismiss them without permission from the authorities.[111] Perhaps the most striking addition, however, pertains to the duties of the maestro di cappella, for it underscores the seriousness of purpose with which the *Fabbrica* pursued the production of new repertoire for the choir:

> The chapel master shall be required every month to compose a mass and a Magnificat and such hymns as shall be necessary, according to the notice given him by the chorus-master, and he shall notify the authorities in charge of music as to his compositions.[112]

This is the first time that the *Fabbrica*'s expectations regarding compositional output were set down in writing, a fact which may explain why the tenures of Ruffo and Pontio were characterized by a more impressive output of sacred repertoire than were those of Hoste da Reggio and Simon Boyleau.

Salaries and benefices

Prior to the reorganization of 1534, adult singers at the Duomo normally received an annual salary of 36 lire 8 soldi, while the boy sopranos were awarded an annual allowance of 12 lire.[113] There were, however, occasional exceptions to this policy. Giovanni Antonio de Vergiate, presumably the most senior member of the choir, received 50 lire 8 soldi per year.[114] In any case, the official reorganization notice of 12 December 1534 specifies new annual salaries of 72 lire for the adults and 12 lire for juvenile singers, and these remained intact until at least 1563.[115] Although the stipends provided for the boys were unchanged, those guaranteed the adult singers constituted an annual raise of almost fifty percent. Even after the reorganization, however, a singer occasionally still received either more or less than the standard salary. Laurentio de Putheo, a 'falsettist' who served the choir from 1534 to 1561, received only 48 lire per annum, while contrabasso Gabriele de Aliardus de Trivultio began collecting an impressive 253 lire and 12 soldi in 1558 after he petitioned the authorities for assistance on account of his 'extreme poverty' and 'the affliction of the children under his care.'[116]

During the 1534 reorganization, Werrecore apparently received no augmentation in salary, and his annual remuneration of 144 lire would remain the standard for the maestri until 1558, when Hoste da Reggio succeeded in securing a raise of 96 lire per year. Each maestro employed thereafter would successfully negotiate a wage either equal or greater than that earned by his predecessor. Ruffo received a remuneration of only 240 lire per year,[117] but Boyleau negotiated a salary of 400 lire upon his return to the chapel in the 1570s. Pontio succeeded in nearly doubling the sum earned by Boyleau with an impressive 737 lire; yet this sharp increase reflects, in part, the high inflation that plagued the city during the 1570s.

If the *Ordinazioni* of the *Fabbrica* are any indication, then it can be said that the selection of organists was handled more casually than that of the singers and the maestri. There are no official appointment notices for the organists, and, as a result, they can only be identified via the surviving pay registers. At the point of the reorganization of 1534, organist Giovanni Stefano de Putheobonello was receiving an annual remuneration of 76 lire and 16 soldi, while his assistant Baptiste de Melegnano was awarded a mere 14 soldi per month. Putheobonello's salary was raised to 100 lire per year in 1546, at which time he also received an additional 11 lire in recognition of his long-standing service.[118] This new salary of 100 lire per annum apparently remained the standard for organists through the early 1570s, although a few exceptions were made in the hopes of attracting local stars to perform on the new organ.[119] When Gioseffo Caimo was stolen away from Sant'Ambrogio in 1577, he was awarded an impressive salary of 115 lire per quarter.[120] Shortly after the construction on the new organ was completed, moreover, the salary of the assistant organist, which had been raised from 16 soldi to a modest 18 soldi per month in 1561,[121] rocketed to 70 lire per year as the assistant assumed the duties for playing the 'old' or second organ,[122] perhaps in the performance of antiphonal music.

Although benefices brought and kept talented musicians in Milan during the fifteenth century,[123] their potential as a recruiting tool for singers seems to have all but dried up during the sixteenth century. Aside from Matthias Werrecore, only two persons appearing on the cappella musicale rosters between 1522 and 1563–Andrea de Germanis, and Giovanni Antonio de Rapis de Busti–held ducal benefices, and both were awarded these benefices prior to the 1535 death of Francesco II Sforza. Andrea de Germanis, a tenor who jointed the Duomo choir in 1542, likely served the Sforza court from 1523 until at least 1531, during which time he acquired two ducal benefices–a ducal canonicate at Santa Maria Adurni's St Blase chapel in 1523[124] and a ducal chaplaincy at Santa Maria della Scala in 1531.[125] Contralto Giovanni Antonio de Rapis de Busti, who served at the Duomo from 1541 to 1557, was appointed to a ducal rectorship at San Silvestro in Porta Nuova in 1525.[126] He also secured a chaplaincy at the Duomo only two years later.[127] Interestingly enough, both of the benefices awarded Rapis were endowed by his uncle, a fact which elucidates the role that family ties played in securing even minor ecclesiastical posts in Milan. Contrary to what the registers seem to suggest, however, there was no dearth of benefices in Milan after the death of Francesco II Sforza. Nor was it impossible for ecclesiastically trained musicians to acquire them. Nicola Vicentino, a Ferrarese musician who served in the private chapel Archbishop Ippolito II D'Este, amassed eight of them and was nominated for eight others between 1554 and 1557 alone.[128] Although he was excused from residency in each case, he did serve as a rector at San Tommaso in terra amara under Archibishop Carlo Borromeo from 1565 to 1578.[129] Vicentino's fluid acquisition of multiple benefices suggests that success was dependent upon the candidate's personal relationship with the individual who ultimately controlled the appointment process, which, with the exception of the royal ducal appointments, appears to have been the Archbishop of Milan himself.[130] Ippolito II, as might be expected, clearly favored his own musicians over the Duomo singers when it came to the awarding of benefices.

Although most of the Duomo singers did not acquire such appointments, several of them did hold chaplaincies that were administrated by the *Fabbrica*. All of these were associated with endowed chapels assigned to altars in the Duomo or other churches in the immediate area, and the majority of them required that the recipient perform various ecclesiastical duties in return for a relatively modest stipend. Singers Giovanni Antonio de Rapis de Busti,[131] Giovanni Petro de Organis[132] and Giovanni Jacobo de Canibus[133] were appointed to chaplaincies in Santa Maria Maggiore, while tenor Francesco da Marliano,[134] contralto Bernardino Gallasino[135], and contralto Fabritio de Baretis[136] held chaplaincies at the churches of Santa Maria presso San Celso, St Victor and the Forty Martyrs, and Sant'Eufemia, respectively. Organis, Marliano, and Rapis each received a six-month stipend of 40 lire from their chaplaincies, while Gallasino collected a six-month stipend of 20 lire from his. In return for his biannual stipend of 40 lire, Organis was required to perform a daily mass at the altar of St Ambrose in the cathedral.[137] Both Marliano and Rapis were expected to say a daily mass in their assigned chapels as well, while Gallasino was held to only three masses per week at St Victor.[138] The exact salary and responsibilities assigned Canibus have not yet surfaced; it is known only that his appointment involved activities in Santa Maria Maggiore.[139] Baretis received 25 lire every six months for unspecified duties at the altar of All Saints in Sant'Eufemia.

Perhaps the most elaborate performance in an endowed chapel at the Duomo occurred in connection to the altar of San Gottardo, which was more commonly known as the altar of the Spirito Santo. A foundation provided by Ambrogio Porro stipulated the performance of a daily plainchant mass there, and, at the outset, this mass required the participation of a cantor, one officiant/custodian, three regular officiants, a custodian/cleric, and three regular clerics.[140] By early 1527 the performance body had been downsized to one cantor, four officiants, and a custodian, perhaps because the salary of the cantor had been raised by twenty lire per annum.[141] Interestingly enough, the cantors who served at this altar during the sixteenth century, which included Giovanni Maria de Castilliono, Carole de Oxio, Vincentio de Braschis, and Donato Mazonzellis, were not members of the cathedral choir.[142] Clearly, however, provisions had been made for a daily plainchant spectacle that communicated the devotion of the benefactor, thus encouraging the attendant public toward donations that insured their own perpetuity. During the 1550s a similar foundation mass was instituted at the altar of Santa Maria del Pilone. There the cantor, Giovanni Antonio de Rubesterijs, was assisted by three officials in a daily sung mass for the soul of Raimondo da Marliano, which, if the salaries are any indication, rivaled that at the altar of San Gottardo in its solemnity and display.[143]

Distribution of Voices

As can be seen from the rosters (Appendix 2), the altus, tenor, and bassus voices of polyphonic works were performed with approximately four singers per part, while around seven sopranos were needed to balance the upper parts. However, it is possible that the soprano parts were divided among the younger singers so that they alternated the singing responsibilities, particularly given their relative lack of experience. Between 1535 and 1550, the total number of singers fluctuated between nineteen and twenty-four, and, with the exception of the boys, replacement of singers occurred relatively infrequently. The sixteenth-century choir was never larger than during the decade falling between 1540 and 1550, when several additional sopranos and tenors were hired. Three extra boy sopranos were hired at half pay in 1547,[144] and they thereafter were replaced by others when their voices changed. In addition, two new tenors were added at the outset of 1549, thus increasing the number of tenors from three to five.[145] Though the latter additions may have resulted, in part, from the reduction of tenor Laurentio de la Strata to half-pay service that same year,[146] they may also reflect the voicing requirements of the currently popular five-part textures, many of which featured a contratenor part in approximately the same range as the tenor.

Between 1550 and 1551, the choir was generally comprised of an adult complement of four contraltos, four tenors, and four basses, as well as seven to nine sopranos, all but one of whom were boys.[147] After Simon Boyleau assumed directorship of the choir in 1551, the number singers for the lower parts was gradually reduced from four to three through natural attrition, while the number of boy sopranos retained remained around six. One adult soprano was employed continuously during this period as well. The proportionally large number of boy sopranos appears somewhat misleading, since some of them were engaged at half pay, while others received a remuneration either 1.5 to 2 times the usual amount, a fact which implies that some of them performed far more frequently than did others.[148] Despite the minor reduction in size that characterized the choir of the 1550s, the *Fabbrica* appears to have been more reluctant to allow the number of tenors to fall below four for long periods of time. In 1559, they even resorted to short-term substitutes, including retired maestro Werrecore, in order to maintain a tenor section of four voices, despite the fact that the number of contraltos and basses generally remained three per section.[149] It is not clear why the choir was reduced slightly in size during the 1550s. The five-voice motets composed by Werrecore for use at the cathedral, which were published in 1555, provide ample evidence that the textural demands for works performed in Milan during this period would not have necessitated a reduction in the number of voices. Perhaps the downsizing of the choir can be attributed to Boyleau's aforementioned lack of attention to administrative matters, for the choir again boasted at least four adult singers of each voice type by 1560. Nonetheless, it would appear that three to four singers of each voice type remained the accepted standard for at least fifteen years thereafter. A list of the singers dating from around 1570 specifies three altos, four tenors, and four basses,[150] and the 1572 ordinances for the choir indicate that the maestro di cappella was responsible for notifying the *Fabbrica* if 'there is missing one or more of the three basses, or the four tenors, or the four contraltos.'[151] Between

1572 and 1576 three basses, four tenors, and four altos continue to appear on the rolls, but by 1576 to 1578 as many as eight to ten tenors are listed frequently.[152] This plethora of tenors perhaps coincides with the introduction of polychoral music in the Duomo, for Urbano Monti reported, in a rare comment on music in the Duomo, that in June 1582 'one made the solo of the choir between the two barriers of the very handsome steeped platforms'[153] found in the center of the church and at the end of the choir.

The Duomo Ceremonial

During Werrecore's tenure, the feasts celebrated at the Duomo were divided, for the purposes of financial management, into five categories: chapter, *Fabbrica*, Santa Tecla, clergy, and diverse. Many of the feasts described in the ceremoniali of the period, including all of those entrusted to the Provost and Canons of the ancient chapter of Santa Tecla, commemorated the dead. These were usually celebrated with a procession around the Duomo that culminated in a sung mass. Some Duomo annuals, however, were commemorated at other local churches in the immediate area, particularly when the deceased for whom the foundation had been established was entombed at a neighboring institution. In most of these cases, the ordinaries, officiants, and other clergy required processed to the church in question and there sang the standard mass.[154] Annual commemorations of the dead occurred at the Duomo or in its environs as often as three times per week, and only those of selected bishops and archbishops were elevated to the status of principal feasts.[155] As a result, the annuals were often performed by clergy capable of singing plainchant, rather than by the members of the Duomo choir itself.[156]

The festal calendar observed at the Duomo during the mid-sixteenth century can be reconstructed from two surviving ceremoniali that can be dated to the years 1543 and 1562.[157] These ceremoniali reveal that the primary feasts on the Duomo's calendar were usually celebrated either with two Vespers and a High Mass or via a procession. While the former practice was employed for the feasts of the Visitation, the Assumption, the Conception BVM, the Presentation BVM, the Epiphany, the Invention of the Cross, Santa Tecla, San Galdino, St James, St Jerome, St Martin, St Catherine, St Jacob, and St Agnes, the latter, which almost always included the singing of litanies and sometimes even culminated in a solemn Mass, was reserved for other selected feasts of particular local significance, including San Bassiano, the Purification BVM (with the Blessing of the Candles), Quadregesima, Palm Sunday, St Gothard, St Gregory, Corpus Christi, and the Dedication of the Church. Additionally, a solemn Mass served to commemorate the feasts of Saints Protasius and Gervaise, St Joseph, All Saints, and the Midnight Vigil of the Nativity, the last of which featured a select group of singers from the Duomo choir.[158] The sixteenth-century choir also sang Mass and Vespers in other local churches, including Sant'Ambrogio, San Dionisio, San Gottardo, Santa Maria dell'Incoronata, San Giovanni ad Conca, Santa Maria della Passione, and San Nazaro on specified feasts, as well as at selected annual commemorations for deceased bishops and archbishops. By the time of Carlo Borromeo's 1577 pastoral visit to the Duomo, the feasts of Saints Peter and Paul,

Saints Nazaro and Celso, the Assumption, and the First Session of the Provincial Council had been added to the processional calendar, and the processions held on the first two occasions typically culminated in a pontifical mass celebrated by Archbishop Carlo Borromeo himself.[159]

Vespers and High Mass, which yielded impressive daily distributions of eight denari to the beneficiaries assigned to the choir by 1572,[160] were clearly central to the Duomo's observances, and must have featured most of the polyphony sung there during the sixteenth century. The importance of these two services with regard to polyphony is further underscored by the 1557 appointment notice for Hoste da Reggio, which notes that the new maestro was to supervise the performance of the Duomo choir at the Divine Offices of Solemn Feasts in other churches, all Vespers services on Solemn Vigils, the feast of the Commemoration of the Dead, and all masses commissioned by the Court of Milan.[161]

It is difficult to determine from the archival and musical evidence just how much the placement of polyphony within the service changed in Milan across the sixteenth century, but the sources certainly imply that the performance traditions remained rather static. The fourth Milan Choirbook, which was copied between 1492 and 1527,[162] contains masses, Magnificats, Vespers hymns, sequences, and motets for the liturgical calendar observed at the Duomo during the late fifteenth and early sixteenth centuries. Many, though certainly not all, of the works contained are intended for Marian feasts. Several annotations found throughout indicate that some of its single motets and motet pairs were sung during the Ingressa (Ambrosian Introit), Offertory, Transitorium (Ambrosian Communion), and Confractorium (roughly corresponding to the Agnus Dei) of the Ambrosian Mass, a practice which is discussed in the cathedral documents as early as 1463.[163] In addition, the repertoire found in the other three Milan choirbooks reveals that motets were also commonly performed during the Elevation. Two documents from Santa Maria della Scala dated 1597 similarly discuss the performance of polyphony during the Offertory,[164] thus confirming that the performance of motets during this section of the mass was a common practice in the region during the sixteenth century. It is clear from the content of *Librone 4*, however, that polyphonic hymns and Magnificats were performed regularly at Vespers, so is not unlikely that some of the motets might have functioned as Vespers polyphony as well. In any case, Mass and Vespers continued to dominate the ceremonial during the latter half of the sixteenth century. An extant list reporting the absences of the Duomo singers from services held between 1 September and 31 December 1608 focuses upon Vespers and High Mass, as well as the occasional Terce.[165]

More problematic to the study of the ceremonial is the conflation of Roman and Ambrosian liturgical items in the surviving polyphony, most of which survives in printed form. The commingling of Ambrosian and Roman texts that Ciceri and Migliavacca found in *Librone 4*[166] seems entirely characteristic of the Duomo's ritual, for it permeates later printed collections associated with the Duomo as well. It appears that although the Ambrosian rite governed the content and order of the Duomo ceremonial, particularly with regard to the readings and other Proper items, the insertion of occasional polyphony on Roman texts appropriate to feasts concordant with the Ambrosian calendar was considered entirely acceptable, if not preferable. Polyphony set to Roman texts was, from a purely practical point of view, more lucrative for the composer who wished to see his work in print. Moreover, it provided the liturgy an additional layer of both textual and musical ornamentation.

Werrecore's 1555 Motet Book

Of the four musicians who served as maestro di cappella between 1522 and 1563, Werrecore appears to have been the most active in collecting and composing new compositions for the cathedral library. If the completion date of 22 June 1527 for the fourth Milan Choirbook (*Librone* 4 or *Mil D* 4) is correct, then Werrecore supervised its copying during the first five years of his tenure.[167] Although *Librone 4* was partially destroyed in a fire during the year 1906, its content has been partially reconstructed, and includes compositions by Josquin, Loyset Compère, Gaspare Weerbecke, and Gaffurius.[168] The cantus firmus techniques and canonic devices employed by these masters clearly influenced Werrecore's style, but he may have found their compositions stylistically outdated, as he also attempted to expand the cathedral's library of printed music at the outset of his tenure.[169] Unfortunately, the records do not include any information regarding the exact nature of his purchases, but it is possible that they included prints with which Werrecore was involved as an editor, including Petrus Schaeffer's *Cantiones quinque vocum selectissimae a primariis* (1539) and Bernardino Calusco's *Mutetarum* (1543).

　　　Werrecore's *Cantuum quinque vocum quos motetta vocant . . . liber primus* (1555), which was printed by Moscheni of Milan while the composer was still in residence at the cathedral, perhaps best reflects the the Duomo's musical traditions during the middle of the sixteenth century. In the tradition of *Librone 4*, Werrecore's collection contains single motets, motet pairs, and three motet cycles on hymns and sequences, the majority of which are intended for either Marian feasts or the most important celebrations of the liturgical calendar (see Table 3.1). The dizzying combination of Ambrosian texts with those from the Roman rite, another characteristic shared with *Librone 4*, may be explained, in part, by the large number of feasts celebrated in other churches of the city, several of which observed the Roman rather than the Ambrosian rite, but it does not begin to account for the Roman texts provided for the Invention of the Cross, Pentecost, Palm Sunday, Easter, and certain Marian feasts. A similar liturgical problem plagues Pietro Pontio's *Modulationem Ecclesiae Maioris Mediolani Mottettorum cum quinque vocibus liber primus* of 1582, which contains nineteen motets on predominantly Roman texts.[170] The introduction of a Pater Noster and Ave Maria at the opening of Pontio's collection and the inclusion of two Marian antiphons at the close suggests that the motets included were intended primarily for use at Vespers and Compline, despite the fact that many of the texts included were derived from other hours of the Roman liturgy. At best it can be postulated that Roman texts appropriate to specific feasts of the Duomo calendar were inserted into Mass or Vespers, and, further, that the conflation of Roman and Ambrosian service items was not troublesome to sixteenth-century listeners.

Although the three motet cycles appear at the close of Werrecore's collection, the collection itself is ordered according to a hierarchy that treats signature as the first priority, cleffing as the second, and final as the third (see Table 3.2). Despite the modernity suggested by the use of such tonal ordering, however, many of the motets betray the ease with which Werrecore embraced the compositional techniques that characterized the Milan Choirbooks. Given the preponderance of tempus imperfectum, prolatione imperfecta in Milanese motets of the period, for example, *Veni sancte spiritus* is distinctive in its use of tempus perfectum, prolatione imperfecta in the prima pars, followed by diminution to proportio dupla in the secunda pars. The plainchant melody appears in the contratenor, but is decorated so that its movement approximates the speed of the other voices, a technique frequently employed by Werrecore. The tempus perfectum signature and the subsequent diminution to proportio dupla, however, are not characteristic of his compositions, and look backward to the generation of Josquin, Weerbecke, Gaffurius, and Compère. Werrecore's setting of *Tu solus* similarly reveals the composer's familiarity with the elevation motet on the same

Table 3.1 Content of Hermann Matthias Werrecore, *Cantuum quinque vocum quos motetta vocant . . . liber primus* (Milano: Francesco e Simone Moscheni, 1555)

Motet	*Liturgical Usage*	*Syst.*	*Cleffing*	*Final*
Veni sancte spiritus	Sequence for Pentecost (Roman)	1 flat	$G_2C_2C_3C_3F_3$	G
O altitudo divitiarum	Romans 11:33 Cap. for Saturday Vespers (Roman)	1flat	$G_2C_2C_3C_3F_3$	F
Alma redemptoris mater	Antiphon BVM	1flat	$G_2C_2C_3C_3F_3$	F
Virgo prudentissima	Antiphon BVM for Assumption (Roman)	1flat	$G_2C_2C_2C_3C_4$	G
Confundatur qui me	Antiphon for Palm Sunday (Roman)	1 flat	$G_2C_2C_3C_3F_3$	F
Tanto tempore	Antiphon, Ingressa, and Psallenda Sts. Philip and James	1 flat	$G_2C_2C_3C_3F_3$	G
Si bona suscepimus	Job 2:10 (Responsory)	-	$G_2C_2C_3C_3C_4$	D
Ave regina caelorum	Antiphon BVM	-	$G_2C_2C_3C_3C_4$	G
Ecce nos relinquimus omnia	Matthew 19:27	-	$G_2C_2C_3C_3F_3$	G
Porta haec clausa erit	Ezekiel 44:2	-	$G_2C_2C_2C_3C_4$	G
Haec dies	Psallenda for Resurrection	-	$G_2C_2C_2C_3F_3$	D
Tu solus	Elevation	-	$G_2C_2C_2C_3C_4$	G

Quid retribuam domino	Antiphon Common of Martyrs and St Stephen (Roman)	-	$C_2C_3C_3C_4F_4$	E
Sana me domine	Antiphon Defunctorum (Roman)	-	$C_2C_3C_3C_4F_4$	A
Proh dolor	Funeral of Alfonso D'Avalos	-	$C_2C_3C_3C_4F_4$	A
Inclina deus aurem tuam	Antiphon for All Souls' Day (Roman); Psallenda Fer IV Adv 6, Feria VI Lazarus, and Day 3 of Litanies	-	$C_2C_3C_3C_4F_4$	E
Inviolata, integra et casta es (cycle)	Antiphon/Sequence BVM (Roman)	1 flat	$C_1\ C_3\ C_4\ F_3\ F_4$	F
Popule meus (cycle)	Adoration of the Cross (Roman)	1 flat	$C_1\ C_3\ C_3\ C_4\ F_4$	G
Ave maris stella (cycle)	Vespers Hymn BVM (Roman)	1 flat	$G_2\ C_2\ C_2\ C_3\ F_3$	G

text by Josquin It features comparable mensural shifts at corresponding positions in the text, as well as the introduction of homophony at the opening of the tripla section (Example 3.1). Werrecore's debt to Josquin, in fact, is evident throughout, and may account, at least in part, for the enthusiasm with which the Milanese humanist Publio Francesco Spinola hailed Werrecore as the worthy descendant of Josquin:

Carmine qui blando longos finire labores, Atque animum Musis exilarare soles, Hermanni modulis studeas, qui Dorcea cantu, Orphea Terpandros aequiparare potest, Quique Linos superat, quicum Pratensis Apollo. Si certet, Musa iudice, victus erit: Mira canit, mirisque modis, mirabitur istos Et Terra, et Pontus, suspicietque modos.

O you, who are wont to end your long labors with a sweet song, and to gladden your soul with the Muses, study the measures of Hermann, whose song equals that of Dorceo. He can be compared to the poet Orpheus Terpandros, and surpasses Linos, as well as the Apollo 'of Pratis.' If he shall strive while the goddess of Music is judge, he will be conquered. He sings wonderously, with wonderous meters: both Earth and Sea will marvel at the rhythms and will admire them.[171]

Spinola, who was engaged in the composition of psalm paraphrases around the time that the ode was written,[172] may also have been inspired by the composer's affective application of tonal types to an interesting combination of standard and uncharacteristic sacred texts. All four of the collection's tribulation motets, for example, are set in low clefs and feature Phrygian modal inflections.

Example 3.1 Werrecore, *Tu solus*, measures 56-69

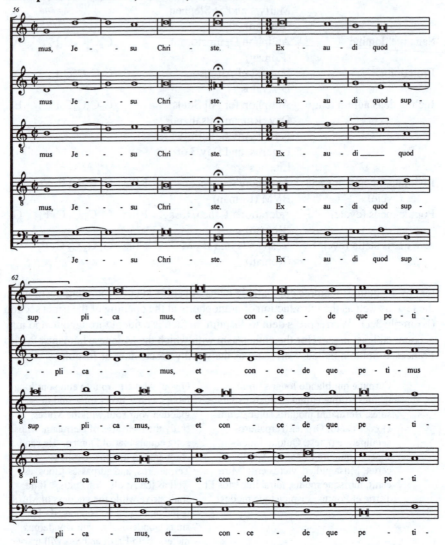

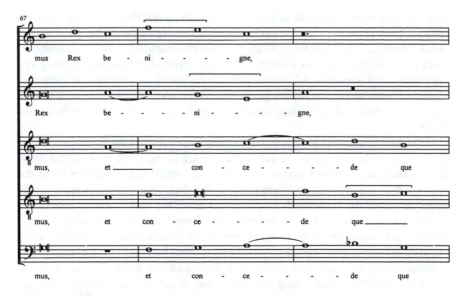

The first of these, *Quid retribuam domino*, is composed on an antiphon for the Common of Martyrs from the Roman rite. The weighty and contemplative nature of its text assuredly motivated the choice of the exclusively low-voice texture, which usually was reserved for lamentation and funeral settings in Milanese compositions from this period.[173] The tonally similar *Inclina Deus, aurem tuam*, makes use of a Roman plainchant for All Souls' Day, and may have been sung during the obsequies for Francesco II Sforza, which were held in the Duomo between 1 November and 19 November 1535. Its occasional text, which cries for mercy upon the afflicted city, is best described as a free paraphrase of Psalms 86 and 64. The funeral motets *Sana me domine* and *Proh dolor*, which employ an A cantus durus tonal type that allows for the commixture of Phrygian, Aeolian and Lydian modalities, were likely written for the funeral of Alfonso D'Avalos. They appear to function as a pair, for they are positioned successively in the print and feature the same cleffing and tone. *Sana me domine* is based upon an antiphon from the Mass for the Dead, while *Proh dolor* is a freely-composed imitative setting of a humanistic text lamenting D'Avalos's passing. The text of the latter, which was discussed at length in Chapter 2 above, appears to be a gloss on the anonymous Proh dolor composed for Maximilian I of Austria, and its use here strengthens the assertion that Werrecore was in the retinue that accompanied Francesco II Sforza to Milan from Austria upon the restoration of the Duchy.

The three motet cycles, *Inviolata, integer et casta es Maria*, *Popule meus* and *Ave maris stella*, contain a number of the features detected in the cycles found in the Milan choirbooks, including tonal organization by mode and cleffing and the use of a hymn or sequence as a unifying textual and musical theme from one motet of the cycle to the next.[174] All three cycles also feature either reduced or expanded voicing in selected motets within them. The reduction of voices is indicated through tacet markings in the silent parts, thus lending additional support to the contention that these motet groups were conceived as cycles. Moreover, when the number of voices is reduced for a given motet of the cycle, the clefs and signatures of the participating voices remain as they were when all the voices were sounding. When the eliminated voices are restored in successive motets of the cycle, their original cleffing and signatures stand (see Table 3.2). Expanded voicing is indicated through the addition of a6 and a7 parts in the appropriate partbooks. When a6 or a7 parts are added to the original five, their clef and signature assignments also remain the same throughout the cycle.

The largest and most ambitious of the three cycles is the seven-part setting of the Marian Vespers hymn *Ave maris stella*. Each of the seven verses of the hymn is conceived as a separate entity, but a sense of overall unity is achieved via the uninterrupted presence of the hymn tune. In the first, fifth, and sixth sections, the hymn is stated in traditional long-note style in the tenor, altus, and cantus primus voices respectively. In contrast, the second and fourth sections feature paraphrased statements of the hymn shared by the soprano and tenor voices, while the third section is characterized by free imitative elaboration of the melody. The culmination of the cycle is a seven-voice setting of the verse 'Sit laus patri' in which the two tenor voices sing the hymn tune in canon at the fourth, while the remaining five voices weave imitative counterpoint around them (Example 3.2). Textural variety is further achieved across the cycle through the reduction and expansion of the number of voices employed. The third and fourth sections are treated to reduced textures of four and three voices respectively, while the sixth and seventh are systematically expanded from five to six and seven voices. The four-section setting of *Popule meus* for the Adoration of the Cross is equally impressive. As in the *Ave maris stella*, textural variety is achieved through the immediate reduction and gradual expansion of voice parts. The final six-voice section, moreover, features the introduction of the ostinato cantus firmus 'Ego deus

Table 3.2 Motet cycles in Werrecore's *Cantuum quinque vocum quos motetta vocant . . . liber primus* (1555)

Motet	Liturgical Usage	Cleffing	Syst.	Final
Inviolata, integra et casta es	Antiphon/ Sequence BVM (Roman)	$C_1 C_3 C_4 F_3 F_4$	1 flat	F
2 p. Quae nunc flagitant (a 3)		$C_1 C_3 C_4$	1 flat	F
3 p. O benigna, ò regina		$C_1 C_3 C_4 F_3 F_4$	1 flat	F
Popule meus	Adoration of the Cross (Roman)	$C_1 C_3 C_3 C_4 F_4$	1 flat	G
2 p. Quid ultra (a 3)		$C_3 C_3 C_4$	1 flat	G
3 p. Ego propter te (a 4)		$C_3 C_3 C_4 F_4$	1 flat	G
4 p. Ego te pavi manna (a 6)		$C_1 C_3 C_3 C_4 C_4 F_4$	1 flat	G
Ave maris stella	Vespers Hymn BVM (Roman)	$G_2 C_2 C_2 C_3 F_3$	1 flat	G
2 p. Sumens illud Ave		$G_2 C_2 C_2 C_3 F_3$	1 flat	G
3 p. Solve vincla (a 4)		$C_2 C_2 C_3 F_3$	1 flat	G
4 p. Mostra te esse matrem (a 3)		$G_2 C_2 C_3$	1 flat	G
5 p. Virgo singularis		$G_2 C_2 C_2 C_3 F_3$	1 flat	G
6 p. Vitam praesta puram (a 6)		$G_2 G_2 C_2 C_2 C_3 F_3$	1 flat	G
7 p. Sit laus Deo patri (a 7)		$G_2 G_2 C_2 C_2 C_3 C_3 F_3$	1 flat	G

Salvador,' which is sounded in alternating soft and natural hexachords in a manner reminiscent of the *Missa Hercules Dux Ferrariae*, three movements of which are found in the third Milan Choirbook.

It is unlikely that the three motet cycles served the same function as did the *motetti missales*. On the one hand, they seem to possess all of the qualities associated with the *motetti missales*, including a single textual theme that is appropriate for several feasts of the liturgical year, motivic material that recurs throughout, unity of clef and mode, and changes in texture through the reduction or addition of voices. On the other hand, however, the cycles include no elevation motet and are textually comprised of successive stanzas of the same hymn or sequence, rather than a series of stanzas from related texts as is common in the *motetti missales*. Since its hymn tune is clearly outlined in each of its seven successive stanzas, *Ave maris stella*, for example, clearly functioned as a polyphonic setting of a Vespers hymn for general use on Marian feasts. It lacks the

Example 3.2 Werrecore, *Ave maris stella*, settima parte, measures 1-13

alternation of plainchant and polyphony that generally characterizes the sixteenth-century polyphonic hymn settings of such composers as Corteccia, Jachet of Mantua, Palestrina, and Victoria, but it features some of the techniques especially favored by Festa, including reduced voicing and canons.

All three of Werrecore's cycles, in fact, contain features of both the polyphonic office hymn and the *motetti missales*. They owe their distinct character to the adaptation of stylistic features borrowed directly from the *motetti missales* to the more universal polyphonic office hymn. The motet cycles in *Librone 4*, in fact, attest to the changing nature of the *motetti missales* during the early sixteenth century. They often consisted of fewer movements and were more loosely united both textually and motivically than were their predecessors, features that may have arisen from attempts to adapt pre-existing material to current practice, as well as from the gradual penetration of Roman influence. For Milanese composers of the post-Sforza generation, the application of compositional styles and techniques associated specifically with the Milan choirbooks may have been viewed as both covertly symbolic and overtly patriotic.

Motets clearly continued to comprise the preferred polyphonic genre in Milan during the first half of the sixteenth century. The majority of the pieces copied in *Librone 4* are motets. Moreover, at least six printed motet collections can be firmly connected to the Milanese court or cathedral between the years 1522 and 1563, while only one mass book demonstrates a potential link to the city. The earliest surviving collections of polyphonic music printed in Milan are the motet collections issued by Castiglione of Milan in 1542 and 1543, a fact which further suggests that the motet was the region's most utilitarian sacred genre. While most of the printed motet collections associated with Milan between 1522 and 1563 can be loosely tied to Santa Maria della Scala through their dedications, organization, and content, Werrecore's 1555 motet book alone stems from the Duomo of Milan. It stands as the single, and, therefore, the most important musical document of performance practice at the Duomo of Milan between 1527, the supposed completion date of *Librone 4*, and 1570, the year in which Vincenzo Ruffo's first book of post-Tridentine masses was issued. The motet cycles contained reflect the continuation and maturation of a musical tradition established under the Sforza that sets Milanese sacred music apart from that of the rest of Italy. Even as it evolved into potential Vespers music, the motet cycle, a genre that was associated specifically with Renaissance Milan, functioned, by its very nature, as an expression of Milanese civic identity, and this particular expression of artistic patriotism was fostered at the Duomo 'in medio ecclesiae.'

The Ruffo Masses

The ordination of Carlo Borromeo as Archbishop of Milan on 15 May 1560 ushered in a new era in the Duomo ceremonial that is marked by the dominance of text intelligibility over all other aspects of the musical experience. Borromeo, who, as papal secretary to Pius IV, all but presided over the final sessions of the Council of Trent, had become actively engaged in the search for an appropriate sacred style by 1564, when he and Cardinal Vitellozzi Vitelli began introducing liturgical reforms at the papal chapel and the Collegium Germanicum in Rome.[175] In 1565 Borromeo held the first of several Provincial Councils aimed at post-Tridentine reform in the diocese of Milan, and sacred music was among the issues addressed. The resulting directive favored the employment of singers trained as ecclesiastics, limited the use of instruments to the organ in all the local churches, sought to purge the liturgy of all secular allusions, and encouraged the composition of polyphony that focused upon clarity of text declamation, thus inspiring the listeners to greater piety.[176] Vincenzo Ruffo was the first maestro subjected to Borromeo's reform program, and, as Lewis Lockwood has ably demonstrated, his compositional career was irreversibly altered by Borromeo's goals of intelligibility and spiritual inspiration.

On 10 March 1565 Borromeo set before Ruffo the task of composing a mass that was 'as clear as possible,'[177] and the result appears to have been one or more of the masses in his *Missae Quatuor Concinate ad Ritum Concilii Mediolani* of 1570. Unlike Ruffo's masses of 1542 and 1557, which relied largely upon the imitation of models by Festa, Jachet of Mantua, and Richafort as the primary compositional device,[178] these masses feature no cantus firmus or polyphonic models. Instead, the movements are unified only by mode, an approach that is less successful in a polyphonic mass than it is in a Magnificat, where the residual plainchant melody serves to rescue even the most elaborate polyphonic setting from incomprehensibility. Almost all of the attention is given over to clarity of declamation, and, as a result, the texture is dominated throughout by a rather monotonous, simultaneous style that is subservient to the natural rhythmic inflection of the text. The pervasive chordal landscapes are relieved by brief passages of paired imitation and alternatim voicings, but the imitative counterpoint usually evaporates rather quickly and the alternatim combinations are somewhat limited by the four-voice texture. Although the modal constructs of each mass are frequently reinforced by clear cadences and subsemitonal inflections that also serve to articulate phrases of the text, mode alone does not succeed in providing the musical comprehensibility and sense of overall design afforded the currently popular imitation technique. Even the descending ostinato introduced in the Christe and Agnus Dei I of the *Missa Quarti toni* fails to save the work from a certain structural monotony.[179]

Ruffo's *Messe a cinque voci* of 1572, which survives only in the form of a second edition printed by Vincenzo Sabbia of Brescia in 1580, abandons the modal theme as an organizational principle, and, instead, offers several masses for general liturgical use. The collection includes a Missa 'Sine nomine', a ferial mass, a 'de Profundis' mass, and a mass for equal voices. As Lewis Lockwood has pointed out, the *Missa de De Profundis* does not appear to be based on a plainchant or polyphonic model, but rather takes its name from the use of low clefs.[180] It is further noteworthy, however, that *De profundus clamavi*, the Cantus sung at Mass on Wednesdays during Lent, was an important liturgical item in the Ambrosian liturgy. Thus, it may be that Ruffo's *Missa de De profundis* was to be performed throughout the Lenten season, or, at the very least, was intended to accompany those masses in which this elaborate plainchant was sung. Such usage appears in keeping with the liturgical ubiquity of the masses found in the volume.

According to the dedication, the *Messe a cinque voci* were commissioned by Borromeo and intended for use both inside and outside the Diocese. Intelligibility, by the composer's own admission, drives the approach to composition, just as it did in the *Missae Quatuor Concinate ad Ritum Concilii Mediolani*.[181] If the *Missa de De Profundis* is at all representative,[182] then it can be said that the *Messe a cinque voci* are characterized by greater rhythmic flexibility and fuller textures. While the Gloria and Credo of the *Missa de De Profundis* feature the simultaneous style almost exclusively, pseudo-imitation is frequently employed in the Kyrie, Sanctus, and Agnus Dei sections. This imitation often follows initially at the interval of a semibreve or breve, with at least two or three voices participating while the others offer complementary counterpoint. Reduced textures and alternatim procedures are explored infrequently, and are reserved primarily for the punctuation of declamatory passages in chordal style.

Although the aforementioned choral ordinances of 1572 specify that the maestro di cappella was to compose a mass, a Magnificat, and the necessary hymns each month, no Magnificats or Vespers hymns that can be tied directly to Ruffo's tenure in Milan have survived. Nonetheless, Ruffo's *Li soavissimi responsorii della Settimana Santa*, which were published by Francesco and Simone Tini in 1586, likely date from his service at the Duomo. In addition to a Mass and Vespers for the lighting of the Easter Candle on Holy Saturday, the Holy Week services at the Duomo included the consecration of the oil and washing of the feet on Maundy Thursday and special oblations to the cross on Good Friday. These observances were held in the Duomo, but the polyphony performed during them certainly was equally serviceable elsewhere. The dedication of *Li soavissimi responsorii*, which was penned by Agostino Resta on 30 October 1585, indicates that the responsories contained were used in the Holy Week services at San Marco in Milan. Nonetheless, they may have been borrowed directly from the Duomo repertoire. According to Resta, the dedicatee Sforza Speciano 'comes every year because of his devotion and at the appointed hour brought the respected music of the Duomo, in order that such sweet harmony from that choir be heard by ours.'[183] No complete set of partbooks for *Li soavissimi responsorii* survives, but text intelligibility likely drove the approach to composition. The dedications of *Il quarto libro di messe a sei voci* (1574) and the *Salmi suavissimi et devotissimi a cinque voci* (1574), both published during Ruffo's first year at Pistoia, betray the continued influence of Borromeo's ideals of intelligibility even after Ruffo left Milan.[184]

Intelligibility would never again dominate musical discourse at the Duomo as it had during Ruffo's tenure. Ruffo's successor Pietro Pontio preferred the imitation mass, a genre which forced the composer to adopt, at least to a limited extent, the style of the pre-existing polyphonic model. After Carlo Borromeo passed on in 1584, moreover, archiepiscopal concerns with devotional music quickly shifted from the intelligible to the inspirational. Passionate artwork that, by its ecstatic nature, enhanced spiritual meditation was valued over simple textures that maintained clarity of expression. Yet Ruffo's masses, more than the music of any other Milanese composer, have come to be identified with post-Tridentine Milan. They represent, more than any other single body of sacred vocal literature, the deleterious effects 'in medio civitatis' of unbridled post-Tridentine fervor.

Notes

1   Maria Luisa Gatti Perer, ' "In medio civitatis" Il centro di Milano tra Cinque e Seicento e il ruolo di Alessandro Bisnati nella sua definizione civile e religiosa,' *Arte Lombarda* 72/1 (1985), 18. Also see Cesare Cesariano, *Di Lucio Vitruvio Pollione de architectura libri dece* (Como: Gotardus da Ponte, 1521), Book V, Chapter LXXIV, page 5.

2   Prior to the erection of the new Santa Maria Maggiore, the fourth-century church of Santa Tecla had served as the cathedral from Easter to October. A parish church with strong attachments to the civic center, Santa Tecla was razed three times and rebuilt twice between 1462 and its final demolition in 1548. For further discussion of the controversy surrounding Santa Tecla, see Evelyn S. Welch, *Art and Authority*, 40-43.

3   Gatti Perer, ' "In medio civitatis," ' 22-23. While the shops of the fourteenth century included many featuring such standard wares as fruit and cloth, those of the fifteenth century were characterized by a heavy population of artisans. For summaries of the history, structure, and function of the *Fabbrica* or governing body that supervises all building operations see Ernesto Brivio, 'Fabbrica del Duomo,' in *Il Duomo di Milano: Dizionario storico artistico e religioso*, ed. Giulia Benati and Anna Maria Roda (Milano: Nuove Edizioni Duomo, 2001), 244-247, and Welch, *Art and Authority*, 71-76.

4   Gatti Perer, ' "In medio civitatis," ' 19.

5   Carlo Ferrari da Passano, *Il Duomo di Milano: Storia della Veneranda Fabbrica* (Milano: Nuove Edizioni Duomo, 1998), 47.

6   Ferrari da Passano, *Il Duomo di Milano*, 47-48. The Verzaro is off the right transept of the Cathedral, and the Porta del Compito now faces the Galleria Vittorio Emmanuele. Many of the shops renting in the Verzaro at the time of its concession in 1549 were relocated to the Piazza Santo Stefano. Gatti Perer, ' "In medio civitatis," ' 23.

7   For the description and location of these altars see Giovanni Battista Sannazzaro, 'Altari,' in *Il Duomo di Milano: Dizionario*, ed, Giulia Benati and Anna Maria Roda (Milano, 2001), 14-25, but especially 19-22.

8   Claudio Sartori, 'La cappella del Duomo dalle origini a Franchino Gaffurio,' *Storia de Milano* (Milano: Giovanni Treccani degli Alfieri, 1957a), IX, 725-734. Also see Claudio Sartori, 'Matteo da Perugia e Bertrand Ferragut, i due primi maestri di cappella del Duomo di Milano,' *Acta Musicologica* XXVIII/1 (1956), 12-27.

9 Sartori, 'La cappella del Duomo,' 746-747.

10 *Ordinazioni* VII (1519-1531), 95r, Archivio della Veneranda Fabbrica del Duomo di Milano (hereafter AVFDM). On Werrecore's Flemish origin see Marco Brusa, 'Hermann Matthias Werrecoren,' 173-179. Much of the other biographical material on Werrecore reported here derives from Getz, "The Milanese Cathedral Choir."

11 *Sforzesco: Registri ducali* 73 (Benefizi 1523-1525), 69r-70r, ASM. This document, which I have transcribed in part in Getz, 'The Milanese Cathedral Choir,' 173, appears in full as Appendix I, Document 5.

12 *Cancelleria dello Stato* 67 (1547 febbraio), f. 59, ASM. The Ottaviano mentioned is likely Ottaviano Bosisio, a contrabasso who served at the Duomo of Milan between 1534 and 1549.

13 This work was discussed at length in Chapter 2. Also see Brusa, 'Hermann Matthias Werrecoren,' 186-192. For the historical details surrounding the Battle of Bicocca itself, see Gino Franceschini, 'Le dominazioni francesi,' 233-240.

14 *Ordinazioni* VII (1519-1531), 95r, AVFDM. A full Latin transcription of this document is provided in Federico Mompellio, 'La capella del Duomo da Matthias Hermann di Vercore a Vincenzo Ruffo,' *Storia di Milano* (Milano: Giovanni Treccani degli Alfieri, 1957a), IX, 749-750

15 Sartori, 'La cappella del Duomo,' 748, claims that the practice of hiring a separate instructor of Latin grammar was begun under Gaffurius. According to the *Vacchette* 391 (1522), 99r, and *Vacchette* 393 (1524), 12r and 58r, AVFDM, Matheo Phamensi (=de Fano) served as 'instructor of grammar to the boys of the cappella musicale' at the outset of Werrecore's tenure. He was succeeded by one Hieronymo de Phano, who obviously was a relative of some sort. The latter instructor appears in the books as late as 1543. See Getz, 'The Milanese Cathedral Choir,' 173.

16 *Ordinazioni* IX (1535-1544), 302r-v, AVFDM.

17 *Ordinazioni* VII (1519-1531), 270v, AVFDM. Werrecore paid L8 Imperial per 'measure' for the property.

18 Ibid., 268v and 270v, AVFDM. The transaction was initiated on 8 March 1530, and is mentioned again in *Ordinazioni* VII (1519-1531), 293r, AVFDM, which is dated 25 May 1531.

19 Records of some of the earliest of these, all of which I have reported in Getz, 'The Milanese Cathedral Choir,' 174-175, include *Ordinazioni* VIII (1532-1534), 68r-v, AVFDM, *Notarile* 5370 (Jo: Agostino Confalconieri), 11 maij 1534, ASM, and *Notarile* 10376 (Battista Abbiate), 20 septembris 1537, ASM, and *Notarile* 10474 (Gio: Francesco Confalconieri), 13 junijs 1538, ASM.

20 'Deinde audito domino Magistro harmano verecorem dicto magnifico Mathia flemengo magistro capella cantorum prefate maioris ecclesie Mediolano requirente a prefatis Reverendis et magnificis dominis prefectis prefate fabrice ut vellint exdem dare aliqua loca in Campo Sancto prefate fabrice aut extra dictum Campum Sanctum pro habitatione ipsius magnifici armani absque oblatione alicuius ficti aut augere ipsi magistro harmano omni anno aliquod sallarium durante dicto eius officio loco pensionis domus . . .' *Ordinazioni* IX (1535-1544), 302r-v, AVFDM.

21 *Ordinazioni* IX (1535-1544), 302r-v, AVFDM.

22 In December 1549 Werrecore was still receiving the L12 monthly salary specified in the 1534 chapel reorganization documents. *Registri* 738 (1544-1550), 191r, AVFDM.

23 The earliest reference to the L16 reimbursement is found in *Vacchette* 404 (1542-1543), 150v, AVFDM. Although no explanation for the reimbursement is provided there, its purpose is clarified by further entries found in *Ordinazioni* X (1545-1552), 81v,

AVFDM, and *Registri* 738 (1544-1550), 77v, AVFDM. Also see Mompellio, 'La cappella del Duomo da Matthias Hermann di Vercore,' 756, on this remuneration.

24 *Vacchette* 741 (1550), 47v, AVFDM.

25 The final salary payment to Werrecore, which was comprised of L70 s6 d9, was made on 18 June 1550. It is specified as 'for five months finishing in the present month of June.' *Vacchette* 471 (1550), 47v, AVFDM. Phalanis's first salary payment, which was made on 14 June 1550, consisted of L12 for the month of June. *Vacchette* 408 (1550-1551), 51v, AVFDM. Also see Mompellio, 'La cappella del Duomo da Matthias Hermann di Vercore,' 762.

26 'Item ordinaverunt et nota*verunt* q*ue* amodo in antea de*b*ent bochalia tria vini ex vino dicte Fabrice singula die D*o*mi*n*o Mathie de Flandria alias ma*gistro* capelle musicor*um* pre*f*ate maioris ecclesie . . .' *Ordinazioni* XIII (1570-1576), 268r, AVFDM.

27 On 30 December 1559 one Domino presbyter Hieronymo de Verukoren received L21 for serving three months as a singer in the cappella musicale. The register entries for this date cover the second half of the year 1559. Given the close relationship between this entry and the letter dated 28 August 1559 discussed below, it is likely that the singer listed is Matthias Werrecore, rather than one of his relatives. *Vacchette* 412 (1558-1559), 123r, AVFDM.

28 'Audito Ma*gistro* Mathia alias ma*gistro* capella cantor*um* pre*f*ata maijoris ecclesiae dicente sit inservisse dicte capelle p*er* annos triginta et ultra et iuventute*m* suam in ea servitute con sumpsissa et ordinem et consuetudine*m* in pre*f*ata v*e*nera*n*da fabrica esse, q*uod* cantores dicte capella inhabiles ad canendu*m* redacti ob infirmitate*m* vel senectutem, quod eius detur medietas sallarij sui, et propterea cum ipse ob eius senectute*m* redactus sit inhabilis ad canendu*m* pentente q*uod* pre*f*ati d*o*mi*n*i p*r*efecti dignent ordinatione que deretero ei ma*gistro* Mathie det*ur* medietas salarij ei soliti dari p*er* agent*es* nom*i*ne pre*f*ate fabrice.' *Ordinazioni* XI (1553-1561), 291r-v, AVFDM.

29 See Mompellio, 'La cappella del Duomo da Matthias Hermann di Vecore,' 756-757, Getz, 'The Milanese Cathedral Choir,' 199-204, and Ganda, 'Giovanni Antonio Castiglione,' 302-306 and 319-320.

30 Davide Daolmi, *Don Nicola Vicentino: Arcimusico a Milano* (Lucca: Liberia Musicale Italiana, 1999), 4-47.

31 *Ordinazioni* XIII (1570-1576), 268r, AVFDM. The system used by the Milanese chapter to record salary payments ensured that all outgoing payments were listed at least twice – once in the *Registri* and once in the *Vacchette*. A substantial number of the cathedral's sixteenth-century *Registri* and *Vacchette* survive, but some of these record only large lump sums awarded the cappella musicale as a whole. This is particularly true of the registers surviving from the years 1565 to 1584. In any case, if Werrecore continued to receive half of his salary during old age, as was customary, then further references to him probably will be found. I currently have compiled annual lists of all of the singers appearing in the pay registers between 1522 and 1563 (Appendix 2).

32 The final salary payment made to Phalanis, which comprised L60, is dated 13 July 1551 and is specified as for five months. *Vacchette* 408 (1550-1551), 145r, AVFDM.

33 'ex vulnere decessit' *Popolazione* p.a. 94 (Registri mortuari 1549-1559), Registro 1551, 3 June 1551, ASM.

34 Boyleau first appears in the Duomo pay records on 31 December 1551, at which time he received his remuneration for the first six months of service. On the same day he was awarded 8 lire for six months of rent on a dwelling, presumably that used to teach the boys of the choir, for which Werrecore had been provided 16 lire per annum. *Vacchette* 408 (1550-1551), 189r and 195v, AVFDM. Early in 1558 Boyleau was succeeded by

Bartolomeo Torresani, better known as Hoste da Reggio. *Vacchette* 412 (1558-1559), 61r-v, AVFDM.

35 Simon Boyleau, *Cantus Simonis Boyleau genere galli, iuvenis in arte musica eximii motetta quatuor vocum* (Venetiis: Hieronynum Scotum, 1544).

36 Simon Boyleau, *Madrigali a quattro voci,* 1546= RISM B4187. Although the printers of the collection are not identified on the title page, Mompellio 'La cappella del Duomo da Matthias Hermann di Vercore,' 762, suggested that the typographical mark is that of Francesco and Simone Moscheni. Mariangela Donà, *La stampa musicale a Milano fino all'anno 1700* (Firenze: Leo S. Olschki, 1961), 27, agreed. However, Jane A. Bernstein, 'The Burning Salamander: Assigning a Printer to Some Sixteenth-Century Music Prints,' *Music Library Association Note*s XLII/3 (1986), 500, assigned the print to Fabriano and Bindoni of Padua, and Lucia Marchi, *Simon Boyleau: studio biografico ed edizione critica dei Madrigali a quattro voci* (1546), discussed at the Università degli Studi di Pavia, Scuola di Paleografia e Filologia Musicale, 1995-1996, 16-21, presents additional evidence that confirms Bernstein's findings. Marchi's thesis contains the most comprehensive biography of Boyleau compiled to date. I very am grateful to the author for sharing a copy of her text with me while my manuscript was in the final stages of preparation.

37 According to Marchi, *Simon Boyleau,* 14-15, Boyleau probably spent the years 1544-1546 in Venice.

38 The madrigal is found in Simon Boyleau, *Il secondo libro de i Madrigali et Canzoni a quattro voci* (Milano: Francesco e Simone Moscheni, 1558). Only the tenor partbook of this collection has survived, but the collection has been catalogued in Emil Vogel, Alfred Einstein, Francois Lesure and Claudio Sartori, *Bibliografia della Musica Italiana Profana pubblicata dal 1500 al 1700* (Pomezia: Staderini 1977), I, 265. The text of the madrigal and a description of its performance within the context of the pompa are found in Antonfrancesco Raineri, *Pompe di Messer Atonfrancesco Raineri* (Milano: Giovanni Antonio Borgia, 1553), n.p. See Chapter 6 below.

39 Simon Boyleau, *Madrigali a IIII, V, VI, VII, et VIII voci* (Milano: Francesco e Simone Moscheni, 1564), Dedication.

40 Marchi, *Simon Boyleau,* 15-16. Also see Lawrence Bernstein, 'The Bibliography of Music in Conrad Gesner's Pandectae (1548),' *Acta Musicologica* XLV (1973), 145.

41 *Vacchette* 409 (1552-1553), 110r, AVFDM.

42 The vestment was made for him at the expense of the chapter, and was kept in the sacristy when not in use. *Ordinazioni* X (1545-1552), 349r, AVFDM.

43 *Vacchette* 409 (1552-1553), 190r; *Vacchette* 410 (1554-1555) , 73r and 149v; and *Vacchette* 411 (1556-1557), 82r, AVFDM.

44 *Vacchette* 409 (1552-1553), 106r, AVFDM.

45 These will be discussed below.

46 'Cum ad aures prefatorum Dominorum prefectorum devenerit, quod Reverendi Domini Ordinarij prefate Venerande Fabrice ecclesiae maijoris Mediolani vociferando vadunt velle amovere Magistrum Sijmonem de Beuliex magistrum Cappelle cantorum predicte ecclesiae absque consensu Dominorum prefectorum Ipsius Fabrice et ne Iura prefate aliquam Iacturam casu patiantur Innocua conserventur et Illexa permaneant. Prefati Magnifici Domini prefecti et huiusmodi Inter eos tentinata Collectisque Inter eos votis, ordinaverunt et ordinant quod si dictus magister Sijmon per prefatos Reverendos Dominos ordinarios ab officio dicte capelle amovebitur sine consensu prefatorum Dominorum prefectorum presentium et pro tempore, que alius magister dicte Capelle qui eligerit sine consensu venerandi Capituli prefate Fabrice, et non servatis servandis,

nunq*uam* admitta*tur* nec admissus Intelliga*tur* pro ma*gistro* dicte Capelle p*er* R*everendos* et Magn*ificos* D*omi*nos p*re*fectos Ipsius Fabrice p*resentes* et p*ro* Tempore nec tali electo ut su*pra*dictum est, nunq*uam* solva*tur* p*er* agentes no*mine* p*refa*te Fabrice aliquod sallarium nec merces, nec esse admissus Intelliga*tur* ad habendu*m* et recipiendu*m* aliquod sallariu*m* nec mercedem, a p*refa*ta Fabrice nec agentibus pro ea.' *Ordinazioni* XI (1553-1561), 222r, AVFDM.

47   The aforementioned notice further indicates that a committee of prefects was formed to secure a replacement. *Ordinazioni* XI (1553-1561), 222r, AVFDM.

48   Boyleau, *Il secondo libro de i Madrigali et Canzoni a quattro voci.*

49   F. 103 inf. (Lettere a S. Carlo Borromeo), 359v, Biblioteca Ambrosiana, Milano (hereafter BAM). See Chapter 6 below.

50   The dates of Boyleau's service at Santa Maria presso San Celso were determined through careful examination of surviving account books and archival sources from Santa Maria presso San Celso housed in the ASDM. For details see Christine Getz, 'Simon Boyleau and the Church of the 'Madonna of Miracles': Educating and Cultivating the Aristocratic Audience in Post-Tridentine Milan,' *Journal of the Royal Music Association* 126/2 (2001), 149-150.

51   *Ordinazioni* XIII (1570-1576), 200r, 204v, 230r, and 255v-256r, and Vacchette 753 (1577-1578), 18r, AVFDM. On 23 August 1574 Boyleau was replaced by Floramonte de Marchesio, the former maestro di cappella at San Lorenzo. Also see Federico Mompellio, 'La cappella del Duomo dal 1573 al 1714,' *Storia di Milano* (Milano: Giovanni Treccani degli Alfieri, 1957b), XVI, 507-509, and Marchi, *Simon Boyleau*, 47-52. Mompellio has unearthed several documents that suggest Boyleau's presence at the Duomo as early as 1572, at which time he was listed as the assistant to Vincenzo Ruffo.

52   Giovanni D'Alessi, 'Una stampa musicale del 1566 dedicata a S. Carlo Borromeo,' *Note d'archivio* IX (1932), 256.

53   On Boyleau's career in Torino see Lucia Marchi, 'La cappella musicale del Duomo di Torino nel tardo Cinquecento e la reggenza di Simon Boyleau' in *Barocco padano 2: Atti del X Convegno internazionale sulla musica sacra nei secoli XVII-XVIII* (Como: A.M.I.S., 2002), 387-407.

54   S. Cordero di Pamparato, 'Emanuele Filiberto di Savoia protettore dei musici,' *Rivista musicale italiana* 35 (1928), 29-30.

55   The suspicions of Oscar Mischiati, 'Recensione di *Sei secoli di musica nel Duomo di Milano* a cura di Graziella De Florentiis [e] Gian Nicola Vessia,' *L'organo* XXVII, 1991-1992, 180, and Barbara Torre, 'Alcune note su uno sconosciuto ritratto di musicista del XVI secolo,' *Rivista italiana di musicologia* XIX/1 (1994), 17, are borne out in a Milanese document that identifies Bartolomeo Torresani as 'qui app*ellatur* hospes q*ui*a filius hospitis fuit, et es regiensis' (who is called Hoste because he is the son of a foreigner/innkeeper, and is from Reggio). *San Calimero* I-93 (Visite pastorali e documenti aggiunti 1567-1604), fasc. 1, ASDM. Moreover, several entries in the Duomo registers, including *Vacchette* 412 (1558-1559), 4v, AVFDM and Vacchette 413 (1560-1564), 54v and 149r, AVFDM, also identify Torresani as Hoste.

56   These include *Il primo libro de madrigali a tre voci* (Milano: Francesco et Simone Moscheni, 1554*); Il secondo libro delli madrigali a quattro voci* (Venezia: Hieronymo Scotto, 1554); *Il terzo libro delli madrigali a quattro voci* (Venezia: Hieronymo Scotto, 1554*); Il primo libro delli madrigali a cinque voci* (Venezia: Hieronymo Scotto, 1554). For information regarding music at the court of Ferrante Gonzaga, see Guglielmo Barblan, 'La vita musicale in Milan nella prima metà del cinquecento,' *Storia di Milano,* IX, 857-876, and Chapters 5 and 6 below.

57   *Notarile* 13010 (Camillo Rho q. Giovanni Antonio 20/11/1553-09/10/1556), 4 septembris
     1555, ASM, and *Santo Calimero* I-93 (Visite pastorali e documenti aggiunti 1567-1604),
     fasc. 1, ASDM.

58   *Metropolitana* XXXIII-406 (Visite pastorali e documenti aggiunti), fasc. 9, ASDM, and
     Ordinazioni XI (1552-1561), 229r-230v, AVFDM. A full Latin transcription of the latter
     appears in Mompellio, 'La cappella del Duomo da Matthias Hermann di Vercore,' 769.

59   Calusco, ed., *Mutetarum.* The collection contains twenty-three motets by Phinot (9),
     Werrecore (3), Lupi (2), Morales, Maistre Jahn, Courtois, Richafort, Brumel, Claudin,
     Tugdual, Penet, and Willaert. See Chapter 2.

60   Matthias Verecorensis, *Cantuum quinque vocum quos motetta vocant . . . liber primus*
     (Mediolani: Francesco et Simone Moscheni, 1555).

61   On 15 February 1558, for example, Hoste was reimbursed L13 s10 d9 for songbooks.
     Vacchette 412 (1558-1559), 4r, AVFDM.

62   *Ordinazioni* XI (1553-1561), 246v-247r, AVFDM. Also see Mompellio, 'La cappella
     del Duomo da Matthias Hermann di Vercore,' 769.

63   *Vacchette* 412 (1558-1559), 61r-v and 94r.

64   *Ordinazioni* XII (1562-1569), 68r-v, AVFDM. Also see Mompellio, 'La cappella del
     Duomo da Matthias Hermann di Vercore,' 769.

65   See Mischiati, 'Recensione,' 150, Torre, 'Alcune note su uno sconosciuto ritratto,' 15-16,
     and Christine Getz, 'New Light on the Milanese Career of Hoste da Reggio,' *Studi
     musicali* XXVII/2 (1998), 299-303.

66   *Popolazione* 96 (Morti-Communi Milano-Registri Mortuari 1564-1569), 5 octobre 1569,
     ASM.

67   See Chapter 2 above.

68   See Flavio Emilio Scogna, 'La musica nel Duomo di Savona,' 261-262, and Flavio
     Emilio Scogna, *Vita musicale a Savona*, 27-28.

69   Maurizio Tarrini, 'Contribuito alla biografia di Vincenzo Ruffo,' 109-111, has
     documented the composer's presence at the Doria court on 14 November 1545 and 12
     January 1546, at which time he received remunerations of 10 scudi for his salary as the
     maestro di cappella.

70   Mons. Giuseppe Turrini, 'Il maestro fiammingo Giovanni Nasco a Verona (1547-1551),'
     Note d'Archivio XIV/4-6 (Luglio-Dicembre 1937), 186-187. Also see Lockwood, *The
     Counter-Reformation and the Masses*, 32.

71   Lockwood, 'The Counter-Reformation and the Sacred Music,' 34-35.

72   Luigi Torri, 'Vincenzo Ruffo, madrigalista e compositore di musica sacra del sec. XVI,'
     Rivista musicale iItaliana III (1896), 642-643, and Lockwood, *The Counter-Reformation
     and the Masses*, 34-37.

73   Lockwood, *The Counter-Reformation and the Masses*, 38-44.

74   Tarrini, 'Contribuito alla biografia di Vincenzo Ruffo,' 114.

75   Lockwood, *The Counter-Reformation and the Masses.* See especially pages 74-135.

76   The full preface is transcribed and translated in Vincenzo Ruffo, *Salmi suavissimi et
     devotissimi a cinque voci*, ed. Mauro Casadei Turroni Monti and Carlo Berlese (Lucca:
     Libreria Musicale Italiana, 1999), XIV and XXXIV.

77   On Ruffo's tenure at Pistoia see Alberto Chiappelli, 'Il maestro Vincenzo Ruffo a
     Pistoia,' *Bulletino Storico Pistoiese* I (1899), 3-10, and Lockwood, *The Counter-
     Reformation and the Masses*, 63-67.

78   See Giuseppe Vale, 'Gli ultimi anni di Vincenzo Ruffo,' *Note d'Archivio* I/1 (Marzo
     1924), 78-81 and especially 80.

79   Russell Eugene Murray, Jr., 'The Voice of the Composer: Theory and Practice in the

Works of Pietro Pontio' (Ph.D. dissertation, University of North Texas, 1989), I, 25-36.

80   Murray, 'The Voice of the Composer', I, 48.

81   Murray, 'The Voice of the Composer', I, 55-57. The processo was held from 24 to 26 July 1569.

82   Murray, 'The Voice of the Composer', I, 54-68.

83   Murray, 'The Voice of the Composer', I, 68-79.

84   Murray, 'The Voice of the Composer', I, 79-94.

85   Murray, 'The Voice of the Composer', I, 96-98.

86   Murray, 'The Voice of the Composer', I, 99-100.

87   Murray, 'The Voice of the Composer', I, 101, calculates Pontio's salary of 125 scudi at five lire and eighteen soldi. According to *Vacchette* 753 (1577-1578), 18r, ASDM, Boyleau's closing salary was 100 lire per quarter.

88   Murray, 'The Voice of the Composer', I, 107-127, and Lockwood, *The Counter-Reformation and the Masses*, 111-113.

89   Murray, 'The Voice of the Composer', I, 124-150.

90   Sartori, 'La musica nel Duomo,' 746-747.

91   *Vacchette* 391 (1522), 71r, AVFDM.

92   'In Domo non li erano Ordenari, né offizii al solito, ma doi o tre preti, li quali cantavano alla meglio che potevano.' Burigozzi, *Cronaca Milanese*, 446.

93   See Table 3.1.

94   ' . . .notandi biscantores *prefate* maioris ecclesie diffitientes in celebratione divinitorum offitiorum.' These individuals include Ambrosio de Fenegroe, who is listed in *Vacchette* 391 (1522), 37r, AVFDM, and Danieli de Pegiis, who is mentioned in *Registri* 717 (1525-1527), 80r-v and 108v; *Vacchette* 397 (1528-1529), 186r, and *Registri* 723 (1532-1533), 36v and 50v, AVFDM. A similar notice from 1513 records payments of 4 lire per year to Johannes Castilliono, chaplain and custodian, for 'listing the singers deficient in the number of hours owed and expected in the celebration of the divine offices.' Here the wording suggests that each singer was expected to perform a given percentage of the total services. *Ordinazioni* VI (1511-1518), 115v, AVFDM.

95   *Ordinazioni* VIII (1532-1534), 98v, AVFDM.

96   *Metropolitana* XXXI-404 (Visite pastorali e documenti aggiunti), Q. 5, doc. 3, ASDM, notes that the ordinaries were expected to sing Terce, High Mass and Vespers, and lists the daily distributions awarded them for performing these duties on specified feasts. Although this document is undated, a comparison with the extant chapter statutes of 1572 and a table of pontifical feasts from the same decade found in *Metropolitana* XXXI-404 (Visite pastorali e documenti aggiunti), Q. 5, ASDM, reveals that it dates from the middle of the century. The distributions allotted are lower than those provided in 1572 and the liturgical demands conform closely to those outlined in the ceremoniali of 1543 and 1562. In addition, certain duties introduced by Carlo Borromeo in connection with the provincial councils and diocesan synods are not mentioned.

97   In 1560 and 1561 one Rocho de Ruschis was receiving an annual salary of 24 lire for taking attendance at the offices. Vacchette 413 (1560-1564), 36v, 58v 118r, AVFDM.

98   *San Fedele* XXII-155 (Santa Maria della Scala: Visite pastorali e documenti aggiunti), q. 13 (Q), ASDM.

99   *Visite pastorali* 8 (Visita pastorale 1578), Archivio Curia Vescovile di Vigevano.

100 *San Fedele* XXII-155 (Santa Maria della Scala: Visite pastorali e documenti aggiunti) q. 13 (Q), ASDM.

101 *Metropolitana* XXXI-404 (Visite pastorali e documenti aggiunti), q. 5, doc. 3, ASDM. Undated statutes for the dignitaries serving in the choir in a sixteenth-century hand. A

comparison of these with the extant chapter statutes of 1572 and a table of pontifical feasts from the same decade found in *Metropolitana* XXXI-404 (Visite pastorali e documenti aggiunti), q. 5, ASDM, confirms that they date from earlier in the century. The distributions allotted are lower and the liturgical demands conform more closely to those outlined in the ceremoniali of 1543 and 1562. Moreover, certain duties introduced by Carlo Borromeo in connection with the provincial councils and diocesan synods are not mentioned.

102 *Ordinazioni* VII (1519-1531), 193r, AVFDM. Mompellio, 'La cappella del Duomo da Matthias Hermann di Vercore,' 753, suggests that this matter may have concerned the choir.

103 *Ordinazioni* VII (1532-1534), 3r-v, AVFDM. For a transcription and translation of this document, see Getz, 'The Milanese Cathedral Choir,' 180.

104 *Ordinazioni* VII (1532-1534), 50r, AVFDM.

105 Ibid., 96r, AVFDM.

106 'Qui infra*scriptis* cantores teneantur cantare singulis horis quibus cantant *domin*i ordinarii preter quando sunt misse pro mortuis. Item q*uod* ipsi cantores teneant*ur* interesse in divinis cum vestibus longis usq*ue* ad tallaria et biretis sacerdotabilus cum cottis albis de super inducti et si contrafecerint pro qualibet vice amittant residentiam illius ebdemode. Item q*uod* deponant rixas quas inter se habent. Item q*uod* non dicant in ipsa eccl*esi*a verba vana nec blasfement et si contrafecerint amittant distributiones illius ebdemode qua tale quod commis*erint*. Item q*uod* non possint deservire per substitutum. Item q*uod* domin*us* Mathias in fabrica teneatur docere pueros et si contrafecerit quod amitat distributiones illius mensis.' *Ordinazioni* VIII (1532-1534), 98v, AVFDM. Also see Getz, 'The Milanese Cathedral Choir,' 181. Other transcriptions of this well-known Latin document appear (without translation) in *Annali della Veneranda fabbrica del Duomo di Milano*, ed. Cantù (Milano: G. Brigola, 1880), III, 256, and Mompellio, 'La cappella del Duomo da Matthias Hermann di Vercore,' 755-756.

107 *Ordinazioni* VIII (1532-1534), 99r-v, AVFDM.

108 'Item q*uod* predicti Cantores non possint se absentare'a, Civitate M*edio*lani sine speciali licentia Inscriptis R*everen*di D*omin*i Deputati provincie p*refa*te ecclesiae pro t*em*pore.' *Ordinazioni* XI (1553-1561), 174r, AVFDM.

109 See Chapter 5 below.

110 Trivutio first appears on the rolls from 1540 to 1544. During the first two years of his tenure, he received a salary of only 12 lire per quarter, a sum 6 lire per quarter less than that assigned his colleagues. *Vacchette* 403 (1540-1551), 105v, AVFDM. On 30 January 1542 his salary was finally raised to 18 lire, the amount normally assigned the adult singers. *Ordinazioni* IX (1535-1544), 256r, AVFDM. These figures suggest that Trivultio either served half time or was engaged as a regular substitute for the years 1540 and 1541. By 1545, however, his name disappears from the rolls of the cappella entirely, but reappears briefly during the years 1546 and 1549. *Registri* 738 (1544-1550), 77v, AVFDM, and *Registri* 738 (1544-1550), 172v, AVFDM. From 1549 to 1558 Trivultio is listed regularly on the pay rosters. See Getz, 'The Milanese Cathedral Choir,' 184.

111 Lockwood's often-quoted translation of the 1572 ordinances can be found in Lockwood, *The Counter-Reformation and the Masses*, 58-60.

112 Ibid., 60.

113 Salary advances were frequent during the 1520s, so the scribe often recorded only the amount of money handed the singer on the day that pay was officially awarded. However, the scribe also occasionally recorded both the amount that had been advanced and the amount being paid, thus making it possible to compute the salaries successfully.

See Getz, 'The Milanese Cathedral Choir,' 179.

114 *Vacchette* 393 (1524), 55v, AVFDM.

115 *Ordinazioni* VIII (1532-1534), 97v-98v, AVFDM. A few individual exceptions are noted. Adult soprano Laurentio de Putheo received only forty soldi, contralto Bernadino Gallasino was awarded 3 lire 4 soldi, and two elderly singers were retained at half pay. According to the registers, 20 soldi were equivalent to a single lira at this time. Mompellio, 'La cappella del Duomo da Matthias Hermann di Vercore,' 755, lists the cappella members without their salaries.

116 Culto p.a. 1049 (Metropolitana: Musicisti), ASM. Trivultio's salary was computed from entries in the *Vacchette* 412 (1558-1559) and 413 (1560-1564), AVFDM.

117 Lockwood, *The Counter-Reformation and the Masses*, 57.

118 *Registri* 738 (15444-1550), 126v, AVFDM.

119 In late 1558 as the decoration of the instrument neared completion, the popular Father Egidio of Sant'Ambrogio was temporarily retained. He received a salary of 105 lire 2 soldi for ten months. *Vacchette* 412 (1558-1559), 98v, AVFDM.

120 *Registri* 753 (1577-1578), 18r and 42r, AVFDM.

121 *Vacchette* 413 (1560-1561), 138v, AVFDM.

122 *Registri* 750 (1571-1572), 49r, AVFDM.

123 For discussion of the benefice as a recruiting tool under the Sforza, see Paul A. Merkley and Merkley, *Music and Patronage*, 370-405, and Lewis Lockwood, *Music in Renaissance Ferrara*, 174-177.

124 *Sforzesco: Registri Ducali* 73 (Benefizi 1523-1525), 11r-v and 19v, ASM.

125 Ibid., 84 (Benefizi 1525-1535), 152r-v, ASM.

126 Ibid., 73 (Benefizi 1523-1525), 253r-v, ASM.

127 *Ordinazioni* VII (1519-1531), 188v-189r, AVFDM.

128 Daolmi, *Don Nicola Vicentino*, 4-47.

129 Ibid., 58-91. The surviving accounts indicate that Vicentino's responsibilities at San Tommaso were non-musical in nature.

130 There were obviously some exceptions. Control of the benefices at Santa Maria della Scala and Sant'Ambrogio in Vigevano, for instance, passed to the Hapsburg princes.

131 *Vacchette* 401 (1536-1537), 31v, AVFDM.

132 *Vacchette* 391 (1522), 24v, AVFDM.

133 *Vacchette* 397 (1528-1529), 182v, AVFDM.

134 *Vacchette* 401 (1536-1537), 28r, AVFDM.

135 *Vacchette* 401 (1536-1537), 32v, AVFDM

136 *Vacchette* 414 (1562-63), 43r, AVFDM.

137 According to Sannazaro, 'Altari,' *Il Duomo di Milano: Dizionario*, 19, the altar of St Ambrose was located in an aisle chapel on the left side of the nave. It was founded by Archbishop Giovanni Visconti around 1426.

138 *Vacchette* 401 (1536-1537), 28r, 31v, and 32v, AVFDM. Also *Vachette* 402-404 (1538-1543) and *Registri* 738 (1544-1550), AVFDM, which contain further entries for these chaplaincies.

139 The only benefice entry that I have discovered thus far for Canibus is dated 31 December 1529. Here Canibus was paid L30 s16 d8 for the past eighteen months of service as a chaplain in Santa Maria Maggiore. It is possible that this amount did not comprise the entire stipend for that period. *Vacchette* 397 (1528-1529), 182v, AVFDM.

140 *Vacchette* 391 (1522), 94r, AVFDM.

141 *Registri* 717 (1525-1527), 106r, AVFDM.

142 See Getz, 'The Milanese Cathedral Choir,' 221-222.

143　The earliest reference I have found to this is dated 16 July 1558. *Vacchette* 412 (1558-1559, 28v, AVFDM.

144　*Registri* 738 (1544-1550), 99r and 100v, AVFDM.

145　Ibid., 172v, AVFDM.

146　Ibid., 191r, AVFDM.

147　*Vacchette* 409 (1552-1553), 51v, 94r, 145r, and 189r, AVFDM.

148　Ibid., 60r, 111r, 154v, and 193v; *Vacchette* 410 (1554-1555), 42r, 78v, 115r, and 154r; and *Vacchette* 411 (1556-1557), 43v, 81r, and 156r, AVFDM.

149　*Vacchette* 214 (1558-1559), 93v and 123v, AVFDM.

150　*Metropolitana* XXXIII-406 (Visite pastorali e documenti aggiunti), fasc. 10 and 11, ASDM.

151　Lockwood, *The Counter-Reformation and the Masses*, 60.

152　Murray, 'The Voice of the Composer,' 105-106.

153　'si faceva il solo del coro tra l'una e l'altra sbarra di bellissime prede machinate . . .' P. 250 sup. (Urbano Monti: Delle cose più notabile successe alla città di Milano, parte terza), 42r-v, Biblioteca Ambrosiana, Milano (hereafter BAM).

154　*Metropolitana* IX-382 (Visite pastorali e documenti aggiunti 1562), ASDM.

155　*Metropolitana* IV-377 (Visite pastorali e documenti aggiunti), q. 9, ASDM. This quire contains a printed copy of the statutes for the cathedral chapter dating from 1572 in which those annuals elevated to the status of a primary feast are listed. Although most of these annuals are carefully described in the earlier ceremoniali, their relative significance to the cathedral calendar is not indicated therein.

156　*Metropolitana* IX-382 (Visite pastorali e documenti aggiunti 1562), ASDM.

157　Ibid. and *Metropolitana* LXXXII-456 (Visite pastorali e documenti aggiunti), q. 22, ASDM. These include a 'Liber festivatum processionum et annualium defuntorum variorum' from 1562 and an 'Annuale 1543' respectively.

158　The pay registers indicate that this practice was initiated during the mid-1550s.

159　*Metropolitana* IV-377 (Visite pastorali e documenti aggiunti), q. 10, ASDM.

160　Ibid., q. 9, ASDM. Twelve denari were set aside for Matutino, a conflated Matins and Lauds observed in many Milanese churches of the sixteenth century, while two to four denari were allotted for the remaining offices. On certain primary feasts, the distributions were doubled or tripled for each office.

161　*Metropolitana* XXXIII-406 (Visite pastorali e documenti aggiunti), q. 9, ASDM, and Ordinazioni XI (1552-1561), 229r-230v, AVFDM. A full Latin transcription of the latter appears in Mompellio, 'La cappella del Duomo di Matthias Hermann di Vercore,' 769.

162　Angelo Ciceri and Eugenio Migliavacca, *Liber Cappelle Ecclesiae Maioris: Quarto Codice di Gaffurio* in *Archivium musices metropolitanum mediolanense* 16 (Milano: La musica Moderna S. p. A., 1968), V, suggest that *Librone* 4 was copied immediately after *Librone* 3 had been completed. On the dating problems associated with *Librone* 3, see Merkley and Merkley, *Music and Patronage*, 322-332, and William F. Prizer, 'Secular Music at Milan during the Early Cinquecento,' 9-16.

163　See Prizer, 'Music at the Court of the Sforza, 150.

164　*San Fedele* XIII-146 (Santa Maria della Scala: Visiti pastorali e documenti aggiunti), 16-18, ASDM.

165　*Metropolitana* XXXIII-406 (Visite pastorali e documenti aggiunti), q. 11, doc. 2, ASDM.

166　Ciceri and Migliavacca, eds., *Liber Cappelle Ecclesiae Maioris*, XI-XII.

167　Ibid., V-VI. Lynn Halpern Ward, 'The Motetti Missales Repertory Reconsidered,' *Journal of the American Musicological Society* XXXIX/3 (1986), 494, presents some compelling evidence for an earlier completion date. However, her analysis of Mil D 4 suggests that she has examined the facsimile edition rather than the original. Study of the original manuscript, which is not currently permitted because of the extensive damage already inflicted by the 1906 fire, would yield additional evidence regarding the order and method of compilation of the manuscript's individual parts. It is especially interesting that most of the identifiable works of Gaffurius appear in the first half of the surviving manuscript pages, while those of the composers associated with Galeazzo Maria and Ascanio Sforza are gathered toward the back.

168   Ward, 'The Motetti Missales Repertory Reconsidered,' 497-502.

169   For details, see Mompellio, 'La cappella del Duomo da Matthias Hermann di Vercore,' 756-757 and Getz, 'The Milanese Cathedral Choir,' 199-204.

170   The print was published by Scotto of Venice. Only the tenor, altus, and quintus partbooks are extant, and can be found in Bologna, Civico Museo Bibliografico Musicale and Modena, Biblioteca Estense. For an inventory of the contents see Murray, 'The Voice of the Composer', II, 6.

171   Bergamo, Biblioteca Civica, Ms. MA 310 (formerly Delta V 35), 43r. It is possible that the copyist accidentally omitted a portion of the text, and I have not identified any concordances.

172   The psalms, which comprised the continuation of a project begun by Marc Antonio Flaminio in 1546, were first published in Basil in 1558. On Spinola's psalm paraphrases see Pio Paschini, 'Un umanista disgraziato,' 98-101, and Alessandro Pastore, *Marcantonio Flaminio, Fortune e sfortune di un chierico nell'Italia del cinquecento* (Milano: Franco Angeli, 1981), 85-89 and 147-148.

173   See the discussion of Ruffo's 1542 motet collection in Chapter 2 above.

174   The characteristics of the motetti missales are outlined in Ward, 'The Motetti Missales Repertory Reconsidered,' and Thomas L. Noblitt, 'The Ambrosian Motetti Missales Repertory,' *Musica Disciplina* XXII (1968), 77-103.

175   See Richard Sherr, 'Competence and incompetence in the papal choir in the age of Palestrina,' *Early Music* XXII/4 (November 1994), 607-629, R. Casimiri, '"Disciplina Musicae" e "Maestri di Capella" dopo il Concilio di Trento nei Maggiori Istituti Ecclesiastici di Roma,' *Note d'Archivio* XII (1935), 1-26, and Lockwood, *The Counter-Reformation and the Masses*, 79-100.

176   The directive is published in Paolo Fabbri, 'La normativa istituzionale,' *La cappella musicale nell'Italian della Controriforma: Atti del Convegno Internazionale di Studi nel IV Centenario di Fondazione della Cappella Musicale di S. Biago di Cento*, ed. Oscar Mischiati and Paolo Russo (Firenze: Leo S. Olschki, 1993), 20. Also see Vincenzo Ruffo, *Seven Masses: Part I* in *Recent Researches in Renaissance Music* XXII, ed. Lewis Lockwood (Madison: A-R Editions, 1979), xi.

177   See Lockwood, *The Counter-Reformation and the Masses*, 93.

178   Ruffo's *Missa Alma redemptoris mater*, published by Scotto of Venice in 1542, appears to be derived from both the plainchant antiphon and Festa's motet a 4. Lockwood, *The Counter-Reformation and the Masses*, 140-142, also detects a possible relationship with Josquin's setting of the antiphon. For the sources of the 1557 imitation masses, see Lockwood, *The Counter-Reformation and the Masses*, 146-172.

179   The ostinato was first noted by Lockwood, *The Counter-Reformation and the Masses*, 189-191.

180   Ibid., 204-205.

181   A transcription of the dedication is found in Lockwood, *The Counter-Reformation and the Masses*, 239-240.

182   A modern edition is found in Ruffo, *Seven Masses: Part II* in *Recent Researches in*

Renaissance Music XXIII, ed. Lockwood, 44-71.

183   '. . .ogn'anno per sua divotione viene, & all'hora faceva venire l'honorata Musica del Duomo, per udire, e dal nostra è da quel coro cosi soave armonia;' The dedication is transcribed in Lockwood, *The Counter-Reformation and the Masses,* 248.

184   The dedication and discourse of *Il quarto libro di messe a sei voci* (1574) is transcribed in Lockwood, *The Counter-Reformation and the Masses*, 240-243. The dedication of the psalm collection is transcribed and discussed in the critical edition of *Vincenzo Ruffo, Salmi suavissimi et devotissimi a cinque voci*, XI-XVII.

Chapter 4

Music in the Civic Processions and Triumphal Progressions

Civic Processions

All roads leading into sixteenth-century Milan via the city gates converged at the Duomo. In the architectural spaces surrounding this Gothic edifice, the offices of church and state both coexisted and commingled, rendering it the epicenter of Milanese public life. Little activity that transpired at the Duomo escaped notice, as can be seen in the rich historical chronicle left to posterity by Gianmarco Burigozzi, a Milanese merchant active in the city between 1500 and 1544.[1] The Duomo was the final destination of every panoply of state that passed through the city's streets. Within its walls, state masses, funerals, and religious celebrations regularly dazzled the eyes and flooded the ears of the city's residents and visitors. In its piazza, mendicant friars who styled themselves after the Dominican monk Girolamo Savonarola preached reform and led the citizens in processions of penitence.[2] Initiated as a monument to the prestige of the ruling Visconti during the late fourteenth century,[3] the Duomo quickly emerged as the city's most widely recognized civic monument. Its ongoing construction demanded the participation of Milanese aristocrats and artisans alike. On its grounds, moreover, human dramas laced with political intrigue and spurred by spiritual reformation unfolded before massive audiences comprised of citizens from every walk of life.

General Processions

If Burgozzi's chronicle at all reflects civic life in sixteenth-century Milan, it can be inferred that every single Imperial victory, catastrophe, or initiative that occurred between 1523 and 1544 was marked by either a state mass or a civic procession, if not both, that culminated at the Duomo. The Venetian accord of 1523, for instance, was celebrated with a procession featuring the singing of laude, and the resulting Imperial victories were commemorated on 1 January 1524 at a state mass in the Duomo honoring the Venetian ambassador.[4] Such celebrations served to turn public attention to events that otherwise might have gone unnoticed in a world in which privacy was a luxury and the dissemination of information was otherwise dependent largely upon the printing press.

During the tenure of Francesco II Sforza, civic celebrations typically were mandated by the ducal authorities. With the election of Pope Paul III in 1534, for example, an order for three days of processions and a Mass of the Holy Spirit in the Duomo was issued by Francesco II and forwarded to all the other major cities in the Duchy, including Cremona, Pavia, Alessandria, Lodi, Tertona, Novara, Como, Vigevano, and Caravaggio.[5] Moreover, similar orders for other comparable occasions were issued by Francesco II, and these usually were similarly distributed throughout the Duchy as well.[6] The ducal penchant for combining general religious processions with a mass of the Holy Spirit in the Duomo appears to have remained standard throughout the sixteenth century. The official registers of ducal missives issued between 1526 and 1562 reveal that numerous processions and masses of the Holy Spirit in the Duomo were ordered by the governors of Milan. While some of these were intended to rouse the citizens in prayer against such threats as the plague,[7] others commemorated important civic or Imperial events, including the 1554 Imperial victory at Siena,[8] the 1557 Imperial victory over the French at Picardy,[9] and the 1560 ordination of Carlo Borromeo as Archbishop of Milan.[10]

The role of the civic procession in marking Imperial events that might otherwise go largely unnoticed by the local population is perhaps most strikingly illustrated by the 1559 obsequy commemorating the death of Charles V, which were held in the Duomo in January 1559. Three years earlier Charles had retired from formal service, conceding the Imperial crown to his son Philip II. Upon his death, which, given his earlier abdication, had no measurable political or economic impact upon the day-to-day business of governing in Milan, a catafalque surrounded by numerous candles was erected in the center of the Duomo. Around two in the morning on 9 January, the bells of the cathedral were sounded. They were echoed by those in all the churches throughout the city until daybreak, when the clergy assembled for a torchlight procession in which the morning hours and the Litany of the Saints were sung. The clergy was then joined by the dignitaries of Milanese state, who were arranged in the following order:

1. The feudatories.
2. The principal members of the Council of War.
3. The governors of the cities of the Imperial State.
4. The commanders of the fortresses of the Imperial State.
5. The Marchese del Pescara, Cavalry General.
6. Vespasiano Gonzaga, Infantry General.
7. Cavalier Confienza, Master of Ceremonies.
8. Consalvo-Fernando di Cordova, Governor of Milan.
9. The Marchese di Saluzzo with the ambassadors of the Dukes of Savoy, Ferrara, and Saluzzo.
10. Francesco Taverna, Grand Chancellor, and Petro Paolo Arrigono, President of the Senate.
11. Other Royal and Ducal Officials of the Imperial State.
12. The ambassadors from the various cities of the State.
13. The Doctors of Medicine and Law with other civic officials.

After a solemn procession of the clergy and dignitaries through the Duomo, the Governor of Milan was led to a seat on the right of the choir that was draped with a black canopy, presumably to the accompaniment of singing. From there he witnessed a Requiem mass sung by Monsignor Alessandro Vesconte, Provost of the Duomo, as well as eulogies given by the Master of Ceremonies and Senator Francesco Grasso.[11] A few days later the Governor of Milan presided over a second Requiem mass in honor of Charles' cousin Mary Tudor, Queen of England. It was sung 'with the same pomp as was the other,' and further featured a eulogy delivered by Senator Pietro Antonio Marliano.[12]

While such civic processions served to draw attention to pivotal moments in the life of the Empire, others functioned as a means of uniting residents in a common cause, be it political, religious, or both. These were often organized according to a prescribed pattern. A ceremoniale for the master of ceremonies at the Milanese court from around 1629 indicates that under the so-called 'Spanish governors,' the first of whom was Don Consalvo-Fernando di Cordova, Duca di Sessa (1558-1564), all general processions commemorating events of state were convened at the Duomo, where a sung Mass of the Holy Spirit was attended by the regular clergy, the secular clergy and the trained students. After the singing of the mass, the processions proceeded to either Sant'Ambrogio, San Celso, or San Simpliciano, as dictated by the governor. The processions were led by the ordinaries, which were followed by the Archbishop, prelates, maestro di coro, and the major and minor readers. During each procession, the *Te Deum* was sung. When the specified destination church was reached, a sermon was delivered, after which a *Benedicamus Dominus Deus* and an 'oration of Israel' were sung before the congregants.[13]

Some civic rituals, however, appear to have evolved from grassroots movements, the result of mendicant friars who successfully exhorted the nervous, war-torn population to penitence. With the initiation of the Turkish campaign in 1532, for example, the Milanese joined 'all Christendom' in praying for a victory. In this particular case, the mendicant friars themselves were largely responsible for initiating and organizing the public devotions, which began with a prayer service in the Duomo on 4 August 1532. Three days of processions from the Duomo to Sant'Ambrogio, the Duomo to Santa Maria presso San Celso, and the Duomo to San Lorenzo followed. During these, the processors accompanied the blessed sacrament while praying and singing 'Eripa me de inimicis meis.'[14]

The Penitential Processions of 1529

Perhaps the most influential of the mendicants with regard to organizing public exercises was Tommaso Spagnolo, a Dominican who arrived in Milan around 1526. According to Burigozzi, Tommaso gave a rousing sermon on 11 April 1529 in which he promised better things for Milan if her citizens would only capture the forgiveness of God through penance. The sermon sparked a series of penitential processions, the first of which was held from 16 to 18 April 1529. Each morning the processors and flagellants, which included 2500 children dressed in white with garlands on their heads and 1200 barefoot men and women dressed in sackcloth, convened at the Duomo, and thereafter processed about the city singing litanies and laude.[15]

An extant register of ducal missives and letters issued between 1526 and 1537 indicates that the official order to convene the procession heralded from the offices of Francesco II Sforza on 15 April 1529. The missive specified the order of the procession as follows:

1. The standard of Sant'Ambrogio.
2. The children under the care of Dominus presbyter Fracesco da Ello and 2 elderly.
3. The ladies dressed in sackcloth.
4. Those of San Simpliciano dressed in sackcloth, with their crucifix.
5. Others dressed in sackcloth, proceeding 2 by 2, with 2 sacerdotes dressed in their robes for every group of forty.
6. The disciplinati in the usual order.
7. The clergy in the usual order.
8. The Reverend Protonotary and the Senate.
9. The Bishop and the 12 officers of the Provision.
10. Other magistrates, decorated corps, and officials in the usual order.
11. The rest of the populace, arranged with the men first and the women second.[16]

According to the ducal missive, the procession visited three specified stations each day. These included Malcontono (prepared by the parish of San Satiro), Carrobio (prepared by the parish of San Lorenzo), and Sant'Ambrogio on the first day; the Hostaria della Balla (prepared by the parish of San Sebastiano), Sant'Eufemia, and Santa Maria presso San Celso on the second day; and the Madonna delli Miracoli (at Santa Maria presso San Celso), the cross of San Jacopo (prepared by Santa Maria della Porta), and Sant'Ambrogio on the third day. At each station the processors genuflected while reciting antiphons and prayers selected by the 'Reverend predicatore,' presumably Tommaso Spagnolo, and then kissed the earth and recited the 'Misericordia.'[17] On the third and final day, the aforementioned body processed from the Duomo to Sant'Ambrogio and back behind the standard of Sant'Ambrogio, accompanied by two shoeless priests, one of whom carried a cross on his shoulders, and eight sacerdotes dressed in linen who bore a tabernacle containing the blessed sacrament. Several representatives from the offices of Archbishop Ippolito II d'Este, some members of the senate, many merchants, and Tommaso himself, all of whom were dressed in sackcloth, were among the participants. The penitence culminated in the Duomo, where the processors left the tabernacle on the altar and heard the Vespers service before departing.
At some point during the proceedings, the processors reportedly circled the city with the tabernacle to the accompaniment of trumpet signals in a re-enactment of Joshua's battle of Jericho. Although it is clear that music played an important role in the procession, it is not currently possible to determine which laude and litanies were sung. However, Burigozzi's descriptions of the clamorous singing of the litany, the trumpet signals and the frequent cries of misericordia invoke a rather fearsome series of musical images.[18]

Penitential fervor, however, did not reach its zenith until the years falling between 1576 and 1584, when the mania surrounding civic processions reached a fever pitch under the direction of Carlo Borromeo, who organized numerous progressions to ward off the plague, to celebrate the city's liberation from it, and to commemorate his provincial councils. The chronicles of the period suggest that these processions in some manner replaced various secular amusements that were considered too frivolous for such a serious age, and the singing of hymns and psalms, an obvious social substitute for the performance of madrigals, figured prominently in most of them. For the sixth provincial council of 1582, for example, the parish priests, clerics, and populace of the diocese were ordered to 'go processionally, singing hymns, psalms, and prayers according to the book that was distributed for that purpose.'[19] In many cases, moreover, religious processions and court entertainments were integrated into a coordinated whole, as was the case with the January 1578 celebration of the liberation from the plague. Three processions, one from the Duomo to San Sebastiano, one from the Duomo to Sant'Ambrogio, and one from the Duomo and back to the same, were organized for the week of 19 to 25 January. The clergy was required to attend all three, and the general population was exhorted to attend the third, which was held in conjunction with an officially sanctioned Forty Hours. During the week candles remained lit in every home in the city, fireworks and instrumental music resounded at court, and proclamations praising the governor, Borromeo, and the Commission of Health for their fine contributions were issued. The final procession from the Duomo reportedly lasted a full ten hours, during which the Milanese, styling themselves after the Israelites, sang a vernacular lauda based on the biblical canticle commemorating the crossing of the Red Sea.[20] At an anniversary celebration of the liberation held two years later, they similarly processed singing Psalms 94, 50, and 102, as well as other antiphons.[21] Such processions embedded the liberation from the plague of 1576 into the collective cultural consciousness and endowed it with a social significance not attached to similar events that had occurred earlier in the century.

Corpus Christi Processions

Tommaso Spagnolo continued to preach frequently in the Duomo following the penitential procession of 1529, encouraging the audience to pray for forgiveness, to organize further processions of penitence, and to celebrate masses for the dead frequently. In his oration of 30 May 1529, he further exhorted the Milanese to observe the feast of Corpus Christi by processing with the sacrament after the high mass, and to repeat the activity each day for the next two days. When the processions were over, the sacrament apparently remained at the altar under the watch of the ordinaries of the Duomo. Each of the other parishes of the city was then advised to hold identical vigils for forty hours, but at different time intervals so that a continuous 'forty hours' would be observed across the city.[22]

The Corpus Christi procession, which was a tradition in many European communities during the late Medieval and Renaissance,[23] was introduced in Milan as early as 1327.[24] Yet it does not appear to have garnered significant civic participation in Milan until after Spagnolo's contrition-inducing oration of 1529. Unfortunately, however, very little information regarding the celebration of Corpus Christi survives from the 1530s, although Burgozzi reports that initially the main procession was held for three days in succession inside the Duomo during the octave of Corpus Christi, beginning on the Sunday devoted to the feast.[25] By the early 1540s, the procession had been moved outdoors and restricted to the Thursday of the octave of Corpus Christi. In order to allow the city to better prepare, the procession was announced in advance by the civic trumpeters serving the governor. The processors departed from the Duomo promptly at 8:30, and accompanied the blessed sacrament to Sant'Ambrogio and back to the Duomo.[26] Some floats and decorations were also commonly used in the outdoor processions of the mid-sixteenth century. Four scudi were spent on "an artillery volley and other decorations" placed in front of the Palazzo Reale in 1567,[27] for example, while the surviving directives for the procession of 12 May 1587 caution against the use of such profane apparati.[28]

Corpus Christi additionally appears to have been observed in some special manner at the court chapel of Santa Maria della Scala by 1542, at which time the Milanese chancery paid remunerations of 52 lire 10 soldi to San Nazaro in Porta Romana and 200 lire to San Giovanni in Cairotta for boy sopranos who were borrowed for the feast.[29] An identical payment of 52 lire 10 soldi was made to San Nazaro for the Corpus Christi celebration of 1567, and the pay records for that year further include an annotation indicating that the sum had been an annual expense for some years.[30] Vincenzo Ruffo's first book of five-voice motets, which was published by Castiglione of Milan while the composer was serving governor Alfonso D'Avalos,[31] contains a setting of the Corpus Christi text *O sacrum convivium* that may have been used for the 1542 court celebration of the feast. The motet, which is constructed on successive points of imitation (Example 4.1), is in high clefs that are suitable to boys' voices. Despite the potential associations suggested by the cleffing, however, it should be noted that the high clefs may also signal a downward transposition by a third in order to retain a modal connection to the plainchant melody on which the motet is based.[32]

In any event, Milanese Corpus Christi celebrations were conducted in the modest manner described above through the early years of Carlo Borromeo's tenure.[33] By 1587, however, the Corpus Christi procession had been transformed into a major civic affair. Although the 1587 procession itself did not begin until 10:00 a.m., it was preceded by three hours of religious preparation. The schools of Christian Doctrine were convened at 7:00 a.m. for two hours of instruction, followed by the confraternities and disciplinati at 9:00 a.m. in the Duomo for services. After processing inside the Duomo with the blessed sacrament, the participants departed for Sant'Ambrogio, where the Litany of the Saints was sung while the sacrament rested on the altar. They then processed past San Giorgio al

Example 4.1 Ruffo, *O sacrum convivium*, measures 1-15

Palazzo and wound their way south toward the Porta Ticinese and Santa Maria Beltrade.[34]

A strict processional protocol was adopted for Corpus Christi around this time and retained through the early seventeenth century. The procession was led by the 'poveri' of San Dionisio and San Martino. They were succeeded by the various penitent orders, the regular clergy, the secular clergy, and the clergy of the Duomo, the last of which included all the ordained singers. The final segment of the processional body consisted of the notaries, the bearers of the miters, the bearers of the thurible and incense, the bearer of the cross with the singers, the ordinaries, the Archbishop, the Bishop, the members of the governor's family in ecclesiastical or academic robes with the prelates, the Senate, the magistrates, the members of the office of the Provision, the remaining members of the governor's family, and, finally, the populace.[35]

The evolution of the Forty Hours observance that became attached to the Corpus Christi processions of this period has been traced to the Archconfraternity of San Sepolcro in Milan, where a service similar to that held at the Duomo in 1529 was observed annually during Holy Week, Pentecost, the Assumption, and Christmas beginning in the year 1527. Thus, the continuous vigil before the sacrament that was introduced at the Duomo in 1529 marks the popularization and extension of a theretofore isolated practice. Forty Hours devotions soon penetrated Italian culture at large, but even as they did, they began shedding their initial identity and relative significance in Milan. At the time of Carlo Borromeo's arrival, many Milanese churches were holding the vigils for weeks or months on end, and these lengthy observances were accompanied by lavish accouterments such as numerous candles and oil lamps. As a result, the ever fastidious Borromeo issued a series of statutes in 1576 that were intended to return the observance to its original Milanese form.[36]

Minor Religious Processions

Several other annual religious processions that were less elaborate than the one associated with Corpus Christi also originated at the Duomo. All of them commemorated specific feasts of the liturgical calendar and culminated in special services that became attached to them. The feast of St Stephen, for example, was marked with a procession to the church of Santo Stefano, where a mass was heard. The feast of St Mark, which was celebrated with a procession from the Duomo to San Francesco, San Vittore, and back, featured the recitation of the litanies. The vigil of the feast of Saints Protasius and Gervaise was commemorated with a procession to San Protasio. The congregants then proceeded on to Sant'Ambrogio, where a Vespers service was celebrated. The feast of St Ambrose was similarly marked by a procession to Sant'Ambrogio, where a mass was thereafter sung. Quadregesima featured a procession of the laity to San Giorgio al Palazzo and then Sant'Ambrogio, where it was joined by the clergy for a procession back to the Duomo. All of these processions were scheduled across the middle of the day and the Duomo singers were evidently required to participate, but the Canonical Hours and the daily High Mass in the Duomo continued when possible, even if in a protracted manner. According to a sixteenth-century ceremoniale from the Duomo:

> When one goes to Santo Stefano, San Protasio, and the aforementioned Sant'Ambrogio at the right time, one sings Terce in the Duomo. Meanwhile, the pontifex or another in his place is dressed, and after Mass they say Sext, Nones and the Compline vigil in this church. Moreover, the regular reader still says those commonly [recited] at his church.[37]

Despite their reduced significance in comparison to Corpus Christi, these minor civic processions marked important annual feasts of the local calendar, and served to bring the community together periodically for the purposes of strengthening its common religious heritage.

The Ambrosian Litany

The only other annual procession treated with the level of significance afforded Corpus Christi in sixteenth-century Milan was the three-day Ambrosian Litany (Triduane Liturgies). Although it is not entirely clear just how the Litany evolved, its observance supposedly served to ward off political and economic oppression. Each morning on the three days following the Ascension, the procession departed from the Duomo, where a benediction was given at the main altar. The participants, which apparently included only members of the clergy, then processed to the Ponte Vedro singing the antiphon 'Convertimini ad me.' Upon their arrival, the processors divided into three choirs according to their clerical status. The first choir was comprised of the Archbishop, ordinaries, and readers. The second consisted of the *maceconici*, while the third included all the remaining members of the clergy. While still at the Ponte, the *maceconici* and an appointed cleric sang the 'Mestorus refugius Deus' in responsorial fashion. This was followed by antiphonal performance of a twelve-fold Kyrie eleison in which the *maceconici* sang three Kyries in low voice to which the *vecchioni* responded in low voice and the readers sang three Kyries in high voice to which the *vecchioni* responded in low voice. Following the singing of this twelve-fold Kyrie, the body processed from the Ponte to selected churches, where its members repeated the performance of the Kyrie, sang and recited specified antiphons and the litany 'Christe liberanos,' and read selected Biblical passages. At the close of each day, the processors returned to the Duomo. There they repeated the twelve-fold Kyrie and sang a short litany in which the Agnus Dei alternated with the 'Gloria Patri,' the verse 'Suscipe deprecationem,' and the 'Benedicamus gratie,' and then remained for the singing of a mass and Vespers by the Duomo choir.[38]

The processional route of the Litany was designed with both the geographic layout of the city and the necessity of departing from and returning to the Duomo in mind. Thus, it was characterized by division of the city into three large pie-shaped segments (see Figure 4.1). Each segment, however, was marked off according to its proximity to one of the city's leading historical landmarks, thereby making it possible to symbolically devote each of the three days to the protection of the respective seats of temporal, ecclesiastical, and Imperial power. The first day's program, which was dedicated to the western area surrounding the Castello Sforzesco, included San Simpliciano, Santo Carpofforo, San Protasio, the Castello, San Vitorello, San Vittore al Corpo, San Martino al Corpo, San Vincenzo in Prato, the Porta Ticinese, Sant'Ambrogio, San Vitale, San Valerie, San Vittore al Treno, and Santa Tecla. The second day's route, which swathed the area immediately north to southeast of the Duomo, featured visits to San Fedele, San Dionysio, San Rocco, San Babila, Santo Stefano, the Porta Romana, San Calimero, Sant'Agata, San Nazaro, Sant'Alessandro, and San Giovanni in Conca. The final day was devoted to the churches in the southern, and, thus, ancient Imperial tier lying between the Porta Romana and Porta Ticinese, which included Sant'Eufemia, San Celso, Santa Maria presso San Celso, Santa Trinità, the Monasterio della Vigna, Sant'Eustorgio, San Lorenzo, San Benesio, San Vito, Santa Maria al Circolo, San Quirico, San Giorgio al Palazzo, San Sebastiano, and Santa Maria Beltrade.

Although participation in the Litany was restricted to the clergy, the heads of all the Milanese families were required to cooperate and no work was to be done during the three days devoted to it. Those living along the processional route were required to clear the processional space of all objects, decorations, and embroidery, and any eating, drinking, or gaming at the event was subject to a fine of 25 scudi.[39] It is noteworthy that the two churches most frequently used by the governor for services, namely San Gottardo in Corte and the royal ducal chapel of Santa Maria della Scala, were not listed for inclusion in the event.[40] This is perhaps due to the

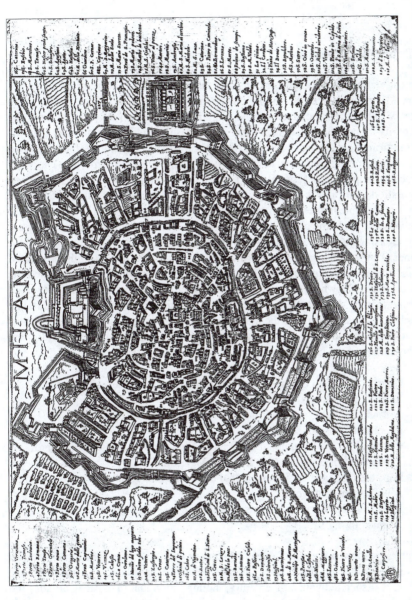

Figure 4.1 1569 Map of Milan, courtesy of the Civica Raccolta delle Stampe 'Achille Bertarelli', Milano.

fact that the human traffic associated with the Litany would have interfered with the liturgical hours and daily masses provided for the gubernatorial retinue in both locations.

The Triumphal Progressions

The most elaborate of the processions that passed through the streets of sixteenth-century Milan en route to the Duomo, however, were mounted in honor of Emperor Charles V and his representatives. The triumphal progression offered Charles V the opportunity to pass through the territories under his control in a manner that diverted attention from the controversial issues of Lutheranism and taxation by focusing upon the financial, military, and territorial strength of the Hapsburg crown. The well-designed triumphal progression relied upon the careful coordination and expert manipulation of art, music, literature, and spectacle. When successful, it not only left an inextinguishable impression of affluence, benignity, and power in its wake, but also communicated a specific political subtext to the host city. The monarchy of Charles V grew increasingly dependent upon the triumphal progression because it was one of the only means by which a sense of control, albeit somewhat artificial, might be exerted over the increasingly unwieldy collection of diverse territories that constituted the Hapsburg state. Nowhere was the Imperial image of unimpeachable authority more important than in Milan, an Imperial fief that constituted Charles' most prized Italian possession. Thus, Milan was the site of at least five progressions during Charles' reign.. These included not only the progressions of Charles and his son Philip, but also the entries of the governors appointed to act in their stead:

1.   Charles V's 1533 triumphal entry into Milan (en route from the papal meeting in Bologna).
2.   Alfonso d'Avalos's 1538 triumphal entry into Milan (upon his appointment as governor).
3.   Charles V's 1541 triumphal entry into Milan (following the liberation of Vienna and prior to the expedition in Algiers).
4.   Ferrante Gonzaga's 1546 triumphal entry into Milan (upon his appointment as governor).
5.   Philip II's 1548 triumphal entry into Milan (as Charles's successor to the Spanish throne).[41]

Each progression was designed to leave the image of a Catholic empire more powerful than ancient Rome in the memory of the Milanese populace. To this end, the ceremonies associated with a given entry, though individual in musical, artistic, and literary detail, were organized according to formats that had proven successful in previous entries. This utilization of stock ceremonial formats in turn influenced musical participation in the ceremonies. A survey of the contemporary accounts of each of the progressions into Milan reveals that music was commonly integrated into three parts of the ceremony – the processional entry into the city, the mass held at the cathedral, and the entertainments hosted by the Milanese court. The processional entry and the cathedral services were strategically important to the ceremonies because they symbolized Charles's dominion over the city as Holy Roman Emperor. The entertainments at court further cemented the emperor's position as a political, military, and religious leader, yet fostered limited social interaction between the Imperial visitors or the incoming gubernatorial party and the established aristocracy. With their emphasis on theater and dance, the court entertainments also provided avenues for the introduction of Milanese artistic traditions. The inclusion of local music, literature, and imagery in them served to facilitate Milan's incorporation into the Empire, and, at the same time, encouraged civic self-esteem amidst the overwhelming onslaught of Imperial imagery.

The Roman Entry

That music was invariably utilized during the same three segments of every triumphal progression – the processional entry, the cathedral services, and the entertainments – was no mere accident, for it served to underscore the most important aspects of a ceremonial tradition that can be traced to ancient Rome, the symbolic seat of Charles's investiture. Charles V maintained the traditional two-headed eagle as his Imperial emblem and chose the columns of Hercules as his personal impresa. These were often iconographically intertwined with his motto 'Plus ultra' and contemporary geographical images of the world over which he reigned.[42] Roman military heroes, including Caesar, Marcus Aurelius, and Trajan were also referentially invoked,[43] perhaps because of the heroic affinities that their careers shared with the Hercules legends.[44] Charles's triumphal progressions perpetuated the Roman military theme by including the three key elements mentioned in the Roman triumphs described by Appian and Plutarch, namely the triumphal progression, the ceremonies in the temple, and the post-progression theatrical performances and tournaments. Of these, the processional entry itself was the most important, and the standard features of its organization were well known to late quattrocento audiences through both the reproduction of antiquarian sources and the dissemination of contemporary studies and artwork devoted to the Roman triumph.[45] Andrea Mantegna's *The Triumphs of Caesar*, a nine-painting series executed for the Mantuan prince Lodovico Gonzaga during the 1490s,[46] is, perhaps, the artistic rendition of the Roman triumph most familiar to modern audiences. Mantegna's series, which depicts Caesar's triumphal progression into Rome, was based upon a number of ancient literary and iconographical sources, including Plutarch's *Triumph of Aemilius Paulus*, Appian's *Triumph of Scipio Africanus*, and the *Arch of Titus* in Rome.[47] It has been recognized as 'the first [modern] attempt at an accurate visual representation of a Roman triumph,' and, thus, reliably represents the Renaissance vision of the Roman triumph.[48] This Renaissance vision was appropriated by Charles V, and, following his investiture as Holy Roman Emperor in 1530, exploited to a degree theretofore untested in early modern Europe.

Charles V's processional entries into Milan usually required the participation of Milanese court dignitaries and local ecclesiastics, as well as members of the

Emperor's retinue. The processions themselves functioned as formal presentations of the Imperial fief to its foreign ruler, and, consequently, symbolized not only the Emperor's ownership of the city, but also the local citizenry's acceptance of his rule. In accordance with the design described in Appian's *Roman History*[49] and Plutarch's *Lives*,[50] as well as the organization recorded in Mantegna's *Triumphs of Caesar*, the trumpeters, wind players, and drummers played fanfares and other musical selections during this event.[51] The surviving contemporary accounts of the Milanese entries provide a number of interesting details regarding the placement of the musicians within the procession itself, as well as the music performed. For example, Alessandro Verini Fiorentino's description of the 1533 royal progression of Charles V mentions not only instrumental music, but also singing. Admittedly, Fiorentino's references to singing may be symbolic rather than factual, arising, as they do, partly from an attempt to preserve the poem's opening image of an angelic choir serenading the devout Charles V. Nonetheless, they also reflect the author's familiarity with the numerous Roman accounts[52] that describe singing and dancing processors:

> But let us return to the Holy Emperor. As he arrived in front of the gates, one heard a roar and furor from the spectators who ran forward to see screaming 'the Empire, the Empire' with great emotion. Children, adults, and elderly of every sort sang and played instruments in the streets in celebration; many had never seen such pomp . . . But let us again return to the Holy Emperor. He did not long remain in that place, but instead, gradually processed towards the Castello, with great honor, and to the accompaniment of singing and the playing of instruments. There everyone made tremendous merriment and excitement with feasting and games. The playing and the noise of the crowds was so loud that it was heard twenty miles away.[53]

The royal entrances of Charles V in 1541, Ferrante Gonzaga in 1546, and Philip II in 1548 similarly opened with processions through the city. Unfortunately, Alberto Albicante's chronicles of the entrances of Charles V in 1541 and Philip II in 1548 concentrate heavily upon the description of the costumes and the decorations rather than the music. However, Juan Cristóbal Calvete's account of the triumphal progression of Philip II notes that the 1548 entry into Milan was led by the trumpeters,[54] a custom which both Appian[55] and Plutarch[56] indicate as appropriate to the Roman triumph. Alonso de Santa Cruz further observes that in the 1548 entry the trumpeters were followed by wind players, drummers, and other instrumentalists,[57] while Alberto de Nobili Volterano adds that 'His Majesty arrived at the gates of the city. A volley was fired from the castle and the trumpets sounded.'[58] Landolfo Verità notes that the 1546 processional entry of newly appointed governor Ferrante Gonzaga was likewise accompanied by the sound of the trumpets and artillery fire,[59] and Gaspare Bugati reports that Charles V's arrival at the city gates during the 1541 entry was similarly announced by a trumpet fanfare.[60]

Even if some members of the audience did not recognize the allusions to the Roman triumphs of Appian and Plutarch suggested by the musical aspects of the entry, they did comprehend the general significance of the trumpeters themselves. The trumpeters, as the employees of the state who delivered every public decree and announced all important civic events, communicated the initiation of a monumental civic exercise by their very presence at the head of the procession. The attention that they commanded was only heightened by their extraordinary costumes, which were specific to the entry in which they were participating, the apparati through which they passed as they led the procession along its designated route, and, of course, the fanfares and the songs that they played.

The Duomo Mass

The second musical event shared by the royal entries was a sung mass in the Duomo of Milan. The cathedral mass not only reinforced the Milanese perception of Charles V as a devout Holy Roman Emperor, but also functioned as a Christian reinterpretation of the formal victory ceremonies that had been held in the ancient Roman temples.[61] Albicante's description of the cathedral mass held during the 1541 triumphal entrance of Charles V is especially explicit with regard to the music performed, and implies that instruments were used to reinforce the voices:

> CAESAR dismounts from his horse. Intent, full of religion, and with great faith he contentedly goes forward step by step. And they anoint his head with the sacred waters. Here one does not see a sorrowful heart because all play and speak, listen and sing. Many instruments resound sweetly, and the tone reverberates to the skies. As he approaches the altar of true sacrifice, the reminder of the vow of Christ, Charles kneels with a sincere heart to these Imperial saints and devotees. And in the middle of the Consistory of the Sacred Clergy and of the faithful, he hears our sacerdotes sing the ritual anew, and remained to thank the eternal Jove.[62]

The accuracy of Albicante's somewhat formulaic description is verified by the accounts of Calvete and Volterano. The former notes that the music was performed by both voices and organ,[63] while the latter succinctly states that:

> [Charles V] dismounted at the Duomo, where the orations would be made for him by the primary singer and the ceremonies made as they had been in similar royal entries; the responses were sung in music. To these His Majesty attended, as always, with great devotion.[64]

A sung mass was also arranged for the entry of Philip II in December 1548. The event was again colorfully recorded by Albicante:

> And inside the Duomo he goes devoted, full of true faith and religion. And with a sincere heart he offers thanks to God, his good intentions rising toward heaven. There was not an empty corner in the cathedral, but [rather] it was full 'to the brim' with people. And each one of them was attentive, desiring to see a King so devoted to God. The ceremony was sung and said sincerely by all the clergy. And thanks expressed to the true maker by perfectly maintained voices. The King then turned, preparing to exit with his retinue, and expressed thanks to God [amidst] the incense and the fragrances . . .[65]

The chronicles detailing the gubernatorial entries of the period mention the mass in the cathedral only in passing, and include very little information regarding musical performance. Verità remarks only that the cathedral mass for the 1546 entry of governor Ferrante Gonzaga featured joyful singing,[66] just as the 1538 entry of governor Alfonso D'Avalos had been marked by song:

> And, by chance, that other gentleman also, [Alfonso d'Avalos], was solemnly received in another time with celebration and song as well.[67]

However, the surviving information on the comparatively modest 1533 entry of Charles V, which occurred while Francesco II Sforza was still presiding as Duke, is more forthcoming. Although Fiorentino merely notes that the 1533 ceremonies included a mass performed in the manner characteristic of other royal entries,[68] Marco Burigozzi further specifies that the mass was performed according to the Ambrosian rite.[69] Burigozzi's observation is noteworthy because it suggests that the distinctly Milanese aspects of the service were highlighted despite Charles's Spanish heritage and Roman titles, perhaps in deference to Francesco II.

The Entertainments at Court

All of the chronicles indicate that the entry processions and the mass in the Duomo were customarily followed by various forms of entertainment that also required music, including banquets, balls, tournaments, musical performances and plays. The events that comprised this stage of the Milanese progression also were modeled upon their Roman predecessors, which typically featured banquets, tournaments, and theatrical presentations. The entertainments designed for Charles V and his representatives served to reinforce previously introduced Imperial themes and symbols, as well as to provide a microscopic view of the city's cultural and social profile. The most elaborate entertainments apparently were prepared for the 1548 entry of prince Philip II, and included banquets, balls, tournaments, games, and two comedies,[70] as well as on Christmas eve a Matins and High Mass in the 'Spanish style' at one of the ducal chapels near the Palazzo Reale, presumably Santa Maria della Scala or San Gottardo in Corte.[71] The entertainments prepared for Philip's entry reflect a calculated attempt to present Milan in a favorable cultural light before the practiced eye of the knowledgeable humanist prince. Philip's retinue for the 1548 entry included his own chapel of 18 singers, 10 trumpeters, 10 additional instrumentalists, a page/scribe, and the renowned organists Antonio and Juan de Cabezón.[72] The presence of such a large and distinguished musical chapel must certainly have pressured the Milanese to furnish entertainments that rivaled those presented at the Spanish court, and, in fact, numerous ecclesiastical and secular musicians equal to the task were on hand. The most famous of these were the virtuoso cornettist Moscatello, who is repeatedly identified in contemporary documents as the leader of the Milanese court's instrumental ensemble during the tenure of Ferrante Gonzaga,[73] the unnamed members of his own band, and the lutenist Pietro Paolo Borrono, who served as a spy at the Milanese court between 1535 and 1556.[74] Borrono's *Intavolatura di lauto*, which was published during the year 1548, may even include some of the dance music performed at the two balls described in Calvete's chronicle of the entry.[75] According to Calvete, the first of the balls featured the dancing of many pavanes and galliardes,[76] two dance types that figure prominently in Borrono's collection.[77] Although it is not at all likely that a single lute served to accompany the dancing, Borrono may have participated or, at the very least, intabulated some of the dances most popular with the attending audience. And even if Borrono's intabulations bear no direct relationship to the festivities, they still reflect the Milanese pavane and galliarde repertoire at the time of Philip's progression.

The Milanese must have put some of their best gambists on display at the second ball, for the performance of several selections on the viola da gamba was, at least from the Spanish visitors' point of view, among its most memorable highlights.[78] Lombardy appears to have been something of a training ground for gambists, and the superiority of its virtuosi was recognized both at home and abroad. Five Cremonese gambists were appointed to the musical chapel of Henry II during the year 1547,[79] and these were followed by others. Thimodeo d'Aqua, a sixth virtuoso gambist who was probably residing in Milan at the time of Philip's 1548 visit, later transferred to the French court as well.[80] Thimodeo, who was among the city's most famous virtuosi, certainly must have been among the gambists featured at the second ball. He also may have joined Borrono and the members of Moscatello's band for the elaborate *intermedi* interspersed between the acts of the two comedies prepared expressly for the royal visit.

The two comedies presented during Philip II's visit included Alessandro Piccolomini's *L'Alessandro* (1543) and Milanese captain of justice Nicolò Secco's *L'Interesse*. Both of the plays included musical *intermedi*, but only a brief description of the music that accompanied Secco's play has survived.[81] It included a prologue in which 'one of seven ancient nymphs crowned Italy,'[82] followed by four *intermedi*, all of which were presented in a Venetian setting that included canals. The first *intermedio* opened with a 'symphony,' after which Bacchus and Silène entered to the accompaniment of instruments. The second featured a choir of seven nymphs and seven shepherds dancing to the accompaniment of instruments. The third and fourth *intermedi* were staged aboard boats floating in the canals, and were performed by six musicians singing to the accompaniment of lutes, zithers, and an organ, and a choir of nine muses, respectively. The *intermedi* concluded with an oration in honor of Philip II given by Mercury,[83] thus making evident Philip's filial role as the representative and messenger of his father, the latter of whom was often symbolized by the god Jupiter.[84] The preparation of Secco's comedy caused the Milanese chancery a good deal of concern because its scenery, which included lifelike replicas of Venetian canals, required extensive reconstruction of the room in which it was to be performed. In addition, a troupe of Florentine actors had been secured for the plays themselves, and various rehearsal and scheduling problems arose as a result.[85]

It is clear that the two plays were intended as the focal points of the entertainments honoring Philip II, since the state banquets, balls, and games were sandwiched between them. Despite their secondary importance to the festivities, however, the banquets, balls, and games were also elaborately staged, largely through the assistance of musical ornamentation. For example, the food served at one of the banquets was presented to the accompaniment of trombones:

> The first and perfect presentation looked like an orderly regiment. All was decorated in gold, as is customary of the people who know how to do things correctly. Soon the dancing begins, although it is not danced as music for trombone. And the arrangement was a beautiful exhibition, as one sees at a well-choreographed joust. [86]

The guests then sat down to the banquet, which was followed by a ball at which the instrumental musicians performed. Other banquets and balls were held, several tournaments were presented, and various outdoor games were played. Each tournament or game was introduced by theatrical trumpet and drum fanfares. Albicante appears to have been especially impressed by the realistic military fanfares featured at one of the tournaments:

> The trumpets sound in a high, horrendous voice, and to every 'tantara' another 'tantara' answers. Therein beats are struck without reparation in every breast and on every brow. [87]

Similar banquets, balls, and tournaments were held during Charles's other royal entries into Milan. According to both Burigozzi and Fiorentino, however, the entertainments presented during the 1533 progression were quite differently placed in that they flanked the previously described rite of the cathedral mass, which was held the day after the royal banquet and before the other court festivities. Both vocal and instrumental music was performed as banquet entertainment,[88] and again was featured during the dancing and games that followed the cathedral ceremonies:

> With great rejoicing, infinite love, and infinite favor, they remained there four days for instrumental music, singing, and great celebration, balls, tournaments, and many games organized by the court, the likes of which had neither been heard nor seen by anyone here or there accustomed to such dancing, singing, and eating. [89]

Such upstaging of the cathedral mass, which generally functioned as the culmination of the entry procession, may have resulted from an attempt to downplay Charles's posture as a Roman victor in favor of Duke Francesco II. During Charles's second royal entry into Milan in 1541, the mass was repositioned so that it occurred at the close of the entry procession and before the secular amusements were introduced. The 1541 entry was characterized by entertainments similar to those planned in 1533 and 1548, but the chronicles offer few details concerning the exact nature of the musical performances. Albicante states only that music was heard at the entrance into the banquet that followed the Duomo mass:

> Everywhere one hears the instruments resound in a harmony that seems a sublime chorus. This display is not done justice by documentation; the major part must be left . . . All the winds [sound] with the errant stars. [90]

Bugati also fails to elaborate upon the specific nature of the music performed during the 1541 entry, but his commentary does suggest that music occupied an important position within the courtly celebrations:

> The Emperor was lodged in this decorated Imperial court, which provided the city with the delightful sounds of bells, trumpets, wind instruments, fireworks, and artillery fire, to say nothing of the volleys from the castle, the festivals, the banquets, the balls, the tournaments, and the other entertainments.[91]

The Impresa and Music

Although the contemporary sources are rife with such descriptions, the descriptions themselves are not particularly useful in identifying the musical selections featured at the various performances mentioned. However, study of the apparati designed for Charles V's Italian progressions may prove useful in determining which of the many surviving ceremonial pieces might have been performed. The decorative themes of each entry were dominated by the Emperor's Roman emblems and *impresa*. These served as a basis for the allegorical embellishment of his latest military and political feats, and provided a central theme around which a number of entries celebrating the same occasion might be designed. Since the decorations for a given entry were fashioned according to a specific occasional interpretation of the emblems and the *impresa*, moreover, separately conceived apparati prepared for the same Imperial event tended toward thematic similarity. This thematic similarity prevailed despite the fact that the Imperial heraldry and its ornamentation were slightly redefined for each entry according to the location in which it was to occur.[92]

The rhetorical and allegorical themes that guided the decorations prepared for a series of progressions commemorating the same occasion are often also reflected in the literary chronicles in which those progressions are recorded. Because the ceremonial motet was the conventional musical avenue for the simultaneous unfolding of political rhetoric and allegorical symbolism, it, like the poetic chronicle, served to reinforce the decorative themes. Several ceremonial motets honoring Charles V were composed for use in the foreign progressions, and they traditionally have been associated with a single entry for which either documentary or circumstantial evidence of their performance at that event survives. Their texts, however, are occasionally specific only in their reference to the triumph being celebrated and its allegorical elaboration, and make no mention of regional or civic themes. It, therefore, is likely that the ceremonial motets heretofore associated with a given entry actually were appropriate for a variety of progressions celebrating the same occasion. Since the triumphal progressions through Italy were a sort of traveling Imperial show that, at least in the case of Philip II, included a chapel of musicians, it is not unlikely that some of the music performed was carried with the royal entourage. This would have made possible the repetition of a given motet in a number of European cities visited by the Imperial party. For example, the processional route of Carlo V's 1533 entry into Milan, which celebrated the peace negotiated by Charles V and Clement VII in Bologna, was decorated with ceremonial draperies, Herculean columns, and Imperial arms bearing inscriptions that referred to Charles V's Roman *impresa*.[93] They assisted in presenting the Emperor as Europe's most sacred and powerful ruler by suggesting a resemblance between Charles V's Holy Roman Empire and Imperial Rome. In Fiorentino's chronicle of the entry, Charles V is repeatedly described not only as Caesar, but also as a celestial being surrounded by an angelic choir.[94] Interestingly enough, the chronicles of the 1530 and 1533 Genovese progressions propose similar analogies.[95] Since the decorative themes of the entries into both Milan and Genoa were imitated by the literary themes of the chronicles that describe them, the texts of the music performed must also have been coordinated with the decorative themes. It, therefore, is possible that Gombert's *Qui colis ausoniam*, which was performed at the 1533 meeting between Charles V and Clement VII in Bologna,[96] was also sung in each of the other cities visited during the Italian tour, which included both Genoa and Milan. Its text celebrates the peace established by the pact between Charles and Clement, and refers to the former as a sacred Caesar.

Qui colis Ausoniam glebae felicis arator	You ploughman who inhabits Italy of fertile soil
Qua Bacchi et Cereris munera sponte fluunt	Where the gifts of Bacchus and Ceres flow
Qui toties fatis gemuisti pressus inquis	of their own accord
	Who so often groaned, weighed down by unjust fates,
Orbe alio assidue dum novus hostis adest	When time and again a new enemy appeared from another world.
Pone aras accende focos pia thura cremato	Set up the altars, kindle the hearth-fires, burn the incense due to the gods,
Gaudia vox lytui cornua sistra sonent.	Let voice, trumpets, horns, sistra sound with joy.
Perpetuum Clemens foedus cum Caesare pacis	Clemens has made a perpetual covenant of peace with Caesar,
Sanciit ut fessae ferret opem patriae	That he might bring assistance to the exhausted fatherland.
Bisfrontisque deam Iani conclusit in aede	And has enclosed the goddess [Pax] in the temple of the two-faced Janus,
Tranquillo aeternum regnet ut haec Latio	That she may reign forever in tranquil Italy.
Quam Caroli sanctique Patris concordia corda	How concordant are the hearts of Charles and the Holy Father.
Quam bene nunc gemino tutus es imperio.	How well protected are you now under their double command.

The 1541 progression celebrated the liberation of Vienna and preceded the ambitious Turkish campaign of that same year. Its organization was apparently especially problematic, for numerous revisions of the list of Milanese dignitaries listed for participation survive in the Milanese state archives.[97] In fact, the attention given to the details in the processional order and the design of the decorations suggest that greater importance was attached to the entry of 1541 than was allotted that of 1533.

This may be due, in part, to the fact that in 1533 the Duchy technically was still invested to the Sforza, whereas by 1541 it had reverted to the Hapsburg dynasty. Some relief from the financial constraints of the early 1530s and the allegiance demanded of the post-Sforza governors may also have come into play. In any case, the *apparati* created for this event, which were designed by architect Giulio Romano, consisted primarily of a number of Roman arches that marked the processional route, the first of which was placed on a bridge outside the Porta Romana. The eight decorative statues adorning it paid tribute to the eight Lombard cities that had once been a part of Imperial Rome – Tortona, Alessandria, Como, Pavia, Cremona, Lodi, Novara, and Milano. Bonner Mitchell has suggested that this arch was intended to convey the fact that Milan viewed itself 'as a territorial nation rather than as a city state.'[98] It probably was further intended as a reference to the city's ancient heritage as an Imperial capital. Additional arches were positioned at civic monuments along the processional route that were associated with Imperial Milan, including the Porta Romana, La Crocetta, and the Porta Ticinese.[99] The final arch, which featured the Emperor in Roman dress mounted on a horse that was trampling an Indian, a Moor, and a Turk, was strategically situated in front of the cathedral.[100] Its placement recalled that of equestrian statues commonly featured in ancient Roman triumphs, which often were positioned in front of the temple in which the religious ceremonies were to be held.[101] In defining a processional route that first passed the ancient civic sites and culminated at the monument to victory in the Piazza of the Duomo, the placement of the arches not only recalled Caesar's victorious return to Rome, but also acknowledged Charles's sacred responsibility as Holy Roman Emperor. Albicante's chronicle of the entry reinforces these images by identifying Charles as the new Caesar, as well as the chief representative of Jupiter, mythical ruler of the heavens and the earth.[102] If such symbolism was musically enforced, then Jean Courtois's *Venite populi terrae*, which was performed during the Emperor's triumphal progression into Cambrai,[103] may have been repeated. The text of the motet pays tribute to Carlo by hailing him as a modern Caesar ruling over many nations, a bearer of peace, and God's sacred representative on earth. Its second section sections features textual parodies on Psalm 150 and the Ave Maria that further reinforce the Emperor's image as a spotless religious leader. The entire text is unspecific enough that it could have easily been reused any number of times.

Venite populi terrae et videte opera dei.	Come all ye nations and see the works of God.
Exultate gaudio et laetitia quia fecit deus prodigia sua magna auferens bella usque ad finem terrae.	Rejoice and be glad because God has performed his great prodigies by ceasing conflict even unto the ends of the earth.
Ecce principes terrae convenerunt in unum et civitas pacis cum duce suo incedit obviam eis.	Behold the princes of the earth have come together in one place, and the city of peace with its commander marches to meet them.
Juvenes et virgenes	Men and women,
senes cum junioribus	Old and young,
cantate canticum novum	Sing a new song.
psallite in jubilatione.	Sound your instruments in jubilation.

Ave Caesar,	Hail Caesar!
ave majestas sacra	Hail sacred majesty!
plena est terra gloria tua	The earth is full of your glory.
benedicta acta dei in secula. Amen.	Blessed are the acts of God forever. Amen

Pierre de Manchicourt's *Nunc enim si centum*, which compares the Emperor to Caesar, leader of the military, and identifies him as the sacred ruler of the Austro-Germanic nations, would also have been thematically suitable.

Nunc enim si centum lingue sint	Now, indeed, were there a hundred tongues
Carole Caesar	(available),
laudes non possum promere rite tuas	I could not adequately praise you, O
qui reges magnos	Emperor Charles,
multos valde que potentes fudisti	who has conquered many great and powerful
summo ast auxilitate Deo.	kings with God's help.
Ne dubitatis letusque tuis	Hesitate not and gladly prepare yourself for
accingere satis quoque hostes	your fares;
plures sunt tibi fide magnis.	have more faith because many are your
	enemies.

Inumeras unus potis es prostrare phalange	Alone you are not able to prostrate
qui cum coelesti federa rege facis	phalanges without number,
	for you did make a pact with the King of
	Heaven.
Austria multa tibi	Much of Austria and all of Germany serve
germania cuncta ministrat	you,
hinc memoram famam	who has memory and fame among those
qui bene vivis habes.	who live in goodness.[104]

Courtois and Manchicourt are both associated with the Franco-Flemish tradition, and their sacred music was widely circulated in the North, as well as in Spain. The performance of either motet at the Milanese festivities may have initiated the resurgence of Milanese enthusiasm for Franco-Flemish compositions that is expressed in the preface to Bernardino Calusco's *Mutetarum divinitatis liber primus*. Calusco's *Mutetarum* was printed in Milan during the year 1543, and is comprised primarily of works by North European composers.[105] As noted earlier, three motets by Hermann Matthias Werrecore, the Duomo's maestro di cappella at the time of the 1541 entry, are also included in the *Mutetarum*. One of these is the five-voice cantus firmus motet *Beati omnes*, which features the baptismal plainchant 'Uxor tua sicut vitis.'[106] The motet, which is based upon the text of Psalm 127, was likely composed for the baptism of Carlo d'Avalos, the seventh son of governor Alfonso d'Avalos. The baptism was one of the numerous festivities held during the Emperor's nine-day stay in Milan following the 1541 progression.[107]

The 1548 triumphal progression of Philip II featured a procession to the main entrances into the city and concluded at the Piazza del Duomo. The decorations that adorned this route included both Roman arches and statues, the latter of which were placed on a bridge near the Porta Ticinese. Volterano describes the statues as four sculptues of gesso, the arms of which represented the eight principal Lombard cities that had been a part of Imperial Rome. The arm associated with a given city was further distinguished by its own individual symbol. For example, the city of Novara was represented by a patent used to order sacrifice, thus alluding to its ancient religious heritage.[108] The function of the 1548 statues recalled that of the images on the 1541 Porta Romana arch, which likewise referred to the eight Lombard cities of the ancient Roman Empire. In placing the gesso statues on a bridge near the Porta Ticinese, which, like the Porta Romana in 1541, marked the beginning of the processional route, a parallel likely was being drawn between the two entries. Philip II was taking unofficial possession of the city, just as Charles had taken official possession in 1541. In fact, a Roman arch bearing Milanese arms and an inscription that hailed Philip as his father's able successor was positioned on the opposite side of the Porta Ticinese bridge. Volterano notes that this arch was approximately forty *braccia* high, and further comments that it was constructed 'with the double proportion adduced by the eye only after a second glance, just as the musical octave fully delights the ear of those who listen carefully.'[109] The double proportion of the arch was possibly intended as an allusion to Philip's recent 'secret' investiture as Duke of Milan, an initiative which had not been particularly well guarded in diplomatic circles.

A number of other Roman arches were also used, at least two of which were placed in the Piazza of the Duomo. The first of these was positioned at the far end of the piazza, and depicted Charles V, two Turks at his feet, supporting the earth. The second was placed directly in front of the main entrance to the Duomo. Its central portion featured a relief that depicted the world held aloft by Hercules and Atlanta, above which Judith Hebrea and David were mounted on the left and right, respectively. The mixture of sacred and secular symbolism is rendered obvious by the inscriptions on the arches. They heralded Philip as the able representative of his father, acclaimed Charles as the Empire's defender of the faith and supreme military commander, and acknowledged Milan's historical and strategic position as an Imperial city of ancient Rome.[110]

Mantuan nobleman Ferrante Gonzaga was serving as the governor of Milan during Philip's 1548 entry, and, as a result, a number of the dignitaries and military personnel who had participated in the Milanese progression were summoned for the succeeding entry into Mantua as well.[111] The *apparati* designed for the entry into Mantua differed from those prepared in Milan primarily in that they underscored the Etruscan heritage of the city, its ties to the poet Virgil, and its position of political significance as the seat of the Gonzaga dynasty. Nonetheless, the overriding theme of the Mantuan *apparati*, like that of the *apparati* designed for Milan, was Philip's position as a representative of the Holy Roman Empire and an able Spanish successor of Charles V.[112] Given both the common participants in the two celebrations and the similarity of the *apparati* used, any ceremonial motets performed during the entry into Mantua would have been equally appropriate for the preceding Milanese festivities. For example, Jachet of Mantua's *Hesperiae ultimae/Philippe, te discendente*, which traditionally is thought to have been composed for the Mantuan progression,[113] may actually have been performed in Milan as well. Its text, which cites Philip as an able religious and military representative of the Holy Roman Emperor, is closely aligned with the themes of both the Milanese and Mantuan decorations.

Hesperiae ultimae invicto Regi	To the invincible ruler of the greatest
Maximi Caesaris inclitae proli	Western lands,
optimo juventutis principi	Successor of the most celebrated Caesar,
honor, victoria, laus et imperium.	Most excellent of the young princes,
	honor, victory, laud, and might.
Philippe, te discendente moerent Hispaniae	O Philip, Spain mourns your absence.
nunc te praesente gaudet Italia	Italy now rejoices in your presence.
ad sese ut properes cupit Germania	Germany desires that you soon occupy the
	North.
Tu desiderium, tu decus es tuis.	Every desire and honor is yours.

Less information is currently available regarding the decorations and inscriptions used during the triumphal progressions of Alfonso D'Avalos, governor of Milan from 1538 to 1546, and Ferrante Gonzaga, governor of Milan from 1546 to 1555. However, Frank Dobbins identified a four-voice ceremonial motet honoring Alfonso d'Avalos in Moderne's *Motetti del Fiore* IV of 1539. It was composed by Ernoul Caussin, maestro di cappella at the church of Santa Maria della Steccata in Parma from 1534 until 1548.[114] Caussin likely became acquainted with D'Avalos between the years 1534 and 1538, at which time the latter was commanding the Imperial forces occupying Piemonte and traveling extensively in Northern Italy on behalf of the Hapsburg state. Caussin's motet, which is entitled *Nomine si vastus* (Example 4.2), lauds D'Avalos's military accomplishments and

Example 4.2 Caussin, *Nomine si vastus*, measures 1-14

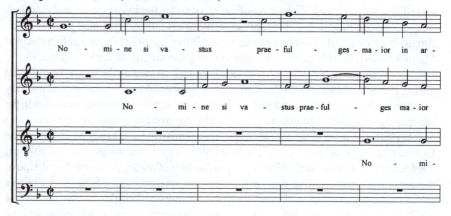

hails him as Caesar's most able general. It probably was performed during D'Avalos's 1538 progression into Milan as the city's governor, an event that occurred approximately one year prior to the publication of Moderne's print.[115]

Nomine si vastus praefulges maior in armis.	If you are huge in name, you shine forth greater in battle.
Et merito Caesar dat tibi prim[us] duci.	And Caesar rightly gives you the prize as commander.
Te peperit Bellona potens de semine martis.	Powerful Bellona gave birth to you from the seed of Mars.
Mars dedit arma prima caetera matris habes.	Mars first gives you military power; you have the rest from your mother.
Me sidum a teneris, genuit natura clientem.	Nature bore me to serve you as a diligent client from my tender years; may you therefore be mindful of me.
Inservire tibi memor ergo me.	To serve you, therefore, is prudent of me.

The identification of ceremonial pieces performed at individual state events during the Renaissance has been dependent primarily upon external documentation that links a given work to a specific progression, while distinguishing clues found in the text of the work itself are treated with secondary importance. This traditional dependence upon archival sources or, more often, circumstantial evidence such as the presence of a composer in a given city in which a progression occurred, undoubtedly is driven by the ambiguity of the texts themselves. They often feature such abstract allegorical and classical symbolism that they can be associated only with an event or achievement in the career of the dedicatee, rather than one of the numerous celebrations of that event or achievement. Given the frequency with which Charles V and Philip II formally entered European cities and the repetitive nature of the allegorical themes associated with those entries, however, such ambiguity appears clearly intended. It guaranteed the ready availability of ceremonial music that could be reused in a number of slightly different ceremonial contexts.

The traveling Imperial show styled after the Roman panoply quickly emerged as a principal form of propaganda during the reign of Charles V. In the Imperial progression, music, art, and literature were thoughtfully combined to create a colorful backdrop against which the Emperor appeared as a one-dimensional pasteboard figure whose movement through the city was controlled by the ceremonial event. The Emperor's seeming otherworldliness within this artificial Roman environment insured his isolation from the populace, yet made possible the application of the religious and military labels necessary to the maintenance of his public image for the duration of each new political or military endeavor. At the same time, the Roman themes suggested a learned prince capable not only of leading in battle, but also of sparring intellectually with the humanists of the day.

Milan, once the jewel of Europe, struggled to redefine its identity during the early sixteenth century. Even as the triumphal progressions of Charles V and his representatives formalized Milan's incorporation into the Empire and served as a mouthpiece for Imperial propaganda, they also increased civic consciousness by bringing the Milanese together as witnesses of an historically informed and culturally sensitive public spectacle that engendered civic pride and restored faith in the city's longevity. Music, as the aural aspect of this public experience, not only underscored the distinctly Roman features of the progression, but also lent its affective properties to the overall aesthetic experience. In the triumphal progression, music shared the power to shape public reaction with the visual and literary arts by supplying a virtual soundtrack for the *tableaux vivante* that unfolded on the urban stage.

The free citizens of ancient Rome customarily sponsored lavish public spectacles, and attached public identity, in part, to the monetary and artistic value of the entertainments that they provided. The quantity and quality of these public spectacles were regarded as barometers of Roman society itself, for they reflected its relative cultural and intellectual achievement during a given period. Charles V, realizing that public display was similarly viewed by Renaissance society, returned periodically to heavily taxed, war-weary Milan with the intention of reviving the city's flagging morale even as he reinvented his own Imperial image. For sixteenth-century Milan, and, indeed, for the Empire itself, the Roman panoply not only functioned as a principal instrument for the proliferation of Imperial propaganda, but also masqueraded as an indication, albeit artificial, of the cultural refinement and elevated financial standing of its society.

Notes

1   Burigozzi, *Cronanca milanese*.
2   Ibid., and Gaspare Bugati, *Histoire universale*.
3   Evelyn Welch, *Art and authority*, 49-69.
4   Burigozzi, *Cronaca milanese*, 440-444.
5   *Sforzesco* 1451 (Milano città e ducato: 1534 settembre-1535 febbraio), n.n., 20 ottobre 1534, ASM.
6   *Sforzesco* 1443 (Milano città e ducato: 1533 febbraio), n.n., 12 febbraio 1533 notes that Francesco II Sforza ordered a Mass of the Purification, while *Sforzesco* 1446 (Milano città e ducato: 1533 giugno-dicembre), n.n., 3 novembre 1533, and *Sforzesco* 1428 (Milano città e ducato: 1530 octobre-novembre), n.n., 3 novembre 1530, ASM reveal that an annual mass of the Holy Spirit was held especially for government officials on November 3. *Sforzesco* 1450 (Milano città e ducato 1534 aprile-agosto), n.n., circa 1 maggio 1534, ASM, contains an order requiring sounding of the bells for three days followed by a clerically organized procession in honor of Christine of Denmark. This was distributed to all of the cities in the duchy.
7   *Registro di Lettere Ducali* 1553-1562, 28v-29r, BTASCM.
8   *Registro di Lettere Ducali*,1553-1562, 38v, BTASCM.
9   Ibid., 100v, BTASCM.
10   Ibid., 188v, BTASCM.
11   *Essequie celebrate nella chiesa del Domo di Milano per Carlo Quinto et per la regina Maria d'Inghilterra* (Milano: Giovanbattista da Ponte e fratelli, 1559), n.p.
12   'con le medesime ceremonie che fu l'altra.' *Essequie celebrate nella chiesa del Domo*, n.p.
13   *Codice* 1252 (Ceremoniale Spagnolo Milanese), 19r, BTASCM. Although the manuscript itself is undated, its latter pages contain the order of ceremonies for a celebration honoring the birth of the prince of Spain in 1629 and the obsequies of Queen Margherita. The oration of Israel likely refers to the song sung by Moses and the Israelites after crossing the Red Sea in Exodus 15: 1-21.
14   A paraphrase of Psalm 58. Burigozzi, *Cronaca milanese*, 511.
15   Burigozzi, *Cronaca milanese*, 487-488.
16   *Registro di Lettere Ducali* 1526-1537, 35r-v, BTASCM.
17   Ibid., 35v-36v, BTASCM.
18   Burigozzi, *Cronaca milanese*, 487-488.
19   ' . . .veghino processionalmente, cantando himni salmi e preci secondo il libretto che percio si è datto fuori.' P. 250 (Urbano Monti: Delle cose più notabili successe alla città de Milano, terza parte), 27r, BAM.
20   P. 248 (Urbano Monti: Delle cose piu notabili successe alla città de Milano, prima parte), 142r-150r, BAM.
21   P. 249 (Urbano Monti: Delle cose più notabili successe alla città de Milano, terza parte), 74r, BAM.
22   Burigozzi, *Cronaca milanese*, 491-492.
23   For example, Reinhard Strohm, *Music in Late Medieval Bruges* (Oxford: Clarendon Press, 1990), 15, notes that a 1417 endowment at St Donatian in Bruges required the

children's cantor 'to assemble the singers to perform a motet during the procession on the octave of the feast of Corpus Christi.' Frank A. D'Accone, *The Civic Muse: Music and Musicians in Siena during the Middle Ages and the Renaissance* (Chicago and London: The University of Chicago Press, 1997), 467, reports that an order for the procession on feast of Corpus Christi is found in the Sienese statutes of 12 May 1456, but postulates that the procession was being held annually before that date. The procession was organized by the Woolen Guild, and included the members of various guilds, the confraternities, and the clergy.

24   Enrico Cattaneo, 'La tradizione ambrosiana,' *Storia di Milano* IX (Milano: Giovanni Treccani degli Alfieri, 1961), 550.

25   Burigozzi, *Cronaca milanese*, 491-492.

26   *Registro di Lettere Ducali* 1537-1545, 200r, BTASCM. The order is for the year 1545, but notes that the procedure described conforms to recent years past. *Registro di Lettere Ducali* 1548-1552, 28r and 127r, BTASCM, contains further notices for the years 1548 and 1552 respectively. In the event of rain, the procession was rescheduled for the following Sunday.

27   'salva di artiglieri et altri addobamenti inanzi à la Porta di questo Palazzo.' *Registri della Cancelleria dello Stato* XXII/16 (Mandati 1566-1567), 206v, ASM.

28   *Fl-2-3 (Diarii ceremoniali)*, 47-49 (Visconti, Gaspare: Disposizioni . . . C.C., number 852), BCM.

29   *Registri della Cancelleria dello Stato* XXII/4 (Mandati 1542-1545), 44r and 47v, ASM.

30   *Registri della Cancelleria dello Stato* XXII/16 (Mandati 1566-1567), 199v, ASM.

31   Ruffo, *Il primo libro de motetti*, dedication.

32   For a discussion of the role of high and mixed clefs in signaling transposition, see Kurtzman, 'Tones, modes, clefs and pitch in Roman cyclic Magnificats,' 641-657.

33   *Registri di Lettere Ducali* 1553-1562, 98r-99r, 103r-131r, 188r, 190v-191v, 215r-216r, and 242v-243r, BTASCM, which contain the orders for 1557-1562. During this period, the procession began at 8:00 a.m. instead of 8:30.

34   Fl-2-3 (Diarii ceremoniali), 47-49 (Visconti, Gaspare: Disposizioni C.C., number 852), BCM.

35   *Codice* 1252 (Ceremoniale Spagnolo Milanese), 21r-24v, BTASCM.

36   Mark S. Weil, 'Devotion of the Forty Hours and Roman Baroque Allusions,' *Journal of the Warburg and Courtauld Institutes* XXXVII (1974), 221-222.

37   'Quando si va, a Santo Stefano, Protasio, et Ambrosio, detto di sopra, essendo buon tempo si canta *terce* in Duomo tanto che si veste il ponti*fice* o vero altro in suo Luoco, e dopo messa si dicono *sext* e *none*s et la vigil compieta in essa chiesa, ultra lettor' ordinaria dette si saper' quelli della sua chiesa ancora.' *Metropolitana* LXXX-456 (Visite pastorali e documenti aggiunti), q. 20, ASDM.

38   *Libro delle litanie secondo l'ordine Sant'Ambrogio per la città di Milano* (Mediolani: al segno della Croce d'Oro, 1546), 1v-90r, Biblioteca Nazionale Braidense, Milano (hereafter BNBM).

39   *Registro di Lettere Ducali* 1553-1562, 96v-97v, BTASCM.

40   *Libro delle Litanie*, 4r-90r.

41   A short essay on the rise of the historical consciousness that spawned the production of such chronicles is found in Gary Ianziti, 'Patronage and the Production of History: The Case of Quattrocento Milan,' in *Patronage, Art and Society in Renaissance Italy* (Oxford: Clarendon Press, 1987), 299-311.

42   On the Imperial emblems, see Silvio Leydi, *Sub umbra imperialis aquilae*, 33-47.

43   See Roy Strong, *Art and Power: Renaissance Festivals 1450-1650* (Berkeley and Los

Angeles: University of California Press, 1984), 75-87.

44   See Leydi, *Sub umbra imperialis aquilae*, 137-143.

45   See Strong, *Art and Power*, 42-50. Also see the discussion in Ronald Lightbown, *Mantegna* (Berkeley and Los Angeles: University of California Press, 1986), 143-145. Some of the widely disseminated quattrocento studies include Livy's *Historia ab urbe condita*, Flavio Biondo's *Roma triumphans*, Roberto Valerio's *De re militari*, Francesco Colonna's *Hypnerotomachia Poliphili*, and Petrarch's *I Trionfi*.

46   The series is now housed in the Royal Collection at Hampton Court Palace. According to Nino Pirotta, *Music and Theatre from Poliziano to Monteverdi*, trans. by Karen Eales (Cambridge: Cambridge University Press, 1982), I, 40-41, six of the panels were used as part of the scenery for four *drammi mescidati* performed at the Mantuan court in 1501.

47   Lightbown, *Mantegna*, 143-145.

48   Strong, *Art and Power*, 46.

49   Appian, *Roman History*, trans. by Horace White (New York: Macmillan Company, 1912), I, 506-509.

50   Plutarch, *Lives of Dion and Brutus, Timoleon and Aemilius Paulus*, trans. by Bernadotte Perrin (Cambridge: Harvard University Press, 1943), VI, 442.

51   Laurana's *Triumph of Alfonso the Great of Naples* (1443), Castello Aragonese, Naples, also depicts the trumpeters at the head of the processing body. According to Robert Payne, *The Roman Triumph* (London, New York, and Toronto: Abelard-Schuman, Ltd., 1962), 22-23, the tradition of placing the trumpeters at the head of the triumphal procession may have been derived from the Etruscan triumph.

52   Appian, *Roman History*, I, 506-507, describes a group of singing and dancing musicians in the triumphal procession of Scipio Africanus, and Plutarch, *Lives*, I, 446-447, comments that the processing troops sang 'divers songs,' 'paeans of victory,' and 'hymns in praise of the achievements of Aemilius' during the triumphs of Aemilius Paulus over Greece. In addition, Payne, *The Roman Triumph*, 28-40, notes that chants and songs were sung by the marching troops in the triumphs of Romulus, Lucretius Trecipitenus, and Aulus Cornelius Cossus.

53   'Ma ritorniamo al Sacro Imperadore// che come giunse drento della porte// si sentiva uno strepito a furore// digente per vedere che coron forte// gridando Imperio, Imperio con gran core// picholi e grandi vechi dognisorte// con festa suoni e canti tutta via// che mai fu vista tanta legia via . . . // Ma ritorniamo al Sacro Imperador// che non si dimoro troppo in quel loco// in verso del Castel con grande honore// con suoni e canti va apoco apoco// dove infinita allegreza e romore// faceva ciaschedun con festa e gioco// tanto era isuoni errumor delle genti// che lontan fu sentito miglia venti . . .' Fiorentino, *La entrata che ha fatta il sacro Carlo Quinto*, s.p.

54   Juan Cristóbal Calvete de Estrella, *El felicísimo viaje del muy alto y muy poderoso Príncipe Don Felipe* (Anvers: Martin Nucio, 1552; reprinted Madrid: Sociedad de Bibliófilos Españoles, 1930), I, 67.

55   Appian, *Roman History*, I, 506-507.

56   Plutarch, *Lives*, VI, 442-443.

57   Alonso de Santa Cruz, *Crónica del Emperador Carlos V* (1551; printed in Madrid: Caracas, Patronato de Húerfanos de Intendencia é Intervención Militare, 1925), 244.

58   'Con questa ordine poi che signor Altezza fu arrivata alla Porta della Città, il castello cominciò una buona salva, et i Trombetti a sonare.' Alberto de Nobili Volterano, *La triomphale entrata del serenissimo prence di Spagna nell'inclitta città di Melano* (Melano: Antonio Borgo, 1548), s.p.

59   Landolfo Verità, *L'entrata in Milano di Don Ferrante Gonzaga* (Milano: Antonio Borgo,

1546), s.p.

60   Bugati, *Histoire universale*, 898.

61   See the discussion in Payne, *The Roman Triumph*, 34-52. Payne suggests that this tradition was introduced by Lucius Taquinius, who held such ceremonies in the temple of Julius Capitolanus.

62   'Dismonta CESAR da Cavallo intento// Pieno di Religione con Fede tanta// E à passo à passo inanzi và contento// (Et nel viso li danno, l'acqua Santa)// Qui non si vede, un cor che Si stia lento// Per che si sona parla s'ode, e canta// Tanti stormenti di soave sono// Ch'in fino al Cielo, ne ribomba il Tuono.// Giunto al'Altar del Sacrificio vero// Che rimembra di Christo, i Santi voti// CARLO s'inchina, con il cor Sincero// Con questi Imperiali Santi, e Devoti// E'en mezo al Concistor, del Sacro Clero,// Et de la Fede, nostra i Sacerdotes// Sente Cantar le Ceremonie noue,// Et possi a ringratiar, l'eterno Giove.' Albicante, *Trattato del'intrar in Milano*, s.p.

63   Calvete, *El felicísimo viaje*, I, 70. Santa Cruz, *Crónica*, 247, remarks that instruments accompanied the voices, but does not specifically identify the instruments.

64   'Et dismontato al Duomo, gli furo dal primiero cantate le oratione, e fatte le ceremonie, che fogliono farsi in simili entrate et i responsi fur cantati in Musica. Alle quali Signor Altezza stette sempre con gran devotione.' Volterano, *La triomphale entrata*, s.p.

65   'Et dentro il Domo se ne va devoto// Piena di vera fede e Religione// Et con gran core à Dio porge il voto// Alzando verso il ciel sue menti bone// Non v'era in Domo, un cantocino voto// Mà pieno et colmo tutto di persone// Et ogn'uno stava attento, col desio// Veder un Re cosi devoto a Dio.// Da tutto'l Clero con sincero core// La ceremonie fur cantata e detto// Et le gratie rendute al ver Fattore// Con le voce mantali be perfette// Il Re si volge poi, à uscir di fore// Con quelli genti di sua corte elette// E rese à Dio, le gratie, incesi, e odori.' Giovanni Alberto Furibondo Albicante, *Al gran Maximiliano d'Austria archiduca. Intrada di Milano di Don Philippo d'Austria, Re di Spagna* (Venetia: Marcolini, 1549), s.p.

66   Verità, *L'entrata in Milano di Don Ferrante Gonzaga*, s.p.

67   'Et per aventura quello altro Signore fu altra volta anche egli con festa e con canti solennemente ricevuto.' Verità, *L'entrata in Milano di Don Ferrante Gonzaga*, s.p. This sentence follows a short description of D'Avalos's funeral, which had been held only a few days before.

68   Fiorentino, *La entrata che ha fatto il sacro Carlo Quinto*, s.p.

69   Burigozzi, *Cronaca milanese*, 513-514. For the convenience of the reader, pagination of the latter publication is given here.

70   Volterano, *La triomphale entrata*, s.p.; Albicante, *Intrada di Milano di Don Philippo d'Austria*, s.p.; Calvete, *El felicísimo viaje*, I, 71-89; and Bugati, *Histoire universale*, 961. According to Leydi, *Sub umbra imperialis aquilae*, 148-152, nearly the entirety of the year 1548 was devoted to the preparations for these events, and extraordinary sums were spent on them.

71   A *Te Deum* with organ responses and vocal solos evidently was among the most memorable musical items. It has been suggested that the description of these services as 'cerimonie alla spagnola' indicates that the Spanish and Milanese cappelle performed them together. See Guglielmo Barblan, 'La vita musicale in Milano nella prima metà del cinquecento,' *Storia di Milano* (Milano: Giovanni Treccani degli Alfieri, 1961), IX, 873, and Marcario Santiago Kastner, 'Il soggiorno italiano di Antonio e Juan de Cabezòn,' *L'Organo* I (January 1960), 60. Both authors refer to Carbonio Besozzi, *Cronaca Milanese*, ed. Cesari Malfatti (Trento, 1967). The Milanese singers who participated were likely those of the royal ducal chapel of Santa Maria dell Scala in Milan.

72 Higinio Anglés, *La Musica en la corte de Carlos V* in *Monumentos de la Música Española* II (Barcelona: Casa Provincial de Caridad Imprenta-Escuela, 1944), 107-109. Also see Kastner, 'Il soggiorno italiano,' 58-61.

73 Moscatello is recorded as a musician at the Milanese court of Ferrante Gonzaga in 1548 by Besozzi, *Cronaca milanese*, 15. According to Raineri, *Pompe*, s.p., Moscatello also participated in the carnevale entertainments at the Milanese court in February 1553. On other documents that place Moscatello at the court between 1542 and 1553, see Chapter 5 below.

74 Borrono is identified as a lutenist at the Milanese court in the preface to Pietro Paolo Borrono, *Intavolatura di lauto* (Venezia: Girolamo Scotto, 1548). However, his name appears in numerous Milanese registri and diplomatic documents issued between the years 1535 and 1556, where he is variously identified as a Milanese soldier and a special agent of Charles V. It is quite evident from the tone and content of these documents that he was serving as a spy. See Chapter 5 below.

75 Borrono, *Intavolatura di lauto*.

76 Calvete, *El felicísimo viaje*, I, 81-85.

77 On the content of the *Intavolatura di lauto*, see Chapter 5 below.

78 Calvete, *El felicísimo viaje*, I, 81-85.

79 The five viola da gambists, more commonly known as the 'five Cremonesi,' included Gabrieli Cherubelli, Gian Battista Cherubelli, Giacomo Philippo Cherubelli, Antonio Maria il Tuono, and Gabriele Sacco, ' The archival documents indicate that they were hired by Henry II in 1547. '. . .che già 4 anni sono al servitio de francesi in corte del Re per sonatore di viola.' *Cancelleria dello Stato di Milano* 135 (1551 ottobre 16-31), 302v, ASM.

80 On 8 November 1554 Thimodeo, who is identified as a Milanese gambist, applied for and was granted permission to serve at the French court. On 9 November 1554 he was granted a safe-conduct for travel to France with the five Cremonese violists. See Chapter 5 below.

81 Calvete, *El felicísimo viaje*, I, 76 and 89, and Volterano, *La triomphale entrata*, s.p. Interestingly enough, a letter from one Signor Elfanzina dated 19 August 1548 in Asti specifically requested that one of Baldessare Castiglione's works be performed for the prince. *Potenze sovrane* 4, fasciolo 2, ASM. Joseph E. Gillet, 'Was Secchi's *Gl'Inganni* performed before Philip of Spain?' *Modern Language Notes* XXXV (1920), 395-401 has successfully demonstrated that *L'Interesse* was the work by Secco performed. Although Calvete does not identify this series of *intermedi* as accompanying Secco's play, he does comment that a room in the palace was constructed especially for them. This information supports the assertion that the *intermedi* described by Calvete accompanied Secco's *L'Interesse* because the surviving archival documentation regarding the preparations clearly indicates that a room in the palace was reconstructed for Secco's play. *Potenze sovrane* 4, fasciolo 2, ASM. Such an assertion is further supported by the fact that Secco's play, like the *intermedi* described by Calvete, is set in Venice. The chancery correspondence regarding the final preparations for Secco's *L'Interesse* survives in the busta *Cancelleria dello Stato di Milano* 91 (1548 dicembre) *Cancelleria dello Stato di Milano* 93 (1548 non datato), ASM.

82 Calvete, *El felicísimo viaje*, I, 74-75. The music of this prologue included vocal selections accompanied by the vihuela. Jean Jacquot, 'Panorama des Fêtes et Cérémonies du Règne,' *Fêtes et Cérémonies au temps de Charles Quint* (Paris: Editions du Centre National de la Recherche Scientifique, 1960), II, 443, also provides a short synopsis of the account recorded in Calvete.

83   According to Calvete, *El felicísimo viaje*, I, 65-66, Mercury was depicted on the principal arch used to decorate the entrance to the ducal palace.

84   Calvete, *El felicísimo viaje*, I, 76, and Jacquot, 'Panorama des Fêtes,' 443.

85   *Potenze sovrane* 4, fascicolo 2, ASM.

86   'Pareva una battaglia in ordinanza// La prima e perfetta imbandigione// Tutta dorata d'oro asimiliglianza// Di quelli che san far le cose bone// Hor si comincia di voltar la danza// Et non si balla a suono di trombone// Et l'ordine facea si bella mostra// Con si vedi in qualche ornata giostra . . .' Albicante, *Intrada di Milano di Don Philippo d'Austria*, s.p.

87   'Suonan le trombe ad'alta voce orrenda// Et tantara a tantara ch'ogni s'affronti// Quivi si menan colpi senza emenda// dandoli sopra i petti, e su le fronte . . .' Albicante, *Intrada di Milano di Don Philippo d'Austria*, s.p.

88   Fiorentino, *La entrata che ha fatto il sacro Carlo Quinto*, s.p.

89   'Quivi con gran letitia quanti// et con amore et carita infinita// stettono quatro di in suoni e canti// e con gran festa di corte bandita// con balli e torniamenti, e giochi tanti// che mai tal cosa fu visto or sentita// che qua, chi la, chi fu che qui andava// che balla o canta, e chi lieto mangiava.' Fiorentino, *La entrata che ha fatto il sacro Carlo Quinto*, s.p.

90   'Ovunque si senton risonar stormenti// Che l'Armonia per, dal sommo choro// Questo apparato, no s'estende incharte// Che non convien lasar, la maggior parte . . .// Tutte le fiffe, con l'erranti stelle.' Albicante, *Trattato del'intrar in Milano di Carlo V*, s.p.

91   'In questa corte Imperialmente apparata, alloggiò esso Imperadotore, facendosi per tutta la città allegrezza di campanile, di trombe, di piffari, di fuochi, e d'artiglieria, per non dir delle salve del castello, delle feste, de' banchetti, delle danze, de' torniamente e d'altro.' Bugati, *Histoire universale*, 899-900.

92   For an overview of the themes that dominated Italian progressions of the sixteenth century, see Bonner Mitchell, *The Majesty of State: Triumphal Progressions of Foreign Sovereigns in Renaissance Italy 1494-1600* (Firenze: Leo S. Olschki, 1986). Leydi, *Sub umbra imperialis aquilae*, 49-182, articulates the individual issues that defined each of the Milanese progressions of Charles V.

93   Fiorentino, *La entrata che ha fatto il sacro Carlo Quinto*, s.p., and Burigozzi, *Cronaca*, 513. Also see Leydi, *Sub umbra imperialis aquilae*, 53.

94   Fiorentino, *La entrata che ha fatto il sacro Carlo Quinto*, s.p.

95   Gorse, 'Between Empire and Republic,' 193-200.

96   Albert Dunning, *Die Staatsmotette 1480-1555*, 147-149, and 333.

97   *Potenze sovrane* 1, ASM.

98   Mitchell, *The Majesty of State*, 175.

99   These arches featured statues symbolizing the rivers of Lombardy, paintings of ancient Roman leaders, and statues of Victory respectively. Although Albicante, *Trattato del'intrar in Milano di Carlo V*, s.p., indicates that the third of the arches was placed 'near' the Porta Ticinese, Mitchell, *The Majesty of State*, 176, has suggested its specific location to be in the Contrada degli Orefici.

100   Albicante, *Trattato del'intrar in Milano di Carlo V*, s.p. and Bugati, *Histoire universale*, 898. Also see Mitchell, *The Majesty of State*, 175-176, which provides a summary of the decorations.

101   Payne, *The Roman Triumph*, 44-45, discusses such use of equestrian statues in the triumph of Papirius Cursor.

102   Albicante, *Trattato del'intrar in Milano di Carlo V*, s.p.

103   See Nanie Bridgman, 'La participation musicale a l'entrée de Charles Quint a Cambrai,' *Fêtes et ceremonies au temps de Charles Quint in les fêtes de la renaissance*, ed. Jean Jacquot (Paris, 1960) , II, 235-254. Also see Dunning, *Die Staatsmotette*, 333.

104   Translation by Laverne J. Wagner. See Pierre de Manchicourt, *Opera Omnia* VI in *Corpus mensurabilis musicae* 55, ed. Laverne J. Wagner (Rome: American Institute of Musicology, 1984), XVII.

105   Calusco, editor. *Mutetarum.*

106   Calusco, ed., *Mutetarum*, number 21. Housed in the Library of Congress, Washington DC.

107   See Chapter 6 below.

108   Volterano, *La triomphale entrata*, s.p.

109   ' . . .con la proportion dupla allegrava l'occhio di riguardanti non altrimenti, che l'ottava nella Musica ampiamente diletta l'orecchia di che ascolta.' Volterano, *La triomphale entrata*, s.p. His description of this arch resembles that of the arch constructed for Philip II's 1549 entry into Antwerp. See William Eisler, 'Celestial Harmonies and Hapsburg Rule: Levels of Meaning in a Triumphal Arch for Philip II in Antwerp,' *Triumphal Celebrations and the Rituals of Statecraft in Papers in Art History from the Pennsylvania State University* IV/1 (University Park: The Pennsylvania State University Press, 1990), 332-356. However, Volterano's account is verified by the Spanish record of Calvete, *El felicísimo viaje*, I, 60, which is also summarized in Jacquot, 'Panorama des Fêtes,' 443. Also see Mitchell, *The Majesty of State*, 183-184.

110   Albicante, *Intrada di Milano di Don Philippo d'Austria*, s.p. Also see Calvete, *El felicísimo viaje*, I, 56-57, and Mitchell, *The Majesty of State*, 184.

111   The Mantuan progression occurred approximately one month after the entry into Milan. See Dunning, *Die Staatsmotette*, 265-266, where an excerpt from pages 256-257 of Ulloa's *Vita dell'invitissimo e sacratissimo Imperator Carlo V* is reproduced.

112   Calvete, *El felicísimo viaje*, I, 100-113.

113   Dunning, *Die Staatsmotette*, 265-267 and 334.

114   Frank Dobbins, *Music in Renaissance Lyons* (Oxford: Clarendon Press, 1992), 181 and 226.

115   *Motetti del Fiore* IV (Lyons: Jacques Moderne, 1539), folios 47-48. Housed in the Bayerische Staatsbibliothek, München.

Chapter 5

Instrumental Music and Musicians under the Early Governors

There are no extant rosters for the court chapel of Francesco II Sforza, but its organization and character can be reconstructed from the numerous state papers, benefice registers, and fiscal books of the Sforzesco in the Archivio di Stato in Milan, as well as from surviving notarial documents in the same archive. These documents indicate that Francesco II employed a number of trumpeters, pifferi,[1] and tamborini,[2] the occasional lutenist and organist, and several singers at his court. The extant sources further demonstrate that the new ducal chapels at Sant'Ambrogio in Vigevano and Santa Maria della Scala in Milan assumed much of the responsibility for the ducal ceremonial, and, as a result, the activities of Francesco's private court chapel were inextricably interwoven with those of the ducal chapels at Santa Maria della Scala and Sant'Ambrogio. Although the patterns of patronage established under Francesco II served as a general model for the Italian governors that followed him, each adapted the design and function of the court chapel to his own personal taste and individual diplomatic training.

After possession of the Duchy of Milan reverted to the Spanish crown in 1535, Charles V appointed a series of resident governors to act on his behalf in Milan, and the city's status was reduced, in effect, to that of an Imperial fiefdom. The basic system of government instituted under the Sforza was retained, with only minor changes in the infrastructure to accommodate the new representatives of the Spanish monarchy. At the outset, the governors themselves were selected from among the Italian aristocracy, with particular preference given to cavalieri who had ably served the Empire on the field of battle and clergymen who were regarded as sympathetic to Hapsburg interests. Thus, Milan's first three governors, Captain Antonio de Leyva (1536), Cardinal Marino Ascanio Caracciolo (1537-1538), and Alfonso D'Avalos, Marchese del Vasto (1538-1546) were, at least on the surface, quite typical of the appointees who occupied the Palazzo Ducale during the sixteenth century. De Leyva and D'Avalos had acquitted themselves successfully as commanders in the Imperial forces on both Italian and foreign soil, while Caracciolo, who received his early ecclesiastical and ambassadorial training in the retinue of the Sforza family, had served Charles V in a string of minor Imperial appointments of increasing political significance.[3] Milan's fourth governor, Ferrante Gonzaga, who brought extensive military and diplomatic experience to the position, sought to control movement and access to the city by renovating the city center, enclosing the city inside a defensive wall, and enacting numerous regulations regarding public conduct. By surrounding himself with non-Milanese appointees, albeit Italian ones, and conducting business in an autonomous manner more suitable to a Mantuan prince, Ferrante succeeded in alienating the Milanese aristocracy to such a degree that, with the exception of his short-lived successor Cristoforo Madruzzo, the Hapsburg princes thereafter studiously avoided Italian appointees, instead favoring Spanish aristocrats who would promote a military and political agenda consonant with Milan's status as an Imperial fiefdom.[4]

In the early gubernatorial culture, instrumental musicians played increasingly diverse aesthetic and social roles. Instrumental musicians, once secondary in status to the singers at the Milanese court, now comprised the core of the court ensemble, and provided all the musical services not already fulfilled by the eight-member ducal chapel at Santa Maria della Scala. As a result, their contributions extended well beyond playing fanfares and other improvised wind music for civic announcements, processions, and dances at the court. Since the duties of the ducal chapel at Santa Maria della Scala were limited to the sacred sphere, many of the court instrumentalists, as will be seen in the succeeding chapter, actually doubled as singer-actors for court entertainments. Still others achieved an internationally recognized level of virtuosity on a particular instrument, thus rendering themselves, perhaps unwittingly, serviceable pawns in the high-stakes game of diplomacy. Given adequate talent, versatility, and tenacity, the instrumental musician who gained entry to the court in sixteenth-century Milan possessed the potential to translate his musical skills into celebrity.

The court had neither the need nor the means to employ all of the city's reputable players. Fortunately, however, the performance of music at local dances and entertainments was a lucrative business in Milan. Many Milanese musicians eschewed the gubernatorial retinue, instead taking to the streets, where they made themselves available for hire by local aristocrats and middle-class merchants seeking to imitate the entertainments associated with the court in their own residences and hostels. The life of the freelance musician was admittedly dangerous, and its history in Milan has been richly preserved precisely because of the peril involved. Serving as a musician at a local party that might well disintegrate into brawl was clearly a pale imitation of the courtly musical venture. Yet the freelance musician forged an identity within middle-class society that was parallel to that of the court musician. This identity was driven by the musician's ability to provide a unique service in return for monetary compensation and potential access to the shifting aristocratic power base. In the end, it might even facilitate his entry into the Milanese court itself. Moscatello, sixteenth-century Milan's most famous virtuoso, successfully positioned himself before the court as the proverbial 'hired gun' whose 'package deal' included his own ensemble of local musicians.

In short, instrumental music thrived in sixteenth-century Milan. It showed little respect for class distinctions, serving much the same function within various levels of Milanese society. Unfortunately, however, much of the literature performed, as might be expected, was transmitted through the oral rather than the written tradition, for only a handful of prints transmitting lute music by Milanese composers survives. Yet the archival sources containing information on instrumental music in sixteenth-century Milan are rich and diverse, and these make possible the successful reconstruction of instrumental activity in Milan, particularly during the middle of the century.

Instrumentalists in the Court Chapel of Francesco II Sforza

During the early years of Francesco II's tenure, the court employed eight trumpeters, each of whom received a monthly salary of 20 lire.[5] On 3 October 1525, for example, the eight trumpeters, designated only as the 'company of trumpeters,' were paid their salary of 20 lire for the previous month of September. They were listed as follows:

Jo. Angelo de Corrigio	Alvisio Marliano
Jo. Petro de Septimo	Alexandro Oldono
Georgio Pisono	Francesco Pisono
Olivero Marliano	Georgio Cattaneo[6]

An analysis of the surviving documentation from the fifty-eight year period spanning 1480 to 1538 indicates not only that the number of trumpeters serving the court was drastically reduced during that time, but also that their salaries were retrenched. In 1480 fifteen trumpeters were serving the court of Milan at a salary of 288 lire per annum. Two of these, designated as 'pro extraordinario,' received an additional sum of 100 lire per year, presumably for extra services rendered.[7] In 1525 only eight positions for trumpeters remained, and each of these was funded at a level of 240 lire per annum. By 9 October 1529 the number of trumpeters had been further reduced to five, for three trumpeters listed on the aforementioned document of 3 October 1525, Jo. Angelo de Corrigio, Olivero Marliano, and Alvisio Marliano, seem to have passed on or been otherwise eliminated.[8] However, this further reduction was likely temporary, since Olivero Marliano resurfaces in the documents of 1530 as a replacement for the 'civic' trumpeter Jacobo da Montebello[9] and a seventh trumpeter named Franzotto is first mentioned that same year as well.[10] In fact, the 1529 reduction in numbers appears to indicate a gradual change in both personnel and appointment types, rather than a reduction in the overall number of trumpeters. A document from 1538 bears this theory out, for it demonstrates that the eight trumpeters had been divided into groups comprised of two court trumpeters and six civic trumpeters with respective salaries of 144 lire and 80 lire per annum:

Trumpeters of the Most Illustrious Signor Marchese	
Agostino Mazadro	L144
Baptista Birago	L144
Other trumpeters of Milan	
Petro da Septimo	L80
Georgio Pisono	L80
Olivero Marliano	L80
Georgio Cattaneo	L80
Camillo de Juliani	L80
Francesco Pisono	L80[11]

The official division of the eight trumpeters into court and civic statuses and the accompanying reduction in annual salaries, though suggested as early as 1530 by Olivero Marliano's reappointment as a 'civic' trumpeter, actually occurred well after

Francesco II's death.   On 2 January 1537, governor Mario Ascanio Caracciolo awarded each of the eight 60 lire in remuneration for their services during the last quarter of the year 1536.[12] The document in which this payment is recorded makes no distinction between trumpeters serving the community and those serving the court. By June 1537, however, the trumpeters had been divided into two distinct groups. Six of the eight, designated as the civic trumpeters, were awarded a stipend of 80 lire for the entire year.[13] Two others from the 1536 group, namely Battista Birago and Agostino Mazadro, reappear in the chancery registers as court trumpeters on 17 December 1538, at which time they were paid 144 lire, which comprised their salary for the current year.[14] Thus, the official division of the trumpeters into civic and court groups can be dated to 1537.

The divided statuses in use by 1537 may reveal something of the nature of the 'pro extraordinario' designation found in the salary rolls as early as 1480. During the reign of Charles V only the court trumpeters and selected drummers were entrusted with the dangerous responsibility of delivering official documents abroad.[15] Since the documents from the early 1530s also contain numerous references to unnamed trumpeters who delivered diplomatic documents,[16] it appears that the 1537 distinction of 'court trumpeter' was intended to financially recognize those already burdened with the ambassadorial responsibilities that initiated the 'pro extraordinario' designation. Moreover, the newly designated court trumpeters clearly served as an integral part of the official   retinue, and traveled with the court on occasion, taking on such responsibilities as those fulfilled by Francesco and Franzotto, two trumpeters in the service of Francesco II who accompanied the Milanese delegation to Venice in October of 1530.[17] In contrast, the civic trumpeters were primarily responsible for the issuing of civic proclamations regarding special activities and newly enacted laws. These were announced by fanfare and read from the steps of the Broletto or town hall in the Piazza Mercanti, which both marked the route from the Duomo to the Castello Sforzesco and was adjacent to the central market. This ostentatious and memorable method of distributing information to the public was employed increasingly during the Hapsburg years as a means of informing the Milanese citizenry.[18] Events of great ceremonial significance, such as the annual Corpus Christi procession from the Duomo to the basilica of Sant'Ambrogio, moreover, were pre-announced in multiple locations. These locations were usually selected according to their architectural prominence within a particular porta, or district, of the city.[19] The civic trumpeter, ensconced within the prescribed architectural space from which the announcement was made, functioned primarily as a muse in the prologue to the panoply of church and state. Yet, as will be seen below, he was occasionally called to participate in the event itself as well.

Governor Caracciolo's 1537 division of the trumpeters into civic and court types appears to have resulted not only from economic and utilitarian necessity, but also from a calculated decision to abandon the patronage style of the Sforza, with its focus upon excessive musical and pictorial display. Upon Francesco I Sforza's accession in 1450, six trumpeters were in the employ of the state, and these were designated as trumpeters of the community.[20] Although Francesco I initially used the designations of civic and court trumpeters,[21] references to 'ducal' or court trumpeters gradually prevailed in the registers, while those to the civic trumpeters eventually faded from view. By May 1450 the registers report twelve positions for ducal trumpeters, and by 1463 these had been expanded to include eighteen. The registers for 1469 list twenty ducal trumpeters at a salary of 22 lire 18 soldi per month,[22] and these twenty receive frequent mention in descriptions of the Sforza ceremonial.[23] In returning to the original plan of six civic trumpeters, the officers of the Spanish crown hailed a new era in which court ceremony, which was directed by the activities of crown-appointed governors, was to assume a somewhat diminished role.

Before this gradual shift in designations, Francesco II's eight trumpeters, whether designated as civic or court, enjoyed an equal and more competitive salary in exchange for which each fulfilled his assigned musical and diplomatic duties. Every new trumpeter apparently was even provided with his own regulation instrument at the outset of his appointment, and these were often acquired abroad. On 12 March 1535, for example, the trumpeter Franzotto, who was appointed at the Milanese court between 1529 and 1530,[24] traveled to Bologna to arrange for the construction of a trumpet to be used by an unspecified new trumpeter:

> . . .And I pay some money to Franzotto, one of your trumpets, so that he might have a trumpet constructed for the new trumpeter . . .'[25]

Franzotto was provided 50 scudi for the new trumpet and 18 scudi for the trip to Bologna in order to acquire it.[26] Such glimpses into daily musical life at the Milanese court of Francesco II are rare, but they do point toward the seriousness with which he maintained the quality of music and ceremony at the Milanese court.

Francesco II employed not only trumpeters, but also pifferi and other instrumentalists; the practice is discussed in a notice from the Provost at Santa Maria della Scala to Francesco II Sforza dated 21 May 1533.[27] Unfortunately, however, none of the pifferi are identified by name in the surviving documents. This is not surprising, as the ratio of trumpeters to pifferi was six to three in 1450 and twenty to four in 1469,[28] thus suggesting that the Sforza traditionally employed far fewer pifferi than they did trumpeters. Despite the numerous general references to tamborini in the documents surviving from Francesco II's reign, moreover, Giovanni Antonio di Piuro, a tamborino stationed at the Castle of Musso in 1532,[29] is the only one mentioned by name. Details about the services performed by the other instrumentalists listed in the documents are not frequently provided either, and information on their personal lives is equally rare. On 10 December 1533, for example, Francesco de Cani and Antonio Maria Vesconte, identified only as instrumentalists at the court, were granted possession of the vacant dockyard of San Jacobo de la Cerea.[30] However, the purpose for which the gift was intended is not disclosed. In any case, Antonio Maria Vesconte was likely a relative of Ludovico Vesconte, a famous virtuoso cornettist from Milan better known as 'Moscatello' who directed the court instrumental ensemble under governor Ferrante Gonzaga (1546-1554).[31]

At least one lutenist, Pietro Paolo Borrono, was present at court during the final year of Francesco II's tenure. Borrono, a spy who served Carlo V in Milan between 1535 and 1554,[32] first appears in the documents just shortly before Francesco

II's death on 1 November 1535. At that time he requested exemption from condemnation by the Senate and a safe-conduct that allowed him to move freely in and out of Milan for an unspecified time. The safe-conduct itself is the first of several requested by Borrono to facilitate various operations that he supervised on behalf of Charles V. Its connection to an exemption from condemnation seems to have arisen from an altercation in which Borrono was involved over a debt for some Milanese property which the court had assisted him in purchasing.[33] It is unclear just how much Borrono contributed to musical life at Francesco II's court. His own collection of lute music was not issued until 1548, but two pavanes by him, 'Malcontenta' and 'Gombertina,' appeared in the *Intabolatura de leuto de diversi autori* published by Milanese printer Giovanni Antonio Castiglione in 1536.[34] The collection, which is dedicated to Battista Visconti, also contains compositions by Francesco da Milano, Giovanni Giacomo Albuzio, Alberto da Mantova, and Paolo da Milano.[35] As the earliest extant print of polyphonic music issued by a Milanese printer, the *Intabolatura de leuto* attests to the city's continued interest in music for lute and viola da gamba. This Milanese predilection for string music can be traced back to the reign of Francesco II's father Ludovico, when at least two or three string musicians were regularly in the employ of the Sforza court.[36] Borrono's presence in 1535 may reflect Francesco II's attempt to economize by employing an individual who might engage in courtly pursuits while also serving the empire's political agenda.

Francesco II's principal organist was Egedio Marliano, a sacristan at the church of Santa Maria delle Grazie in Milan. Egedio first appears in the documents for 5 through 9 December 1531, at which time he accompanied several singers from the newly expanded ducal chapel at Santa Maria della Scala in Milan to the newly organized ducal chapel at Sant'Ambrogio in Vigevano, presumably to participate in services for the feast of the Immaculate Conception. Egidio's trip to Vigevano lasted six days, for which he was awarded a travel remuneration of 10 lire and 10 soldi.[37] Although the documents do not specify his exact role in the festivities, additional records confirm that the position of organist at Sant'Ambrogio in Vigevano was not founded until 1533,[38] thus suggesting that Egidio was filling in there until such time as the official organ position could be created. Two months prior to the founding of the organ position at Vigevano, in fact, Egidio received another salary payment of 50 lire for services as organist from the court treasury. Although the document does not specify where Egidio had been playing, the list on which the payment is found contains several other names, including one Stephano, a chaplain at Sant'Ambrogio in Vigevano.[39] Further evidence that Egidio was serving as organist at Sant'Ambrogio in Vigevano at least part of the time is found in an autograph letter dated 25 July 1531 that was written by Egidio in Vigevano to Francesco II in Milan:

> Most Illustrious and Excellent Signor and My Patron
> In the past days I've been told by the Reverend Monsignor our bishop and my patron that I should return the organ to that place where it was. And, moreover, your Excellency told me this at the proper time in order that I advised your Most Illustrious Lordship that I executed all that which your Excellency had planned upon your departure. I do not fail, however, to serve the church with the little organetto

until such time that you will provide for the repair of that other as is your desire. Not the least among the faithful servants and subjects of your Excellency, Priest Victorio and I commend ourselves to the good grace of your Excellency and with faithful hearts we pray to God for that which is able to achieve the favorable desire and every perpetual happiness which benefits. Amen. In Vigevano on 25 July 1531.

From Your Most Illustrious Excellency's most faithful subject and servant Priest Egidio, musician and organist[40]

No further mention of Egidio is found until 16 March 1560, when the deputies of the *Fabbrica* of the Duomo of Milan informed Carlo Borromeo that they had intended to hire the reputable Egidio of Sant'Ambrogio to play their new organ, but, unfortunately, he had recently passed on.[41] The pay registers of the Duomo, in fact, indicate that Egidio already had been employed temporarily as the Duomo organist for nearly ten months prior to his passing.[42]

Three other musicians are mentioned in the documents, but the services performed by each remain unclear. Two of these, Jachetto and Il Pretino, contacted the office of the *biade* requesting payment of their salaries on 4 May 1532. Il Pretino is likely Egidio, the ducal organist mentioned above who performed for court functions at Santa Maria delle Grazie and Sant'Ambrogio in Vigevano. Jachetto may be Jachet de Berchem, a composer loosely associated with northern Italy during the final years of Francesco II's reign. Although Berchem's exact whereabouts during the early 1530s are unknown, he made several visits to Venice and his works began appearing in collections issued by Venetian printers around 1538. The archival and musical evidence unearthed to date reveals that Berchem maintained some connections to Francesco's Este relatives that cannot yet be fully explained.[43] Thus, the possibility that he was employed at the Milanese court during the early years of his career cannot yet be ruled out. The third musician mentioned is Monzino, who appears to have been either some sort of maestro di cappella or the director of the court band. On 25 February 1531, Milanese court treasurer Hieronymo Brebbia notified Francesco II Sforza that he had attempted to pay Monzino the provision set aside for the musicians as ordered, but had been unable to do so because the order of payment had not been properly counter-signed.[44] Nothing further can be found in the documents regarding the affair.

Instrumental Musicians at the Court of Alfonso D'Avalos

The tenures of governors De Leyva (1536) and Caracciolo (1537-1538) were far too brief to have a measurable effect upon cultural life in sixteenth-century Milan. Neither governor, however, demonstrated a particular affinity for music. Caracciolo, in fact, appears to have been ultimately responsible for diminishing the salaries and visibility of the trumpeters' corps. The archival evidence indicates that the trumpeters who served Francesco II Sforza for the handsome remuneration of 20 lire per month continued to do so under De Leyva.[45] By June 1537, however, Caracciolo had divided the eight into six civic trumpeters and two court trumpeters with stipends of 80 lire[46] and 144 lire,[47] respectively.   Apparently, the newly designated civic trumpeters immediately protested and requested reinstatement of their previous status.[48]   In fact, trumpeters Joanedro Cozo and Giovanni Antonio Birago may even have resigned in indignation, for both musicians disappeared from the rosters sometime between January 1537, at which time all the court trumpeters were paid the customary salary for the remainder of the previous year, and June 1537, when the changes in status were officially applied to the salaries (See Table 5.1).   In any case, the protests of the civic trumpeters apparently went unheeded, as the new system of division instituted by Caracciolo was retained by his successor Alfonso d'Avalos, Marchese del Vasto, who served as governor of Milan from 1538 to 1546.   The initial furor over the matter, in fact, appears to have dissipated entirely, for the rosters from D'Avalos's tenure show no further changes in personnel among the trumpeters.[49]   Although only the civic trumpeters registered a formal objection to the change in status, the court trumpeters were also adversely affected.   They suffered a reduction in pay of over 100 lire per annum, despite the fact that they presumably continued to perform services similar to those assigned them by Francesco II Sforza.

Table 5.1 Rosters and annual salaries of trumpeters at the Milanese court 1536-1569

Court trumpeters 1535- 1537

Augustino Mazadro	L240
Battista Birago	L240
Georgio Cattaneo	L240
Giorgio Pisono	L240
Camillo di Giuliani	L240
Petro da Septimo	L240
Giovanni Antonio Birago	L240
Joanedro Cozo	L240

Court and civic trumpeters 1537-1548

Augustino Mazadro, court	L144
Battista Birago, court	L144
Georgio Cattaneo, civic	L80
Giorgio Pisono, civic	L80
C amillo di Giuliani, civic	L80
Petro da Septimo, civic	L80
Francesco Pisono, civic	L80
Olivero Marliano	L80

Court and civic trumpeters May 1549

Augustino Mazadro, court	L144
Battista Birago, court	L144
Georgio Cattaneo, civic	L80
Giorgio Pisono, civic	L80

Camillo di Giuliani, civic	L80
Petro da Septimo, civic	L80
Francesco Pisono, civic	L80
Bartolomeo Oldano, civic	L80

Court and civic trumpeters April 1550

Augustino Mazadro, court	L144
Battista Birago, court	L144
Georgio Cattaneo, civic	L80
Giorgio Pisono, civic	L80
Giovanni Andrea Pisono, civic	L80
Petro da Septimo, civic	L80
Francesco Pisono, civic	L80
Bartolomeo Oldano, civic	L80

Court and civic trumpeters October 1558

Augustino Mazadro, court	L144
Battista Birago, court	L144
Georgio Cattaneo, civic	L80
Hieronymo Pisono, civic	L80
Giovanni Andrea Pisono, civic	L80
Francesco Gariboldo, civic	L80
Francesco Pisono, civic	L80
Bartolomeo Oldano, civic	L80

Court and civic trumpeters February 1564

Augustino Mazadro, court	L144
Battista Birago, court	L144
Georgio Cattaneo, civic	L80
Giovanni Ambrogio Pisono, civic	L80
Giovanni Andrea Pisono, civic	L80
Francesco Garibaldo, civic	L80
Francesco Pisono, civic	L80
Francesco Garibaldo, civic	L80

Court and civic trumpeters March 1569

Augustino Mazadro, court	L144
Battista Birago, court	L144
Giovanni Rho, civic	L80
Giovanni Ambrogio Pisono, civic	L80
Giovanni Andrea Pisono, civic	L80
Francesco Garibaldo, civic	L80
Giovanni Andrea Samarata, civic	L80
Bartolomeo Oldano, civic	L80

Caracciolo obviously intended that the civic trumpeters be responsible for announcing proclamations via fanfares and playing for civic ceremonies, thus leaving the court trumpeters free to travel with the court and deliver sensitive documents abroad. The registers of ducal letters and missives for the years 1537 through 1562 contain numerous missives containing a notation that indicates where and by whom the civic missives were publicly read.[50] The delivery of them was invariably entrusted to a civic trumpeter, who frequently read the missive from the steps of the Broletto (town hall) in the Piazza Mercanti or at one of the porte that marked off the various districts of the city.

The two court trumpeters, Agostino Mazadro and Battista Birago, evidently received higher pay because their duties at the court included not only playing for court ceremonies and entertainments, but also transporting sensitive communiques, sometimes behind enemy lines. During D'Avalos's tenure, Battista Birago appears to have been especially active in the latter regard. In 1539, for example, an order was issued by the Milanese chancery mandating that he be supplied by the *biada* (provisioner) at Nizza with horses, grain, food, and other necessities during his stay in that city.[51] Further, an order for reimbursement dated 18 October 1544 indicates that Birago was paid 18 scudi for expenses incurred while transporting 'certain of our extremely important letters' from Torino.[52] In 1545 Birago is found traveling in north Italy near Como on two separate occasions. In the first instance, he was advanced cash from the treasuries in Pelizono and Mariano for trips to be made between those two cities and Como.[53] In the second, he was awarded a considerable sum from the *biada* at Pelizono and Mariano, presumably to pay for food and lodging while on an official mission in the Swiss canton of the Grisons:

> On 16 May 1545 from Genoa. A mandate to the Magistrate that he give license to Battista, trumpeter, to remove 100 lire from the cash holdings of the biada at Pelizono and Mariano. And to use them to operate in the jurisdiction of the Grisons gratis and without payment of bills . . .[54]

Although the exact purpose of these trips is intentionally unclear in the surviving account books, it is evident that Birago was transporting documents for the state. The chancery normally issued such orders only for officers of the court who were traveling on behalf of the Empire.

In addition to the civic and state trumpeters, D'Avalos apparently had access to the instrumental band of Moscatello, a virtuoso cornettist who rose to prominence as a musician of D'Avalos's successor, Ferrante Gonzaga. Moscatello's association with Ferrante Gonzaga has heretofore rested primarily in the historical chronicle of Cerbonio Besozzi, who identified Moscatello as a musician of Ferrante in the course of his account of Maximilian II of Austria's 1548 royal entry into Trent.[55] Moscatello was further described by contemporaries Cosimo Bartoli and Antonfrancesco Raineri as a virtuoso cornettist and director of a company of skilled instrumental musicians respectively,[56] and, in point of fact, the archival records bear these contemporary biographical statements out. The extant documents, which include not only chancery papers but also several autographs, reveal that Moscatello's Christian name was

Ludovico Visconte. He appears to have commanded a company of wind players, several of whom may have been relatives, that were contracted first by Alfonso D'Avalos, and then by Ferrante Gonzaga.

The earliest document connecting Moscatello to the Milanese court is an autograph letter to Alfonso D'Avalos dated 12 April 1543 in which the cornettist, who was then in Polesino, a small city near Mantua, on unspecified business, requested that D'Avalos allow Giovanni Petro of the notary to conduct some grain through Milan en route to the Po. According to Moscatello, he owed Giovanni Petro compensation for a favor, and was confident that D'Avalos, as his only patron, would act faithfully on his behalf.[57] Moscatello's confidence in D'Avalos's support in this affair is striking, and suggests that the cornettist commanded great respect at the Milanese court even during the earliest stages of his musical career. Unfortunately, however, Moscatello is not mentioned in the documents again until 1545, when he is listed among several individuals who reportedly had sold property to one messer Bernardino of the Compagnia of Santo Jacobo.[58] Yet he obviously remained at the Milanese court following the death of D'Avalos, for numerous documents recording his activities there survive from the years 1548 through 1553.

The nature of Moscatello's services to D'Avalos is not discussed in detail in the documents, and, as a result, they must be inferred from the extant archival information regarding the ducal ceremonial. The most auspicious public event sponsored by the Milanese court during D'Avalos's tenure was the royal entrance of Charles V in August 1541. The highlights of the Emperor's ten-day visit included both the royal entry itself and the baptism of D'Avalos's son Carlo, for whom the emperor stood as sponsor. The former event was marked by a processional entry through the streets of the city, a high mass in the Duomo, and a royal banquet at the adjacent Palazzo Ducale. Giovanni Alberto Furibondo Albicante's poetic chronicle of the entry notes that instruments were heard both during the Duomo mass and in the banquet hall, and, at one point, even identifies these instruments as winds.

> CAESAR dismounts from his horse, intent,
> Full of piety, with great faith,
> And step by step goes contentedly.
> (And they anoint his head with the sacred waters.)
> Here one does not see a sorrowful heart
> Because they play, speak, listen, and sing.
> Many instruments resound sweetly,
> And the tone reverberates to the skies . . .
> Resplendent is the court, the accommodations,
> Rooms, and halls; of gold brocade
> The tapestries on the floor; others of silver
> With delicately worked embroidery.
> Everywhere one hears the instruments resound
> With harmony that seems a sublime chorus.
> It is not possible to document this setting properly
> Because the greater part is not worth leaving [out].
> Having spoken [to] the whole grand court,

That unique splendor of the distinguished VAST(O) . . .
All the fifes, with the errant stars.[59]

D'Avalos undoubtedly sought to impress the emperor with the so-called 'splendors' offered by the Milanese court, and, consequently, Moscatello's band must have performed much of the secular music heard during the celebrations. As will be seen below, the ensemble is found among the musicians who participated in a number of other official events hosted by the Milanese court throughout the succeeding decade, including the 1548 entry of Maximilian II of Austria[60] and the carnival entertainments of 1553.[61]

D'Avalos's chief court musician, Vincenzo Ruffo, may have participated in the 1541 entry as well. Although Ruffo traditionally has been regarded as a maestro who contributed primarily to the development of the madrigal and sacred vocal genres, he must have had some professional experience as a gambist. His *Capricci in musica a tre . . .a commodo de virtuosi* (1564), which were published in Milan just shortly after he had been appointed maestro di cappello at the Duomo[62] betray more than a passing familiarity with the idiomatic characteristics of sixteenth-century stringed instruments. Thus, Ruffo likely contributed both vocally and instrumentally to musical life at the D'Avalos court during his brief one to two-year tenure.

Ruffo's short stay in Milan may have been due, in part, to Maria d'Aragona and Alfonso d'Avalos's comparative disinterest in musical pursuits in the face of their literary ones. The archival and printed evidence suggests, in fact, that their attentions in Milan were focused primarily upon the letterati available to them, including Pietro Aretino, Luca Contile, Niccolò Franco, Girolamo Muzio, Marcantonio Maioragio, and Giovanni Alberto Furibondo Albicante. An extant document surviving from D'Avalos's tenure in Milan reveals that even the revered lutenist Francesco da Milano, who spent the greater part of his career in Rome, was forced to resort to extreme measures in order to garner the support of the military commander. On 24 June 1542, Marguerite of Austria wrote to D'Avalos on behalf of Francesco da Milano, musician, and Gabriele Casato, doctor, requesting that they not be further impeded from taking possession of several small benefices that had been granted them by Pope Paul III. She enjoined D'Avalos to turn the matter over to the apostolic commission, a request which suggests that the Milanese state itself was partially responsible for the difficulties.[63] It is not clear where the benefices were located. Francesco da Milano previously had held a canonry at San Nazaro in Brolio and a prebend at San Arderico, but apparently renounced both of them in favor of his brother before marrying in 1538.[64]

Instrumental Musicians at the Court of Ferrante Gonzaga

D'Avalos's successor Ferrante Gonzaga apparently maintained the tradition of depending heavily upon brass and wind players. Two court and six civic trumpeters continued to serve in the city of Milan throughout their tenures. In addition, a number of trumpeters, fifers, and drummers were employed in the peripheral castles and fortresses, including a fifer and two drummers at the fortress in Milan, a fifer and two drummers at the castle in Piacenza, and a drummer at the castle of Novara. A special trumpeter also was assigned to the headquarters of the captain of justice,[65] and a trumpeter was provided to the infantry as well.[66] These appointments were essentially military in nature, and may have existed prior to Ferrante's ascension to the seat of governor. However, other efforts to improve conditions in the Milanese trumpet corps may be detected during Ferrante's tenure, and these suggest that he took more than a passing interest in the personal welfare of his musical employees. First of all, financial provisions, albeit meager, were made for the families of trumpeters who died in service. The heirs of civic trumpeters Olivero Marliano and Petro da Septimo, for example, collected 20 lire for the final quarter of service, despite that fact the entire quarter was not served in either case.[67] Secondly, the banners of the civic trumpeters were refurbished in 1551 under the supervision of Battista Birago.[68] Finally, alternate routes of travel and payment were designed for trumpeters facing potential harassment, interception, capture, and financial setback while serving as couriers for the Milanese state.[69]

Hoste da Reggio, Ferrante's principal singer-composer, was joined at the Milanese court by Moscatello and his band, which functioned as the core instrumental ensemble there between 1548 and 1554. Although the ensemble was paid from the state treasury during this period,[70] Moscatello evidently managed the band, acted as its chief negotiator, and exercised considerable influence over its membership. The surviving correspondence regarding the band is either addressed to him or makes direct reference to him, and its language often suggests that he invariably acted on behalf of the group.

The ensemble apparently traveled with the gubernatorial retinue and was featured regularly in court entertainments, where its members played a variety of roles. In 1548 the band presumably accompanied Ferrante Gonzaga to Trent, where it participated in the entertainments held at the Trivulzio palace, for the royal entry of Maximilian II, son of Ferdinand of Austria.[71] Nine of them also appeared in the *Dei poeti amorosi*, one of two pompe held in Milan during the carnival week of February 10 through 16 in 1553. According to Antonfrancesco Raineri, who attended the celebrations as a guest of Carlo Visconti, the nine members of Moscatello's band played the role of the muses during the entrata:

> There followed the nine muses, which were the excellent Moscatello with his company, the most exceptional musicians, each of which came playing musical instruments, the one diverse from the other.[72]

The ensemble's intense activity was cut short by Moscatello's death in late 1553 or early 1554, for references to it disappear from the documents after January 1554. Moreover, a supplication on behalf of Moscatello's wife and eight surviving children that requests relief from mounting debts accrued by them was submitted to the Milanese chancery on 11 May 1557,[73] and this confirms that his guidance had been absent from the ensemble for some time. However, Moscatello and his band are mentioned in at least ten Milanese archival documents surviving from the years 1551 to 1554, and these documents underscore both the professional trends and the ongoing concerns faced by Milanese musicians during the Ferrante's tenure as governor.

The most mundane of the ongoing concerns was the Milanese chancery's increasing lack of attention to the timely remuneration of the instrumental musicians in Ferrante's service. The problem seems to have become particularly acute in the year 1553, during which both the trumpeters[74] and Moscatello's corps[75] formally approached the chancery to request payment of salaries long overdue. A flurry of correspondence from the months of February and October 1553 between Ferrante Gonzaga and President Francesco Grasso regarding the payment of the trumpeters and wind players, respectively, reveals that several issues contributed to the difficulties, including Ferrante's failure to file a formal directive to pay, Grasso's reluctance to order payment from sums for which the monetary source was not clearly specified, and a shortage of funds itself.[76] In fact, after making repeated requests to Ferrante on behalf of the trumpeters in early February 1553, Grasso notified the chancery on 19 February that he had paid them only half of the remuneration due:

> President Grasso writes of having given the trumpeters of your excellency the half of
> that suited to them, and that he petitions also for the remainder as is the better manner
> of it now.[77]

Although it is not clear exactly how the matter of the trumpeters' remaining salary was resolved, it is obvious not only that the musicians had reached the threshold of their frustration, but also that Grasso was growing weary of the disorganized manner in which the orders to pay were handled.

Lombard Musicians Serving Abroad

Such issues may have indirectly encouraged some musicians to seek their fortunes abroad. In late 1553, Orfeo, a trombone player in Moscatello's wind band,[78] sought Ferrante's permission to enter the service of the Archduke Ferdinand of Austria. Moscatello protested vociferously, noting that Orfeo's absence would adversely affect the quality of the music at court:

> Most illustrious, excellent, and honored signor patron
> In the past days Camillo, trumpet of your Excellency, was sought, together with one
> of my company, a trombone named Orfeo. And I, having heard such thing,
> immediately gave him permission to go with Camillo and with the representative of
> Signor Aloisio of Lamara so that he remained in the service of that one. Now again I
> understand to be here one of the Counts of Lodrono who must come or send to your
> excellency for permission for the aforementioned Orfeo my companion in order to
> send him into the service of the Most Illustrious Archduke of Austria, which thing
> will be in grand damage to the music of your Excellency. And because of this and
> wishing to remain true to our office, servitude and honesty, in the face of this I was
> not able to fail to give notice to your Excellency so that when this gentleman comes,
> you may give him that response which seems best in order that our good consort is
> not lost, which I hold with hands and feet in honor of your Excellency, to whom with

a good heart I kiss the hands and recommend myself to your good grace. From your Most Illustrious and Excellent signory's servant in Milan on 1 February 1553. Ludovico Visconte, called Moscatello.[79]

The voyage that Orfeo and Camillo had made previously with Signor Aloisio Lamara apparently occurred during the year 1550, for at that time Camillo renounced his position as a civic trumpeter in favor of Giovanni Andrea Pisono in order, as the chancery registers put it, to 'better serve us.'[80] It is not clear where the two musicians went or what they were doing at that time, but by 1553 they obviously had returned to Milan as internationally respected performers. Ferrante, perhaps eager to showcase Orfeo's talents, gave him permission to go to Austria, despite Moscatello's ardent protests. Moreover, Camillo likely was sent with him. When a Milanese commission subsequently investigated one Giovanni Antonio Brena's request for a patent on a harpsichord that could be raised and lowered in pitch, both Orfeo and Camillo testified to having heard an harpsichord that could be raised or lowered in pitch by a tone and an organ that could be raised and lowered as much as three tones while in the Archduke's service.[81] The chancery hearing regarding the harpsichord patent occurred in April 1569, but the two musicians may already have been back in Milan for some time. Camillo was in northern Italy on 11 February 1557, at which time the chancery awarded him six scudi for travel on official government business.[82]

Most of the Lombard musicians who traveled abroad via Milan during this period sought their fortunes in France rather than in Austria. The French court, in fact, appears to have been an especially popular destination for string players, despite the political ramifications and potential legal difficulties associated with travel to France. Five Cremonese 'violists,' Gabrieli Cherubelli, Gian Battista Cherubelli, Giacomo Philippo Cherubelli, Antonio Maria il Tuono, and Gabriele Sacco, were employed at the French court during Ferrante's tenure. According to the Milanese archival documents, the 'five Cremonesi' were hired by Henry II in 1547.[83] They first appeared in the Milanese chancery approximately one year later, at which time they arrived in Lombardy carrying a license from Henry II granting them permission to remain in Cremona for four to five months in order to visit their wives and children. The documents suggest, but do not clearly state, that the Milanese chancery was amenable to this request.[84] In 1551 the five Cremonesi again returned to Cremona on leave from the French court, but this time their arrival in the Duchy was met with charges of collusion. On 23 October 1551 they appeared before the chancery to contest an accusation that they were in violation of a recent decree that warned citizens against providing assistance to the French crown. The misunderstanding seems to have arisen specifically from the interpretation of the phrase of the decree that read 'in service of the French.' In spirit, the decree referred to those who were supplying military or political aid. Consequently, the Cremonesi argued that they were serving Henry II with their art, which was an honest means of maintaining their wives and children, rather than with arms, which was clearly prohibited.[85] It was decided that they would be permitted to remain in the Duchy, and a safe-conduct informing all officers of the state that they were not to be harassed during their visit was issued.[86]

The five Cremonesi were not the only musicians to ignite the suspicions of the chancery with regard to the aforementioned decree. In April 1554 an investigation was launched against a wind player named Pietro who was soliciting recommendations to the French king in the hopes of obtaining a position at the French court. The tempest over Pietro seems to have dissipated quite quickly, however, once the chancery had verified the fact that Pietro had been seeking a musical position that he was not even likely to be granted.[87] Following the incident involving Pietro, the exchange of musicians with the French court appears to have flowed a bit more freely for reasons that are not entirely clear. On 9 November 1554 the five Cremonesi again appeared in the chancery, this time to request safe-conducts allowing them to return unharmed to the French court.[88] Safe-conducts providing for travel to the French court were immediately granted to them, as well as to a Milanese gambist named Thimodeo d'Aqua who was also employed there.[89] It is likely that the Cremonesi had only recently recruited Thimodeo, for just the day before Thimodeo had applied to the Milanese chancery for permission to accept a position at the French court.[90] Little is known regarding Thimodeo's activities in Milan prior to his request for permission to travel abroad, but he must have been a gambist of some reputation. He is among the Milanese musicians mentioned in the *Rime* of sixteenth-century historian Giovanni Paolo Lomazzo.[91]

The deep suspicion with which Milanese citizens who interacted with the French were regarded during this period is further illustrated by the case of a Milanese drummer named Francesco Guazzo. In 1554 Guazzo returned to Milan from a position at the French court, and was immediately arrested, incarcerated, and tortured on suspicion of spying. Despite his professed innocence, Guazzo was summarily convicted by the Milanese senate and exiled. However, the conviction was based primarily upon the flimsy accusations of a single Milanese official, and, as a result, it was later overturned and Guazzo was granted a pardon.[92]

Musicians and the Arms Laws

Many other musicians found their way into the Milanese chancery during Ferrante's tenure, but most of these eked out a living playing independently contracted events in the local area. Such musicians rarely sought safe-conducts, and only encountered the chancery if required to appear in legal defense of themselves or their colleagues. During the 1540s and 1550s it was illegal for musicians to perform at inns or private parties to which the guests carried swords, lances, spears, daggers, small hand-held swords, or other prohibited arms, including the newly popular harquebus. The penalty for violation of this decree was 25 scudi (that is, 133 lire) or three lashes of the whip, fines which most freelance musicians were both unable and unwilling to pay.[93] The proliferation and control of arms was of general concern to the state in early modern Europe, and numerous ordinances limiting their usage were enacted by the Spanish crown in order to curb the assembling of makeshift armies for the purposes of revolt or banditry.[94] This particular law, however, no doubt arose from the conventional wisdom that mixing weapons with levity, dancing, and alcohol had tragic consequences, for the chancery documents are filled with gruesome descriptions of brawls over minor issues that erupted between the armed guests and even the musicians themselves during local parties and dances. The case of Francesco Brugora and Giovanni Domenico Cytharedore, two Basilean gambists, serves to illustrate this point. In 1547 the two musicians were playing at a party in Rozzano when two guests of the same surname began bickering. The argument evidently escalated to a heated brawl, during which one Marco Veronese was struck on the head with a gardening knife, supposedly by reveler Francesco Vercellesi. Francesco fled to the cathedral with the aforementioned Marco in hot pursuit. The two gambists thereafter ceased playing, drew their swords, and rushed to Marco's aid. They arrived at the cathedral to find Francesco mortally wounded, presumably by Marco, having suffered two blows to the back, one behind the left ear, and one in the flank 'with great effusion of blood.' Although the two gambists were not convicted of murdering Francesco, they initially were fined 25 scudi (or three lashes of the whip) for not ceasing to play immediately when prohibited arms were displayed by the guests. Interestingly enough, the illegal swords that the two gambists were themselves carrying received only passing mention in the proceedings because the musicians claimed to have had no other mode of defending themselves. In the end, however, both musicians failed to appear in court, and, as a result were banished from the state.[95] They then resorted to the standard tactic of filing a supplication, a measure which usually tied the matter up in the courts for quite some time. Their supplications were read and their character witnesses heard in the Milanese chancery on 25 February 1549, some two years after the incident occurred, and they were granted a pardon that same day.[96]

Applying for a pardon usually entailed the submission of a notarized supplication pleading the 'trustworthy voice and sound reputation' of the supplicant along with the names of reliable character witnesses. Once the supplicant had secured a hearing, his supplication was read before the chancery and his character witnesses were examined. Eye witness accounts or statements made during inquisitions were sometimes considered by the chancery as well. Legal historians have detected no formula that guaranteed success to the supplicant, and note that pardons appear to have been granted to one person and denied another for no apparent reason.[97] The process itself was not inexpensive, as the pardon of the Basilean gambists notes that the fees for their case, which were to be remitted by the state, totaled at ten scudi (that is, 55 lire) per year.[98] A survey of the documents pertaining to the arrest of musicians between 1536 and 1556 reveals that the standard case was processed in one to two years, though homicide cases sometimes required greater persistence. (See Table 5.2.) Giovanni Paolo de Mantova, a lutenist accused of homicide in 1546, submitted four separate supplications to the chancery before disappearing from the records in 1548, and Petro de Olthosio, a musician arrested for homicide in 1536 was imprisoned until his pardon in 1540.

Ferrante Gonzaga's Milanese court instrumentalists were no less susceptible to prosecution, but the evidence suggests that their cases were processed much more quickly. In 1547, for example, Johannes 'Il Greco' and Paolino Veggio, two instrumentalists in the service of Ferrante Gonzaga,[99] were arrested for performing at a dance in Verme to which several revelers had carried illegal spears. The details of their case were admittedly far more mundane than those of the two Basilean gambists, for no violence was attached to the affair. Further, they claimed to have been unaware that anyone had been armed. However, while the aforementioned Basilean gambists waited nearly two years from the date of arrest for their pardon, Il Greco and Paolino were detained for approximately one week. Their character witnesses were heard by the chancery immediately after their arrest and before their supplication was even submitted, a noteworthy irregularity in procedure.[100] The documents suggest that the standard fine of 25 scudi was initially imposed, but the two musicians appeared five days later to plead their case a second time on the grounds of penury.[101] The second appeal was successful and the incident was entirely omitted from the official registers. Moreover, the whole process took less than a week.[102] This is particularly significant because it was not Il Greco's first brush with the law. In October 1541 Il Greco had been sleeping with his colleague Matteo da Palemo in a room in Abbiategrasso when he was awakened by a disturbance at the door. Apparently Matteo's Bolognese attendant Sylvester de Raimondi had wished to bring a woman into the room, and, upon being denied access, had thrown a lamp in Matteo's face. The drowsy Il Greco, rushing to his colleague Matteo's defense, hit the offending Sylvester over the head with a knife and knocked him down a flight of stairs. Sylvester passed on sixty days later, but not before personally pardoning Il Greco, who was not, in his estimation, directly responsible for the initial disturbance. On the basis of both Il Greco's account and Sylvester's pardon, the Milanese chancery notified the local Captain of Justice that all proceedings regarding the matter were to be terminated. The supplication and pardon are dated 11 May 1542.[103]

Moscatello himself was twice involved in legal proceedings in the chancery that appear to have dissolved rather quickly. Neither case, however, involved musicians. He is incriminated in a supplication read in chancery on 6 March 1551 alleging that he was among a crowd that attacked a virtually defenseless Jacomo Filippo Trincherio, maker of gloves. Apparently, Jacomo had been imprisoned since 1549 for cutting the ear of Moscatello's father-in law with a gardening spade in self-defense. According to Jacomo, Moscatello's father-in law started the fight, and he and his cronies, which included Moscatello, were armed with daggers.[104] Aside from Jacomo's renewed imprisonment, little seems to have come of the matter. On 10 October 1552 Moscatello himself appeared in the chancery, but this time as a character witness for P. Francesco Abbiate, a soldier who retaliated after being hit over the head with a club by his nephew.[105]

The chancery documents pertaining to the arrest, inquisition, imprisonment, fining, and punishment of musicians between 1536 and 1556 (Table 5.2) reveal that from 1536 to 1547 musicians were prosecuted only for homicide. Between 1547 and 1548, however, those musicians who performed at events in which brawling or violence occurred were prosecuted as well. This phenomenon likely arose from a decided attempt on Ferrante's part to more strictly enforce the arms restrictions that had been in place since the tenure of his predecessor Alfonso D'Avalos. After 1548, interest in prosecuting arms law offenders declined until 1553, at which time the effort to squelch arms violations was redoubled. In 1553, however, Ferrante appears to have chosen a new tack. Instead of focusing upon the musicians who violated the decree, he turned his attention to those who brought the weapons. This initiative perhaps reflects a certain amount of financial acumen on Ferrante's part. The fee for carrying an illegal weapon to a private party or public hostel at which dancing occurred was 100 scudi, a fine four times the 25 scudi exacted from musicians who played at such events.[106] Moreover, those carrying the illegal weapons may have been more likely to produce the desired fine than were the penurious freelance musicians who inevitably flooded the chancery courts with requests for pardon. Freelance musicians were still arrested for playing at events to which illegal arms were carried on occasion. Nonetheless, one of the three documented arrests made between 1553 and 1556, namely that of Stefano Rossi, was motivated by the fact that the musician himself was carrying an illegal sword, rather than by the fact that he was playing at an event to which arms had been carried.[107]

Musicians may have felt that they had good reason to carry such weapons. In June 1550 a cittern player named Alberto Camaccio was struck on the head with the butt of a harquebus and murdered by a passer-by who merely wished to try out his instrument.[108] Three years later Giovanni Francesco de Volpi, a gambist, was attacked and stabbed to death by three revelers when he ceased playing at a party because his contractual obligations had been fulfilled and he wished to be paid for

Table 5.2 Musicians arrested for arms violations or violent acts 1536-1556

Musician(s)	Offense	Arrested	Pardon?	Pardon Date
Jo. Francesco Stavolis, piffero	Homicide	February 1536	yes	4 November 1539
Petrus de Olthosio, sonatore	Homicide	December 1536	yes	3 September 1540
Jacopo Philippo Maynero, organist	Homicide	1538	no	-----
Johannes Greco, trumpeter	Homicide	October 1541	yes	11 May 1542
Giovanni Paolo de Mantova, lutenist	Homicide	May 1546	no	-----
Ludovico Storaci, keyboardist	Arms	May 1547	no	-----
Baptiste de Curte, violist and Ambrogio Calegario, violist	Arms	May 1547	no	-----
Francesco Brugora, violist and Gio. Domenico Cytharedo, violist	Arms	July 1547	yes	25 February 1549
Johannes "Il Greco," trumpeter, and Paolino Veggio	Arms	July 1547	yes	18 July 1547
Stefano, tamborino	Physical violence	July 1547	yes	13 April 1548
Donato Siciano and Togneto della Viola, onatori	Arms	September 1547	yes	24 November 1547
Three unnamed musicians	Arms	not indicated (Supp. Nov. 1547)	no	-----
Marc Antonio, lutenist	Physical violence	January 1548	yes	27 February 1558

Benedetto Maiochi "il violino," sonatore	Arms	not indicated (Supp. January 1548)	no	----
Paolino Falchino, sonatore	Arms	not indicated (Supp. July 1548)	no	----
Hieronymo Guissano, lutenist	Homicide	July 1549	yes	1 April 1551
Francesco Rigamonte, sonatore	Homicide	July 1549	yes	18 June 1551
Jo. Paolo de la Tera, lutenist	Physical violence	not indicated (Supp. Jan 1552)	no	----
Francesco "il violino"	not indicated	not indicated	yes	10 December 1553
Stefano Rossi, sonatore	Arms	July 1553	yes	15 January 1554
Antonio Mogina, Gio. Francesco Molinari, Antonio Maria di Arcosi, Gio. Maria de Vigna, Pompeo di Vigna, and Laurentio Mogina, sonatori	Arms	February 1554	no	----
Cesare Ventuaria and Antonio Barbetti	Arms	August 1554	no	----

them before performing additional numbers.[109]   Many of the individuals who sponsored or attended private parties and local dances held in the Duchy evidently lacked self-control, and the musicians who entertained them were at their mercy. By 1548 the professional lutenists, violists, keyboardists, and bagpipers in Milan had formed a society aimed at combating some of the challenges of the profession, and membership in it was a goal of most aspiring local musicians.[110]

Both the society for lutenists, violists, keyboardists, and bagpipers and the large number of freelance musicians who appeared in the chancery during Ferrante's tenure suggest the presence of a considerable body of professional musicians, many of whom were connected to neither the court nor the church. While many of these obviously were contracted for dances and parties in the area, others evidently served as private music instructors for wealthy Milanese families. In a supplication dated 7 November 1548, for example, Pelina di Lumelina, the widow of Signor Giovanni Marino, requested that the chancery augment the annual allowance allotted her family of four daughters and a son from 700 scudi per year to 1200 scudi. Her list of yearly living expenses included 12 scudi for a teacher of singing.[111]

Instrumental Musicians at the Courts of Ferdinando-Alvarez de Toledo, Cristoforo Madruzzo, and Consalvo-Fernando di Cordova, Duke of Sessa

With the ascension of interim governor Ferdinando-Alvarez de Toledo, Duke of Alba, in June 1555, the mention of musicians other than the trumpeters or the occasional violator of an arms ordinance virtually disappears from the chancery registers and documents. Moreover, the successive tenure of Cardinal Cristoforo Madruzzo, which lasted from January 1556 until September 1557, is equally infertile with regard to the archival sources.   Although the lacuna of documentary evidence regarding instrumental musicians at Madruzzo's court is somewhat surprising, given his long-standing reputation as a patron of music, art, and letters,[112] it may be attributed to two factors. First, Madruzzo, who was primarily occupied with the ongoing threat of French infiltration, demonstrated a decided disinterest in prosecuting musicians violating arms laws during his Milanese tenure. Secondly, Madruzzo's energies in cultivating the arts and letters were concentrated primarily upon his residence in Trent. Aside from the trumpeters,[113] only two court musicians are mentioned by name in the documents surviving from Madruzzo's tenure, but these musicians were treated with the same regard that had previously been afforded the court's most prominent literary figures.   On 30 January 1557, Hercole Trezzo, identified only as 'one of our musicians,'was awarded the place in the guard of the court of Milan formerly belonging to the recently deceased Milanese poet Giovanni Alberto Furibondo Albicante. Trezzo, like Albicante, was further placed on the role of the guard with a monthly salary of 20 lire.[114] Around that same time, George Gariver, another of the court's musicians, was moved from his lodging in the infantry of the bargello to a place more appropriate to his occupation.[115]

Madruzzo's successor, Don Consalvo-Fernando di Cordova, Duke of Sessa, held the post of governor from 1558 until 1564, but was absent from the city for at least three years. Despite his extended absence, however, Cordova restored, in some measure, Ferrante Gonzaga's patriarchal spirit to the Palazzo Reale. Cordova did not share Ferrante's Milanese agendas of an autonomous Spanish-Italian province and an ambitious civic expansion and fortification program, but he did recognize the value of spectacle and display in retaining a princely image.[116] In early 1563, for example, Consalvo allotted a nealy scandalous 390 lire for four flags for the trumpeters.[117] Alvarez-Ossorio Alvariño has observed that Cordova's humansitic proclivities were closer to those of Alfonso D'Avalos and his son Francesco Ferdinando than to those of Ferrante Gonzaga,[118] but herein lay the link in tradition, for Francesco Ferdinand, the spouse of Isabella Gonzaga and very much the Mantuan-styled prince, served as Cordova's interim governor during his protracted absence. The young D'Avalos, in fact, was probably responsible for introducing Giaches de Wert, Cordova's maestro di cappella, at the Milanese court, and, as will be seen below, was actively engaged in the performance of secular song. But even before D'Avalos took the reins of government from Cordova, string musicians seem to have been flocking to Milan. Several violists from Pavia accompanied Cordova's retinue to Vigevano in November 1558, and the virtuoso Timodeo d'Aqua returned from France at his behest for the carnival of 1559. By 1562 Fabritio Dentice even may have been present.[119] On 14 April 1565, moreover, Wert sent Alfonso Gonzaga, Duke of Mantua, a Miserere, a Benedictus, five motets, a madrigal, and some lamentations from Milan, remarking that the Benedictus and the Miserere 'work well when performed with viols, as we do here.'[120]

Pietro Paolo Borrono, Lutenist and Spy

The lutenist Pietro Paolo Borrono is perhaps the most enigmatic of the so-called instrumental musicians associated with the Milanese court during the governorships of Alfonso D'Avalos, Ferrante Gonzaga, Ferdinando-Alvarez de Toledo, and Cristoforo Madruzzo.[121] Geo Pistarono's early research on Borrono, which focused upon his possible participation in a plot to eliminate Cardinal Alessandro Farnese, suggested that the lutenist served as some sort of special agent of Ferrante Gonzaga by using his musical profession as a cover.[122] In a more recent study, Alessandra Bollini attempted, in part, to refute Pistarono by painting Borrono as a military man with strong loyalties to the Gonzaga, but her research is based on selected state documents, rather than the full range of materials available.[123] The extant archival documentation reveals, in fact, that Borrono was actually employed by Charles V rather than Ferrante Gonzaga. Although the sources make no reference to his lute playing, moreover, they strongly support Pistarono's general impression of the lutenist's activities. Borrono first appears in the Milanese archival documents in October 1534, when he requested an exemption from condemnation and a safe-conduct from the Milanese state.[124] Aside from the fact that he contributed two pavanes to Giovanni Antonio Castiglione's *Intabolatura de leuto* of 1536, however, little else is know of his activity in Milan before 1542. On 12 October 1542 he was granted a safe-conduct that insured him not only free movement within the Duchy, but also any assistance from local officials deemed necessary in his unspecified duties on behalf of the Imperial chamber:

Alfonso et cetera. Being expedient at present to send the noble Pietro Paolo Borrono for several important things to the service of the Imperial chamber, and desiring that he be protected and helped in every location where it will be necessary for him to go, and in order that he is able to execute his mission more easily and with greater speed, through the present we command any gentlemen, governors, commanders of the castles, mayors, and other imperial officials, and the deputies, counsels, municipal officers, and men of the city, villages and localities of the State of Milan, to whom this [safe-conduct] will be shown, that, being sought by the aforementioned Borrono, they extend him every protection and assistance expedient to the execution of his commission, and in such not fail to fulfill the service of His Majesty and to satisfy our intentions. From Chorio on 12 Ottobre 1542. The Marchese del Vasto. Agostino da Monte. And Taverna.[125]

During D'Avalos's tenure, however, Borrono evidently was declared an outlaw of the state for 'several charges leveled against him of not having administered faithfully the things of the imperial chamber.'[126] The undated document that relays this information further notes that Borrono exonerated himself and thereafter was issued another safe-conduct.[127] This turn of events may explain the existence of a second safe-conduct dated 30 June 1544 that is virtually identical to that issued on 12 October 1542.[128]

Borrono disappears from the Milanese archival documents between 1544 and 1548, only to re-emerge as an even more mysterious figure, for between 8 July 1548[129] and 6 April 1554[130] he is mentioned in over fifty chancery documents. While many of these record payments of between 20 and 250 scudi for 'secret commissions in service of His Majesty,' others report on his movements throughout the Duchy and make rather nebulous references to his activities. None of them, however, mention that he is a lutenist, thus suggesting that he may not have relied upon this secondary profession in order to mask his covert activities. In fact, he is more often styled as a soldier, and was placed on the rolls of the soldiers of the castello with a monthly salary of ten scudi beginning in November 1550.[131]

By 1552 Borrono had obtained permission to carry an harquebus,[132] despite the fact that citizens normally were not permitted to carry such weapons within the boundaries of the state. Moreover, he had a number of assistants in his employ, including his son Giovanni Battista,[133] and moved about the Duchy with uncommon freedom. In fact, Grand Chancellor Francesco Taverna was reminded in an unsigned notice written in early June 1552 that Borrono's activities traditionally were kept secret and accommodated without question.[134] Nonetheless, the latitude that Borrono had enjoyed in Milan between 1548 and 1552 was greatly diminished at the close of 1552 by a chancery scandal in which he was accused of engineering the alteration of a safe-conduct. A transcript of a confession that likely was narrated by Battista Suico, the Captain of Justice who prepared the safe-conduct on 1 December 1552,[135] reveals not only that Borrono had attempted to circumvent standard chancery procedures, but also that he indeed was involved in an ongoing plot to assassinate Cardinal Farnese. Suico's confession was supported by the corroborating testimony of chancery secretary Agostino da Monte, who indicated that he had assumed Borrono to be acting on the secret orders of Ferrante Gonzaga.[136] Although a sudden sharp decline in the number of documents referring to Borrono suggests that his activities were greatly curtailed following the safe-conduct scandal, it does not appear that he was specifically penalized for his actions. Grand Chancellor Taverna may have borne most of the blame himself. When Taverna was brought up on charges of treason for his mismanagement of the chancery in 1556, the incident was listed among the accusations and reviewed during the testimony.[137]

The fallout from Taverna's trial does appear to have affected Borrono's reputation and, in turn, his finances. A document dated 18 November 1556 indicates that his pension of 10 scudi per month was suspended for approximately a year before being reinstated and raised in value on the orders of Charles V.[138] Despite the restoration of this handsome gratuity, however, Borrono apparently fell into monetary difficulty. In July 1559 he and his son Giovanni Battista were denounced before the Milanese senate by Nicolò Ardentino, a friar to whom he supposedly owed over 80 scudi. The issue apparently was not resolved immediately, for Borrono submitted a supplication for clemency to the Milanese chancery in January 1564, claiming that the Captain of Justice had unfairly harassed him and ordered him arrested for a fallacious debt owed Ardentino. Borrono, who was over seventy and in ill health at the time the supplication was filed,[139] evidently was no longer the imperial chamber's darling.

Borrono's absence from the Milanese court between 1544 and 1548 likely corresponds with the period in which he was engaged in the preparation of his *Intavolatura di lauto*. Perhaps the *Intavolatura* was Borrono's response to boredom during a fallow period in his career as a spy. It may even have been compiled to meet financial needs not currently supplied by the Milanese state. The volume was printed in both Milan and Venice, two regions that typically issued mutually exclusive printing privileges, during the year 1548. Jane Bernstein postulates that the earliest version was prepared by Giovanni Antonio Castiglione of Milan because his edition contains a dedication to Count Ippolito del Mayno that is signed by Borrono's son Giovanni Battista, as well as a reference to the privilege extended Borrono by Pope Paul III.[140] The version issued by Scotto of Venice, although identical in content to Castiglione's save the omission of one piece, lacks both a dedication and a statement of privilege. Moreover, the designation 'opera novissima,' which is found on the title page of the Castiglione edition, is dropped from that of Scotto print.[141]

Nearly half of the compositions contained in the *Intavolatura* of 1548 are actually by Francesco da Milano, a feature which is acknowledged on the title page of Castiglione's edition, but is ignored entirely on that of the version issued by Scotto. In fact, all but two of the numerous fantasie contained are by Francesco da Milano. The bulk of Borrono's contribution to the collection rests in the numerous pavanes and saltarelli on popular tunes (Example 5.1) that are grouped in smaller

Example 5.1 Borrono, *Saltarello terzo detto della Duchessa*, measures 1-15

series, possibly reflecting their arrangement for practical use at the Milanese court. However, Borrono also supplied seven arrangements of popular chansons and motets by Claudin de Sermisy, Josquin, Jean Mouton, and Willaert, and these are representative of intabulations found in many Italian collections of the mid-sixteenth century. Borrono's intabulation of Mouton's *Noe, noe, noe Psallite* (Example 5.2) reveals that the composer likely was somewhat technically limited as a player, for it lacks the improvisatory idiomatic writing that characterizes the works of Francesco da Milano and Luis Milán. The model's points of imitation are intitally retained, but in each instance they quickly give way to free counterpoint. Even so, the counterpoint is often note-against-note, for semiminims, fusae, and other intricate rhythmic decorations are used quite sparingly. In addition, the voice leading is sometimes rather angular, the chordal content is diluted to the bare necessities, and octave doublings are often reduced to unisons. Borrono, a soldier and spy by trade, apparently engaged in music-making as a hobby and made use of his musical skills only as they served his entrepreneurial interests. The *Intavolatura*'s strong reliance on dances and works by Francesco da Milano suggests that Borrono may have been as much a collector of lute music as an actual composer of it. An abbreviated edition of the *Intavolatura* was reissued in 1563, just shortly before Borrono's final appearance in the archival documents. Yet the *Intavolatura* certainly was not Borrono's only contribution to the genre. His works had appeared in Milan as early as 1536 in the *Intabolatura de leuto de diversi autori* printed by Giovanni Antonio Castiglione.

Example 5.2 Borrono, *Noe, noe noe Psallite*, measures 1-25

The Influence of the Milanese Dance Masters

That Borrono's own contribution to the *Intavolatura* of 1548 is so heavily dependent upon pavanes and saltarelli comes as no surprise, for sixteenth-century Milan was especially noted for its contributions to the art of dance. This is particularly true for the second half of the century, at which time Cesare Negri 'detto il Trombone' and his students resided in the immediate vicinity of the Palazzo Reale.[142]   When the prominent Milanese dancing master Pompeo Diobono accepted a position at the French court in 1554, Negri, then about eighteen years old, assumed the directorship of Diobono's school. He thereafter achieved a fame unrivaled by any other Milanese dancer of the Renaissance. During the succeeding fifty years, Negri served nearly all of the Spanish governors as either a private teacher or a court performer, if not both. His services were enlisted, moreover, whenever a foreign prince visited the city, and prospective virtuosi from all over the peninsula traveled to Milan to study with him.[143]

If the 1574 progressions of Henry III en route from Poland are any indication of Negri's reputation, then it can be said the he was by far the most famous Milanese court entertainer of the period. On 6 August 1574 Don Antonio de Guzman y Zuniga, Marchese d'Ayamonte, the current governor of Milan, traveled to Cremona to pay respects to the French king, and Negri and three of his pupils accompanied him. Representatives of many of the north Italian courts were assembled there, and Negri and his dancers performed at least twice for them during the succeeding week.[144] Three years earlier, Negri had spent eight days at the castello in Vigevano giving dancing instruction and thereafter mounting a special mascherata for the visiting Don Juan of Austria.[145] In 1582, moreover, he danced before Emanuele Filiberto, Duke of Savoy.[146]

The dance most often memorialized in the accounts of the period is the galliard, and it is clear that this dance, along with its relatives the pavane and saltarello, attracted the most attention at court because of the inherent potential for virtuosic display. The running steps and leaps that characterized both the galliard and the saltarello encouraged both creative footwork and interesting choreography, while the processional style of the pavane provided a fitting introduction to the lively galliard or saltarello that followed. As Negri's *Le Gratie d'Amore* of 1602 so readily demonstrates, the Milanese, mesmerized by the adroit maneuvers of Negri and his disciples as they performed galliards on the dance floor, could not resist the call to the dance, and to dance well. Eight of Negri's students opened dancing schools in Milan, and others taught in Venice, Padua, Bergamo, Bologna, and Turin.[147] Thus, dance music, which had always occupied a position of importance at the Milanese court, acquired unparalleled prominence during the latter half of the sixteenth century. At least two of Negri's pupils, Michele Angelo Varade and Cesare Agosto, were as well known for their skill in playing dance music as they were for their balletic achievements.[148]

Although the printed music points to a particularly strong lute tradition at the Milanese court, the archival documentation reveals that while the lute played a central role in courtly entertainments, wind music was equally prominent there. Yet the archival evidence also demonstrates that courtly pursuits frame only a fragment of the story in a city as large as Milan. Numerous instrumental musicians plied their trade at festivals, private parties, and hostelries throughout the city. Moreover, several shops in the city center specialized specifically in instrument production. In 1550, for example, Duke Francesco Gonzaga contacted Ferrante Gonzaga to request the trombonist Orfeo's assistance in locating a new trombone to be used at the court in Mantua. He further notes that 'we are informed that there is a beautiful one in a shop of a German merchant that is at the other side of Broletto nuovo.'[149] Apparently, such shops catered to a healthy market that drew on a large number of active consumers and a wide variety of musical venues in the local area. Milan boasted a variety of civic spaces, many of which were public, that were appropriate for the performance of instrumental music. These urban spaces were defined largely by their civic function, and, as a result, were frequented by audiences that differed markedly in social pedigree, educational background, and financial standing. Yet the instrumental music performed in them frequently defies recovery because it formed part of the popular improvisatory tradition that prevailed throughout much of sixteenth-century Italy. This improvisatory tradition remained, by its very nature, unfettered by class distinctions, and permeated music-making at every level of Milanese society.

Notes

1   Players of the trombone, shawm, recorder, cornetto, and other wind instruments.

2   Pipe and tabor players.

3   On the career of Caracciolo, see G. de Caro, 'Caracciolo, Marino Ascanio,' *Dizionario biografico degli Italiani* (Roma: Società Grafica Romana, 1976), XIX, 414-425.

4   Cesare Mozarelli, 'Patrizi governatori nello stato di Milano a mezzo il cinquecento. Il caso di Ferrante Gonzaga' in *L'Italia degli Austrias. Monarchia cattolica e domini italiani nei secoli XVI e XVII*, ed. Gianvittorio Signorotto (Mantova: Edizioni Centro Federico Odorici, 1993), 119-134.

5   *Sforzesco* 1422 (Milano città e ducato 1523-1525), Busta 1525, n.n., ASM, and *Sforzesco: Registri Ducali* 26 (Affari fiscali 1522-1538), 122r, ASM.

6   *Sforzesco* 1422 (Milano città e ducato 1523-1525), Busta 1525, n.n., ASM.

7   Merkley and Merkley, *Music and Patronage*, 372.

8   *Sforzesco* 1424 (Milano città e ducato 1527-1529), Busta ottobre 1529, n.n., ASM.

9   *Sforzesco* 1429 (Milano città e ducato 1530 dicembre e 1530 senza dato), Busta 1530 senza dato), n.n. ASM.

10   *Sforzesco* 1471 (Potenze sovrani: Francesco II Sforza 1499-1535), 19, ASM.

11   *Sforzesco: Registri Ducali* 26 (Affari fiscali 1522-1538), 135r, ASM.

12   The eight trumpeters listed include Augostino Mazadro, Battista Birago, Georgio Cattaneo, Giorgio Pisono, Camillo de Giuliani, Petro da Septimo, Giovanni Antonio Birago, and Joanedra Cozo. *Registri della Cancelleria dello Stato* XXII/1 (Mandati 1536-1538), 29v-30r, ASM. Also see the passing reference to this document in Barblan, 'La vita musicale in Milano,' 877.

13   Georgio Cattaneo, Giorgio Pisono, Camillo de Giuliani, Petro da Septimo, Francesco Pisono, and Olivero Marliano. Here, Francesco Pisono and Olivero Marliano, both of whom had served Francesco II Sforza, reappear as replacements for Giovanni Antonio Birago and Joandra Cozo. Their whereabouts during the year 1536 are unknown. *Registri della Cancelleria dello Stato* XXII/1 (Mandati 1536-1538), 77r, ASM. See also the brief reference to this document in Barblan, 'La vita musicale in Milano,' 878.

14   *Registri della Cancelleria dello Stato* XXII/2 (Mandati 1538-1540), 45r, ASM. Also see Barblan, 'La vita musicale in Milano,' 878.

15   For example, *Sforzesco* 1435 (Milano città e ducato 1531 December), Busta 2, n.n., ASM contains a number of references to an unnamed trumpeter entrusted with the dispatch of messages between Milan and Vigevano.

16   *Sforzesco* 1436 (Milano città e ducato 1532 gennaio e febbraio), n.n., ASM, mentions a trumpeter traveling to Naples; *Sforzesco* 934 (Potenze estere: Ferrara 1525-1529), n.n., ASM, makes reference to a trumpeter traveling to Ferrara; and *Sforzesco* 1440 (Milano città e ducato 1532 6 agosto-31 ottobre), Busta 1, n.n., ASM, mentions a trumpeter sent to Codogno with military orders.

17   The Francesco mentioned is likely Francesco Pisono, one of the five trumpeters already listed in the 9 October 1529 document. Franzotto, however, was apparently a recent hire, for his name is not found on any of the earlier rolls. *Sforzesco* 1471 (Potenze sovrane: Francesco II Sforza 1499-1535), 19, ASM.

18   A number of the decrees recorded in the ducal registers between 1537 and 1545 close with a notation indicating that they were published from the stairs of the Broletto by one of the civic trumpeters. See for example, *Registri di lettere ducali* 1537-1545, 130v, BTASCM, which reads 'Publicarum ad Schala palatij broleti communitas Mediolani per Georgium Pisonum preconem die Jovis duodecimo mai MDXLI sono Tube' praemisso.'

19   *Registri di letters ducali* 1539-1552, 127r, BTASCM. Each district of the city was determined according to radii drawn from the focal point of the Duomo to one of the city's major gates, or porte. The resulting pie-shaped districts were named for the porte to which they were attached. For the layout of the city during this period, see Figure 4.1.

20   Barblan, 'La vita musicale in Milano,' 788.

21   Ibid., 789.

22   Ibid., 789-790.

23   Ibid., 790-800, and Merkley and Merkley, *Music and Patronage*, 299-319.

24   Franzotto is not found among the trumpeters in the salary records from 1529. His name first appears on a list of members of the delegation to Venice dated 13 September 1530. *Sforzesco* 1471 (Potenze sovrani: Francesco II Sforza 1499-1535), 19, ASM.

25   '. . .Et ch'io paga alcuni danari a Franzotto uno de li Suoi trombeti et che faci far' li fornimenti di una tromba per il novo trombeta . . .' Excerpt from a letter to Francesco II Sforza from treasurer Hieronymo Brebbia dated 12 March 1535. *Sforzesco* 1452 (1535 marzo), Busta 1, n.n., ASM.

26   Insert in a letter to Francesco II Sforza from treasurer Hieronymo Brebbia dated 13 March 1535. *Sforzesco* 1452 (1535 marzo), Busta 1, n.n., ASM.

27   *Sforzesco* 1444 (Milano città e ducato 1533 marzo ed aprile), busta marzo, n.n., ASM. The document was filed in the wrong busta.

28   Barblan, 'La vita musicale in Milano,' 796. William F. Prizer, 'Music at the Court of the Sforza,' 151, notes that there may have been as many as six pifferi at the Sforza court by 1469.

29   *Sforzesco* 1436 (Milano città e ducato 1532 gennaio e febbraio), Busta 3, n.n., ASM.

30   *Sforzesco* 1429 (Milano città e ducato 1530 dicembre e 1530 senza dato), Busta 1, n.n., ASM.

31   See Chapter 6 below.

32   The theory that Borrono served as a spy was first advanced in Geo Pistarino, 'Un episodio della vita di Pietro Paolo Borrono,' *Rivista musicale italiana* 51 (1949), 299-305. As will be seen below, the archival evidence bears this theory out.

33   *Sforzesco* 1451 (Milano città e ducato 1534 settembre-1535 febbraio), Busta 1534 ottobre, n.n., ASM.

34   Barblan, 'La vita musicale in Milano,' 883.

35   Donà, *La stampa musicale a Milano*, 20-21.

36   Barblan, 'La vita musicale in Milano,' 801-809, and Prizer, 'Music at the Court of the Sforza,' 153-154 and 182-183. Also see Francesco Degrada, 'Musica e musicisti nell'età di Ludovico il Moro,' *Milano nell'età di Ludovico il Moro: atti del Convegno internazionale*, 28 febbraio-4 marzo 1983 (Milano: Commune di Milano, Archivio storico civico e Biblioteca Trivulziana, 1983), II, 409-415.

37   *Culto* p.a. 2216 (Vescovi e Vescovati: Vigevano 1530-1672), Busta 1530-1538, n.n., ASM.

38   *Masso* 5, numero 6 (Mensa Vescovile), AVV.
39   *Sforzesco* 1445 (Milano città e ducato 1533, 21 aprile -30 maggio), Busta 1533 aprile,
      n.n., ASM.
40   'Ill*ustrissi*mo et ex*cellentissi*mo si*gno*re et patron mio precipuo. Alli giorni passati quella
      mi fece dire p*e*r il Reverendissimo monsignor nostro episcopo et patrono mio: chio
      dovesse to*rna*re via lorgano da quello loco dove era et oltra questo vostra ex*cellen*tia me
      lo dise de propria loca: si che per tanto haviso vostra Ill*ustrissi*ma si*gno*ria chio exeguito
      tuto quello me ha imposto vostra ex*cellen*tia alla partita sua non Manco pero de servir alla
      giesa con lorganeto picolo insin atanto che Lei provedara de far' refar' questo altro
      sicome con il desiderio vostro: non oltro fra Li fidelissimi servitori e subditi de vostra
      ex*cellen*tia io: e p*re*te victor' se vi comadamo alla bona gratia de vostra ex*cellen*tia e de
      continuo di core pregamo dio che quella possa conseguire loptato desiderio et *omnia*
      perpetua felicita quod utinaz' amen: In Vigevano die 25 luij 1531.   Da *vostra*
      Ill*ustrissi*ma ex*cellen*tia El fidelissimo subdito et servitor' prete Zilio Musico et
      organista.'   Autografi 94/1 (Musicisti), 41, ASM.
41   F. 36 inf., 26r-27r, BAM. See Appendix I, Document 6.
42   On 17 August 1559 105 lire and 2 soldi were paid Egidio's brother-in-law for ten months
      of service finishing in August 1559. *Vacchette* 412 (1558-1159),   AVFDM.
43   See George Nugent, 'Berchem, Jachet de,' *The New Grove Dictionary of Music and
      Musicians*, 2nd edn (London and New York: Macmillan Publishers, Ltd., 2001), III, 304-
      306, and Jo Ann Taricani, 'The Early Works of Jacquet de Berchem: Emulation and
      Parody,' *Revue Belge de Musicologie* 46 (1992), 53-79.
44   *Sforzesco* 1431 (Milano città e ducato 1531 febbraio), n.n., ASM. See Appendix I,
      Document 1.
45   *Registri della Cancelleria dello Stato* XXII/1 (Mandati 1536-1538), 29v-30r, ASM. Also
      see the passing reference to this document in Guglielmo Barblan, 'La vita musicale in
      Milano, 877. Here each of the eight trumpeters received a payment of L60 for the last
      quarter of 1536.
46   *Registri della Cancelleria dello Stato* XXII/1 (Mandati 1536-1538), 77r, ASM. See also
      the brief reference to this document in Barblan, 'La vita musicale in Milano,' 878. Table
      5.1 contains a list of the trumpeters who served the Milanese court from 1536-1569.
47   *Registri della Cancelleria dello Stato* XXII/2 (Mandati 1538-1540), 45r, ASM, and
      Sforzesco: Registri ducali 26 (Affari fiscali 1522-1538), ASM. Also see Barblan, 'La vita
      musicale in Milano,' 878.
48   *Cancelleria dello Stato di Milano* (1542 non datato), 111, ASM. Although this document
      is undated, the content is concerned with events that properly place it in the year 1538.
49   *Registri della Cancelleria dello Stato* XXII/2-5 (Mandati 1536-1546), ASM.
50   *Registro di Lettere Ducali* 1537-1545, BTASCM, *Registro di Lettere Ducali* 1539-1552,
      BTASCM; and *Registro di Lettere Ducali* 1553-1562, BTASCM.
51   *Cancelleria dello Stato di Milano* 27 (1539 agosto), 47, ASM.
52   'certe *lettere no*stre importantissime.' *Registri della Cancelleria dello Stato* XXII/4
      (Mandati 1542-1545), 139r, ASM. During this period, one scudo was equivalent to
      approximately 5.5 lire.
53   *Cancelleria dello Stato di Milano* 56 (1545 febbraio), 62, ASM. The sums advanced
      Birago are recorded only as twenty at Pelizono and thirty at Mariano. Because the earlier
      sums were given in scudi, it is likely that scudi were intended here.
54   'Adi 16 Maggio 1545 in Genoa un man*da*to al Magi*stra*to che faccia licentia a Battista
      Trombetta di poter levar della Cassina di Pelizoni et Mariano somme cento de biada. Et
      farle condurre nel paese di Si*gno*ri Grisoni gratis et senza pagamento di tratta . . .'

Registri della Cancelleria dello Stato di Milano XXII/4 (Mandati 1542-1545), 165v, ASM.

55	Besozzi, *Cronana milanese*, 15.

56	Guglielmo Barblan, 'La vita musicale' , 859-860.

57	*Famiglie* 205 (Visconti 1500-1550), Ludovico Visconti, 12 aprile 1543, ASM. A full transcription and translation of the document is found in Appendix I, Document 7. A document of 18 February 1542 in which one No*b*ile Ludovico Vicecomite was awarded an annual salary of 100 lire for extraordinary services to the chancery likely refers to a member of the noble family, rather than to the cornettist. *Registri della Cancelleria dello Stato di Milano* I-2 (Privilegi), 38r-v, ASM.

58	*Cancelleria dello Stato do Milano* 59 (1545 ottobre-decembre), Busta ottobre, 140, ASM.

59	'Dismonta CESAR da Cavallo intento// Pieno di Religione con Fede tanta// E à passo à passo inanzi và contento// (Et nel viso li danno, l'acqua Santa)// Qui non si vede, un cor che Si stia lento// Per che si sona parla s'ode e canta// Tanti stormenti, di soave sono// Ch'in fin al Cielo, ne ribomba il Tuono . . . // Risplendon per la corte i Loggiamenti// Camere e sale, de Brocati d'oro// In terra li Tapeti, altri gli Argenti// Con gran Recami de sottil Lavoro,// Ovunque si senton risonar stormenti// Che l'Armonia per, dal sommo choro// Questo apparato, no s'estende incharte// Che non convien lasar, la maggior parte// Havea parlato, la gran Corte intiera// Quel Unico splendor del VASTO eletto . . . // Tutte le fiffe, con l'erante stelle.' Albicante, *Trattato del'intrar in Milano di Carlo V*, n.p.

60	Besozzi, *Cronaca milanese*, 15.

61	Antonfrancesco Raineri, *Pompe de Messer Antonfrancesco Raineri* (Milano: Giovanni Antonio Borgia, 1553; Biblioteca Trivulziana ed Archvio Storico Civico, Milano H. 1484), n.p.

62	Vincenzo Ruffo, *Capricci in musica a tre . . . a commodo de virtuosi* (Milano: Francesco Moscheni, 1564).

63	*Potenze estere* 2 (Austria), s.p., ASM. See Appendix I, Document 8 for a full transcription and translation.

64	See Franco Pavan, 'Francesco Canova and his Family in Milan: New Documents,' *Journal of the Lute Society of America* XXIV (1991), 5-12.

65	*Registri della Cancelleria dello Stato di Milano* XV-6 (Missive 1548-1549), 192r-194v, ASM; *Registri della Cancelleria dello Stato di Milano* XV-7 (Missive 1549-1550), 142v-146r, ASM; *Registri della Cancelleria dello Stato di Milano* XXII-9 (Mandati 1549-1552), 171v-173v; and *Registri della Cancelleria dello Stato di Milano* XV-8 (Missive 1550-1552), 254v, ASM. The musicians at the castles of Milan and Piacenza were paid 33 lire per year and 3 scudi per year respectively, while the trumpeter at the headquarters of the Captain of Justice received 30 lire per year.

66	*Registri della Cancelleria dello Stato di Milano* XV-6 (Missive 1548-1549), 2v, ASM, and *Registri della Cancelleria dello Stato di Milano* XV-6 (Missive 1548-1549), 103v, ASM. The infantry trumpeter was awarded an annual remuneration of 50 scudi and 45 soldi, a sum, incidentally, that dwarfed the annual salaries of the court and civic trumpeters.

67	*Registri della Cancelleria dello Stato di Milano* XXII–8 (Mandati 1548-1549), 124v, ASM, and *Registri della Cancelleria dello Stato di Milano* XXII-10 (Mandati 1552-1555), 44r, ASM. Marliano died on 9 March 1549, but his son received a remuneration of 20 lire for the first full quarter of the year. Settimo passed on at the outset of 1552, and his heirs received his remuneration for the first quarter of the year.

68	*Registri della Cancelleria dello Stato di Milano* XXII-9 (Mandati 1549-1552), 157r, ASM, and *Registri della Cancelleria dello Stato di Milano* XXII-9 (Mandati 1549-

1552), 232r, ASM. On 12 March 1551 Birago was reimbursed 39 lire 5 soldi for the refurbishment of six bandieri. He received a second reimbursement of an unspecified amount for the same project on 27 May 1551.

69   *Cancelleria dello Stato di Milano* 147 (1552 aprile), 183 and 314, ASM.

70   In a letter to Ferrante Gonzaga dated 23 October 1553, for example, Francesco Grasso requests a directive regarding the funds from which he should pay Moscatello and his musicans for services rendered. 'Il Mede*s*imo dico nel particolar' di Moscatello et musici; per quali con una sua di xii di questo *vostra* eccellen*z*a mi commanda ch'io vegga di farli satisfare *p*er via di qualche straordinarij.' *Cancelleria dello Stato di Milano* 170 (1553 ottobre 16-31), 361, ASM.

71   Besozzi, *Cronaca milanese*, 15.

72   'Seguivano le nove muse; le quali erano l'eccellente Moscatello, con i suoi compagni, musicisti rarissimi, et ciascuno d'essi veniva sonando instrumenti musicali, diversi l'un dal'altro.' Raineri, *Pompe*, n.p.

73   All eight children were under the age of ten. *Famiglie* 206 (Visconti 1550-1600), n.n. ASM.

74   *Cancelleria dello Stato di Milano* 156 (1553 febbraio 1-20), 525, ASM.

75   Moscatello appeared in chancery twice during March 1553 and twice during October 1553 to request payment of overdue salaries. *Cancelleria dello Stato di Milano* 157 (1553 marzo), 211 and 481, ASM, and *Cancelleria dello Stato di Milano* 169 (1553 ottobre 1-15), 373 and 543v, ASM.

76   *Cancelleria dello Stato di Milano* 156 (1553 febbraio 1-20), 183, 271, 276, 302, and 407, ASM, and *Cancelleria dello Stato di Milano* 170 (1553 ottobre 16-31), 361, ASM.

77   'Il Presidente Grasso scrive haver fatto dar' a gli trombetti de *vostra* Eccellen*z*a la meta di quella si le doneva: et che si supplica anche al resto come ci sia il modo meglio d'hora.' *Cancelleria dello Stato di Milano* 156 (febbraio 1-20), 525, ASM.

78   Both Orfeo and Moscatello are immortalized in the poem 'A Claudio da Coreggio Musico' of Giovanni Paolo Lomazzo, *Libro terzo dei grotteschi*, 165-166. Although Laura Mauri Vigevani, 'Orfeo Vecchi, Maestro di Cappella di S. Maria della Scala,' 352-353 suggests that Orfeo may have been the father of the composer Orfeo Veccchi, the archival evidence does not bear this theory out. *Autografi* 93, Cartella II (Artisti diversi), 'Cornaro, Orfeo', ASM, contains a supplication from Orfeo Cornaro's only son Giovanni Paolo requesting that his father's unpaid salary be awarded him and applied to his father's debts.

79   'Ill*u*stri*s*simo et Eccel*l*en*t*issimo Signo*r* Patrono hono*r*issimo. Alli giorni passati fu recercato Camillo trombetta di *vostra* ec*c*ellen*t*ia insieme co*n* uno de li mei compagni trombono detto Orffeo. Et havendo io intese tal cossa gli fecce *q*uella subita permixione potej co*n* Camillo et co*n* lo bravo del signo*r* Aloysio di lamara tanto ch*e* e restato al se*r*vitio di *q*uella. Hora di novo intendo esse*r*e qua uno de li signo*r*i Conti di Lodrono quale deve venir' ove*r*o mandar' da *vostra* ec*c*ellen*t*ia *p*er have*r*e licenti*a p*er lo detto Orffeo mio compa*g*no da mandarlo al se*r*vitio del Illustrissimo Archiduca de Austria la quale cossa saria in grande danno di la musica di *vostra* ec*c*ellen*t*ia et *p*er tanto per no*n* mancar del offitio servitute et honor' mio *v*erso *q*uella non ho volutto mancar di dar' aviso a *vostra* ec*c*ellen*t*ia accio venendo esso signo*r* gli fatia *q*uella risposta ch*e* a *q*uella pareva accio che no*n* si perda el n*o*stro bon concerto qual' tengo co*n* mane et piedi in honor' di *vostra* ec*c*ellen*t*ia alla *q*uale di bono cor' baso le mane et in sua bona gra*t*ia me li raccoma*n*do. Da Milano lo *p*rimo di Dicemb*r*e M.D. LIII. Da *vostra* Illustri*s*sim*a* et Eccel*l*en*t*issima signoria se*r*vitore, Ludovico Visconte detto Moscatello.' *Famiglie* 206 (Visconti 1550-1600), ASM.

80   *Registri della Cancelleria dello Stato* XV-7 (Missive 1549-1550), 170r, ASM. The entry is dated 23 April 1550.

81   *Materie* 822 (Busta 9: Pianoforte), foglio 7, BTASCM.

82   *Registri della Cancelleria dello Stato di Milano* XXII-11 (Mandati 1555-1558), 95v, ASM.

83   ' . . .che già 4 anni sono al servitio de francesi in corte del Re per sonatore di viola.' *Cancelleria dello Stato di Milano* 135 (1551 ottobre 16-31), 302v, ASM.

84   Ibid., 81 (1548 marzo), 169-170, ASM.

85   Ibid., 135 (1551 ottobre 16-31), 302v, ASM.

86   Ibid., 136 (1551 novembre 1-15), 372, ASM..

87   ' . . .ch'era di servir' sua Maesta ch'é ben vero, ch'un Pietro piffero qual habita fuori di Pandino gli haveva ricercato lettere, et favore col detto camillo suo fratello per andar' al servitio di francesi, ma che lui non se ne volse impacciar.'' *Cancelleria dello Stato di Milano* 180 (1554 aprile), 11.

88   *Cancelleria dello Stato di Milano* 188 (1554 novembre), 130, ASM.

89   *Registri della Cancelleria dello Stato di Milano* XXI-1 (Patenti, Salvocondotti, etc. 1552-1555), 78r-v, ASM.

90   *Cancelleria dello Stato di Milano* 188 (1554 novembre), 100, ASM.

91   Giovanni Paolo Lomazzo, *Rime . . .de le cose sacre, di Prencipi, di Signori, et huomini letterati, di pittori* (Milano: Pacifico Pontio, 1587), 164. I am grateful to Agostino Ziino for calling my attention to this text.

92   *Cancelleria dello Stato di Milano* 189 (1554 dicembre 1-15), n.n., ASM, and *Registri della Cancelleria dello Stato di Milano* IV-12 (Grazie, donazioni, e privilegi 1554-1555), 65r-v, ASM. The texts of the two documents are nearly identical.

93   According to the documents from Ferrante's tenure, this law originated under Alfonso D'Avalos, Marchese del Vasto, governor of Milan from 1538-1546. *Cancelleria dello Stato di Milano* 73 (1547 agosto), 506, ASM. A late sixteenth-century version of the decree is preserved in *Gride* 19/1, no. 85, BTASCM.

94   See Julius R. Ruff, *Violence in Early Modern Europe* (Cambridge: Cambridge University Press, 2001), 44-52.

95   According to archival documents dating from the era, a scudo was equivalent to 5.5 lire. Thus, the 25 scudi fine was roughly equivalent to or exceeded a court or cathedral musician's annual salary.

96   *Cancelleria dello Stato di Milano* 96 (1549 febbraio), 517-519, and *Registri della Cancelleria dello Stato di Milano* (Grazie, donazioni, privilegi 1548-1549), 223r-224v, ASM. A transcription of the section of the pardon that describes the events leading up to the pardon itself is transcribed in Appendix I, Document 9.

97   Gian Paolo Massetto, 'Monarchia spagnola, senato e governatori: la questione delle grazie nel Ducato di Milano. Secoli XVI-XVII,' *Archivio Storico lombardo*, Serie 11, VII (1990), 75-112, but see in particular 76-77.

98   *Registri della Cancelleria dello Stato di Milano* (Grazie, donazioni, privilegi 1548-1549), 223r-224v, ASM.

99   Il Greco apparently had been employed at the Milanese court for some time. He is found in a list of the dependents of Francesco Sforza who traveled in the Milanese delegation to Loreto and Venice in 1530. *Sforzesco* 1471 (Potenze sovrane: Francesco II Sforza 1499-1535), 19, ASM. There are two copies of this list. One appears to be the original master and the other a fair copy.

100   *Cancelleria dello Stato di Milano* 72 (1547 luglio), 169, 188r, and 212r, ASM. These comprise the character witness testimony dated 12 July 1547, a chancery entry noting

that the testimony had been heard dated 13 July 1547, and a second chancery entry noting that a supplication had been read dated 14 July 1547.

101 *Cancelleria dello Stato di Milano* 72 (1547 luglio), 244r, ASM.

102 Ibid., 72 (1547 luglio), 297r, ASM.

103 Ibid., 38 (1542 maggio-giugno), 89, and *Registri della Cancelleria dello Stato di Milano* IV-3 (Grazie, donazioni, privilegi 1542-1543), 94r-95v.

104 Ibid., 126 (1551 marzo), 106, ASM.

105 Ibid., 151 (1552 settembre ed ottobre), busta ottobre, 250.

106 For example, *Cancelleria dello Stato di Milano* 183 (1554 giugno), 263 and 267, and *Cancelleria dello Stato di Milano* 185 (1554 agosto), 52 and 269, ASM concern cases in which citizens were arrested for carrying illegal arms to private parties or public hostels at which dances were held.

107 *Cancelleria dello Stato di Milano* 175 (1554 gennaio 1-15), 325 and 337 and *Registri della Cancelleria dello Stato di Milano* XV-10 (Missive 1550-1555), 80v, ASM.

108 Ibid., 131 (1551 agosto), 11, and *Registri della Cancelleria dello Stato di Milano* IV-9 (Grazie, donazioni, e privilegi 1550-1552), 218r-219r, ASM.

109 *Cancelleria dello Stato di Milano* 178 (1554 febbraio-marzo), II/13, and *Registri della Cancelleria dello Stato di Milano* IV-11 (Grazie, donazioni, e privilegi 1553-1554), 152v-154r.

110 In 1548, for example, Henrico Parazozero arranged for his son Giovanni Ambrogio to study lute with one Magister Battista de Giramis. The contract specified that five scudi were to be paid in advance and the other five when Giovanni Ambrogio was deemed sufficient. Part of the measure of sufficiency was to include earning membership in the society. *Notarile* 7023 (Benedetto di Castiglione), 22 octobris 1548, ASM.

111 *Cancelleria dello Stato di Milano* 90 (1548 November), 71, ASM.

112 On Madruzzo as a patron see Renato Lunelli, 'Contribuiti trentini alle relazioni musicali fra l'Italia e la Germania nel Rinascimento,' *Acta musicologica* XXI (1949), 41-71, but especially pages 55-70. Also see Laura Dal Prà, *I Madruzzo e l'Europa 1539-1658* (Milano: Charta, 1993), which was prepared especially for an Italian exhibition of artistic works associated with the family.

113 *Registri della Cancelleria dello Stato* XXII-12 (Mandati 1558), 24r, ASM.

114 *Cancelleria dello Stato di Milano* 215 (1557 gennaio), n.n., ASM, and *Registri della Cancelleria dello Stato di Milano* XV-13 (Missive 1556-1557), 204r-v, ASM.

115 Ibid., 215 (1557 gennaio), n.n., ASM The letter to Madruzzo regarding this matter is dated 30 January 1557.

116 On the Duke of Sessa as governor, see Antonio Alvarez-Ossorio Alvariño, *Milán y el legado de Felipe II: Gobernadores y corte provincial en la Lombardià de los Austrias* (Madrid: Sociedad estatal per la Commemoracíon de los centenaries de Felipe II y Carlos V, 2001), 43-161.

117 *Registri della Cancelleria dello Stato* XXII-14 (Mandati 1563-1564), 107v, ASM.

118 Alvarez-Ossorio Alvariño, *Milán y el legado de Felipe II*, 50-51 and 117-120.

119 Ibid., 122. On Dentice see *Da Napoli a Parma: itinerari di un musicista aristocratico. Opere vocali di Fabritio Dentice*, ed Dinko Fabris (Milano: Skira Editore, 1998), 43. The document Firenze, Archivio di Stato, Ducato di Urbino, Cl. 1, Div. G, busta 194 (carteggio Milano), f. 234 to which Fabris refers is among the correspondence of the Lonate family. While it demonstrates that Dentice was in Milan, it does not confirm that he was employed by the Marchese di Pescara as Fabris suggests.

120 'Se Vostro Signoria farà cantare quest cose con le viole riesceranno bene che cosi faciamo qua.' From a letter transcribed in Iain Fenlon, *Giaches de Wert: Letters and*

Documents (Abbeville: Èditions Klincksieck, 1999), 88.

121 For the basic biographical information on Borrono, see Alessandra Bollini, 'L'attività liutistica a Milano dal 1450 al 1550: nuovi documenti,' *Rivista italiana di musicologia* XXI/1 (1986), 52-60.

122 Pistarono, 'Un episodio della vita di Pietro Paolo Borrono,' 299-305. In three letters to his brother Ottaviano Farnese written in March 1551, Cardinal Alessandro Farnese reports that Borrono, then posing as a lutenist in Rome, confessed to the attempted plot and subsequently revealed Milanese state secrets.

123 Bollini, 'L'attività liutistica a Milano,' 52-60.

124 See Chapter 2 above.

125 'Alphonsus et c*et*era. Essendo espediente mandar' di p*r*esente il nob*i*le Pietro Paolo Borrono per alcune cose importanti al ser*vi*tio della Ces*a*rea camera, et desiderando noi che sia favorito et aiutato in ogni loco dove gli occorrera andare, accio piu facilmente et co*n* maggior' celerita possa preficer' l'impresa sua.   Per tenore de la presente co*m*mandiamo a qualunche sig*n*ori, Gover*n*atori, Castellani, Pod*es*tà et altri offi*c*iali ces*a*rei et alli deputati, consuli, co*mun*i, et ho*mi*ni de le città, terre, et lochi dil stato di M*i*lano, à quali sarano esshibite queste n*os*tre, che essendo ricercati dal p*re*fato Borrono gli prestino ogni favor' et aiuto op*o*rtuno per executione de la co*m*missione sua, et in cio non manchino per ricercar' così il ser*vi*tio di S*u*a M*a*esta et esser*e* n*os*tra mente. Dat*um* in Chorio alli XII de ottobre 1542. El Marchese del Vasto. Aug*us*t*i*nus Mont*us*. ut*er*que Taberna.' *Sforzesco: Registri Ducali* 143 (Salvicondotti, patenti 1538-1546), 120v-121r; restamped 242v-243r, ASM. Also see Bollini, L'attività liutistica a Milano,' 52-53.

126 '. . .per alcune imputationi dateli di non haver' administrato fidelmente le cose della Cesarea Camera.' *Famiglie* 27 (Bor-Bos), Borrono, ASM. Also see Bollini, 'L'attività liutistica,' 54.

127 *Famiglie* 27 (Bor-Bos), Borrono, ASM. Also see Bollini, 'L'attività liutistica a Milano,' 54.

128 *Sforzesco: Registri Ducali* 143 (Salvicondotti, patenti 1538-1546), 154v-155r; restamped 304v-305r, ASM.

129 *Registri della Cancelleria dello Stato di Milano* XXII-8 (Mandati 1548-1549), 30r, ASM. On this date he was advanced 20 scudi to execute a commission for His Majesty.

130 *Cancelleria dello Stato di Milano* 180 (1554 aprile), 248, ASM.

131 *Registri della Cancelleria dello Stato di Milano* XV-8 (Missive 1550-1552), 13v, ASM, and *Registri della Cancelleria dello Stato di Milano* XV-8 (Missive 1550-1552), 234v, ASM The former document is transcribed in Bollini, 'L'attività liutenistica a Milano,' 55.

132 *Cancelleria dello Stato di Milano* 146 (1552 marzo 16-31), 171, ASM.

133 *Registri della Cancelleria dello Stato di Milano* XXII-9 (Mandati 1549-1552), 169r, ASM. On 7 April 1551, the chancery gave 30 scudi to Giovanni Battista Borrono for a secret commission of His Majesty being directed by his father. *Cancelleria dello Stato di Milano* 146 (1552 marzo 16-31), 130, ASM, notes that a pardon is to be provided one of Borrono's men.

134 *Cancelleria dello Stato di Milano* 149 (1552 giugno), 2a, ASM.

135 *Gonzaga di Guastalla* 3, busta 1556, ASP.

136 *Sforzesco* 1607 (Potenze sovrane ed altre voci), n.n., ASM. The transcript of Suico's testimony appears as Appendix I, Document 10.

137 *Gonzaga di Guastalla* 3, busta 1556, ASP.

138 *Registri della Cancelleria dello Stato* XV-13 (Missive 1556-1557), 90r-v, ASM.

139 *Famiglie* 27 (Bor-Bos), Borrono, ASM. See Bollini, 'L'attivita liutistica a Milano,' 58-60.

140 Jane A. Bernstein, *Music Printing in Renaissance Venice: The Scotto Press (1539-1572)* (New York: Oxford University Press, 1999), 359.

141 The content of both editions is outlined in Howard Mayer Brown, *Instrumental Music Printed before 1600* (Cambridge: Harvard University Press, 1965), 110-111. Also see Bernstein, *Music Printing in Renaissance Venice*, 359-360. The Castiglione edition contains a Fantasia by Francesco da Milano that is omitted from the Scotto print.

142 Katherine Tucker McGinnis, 'Moving in High Circles: Courts, Dances, and Dancing Masters in Italy in the Long Sixteenth Century' (Ph.D. dissertation, University of North Carolina at Chapel Hill, 2001), 352-356.

143 On Negri's career in Milan, see McGinnis, 'Moving in High Circles', 278-299.

144 Laurie Stras, "Onde havrà'l mond'esempio et vera historia:" Musical Echoes of Henry III's Progress through Italy,' *Acta Musicologica* 72/1 (2000), 18, and McGinnis, 'Moving in High Circles', 285-286.

145 McGinnis, 'Moving in High Circles', 284.

146 Ibid., 286.

147 Ibid., 294.

148 Ibid., 292-293 and 295.

149 'siamo informati che ve n'è un bello a una bottega di un mercante Thedesco che è dall'altro lato di Bronetto nuovo.' This document is reported in A. Bertolotti, *Musici alla Corte di Mantova dal secolo XV al XVIII* (Milano: G. Ricordi, 1890; reprinted Genève: Minkoff, 1978), 158.

Chapter 6

The Collective Culture of Secular Song

I generally condemn the game, but not so telling short stories, on account of not seeming that we wish to rob or imitate Boccaccio. If you control yourselves in my manner we will sing and tell stories at the same time, because where one encounters others singing dryly by speaking alone, we say it once again. This is beautiful. And [through] similar idle chatter, we will consider a bit more fully poetry, jests, short stories and other little fantasies in reasoned discourse. In so doing, it will incline us to order, and suitably. And thus nourishing the body with a sweet repose, we still will graze the soul in soft delicacy, [and], indeed, in divine food.[1]

Thus Hoste da Reggio, Ferrante Gonzaga's chief singer-composer, introduces the singing of the first madrigal in Antonfrancesco Doni's celebrated *Dialogo della musica* of 1544. The imaginary journey into the study of the madrigal that follows, plunges the reader into the intellectual milieu of Doni's Piacentine *Accademia Ortolana*. Yet Doni's four interlocutors, who dedicate themselves throughout to the examination of sixteenth-century madrigals, include not only Hoste da Reggio, but also the Lombard composer Michele Varotti.[2] Lombard literary philosophy permeates the *Dialogo*, and its subject matter reflects the Milanese penchant for short expository forms in which content is driven primarily by symbol and allusion. The madrigal and the motet, in fact, predominated in sixteenth-century Milan, while more extended forms, such as the mass and Magnificat, only received marked attention after the elevation of Cardinal Carlo Borromeo as Archbishop of Milan in 1560.

Although secular singing was clearly an important form of entertainment fostered at the Milanese court, singers appear less prominent than instrumentalists in the surviving documentary evidence, perhaps because, as will be seen below, many of the instrumentalists who served at court were capable of doubling as singers. Yet Francesco II Sforza and many of the early governors who succeeded him seem to have made a point of retaining the services of at least one prominent composer of vocal polyphony, and, interestingly enough, most of the composers that they chose were employed either concurrently or thereafter as maestri di cappella at the Duomo as well. For example, Matthias Werrecore, who is identified as one of Francesco II Sforza's singers in a document of 1524, served as maestro di cappella at the Duomo from 1522 until 1550. Vincenzo Ruffo, the principal composer found in the household of Alfonso D'Avalos, returned to Milan in 1563 as maestro di cappella at the Duomo after an absence of some twenty years. Both Simon Boyleau and Hoste da Reggio, madrigalists who served Ferrante Gonzaga in 1553 and 1554, respectively, held the position of maestro between the years 1550 and 1563. Only Massimo Troiano, a Neapolitan composer who is found in the retinue of governor Consalvo-Fernando di

Cordova, Duke of Sessa, and Giaches de Wert, who served Cordova as maestro di cappella of his court chapel, had no demonstrable connection with the Duomo.

Singers and Song at the Court of Francesco II Sforza

A number of singers were employed by Francesco II Sforza, and most of these, like those of his ancestors, were supported by ducal benefices held in the surrounding region.[3] In fact, most of Francesco II's singers can be identified only through the benefice documents, for no complete list of the ducal singers survives from Francesco II's tenure. Francesco II's singers can be divided into two types, namely those of Italian heritage and those of Flemish or German background. The Italian singers include Giovanni Maria del Corte, Gabriele Barni, and Giovanni Antonio de Rapis de Busti. Giovanni Maria del Corte presumably was awarded the vacant canonicate and cantoria at San Theodoro in Pavia shortly after his nomination in January 1531, although the documents are not entirely clear on this point.[4] Gabriele Barni, a Milanese singer, was awarded a ducal canonicate at San Quirino et Judith in Lodi on 28 February 1528.[5] Barni held the canonicate for only a little over a month, as the records indicate that he had passed on by 31 March of that same year.[6] Interestingly enough, his canonicate was inherited from an indisposed relative named Alvisio Barni,[7] and was relinquished to one Battista Barni following his death.[8] Giovanni Antonio de Rapis de Busti, a Milanese contralto, was awarded a ducal benefice as rector at San Sylvestro in Porta Nuova in 1525,[9] and acquired a second chaplaincy through the diocese of Milan at Santa Maria Maggiore just two years later.[10] The latter chaplaincy required that Rapis say a daily mass in exchange for a stipend of 80 lire per annum.[11] Rapis appears to have remained in Milan following Francesco II's death, and was appointed to the cathedral choir at the Duomo of Milan in 1541. Both of Rapis' benefices were bequeathed to him by an uncle named Thome de Burgontiis. This fact, when considered in light of the circumstances surrounding Barni's appointment, suggests that many of the benefices awarded singers during Francesco II's tenure were acquired via familial ties to the recently deceased holders.

The most prominent of Francesco II's Flemish singers was Hermann Matthias Werrecore, maestro di cappella at the Duomo of Milan from 1522 until 1550. Werrecore, identified in the documents as 'our singer,' was awarded a canonicate in the collegiate church of St Michael of Busto in Gallerate in 1524.[12] Others ducal singers included Guglielmus Dibbons, a Fleming who served Francesco II from approximately 1523 until his death around 1535, and Otto 'cantore,' presumably also of northern origins. Little is known regarding Gugliemus other than that he lived in the vicinity of San Paolo in Milan and passed on shortly before Francesco II. Guglielmus left no heirs, thus causing the Milanese chancery some minor fiscal difficulties regarding the proper disposal of his estate.[13] Even less is known regarding Otto; the documents report only that he accompanied the Milanese delegation to Venice in 1531.[14] It is possible that he may be the contrabasso Ottaviano Bosisio who first appears on the rolls of the Duomo choir in 1534.[15] The ties between Francesco

II's retinue and the Duomo were evidently strong, for at least two of Francesco II's other singers moved from the court to the Duomo choir following his death on 1 November 1535. Moreover, records from the Milanese chancery hearings of 9 February 1547 report that 'Matthais maestro di cappella at the Duomo, and Ottaviano, contrabasso, requested that they be released of extraordinary duties, as was done during the time of the signor Marchese [del Vasto].'[16] These extraordinary duties, though unspecified, were clearly attached to the Milanese court and had been waived before. Examination of the Duomo rosters for 1547 reveals that the individuals in question were none other that Matthias Werrecore and Ottaviano Bosisio, suggesting thus that both singers maintained a long-standing relationship with the court that stretched back to 1524, the year in which Werrecore was awarded his ducal benefice.

Tenor and presbyter Andrea de Germanis apparently was one of Francesco's favorite singers.[17] He was awarded the ducal chaplaincy at the altar of St Blase in Santa Maria Adurni in Pavia in 1523,[18] and was nominated for the canonicate and cantoria at San Theodoro in Pavia in 1530. However, the notice of award at San Theodoro was cancelled,[19] presumably in favor of the singer Giovanni Maria del Corte. Instead, Germanis was elected to a more prestigious canonicate in the newly expanded ducal chapel at Santa Maria della Scala in October 1531. The benefice register specifies that Germanis was to hold one of the three dignitary appointments at Santa Maria della Scala,[20] which included positions for a Provost, an Archpriest, and an Archdeacon. Since Hieronymo de Matia was serving as Provost at the time, Germanis most certainly held one of the latter two positions. Given the chapel's devotion to the preservation of the Ambrosian rite and Germanis' vocal abilities, it is most likely that he served in the capacity of Archpriest, a position in which he would have been responsible for singing major portions of the liturgy. Following his appointment at Santa Maria della Scala, Germanis disappears from the Milanese records for nine years, only to resurface as a tenor at the Duomo of Milan in 1542.[21]

Although Francesco II employed several singers at his court, the only surviving secular polyphony associated with his reign is preserved in Werrecore's *La bataglia tagliana*, which was published by Antonio Gardane of Venice in 1549. In addition to the well-known tripartite 'alla bataglia' which Gardane offered his patron Alessandro Zamberti after hearing a French battle piece 'so elegantly sung by Messer Sebastiano and by his companions' that it seemed 'as if they had been born and raised in the middle of France,'[22] the print contains three other villotte that also quote a variety of popular Italian songs.[23] Like *La bataglia tagliana*, the villotte are homophonic in texture and rather static in their harmonic content. Most of the musical interest is derived from the inventive combination of the various folksongs, the lascivious subtexts, the clever onomatopoeic devices, and the juxtaposition of duple and triple rhythmic patterns. That these villotte, albeit amusing, alone represent the secular output of Francesco's court is, at first glance, rather puzzling, particularly given Francesco's strong ties to Ippolito II D'Este, through whom he became acquainted with the vocal compositions of both Willaert and Maistre Jhan.[24] Francesco's approach to musical patronage, however, takes that of his father Ludovico as a model. Francesco appears to have focused his energies upon the maintenance of a small coterie of performers who could make themselves available for the singing of songs that he acquired from various sources, rather than the cultivation of a group of composers who might supply the court with a challenging and distinctive repertoire. These performers were supported by ecclesiastical benefices when possible, and Werrecore was the only one among them with an established reputation as a composer.

Before Ferrante Gonzaga

Upon Francesco's death, the ducal privilege of nominating singers to ecclesiastical benefices was extended, in a number of cases, to the governors of Milan, but local musicians seem not to have benefited during the succeeding years. Benefices certainly remained plentiful, but, as the case of Nicola Vicentino demonstrates, they were more easily acquired by musicians who served in the Ferrarese retinue of the Archbishop of Milan than by musicians associated with the gubernatorial court. [25] Consequently, the number of trained singers employed by the court diminished in favor of instrumentalists who were capable of performing a variety of musical tasks. Even so, at least one composer of vocal polyphony was regularly retained at the gubernatorial court during the early Hapsburg years, thus insuring the continued proliferation of vocal genres.

The aforementioned literary proclivities of Alfonso D'Avalos and Maria D'Aragona should have provided an ideal environment for the cultivation of the madrigal in Milan during the early 1540s, particularly since Ruffo, the musician and 'familiare' in their employ during the year 1542, later distinguished himself as a madrigalist and maestro at the prestigious Accademia Filharmonica in Verona. D'Avalos, however, patronized sacred music, for the most part, during his Milanese tenure, and, as a result, Ruffo poured his efforts into *Il primo libro de motetti a cinque voci*. Most of Ruffo's early interaction with the madrigal dates from his service to Andrea Doria of Genoa (1545-1546) and his subsequent association with the Accademia Filharmonica of Verona (1547-1552). Ruffo's first anthology of black-note madrigals was published in Venice in 1545, and approximately 225 more madrigals followed between the years 1545 and 1560.[26] It is, of course, possible that some of the madrigals of the 1545 book were composed in Milan, and, further, that two works printed earlier, *Ma chi debbo lamentarmi* and *Alcun non può saper*, also date from his Milanese tenure. That the quality of *Ma chi debbo lamentarmi* alone earned Ruffo a place in Doni's *Dialogo della musica* of 1544 seems somewhat implausible, but the numerous individual dedications of Ruffo's madrigals point toward Verona rather than Milan, thus suggesting that Ruffo became interested in the genre only after the publication of his *Il primo libro de motetti a cinque voci* in 1542 and his subsequent removal to Savona.[27]

Secular Entertainments at the Court of Ferrante Gonzaga

Despite the reported presence of Orlando di Lasso from 1546 to 1549,[28] there is scant documentary evidence of increased secular music-making at the Milanese court when

Ferrante Gonzaga first assumed the governorship upon D'Avalos's death in 1546. By 1548, however, Moscatello and his wind band,[29] who had also served D'Avalos, appear to have established themselves as a fairly permanent court ensemble. This phenomenon, combined with the arrival of composers Hoste da Reggio and Simon Boyleau, not only encouraged the proliferation of dance and lute music, as is evidenced in Petro Paolo Borrono's aforementioned *Intavolatura di lauto* of 1548, but also fostered the cultivation of the madrigal and other similar genres. The method by which madrigals and other incidental pieces were integrated into court entertainments during the Gonzaga years can be seen in a pair of events held at the Milanese court during the pre-Lenten carnival season of 1553. The first of the two, entitled the *Pompe dei corrieri amorosi* (*Pomp of the Amorous Couriers*), was held on Sunday 10 February 1553. Twelve horsemen, dressed as sacerdotes from the temple of Venus, processed two by two from the palace of Carlo Visconti to the court:

> dressed they exited with the guide upon the sounding of the horn, and two by two in beautiful order, passing through the middle of the city, they rode to court, where in a grand hall one found the Most Illustrious and Excellent Madame Princess . . .[30]

There they were formally introduced before a large gold enamel decoration, which, when illuminated by fire, revealed the phrase 'Ardor and Snare.' Each of the horsemen then stood before the decoration and delivered a poem, the text of which was printed in a special memorial volume that immortalized one of the ladies present. It is unclear whether any of the poems were sung, but it is likely that at least some music was used, as the second entertainment, *Dei poeti amorosi* (*Of the Amorous Poets*), made thoroughgoing use of it.[31]

Dei poeti amorosi celebrated poets who had honored the beauty of Milanese women through the ages. It was presented at court on Thursday 14 February 1553 in a large hall surrounded by columns and draped with blue cloth. According to Antonfrancesco Raineri, most of the lords and nobles of Milan and their ladies were present. A dinner sponsored Francesco Grasso, president of the senate, preceded the entertainments, which themselves culminated with a ball. At six in the evening the poets, masked and dressed as Cardinals, suddenly appeared led by cupids, Apollo, and the nine muses. The roles of the nine muses were played by Moscatello and the members of his band, each of whom carried a different instrument. The nine were dressed in costumes of white silk and muslin trimmed in gold, black, yellow and crimson, and they wore crimson and gold capes over their left shoulders. Their blond wigs were decked with laurel wreathes and crowns shaped as rays of gold, and this attire was completed by matching boots embossed in silver and pearl necklaces. Raineri, who was among the guests, described the entry of the musical muses as follows:

> There began in the aforementioned court the most superb mascherata, with such beautiful order, silence, and universal astonishment of the bystanders. And it traveled round it three times, the aforementioned musicians promenading and playing with the most sweet harmony, at they end of which they all stopped in the full view of the

ladies and noblewomen. And the muses formed a row in front of the poets near Apollo, the three most ancient on the left hand and the modern on the right, each in his place, and [Apollo], playing the lyre with a plectra of gold, sweetly sang the following stanzas.[32]

The text sung by Apollo was a *strambotto* entitled 'Donna gentil, ch'Amor in grembo havete.' Although all five stanzas of the *strambotto* were preserved by Raineri, the music to which they were sung cannot be identified. However, the text itself mentions a number of the poets featured in the entertainment, including Dante, Boccaccio, Bembo and Sannazaro, and appears to have been composed especially for the event. Given the schematic regularity and general popularity of the *strambotto* in early sixteenth-century Italy, 'Donna gentil' was likely performed to a pre-existing melody that was appropriate to the singing of any number of *ottave rime*. The text may also have been sung to a melody improvised over a standard bass. In any event, Raineri's narration of the performance continues as follows:

> After those were finished, a circle was formed by the muses around Apollo, and they surrounded him, all genuflecting around him, while he remained standing with great dignity before those ladies and noblewomen; and after a lovely ricercare in which the musical instruments played together, the muses sang the following madrigal:
> *Amar' cari tacendo Occhi beati;*
> *Et sofferir' tacendo;*
> *Et non chieder morendo anco mercede;*
> *E' più grave dolor, ch'altri non crede.*
> *Amor' che'n tutti i lati*
> *Mi vai serrando il cor, l'anima aprendo*
> *Perche mi chiudi ancora*
> *La labra algenti? E vuoi ch'io taccia e mora?*
> After the madrigal was sung and repeated another time, the muses rose to their feet and circled the court anew in beautiful order, playing those diverse instruments in very pleasing harmony. And a little later they departed behind the little cupids, who turned leaping and frolicking as before.[33]

During the final segment of the entertainment, each masked poet recited his stanza before the ladies, and then presented them small gifts of unadorned gold. In addition, a written copy of each stanza was given to the lady to whom it was dedicated.[34]

Because the Milanese obsessively memorialized important civic progressions via detailed chronicles of them, the entire text of the madrigal 'Amar cari tacendo, occhi beati' is preserved in the account of Antonfrancesco Raineri. Raineri does not identify the author of the musical setting that was sung during the entertainments, but a version of it is found in Simon Boyleau's *Secondo libro de i Madrigali et Canzoni a quattro voci*, which was published by Moscheni and Pozzo of Milan in 1558. Unfortunately, however, only the tenor partbook of this collection survives, so it is not possible to examine the work at length.[35] In 1553 Boyleau was serving as the maestro di cappella at the Duomo of Milan, a position which he held between 1551 and 1557.[36] Although it is not clear when Boyleau arrived in Milan, he does seem to have maintained a relationship to the Gonzaga family throughout his life. His 1564 madrigal book, which is devoted to pieces composed for specific members of Milanese society, was dedicated to Ferrante's son Cesare.[37] Thus, the setting by Boyleau is probably the one that was performed during the 1553 entertainments.

Secular Entertainments at the Court of Don Consalvo-Fernando di Cordova, Duke of Sessa

Apparently, the Milanese court sponsored entertainments similar to those commemorated by Raineri every carnival season, and an even more elaborate event is recorded for the year 1559, by which time Don Consalvo-Fernando di Cordova, Duke of Sessa, had taken office.[38] Like the *Pompe* of 1553, the 1559 entertainment was held on the Sunday of carnival and celebrated the gallantry of love in a manner reminiscent of the *stile dolce nuovo*. In this particular case, however, the central protagonist was a sorrowful lady tormented by the vices of ingratitude, instability, and fraud. In an attempt to free her, several cavalieri chosen from among the nobility executed their skills in a series of staged jousts that were overlaid with well-known allegorical and mythological scenes, including the standard entrance of Apollo and the nine muses and Orpheus's musical mesmerism of the underworld.

One of the principal highlights of the 1559 entertainment was its apparati, which were designed by architect Leone Aretino and a corps of engineers especially for the host palace of the Marchese of Cassano. According to chronicler Ascanio Certorio degli Ortensi, the central stage featured the City of Dis under a star-studded sky with moveable clouds that could be lit by the sun. The turbulent river Acheron, studded with a little boat and skulked by two fearsome serpents, divided the city. To the right were the Elysian fields dotted with loggias, fountains, temples, and trees from which the sounds of birds and instruments could be heard. On the left was a Doric temple dedicated to Venus Matron and a single tall pine to which was affixed a queen's crown with a cap of gold. In addition, the stage featured a central piazza area divided by a wooden bar that was intended especially for the sparring of the cavalieri. This central piazza was surrounded by loggias hung with cloth in which the Milanese noblewomen were seated. According to Ortensi, the stage also had an infinite number of steps upon which the female viewers could sit to watch and listen, thus allowing them to become virtually at one with the drama.[39]

Music was integrated into the performance throughout, but primarily served to provide sounding tableaux that ornamented the drama proper. At the chiming of the introductory bell, for instance, the veil that covered the temple lifted to reveal the three principal cavalieri armed in gold and silver as there sounded:

> an excellent music of bowed viols, trombones, cornets, and voices, whose players, dressed in long garments of white voile, were seated in an orderly arrangement on the steps of the temple playing their instruments so sweetly and harmoniously . . .[40]

The various processional entrances of other cavalieri were similarly accompanied by 'a concert of the most divine music on various instruments.'[41] The scene in the underworld, where the vices would finally be carried off in Caron's boat, was introduced by the singing of a nine-stanza *strambotto* entitled 'Da l'ombre Stigie, e da Tartarei chiostri'in which the mythological Orfeo accompanied himself on the lyre. As was the case in many of the other musical segments, Orfeo's presence was merely decorative and referential, and served no purpose in forwarding the primary action of the scene.[42] The roles of Apollo and the nine muses, all performed by instrumental musicians, impacted the dramatic action more directly. In the closing scene, which took place in the fields of Elysium after the fires of hell had swallowed up the vices, Apollo and the diversely attired muses first received the sorrowful lady in an amorous concert of instruments and song. They then led her down the steps processionally and encircled her for the singing of a madrigal entitled 'Da lieti campi e da fiorite rive,' which they performed themselves. Thereafter, they conducted her into to the Elysian fields as they sang and played.[43] The nine muses, incidentally, reappeared later in the evening during the course of a separate mascherata organized by governor Cordova as a short interlude at the ball. The central character of the separate mascherata was one Dio Pane, who sang a canzone entitled 'Da lieti e verdi campi' to the accompaniment of the nine muses, each of whom played a different instrument, as fourteen masked satyrs and fauns, who were chosen from among the governor's cohorts, looked on.[44]

Art and music were also integrated into a dramatic postlude, as well as into the concluding banquet and ball. The postlude, which glorified the seven liberal arts and had little in common with the drama that preceded it, featured nine processing noblewomen, each of whom represented one of the arts via her dress and props, escorted by elderly gentlemen. The procession itself was led by a lady dressed as Saffo who declaimed a text entitled 'Amene valli, e lati campi aperti' to the accompaniment of a lyre and thereafter was led, like the sorrowful lady, to the fields of Elysius, where she witnessed a final choreographed battle of the cavalieri.[45] At the banquet that followed, the dishes were presented in a processional style in which the pages carrying the plates of food were succeeded by another bearing a tondo or vase inscribed with a motto relating to the themes of the preceding drama. Each presentation was made to the accompaniment of specific types of instruments, all of which joined together for a rousing finale as the desserts were distributed. A ball for the participants that included the aforementioned mascherata that was organized by the governor closed the entertainment.[46]

The accounts of such entertainments suggest that the governors who succeeded Francesco II persisted in hiring only one or two singer-composers and a larger corps of instrumentalists because most of the instrumentalists were capable of doubling as singers for these miniature dramas. In the 1553 performance of 'Donna gentil, ch'Amor in grembo havete,' for example, Apollo accompanied himself on some sort of lyre, thus indicating that the string musician who played this role was a singer as well. A similar conclusion can be drawn for the song performed by Orfeo during the 1559 entertainment. Further, members of Moscatello's wind band sang Boyleau's madrigal 'Amor' cari tacendo, occhi beati' during the 1553 entertainments, and, in Raineri's estimation, performed it beautifully. Likewise, the instrumentalists appear to have competently sung the madrigal 'Da lieti campi e da fiorite rive,' which was probably penned by governor Cordova's court composer Massimo Troiano, at the

1559 entertainment. Given the diverse abilities of the instrumentalists, there apparently was little need of musicians who specialized only as vocal performers for the rendition of secular pieces. After all, eight trained singers who specialized in the Ambrosian rite had been permanently available for the performance of liturgical music since the 1531 founding of the royal ducal chapel at Santa Maria della Scala.

That governor Cordova's singers and courtiers also participated in madrigal singing apart from theatrical entertainments is evident from a letter written by Giaches de Wert, who served as Cordova's maestro di cappella from at least 1563 to 1564, to Don Alfonso Gonzaga in Novellara. On 10 June 1563, Wert reports that Isabella Gonzaga's spouse Francesco Ferdinando D'Avalos, Marchese de Pescara, who was serving as Cordova's temporary deputy in Milan, joined the musicians and several officers of the Milanese garrison in some lively singing of some sort of polyphonic song:

> . . .Oratio Tuttavilla still sang in this half that we sang so well that upon finishing his card game, the Marchese came to hear our beautiful music and, in order to tidy up Oratio's singing, wished to sing also, so that [the music] dissolved into laughter because I needed to correct them passage by passage. The Marchese said that Oratio made a mistake, and Orazio said that it was the Marchese. Count Manfredino pronounced the sentence, stating that neither of them knew what he was doing . . .[47]

D'Avalos, in fact, seems to have instigated number of such musical evenings at the court, and was likely responsible for Wert's appointment in Milan. Even after governor Cordova was removed in favor of Don Gabriele de la Cueva, Duke of Albuquerque, in April 1564, Wert was retained as maestro di cappella for at least a year. Interestingly enough, D'Avalos also remained at the court, and Wert reports that on Saturday, 4 November 1564 at 11:00 p.m. the Marchese 'came down to the picture gallery with [Don Cesare, Don Carlo, and the Conte Manfredino] and wished to sing, but there weren't many of us.'[48]

Wert's own madrigals may well have been among the compositions sung in the Palazzo Reale during these years, for his *Madrigali a cinque voci . . . Liber III*, which was printed by Antonio Gardane of Venice in 1563, is dedicated to Cordova.[49] It contains fifteen madrigals on sonnets, dialogues, and canzone by such poets as Ariosto, Sannazaro, and Petrarch, and reflects the changing face of the madrigal during the two decades falling between 1550 and 1570. All of the works contained are cast in the increasingly typical alla breve mensuration, but each is individual in its approach to texture and its harmonic style. The declamatory chordal style characteristic of the Milanese madrigal is frequently employed as a special effect, but imitative procedures are far more predominant than in the Milanese madrigals printed by Moscheni and Scotto during the previous decade. And while some of the madrigals feature tentative use of daring chromaticism, others are almost entirely devoid of harmonic experimentation. Both harmonic and figural madrigalisms abound throughout, and are reminiscent of those found in Rore's works of the 1550s.

The collection opens with a madrigal dedicated to Cordova that likens D'Avalos and Cordova to Castor and Pollux, respectively, and on this basis Iain

Fenlon has suggested that it was intended to commemorate Cordova's return to Milan in March 1563 following a three-year absence in which D'Avalos served in his stead.[50] There is, however, no record of a special court celebration of that event. Four other pieces in the collection, moreover, also carry individual dedications. Three of these are devoted to members of the Gonzaga family – Alfonso Gonzaga, Camillo Gonzaga (with his spouse Barbara Borromea), and Francesco Ferdinando D'Avalos, while the fourth acclaims Alfonso II d'Este, Duke of Ferrara. All four patrons, like Cordova, provided Wert financial support during the course of his career.

The Moscheni and Scotto Prints

The arrival of the printers Francesco and Simone Moscheni in Milan during the year 1553 marked a turning point in Ferrante Gonzaga's musical patronage that not only would come to distinguish his Milanese tenure, but also would influence the succeeding history of Milanese music printing. The Bergamasque Moscheni, who specialized in the printing of Greek, Latin, and Italian texts, launched their careers in Alessandria and later set up shop in Pavia.[51] On 16 December 1553, at which time they evidently were still operating in Pavia, the Moscheni were given leave to print several books in Milan.[52] Shortly thereafter they must have relocated to Milan, for on 10 March 1554 they secured an exclusive twelve-year privilege granting them permission to print Greek, Latin, and Italian texts in the city.[53] Nine days later they were further awarded a ten-year exemption from personal and business taxes because of the great expense incurred in setting up their practice. The exemption was extended to the twelve persons on their staff as well, on the condition that they practice their art of printing from 'a type newly corrected and very elegant' in Milan, thus bringing honor to the city.[54] Although the privileges make no reference to music printing, circumstances seem to have dictated that the art was soon to become a major contribution of the Moscheni press. During the twelve years that the Moscheni brothers operated in Milan, they issued a dozen prints, most of which were dedicated to locally composed motets and madrigals. The persistence with which they pursued the craft of printing polyphony, moreover, initiated a significant spurt of growth in the Milanese music printing industry, which thereafter blossomed into a thriving and competitive trade.

The Moscheni's first musical project was Hoste da Reggio's *Il primo libro de madrigali a tre voci*, which was dedicated to Ferrante Gonzaga's daughter Hippolita. The dedication itself indicates that the book was intended as a wedding gift in celebration of Hippolita's second marriage to Antonio Carafa de Mandragone in 1554.[55] It further suggests that the young Princess, who was trained in classical studies under the tutelage of her uncle Cardinal Ercole Gonzaga,[56] had already sung a number of the pieces contained with her friends.[57] The madrigals of *Il primo libro de madrigali a tre voci* are typical of those found in Hoste's other collections. Although the origin of several texts selected is unclear, those of identifiable authorship reveal an affinity for the poetry of Ariosto, Petrarch, and Cassola. The settings themselves show a tendency towards specific clef and system combinations, a characteristic which is clarified by Antonio

Table 6.1 A comparison of the 1554 and 1562 editions of Hoste da Reggio, *Il primo libro de madrigali a tre voci*

1554 Ordering

Text
Perche la vit'è breve
2 pars. Occhi leggiadri
Nasce la pena mia
S'el dolce sguardo
Canzon mia ferm'in campo
Madonna pio che'uccider
Consumando mio vo
Et le parole, ch'ogni dur' affetto
O candidetta come lo camino
Crudel di che peccat'a dolert'hai
Chi vi parl'è felice
Occhi leggiadri
Poi che sento di me
Quel pudico desio
O quant'invan si spargon
Nov'angeletta sovra l'ale accorta
Madon'hai torto a dirmi*
Dhe se pensavi*
Sic praesans testatur (Nativity)
Ego vero orationem mean (Pro defunctis)
Pastores qui audierunt (Epiphany)
Tua est potentia (From Machabees)
Scriptum est enim (Purification)
2p. Postquam autem

1562 Ordering

Text	Signature	System	Cleffing	Final
Perche la vit'è breve	C	1 flat	C1C2C4	G
2 pars. Occhi leggiadri	C	1 flat	C1C2C4	G
O quant' invan	C	1 flat	C1C2C4	G
Madonna pio che'uccider	C	1 flat	C1C2C4	D
Nasce la pena mia	C	1 flat	C1C2C4	A
Consumando mio vo	C	0	C1C3C4	D
S'el dolce sguardo	C	0	C1C3C4	A
Occhi leggiadri	C	0	C1C3C4	A
Canzon mia ferm'in campo	C	0	C1C3C4	C
O candidetta	C	0	C1C3C4	C
Nov' angeletta sovra l'ale	C	0	C1C3C4	G
Et le parole	C	0	G2C3C3	C
Chi vi parl'è felice	C	0	C1C3C4	C
Crudel di che peccat'a	C	0	G2C2C3	G
Quel pudico desio	C	0	C2C3C4	A
Poi che sento di me	C	0	G2C2C3	A
*omitted in 1562				
*omitted in 1562				
Ego vero orationem	C	0	C1C3C4	E
Scriptum est enim	C	1 flat	G2C2C3	F
2p. Postquam autem	C	1 flat	G2C2C3	F
Tua est potentia	C	0	C1C3C4	G
Pastores qui audierunt	C	0	C1C3C4	G
Sic praesans testatur	C	1 flat	C2C3F3	G

Gardane's reorganization for the 1562 reprint, as well as a decided preference for the popular *a note nere* signature (see Table 6.1).[58] Both declamatory chordal writing and imitative techniques are employed, and affective treatment relies primarily, although not exclusively, upon the introduction of occasional pungent dissonances within the textural fabric. However, *Il primo libro de madrigali a tre voci* is somewhat unique in its employment of only three voices. The transparent texture inherent in the reduced voicing not only provides the illusion of clean theatrical recitation, but also insures ease of performance and a facile transformation of the material into a successful solo for voice and lute. In *Occhi leggiadri*, for example, the primary mode of presentation is chordal, with all of the voices moving at approximately the same rhythmic speed. The opening quattrain of Cassola's canzona, which features alternating seven and eleven-syllable lines, is set to unencumbered chordal declamation that is entirely devoid of repetition. Each of the three seven-syllable lines that follow, however, are repeated in a similar declamatory fashion, thus creating an artificial balance between the two sections of the poem while simultaneously lending a quality of breathless excitement to its climactic latter half. Although clarity of declamation is paramount, madrigalisms such as the brief decoration on 'leggiadri' (charming) accentuate a few individual words. The overriding simplicity of the setting seems to be driven primarily by a need to tailor the work to the skills of Hippolita and her fellow amateur performers, as well as by the possibility that the piece might be rendered as a solo with instrumental accompaniment (Example 6.1).

Il primo libro de madrigali a tre voci is just one of four madrigal books containing works by Hoste that were issued in 1554.[59] The other three, which feature four and five-voice madrigals, were printed by Girolamo Scotto of Venice. Yet all four books identify Hoste as a musician in the service of Ferrante Gonzaga, and three of the four, including the collection for Hippolita, are dedicated to members of Ferrante's immediate family.[60] As has been noted above, Hoste, who often is identified in Milanese sources by his Christian name of Bartolomeo Torresani, first appears in the Milanese archival documents in 1555, when he was awarded an ecclesiastical benefice at San Calimero, a Milanese church that would later sponsor of Carlo Borromeo's Scuola of San Michele. Hoste's duties there evidently were minimal, however, as he was required only to perform one festal mass per year in addition to the occasional mass for the faithful.[61] From 1558 until 1563 Hoste also served as maestro di cappella at the Duomo of Milan, and, with the exception of a brief foray at Santa Maria Maggiore in Bergamo between June 1567 and June 1568, appears to have remained at San Calimero until his death on 5 October 1569.[62] Hoste's relationship with the Gonzaga stretches at least back to 1547, the year in which his *Primo libro de madrigali a quattro voci*, which was dedicated to Cardinal Ercole Gonzaga, was issued by Gardane of Venice.[63]

Example 6.1 Hoste da Reggio, *Occhi leggiadri*, measures 1-8

Aside from the 1547 dedication to Ercole Gonzaga, however, there is no documentary evidence of Hoste's interaction with the Gonzaga before the dedications of madrigal collections of 1554 were penned. Thus, it appears likely that Hoste came to the Milanese court via Mantua, and, further, that Ferrante himself arranged for the mass publication of Hoste's extant madrigals in 1554. It is not clear why the bulk of the business of publishing Hoste's works was awarded the Scotto firm rather than the Milanese Moscheni, but it is likely that the Moscheni, having established themselves in the city only recently, were not prepared to handle the sizeable output. Moreover, the new Milanese firm, while practiced in the art of printing books in the classical languages, was a fledgling in the specialized art of music printing.

Hoste's *Il secondo libro delli madrigali a quattro voci*, which was among the three collections printed by Scotto in 1554, is dedicated to Ferrante's spouse Isabella de Capua, and, according to the dedication, the madrigals contained were 'born' in Isabella's 'shadow.'[64] The collection includes twenty works, and is organized according to system, cleffing and mode. Although the poetic sources of many of the texts have not been identified, the poetry of Ariosto figures prominently among those that are identifiable.[65] Interestingly enough, the addition of a fourth voice to the musical texture does not initiate marked changes in the composer's approach to setting the texts. Passages of homophonic declamation abound, and are often employed to introduce the initial line of text, to underscore particularly significant phrases, and to preserve the natural inflection of the text. When imitation is introduced, it is often quickly absorbed into a chordal texture. Expression is achieved largely through rhythmic and chromatic inflections, rather than by the excessive introduction of text painting. The chromatic inflections employed, however, are incidental to the long-term harmonic structure, and never reach the level of adventurousness associated with Rore and Vicentino.

Il secondo libro delli madrigali a quattro voci concludes with an eight-stanza recitation to the goddess Chastity that reportedly was delivered by Isabella herself, perhaps at one of the court's annual carnival celebrations (Example 6.2). The stanzas are organized in ottava rima, a typical pattern employed in Milanese theatrical pieces of the period. Even from a purely musical standpoint, however, the recitation is a bona fide theatrical piece. It is comprised largely of homophonic, treble-dominated declamation harmonized in falsobordone, although passages of pseudo-imitation are employed occasionally for the purposes of heightened text expression. The individual lines of text are frequently harmonically elided, but fusa rests in the superius serve to mark them off from one another, while simultaneous rests in all the parts supply the necessary grammatical punctuation. Repetition, either of text or of text and music, is utilized to underscore particularly significant phrases of text, as well as to mark off the final line of each stanza. The natural flow of the declamation is paramount throughout, and is carefully preserved via the rhythmic displacement of regular duple accents and the frequent introduction of chromatic inflections.

Example 6.2 Hoste da Reggio, *Dal di che conobb'io*, **measures 1-7**

Of the three collections of Hoste's madrigals printed by Scotto in 1554, *Il primo libro delli madrigali a cinque voci*, which was dedicated to Ferrante Gonzaga, is perhaps the most interesting musical document surviving from this period in the social history of the Milanese court. It is Hoste's only collection for five voices, and appears to be organized around the themes of war and government that characterized Ferrante's career. It features various military frontispieces, one of which depicts a general in conference with his soldiers in an encampment bordering a bay in which battleships stand ready (Figure 6.1), and its dedication, which was penned by the composer himself, indicates that the madrigals contained were collected and printed for Ferrante:

> . . .under your most glorious name, hoping that if those are not worthy of the support given me by Your Excellency, they will at least satisfy a certain ambition that I entertain. And I want to be clearly understood, since I had a chance to find a patron of

such greatness. Your Excellency, therefore, you deign to receive willingly my good wish that still when, bathed in sweat and blood, you will be divested of the victorious arms and of things serious and lofty, you will be permitted to descend to the low and the light.[66]

The divesting of 'the victorious arms and of things serious and lofty' to which Hoste refers here rings with an immediacy that stretches beyond Ferrante's illustrious military career. In 1554 Ferrante was, in fact, the object of an Imperial investigation into his gubernatorial policies and operating procedures. The investigation was initiated by complaints from castellano Don Giovanni da Luna and Grand Chancellor Francesco Taverna, as well as by damaging auxiliary corroboration from Don Raimondo di Cardona, the treasurer of the armies, and Camillo Castiglione, the vicar of provisions. After Ferrante had been removed from office, the Imperial investigations into Milanese affairs reached beyond Ferrante to other officials serving the chancery, including Grand Chancellor Taverna himself and chancery secretary Agostino da Monte. Ferrante's political forces evidently had been arrayed against those of the conspirators for some time before the storm actually broke, for similar images of an embattled Ferrante Gonzaga had already been painted the previous year in a contemporary text preserved in the Biblioteca Ambrosiana. The text describes an imaginary allegorical joust between Ferrante and his political enemies which supposedly took place during the year 1553.[67] Even if Hoste da Reggio was not privy to the Ambrosian text itself, *Il primo libro delli madrigali a cinque voci*'s general theme of Ferrante as the victorious commander-in-chief most certainly reflects much of the court-sponsored propaganda of the period.

ALTVS

De l'Hoſte da Reggio,

MAESTRO DELLA MVSICA,

DELLO ILLVSTRISS. ET ECCELLENTISS.

DON FERRANTE GONZAGA.

IL PRIMO LIBRO DELLI MADRIGALI,

A CINQVE VOCE.

NOVAMENTE DA LI SVOI PROPRII EXEMPLARI,

CORRETTI, ET POSTI IN LVCE.

Venetiis apud Hieronymum Scotum

MDLIIII

Figure 6.1 Frontispiece of Hoste da Reggio, *Il primo libro delli madrigali a cinque voci* (Venice: Hieronymo Scotto, 1554). Courtesy of the Civico Museo Bibliografico Musicale, Bologna. All rights reserved.

Central to Hoste's collection in honor of Ferrante is the madrigal 'Se altra ragioni ti mosse al canto e al suono,' which lauds the beleaguered governor through an affective setting of a text styled after that of the state motet:

Se altra ragioni ti mosse al canto e al suono	If another reason moved you to singing and to playing,
Milan citta de d'oro	Milan, the city of gold,
Quando giove del suo sublime trono	When Jove from his sublime throne
De passati travagli alma ristoro	restored the soul from past afflictions,
Il gran ferrando ti mando per duce,	the great Ferrante he sent as Duke.
Hor che non minor gloria a te conduce	Now that no small glory leads
Quella beata schiera	that blessed rank
E quei felici spirti peregrini	and those felicitous wandering spirits to you,
Godi giosci e spera	you delight, rejoice and hope
Che mentr'egli d'astrica regge gl'honori	that while he of Austria bears the honors,
Questi ferrando in secreti alti e divini	these joust Ferrante in deep and divine
Torneran di trofei palme et allori.	secrets of trophies, palms, and laurels.[68]

Unfortunately, only four of the five partbooks of *Il primo libro delli madrigali a cinque voci* are extant, so it is impossible to evaluate the full effect of the musical setting. The frequent introduction of dotted rhythms underscores the military overtone of the text, while subtle chromatic inflections serve to enhance its rhetorical delivery. As in many of Hoste's extant madrigals, however, harmonic shading seems to take precedence over figural text painting in communicating the intricacies of the text. Many of the other madrigals of *Il primo libro delli madrigali a cinque voci* make similarly veiled references to Ferrante's military prowess and political difficulties, but these are often couched in the context of the typical madrigalian themes of love and longing. For example, although the opening strains of Petrarch's 'Passa la nave mia,' portend an innocuous lament by a grief-stricken lover, the ottava, when considered within the context of the dedication, alludes to the usurpation of Ferrante's Milanese appointment. The references to the enemy seem pointed at none other than Grand Chancellor Taverna, who not only engineered Ferrante's downfall, but also managed the affairs of the Milanese state for a brief period following his recall.

Passa la nave mia Colma d'oblio	My ship, full of oblivion, passes
Per aspro mai a mezzanote il verno	through the rugged sea between Scylla and Carybdis at midnight during winter.
Infra scill'e carridd'et al governo	And at the helm sits the gentleman,
Sied'il signor anz'l nemico mio	indeed, my enemy.
A ciascun rem'in pensier pront'e rio	To anyone holding his oar alertly and rightly
Che la tempesta e'l fin par ch'abb'a scherno	the tempest and death seem a mockery.
La vela rompe un vent'humi d'eterno	The sea is broken by a wind carrying the essence of eternity,
Di sospir di speranz'e e desio.	of whispers, expectations, and desires.

That Hoste da Reggio lamented Ferrante's impending dismissal so publicly is not entirely implausible, for his resignation marked the end of a very successful period in the production and publication of the composer's works. Although Hoste's *Il primo libro de madrigali a tre voci* of 1554 was reissued with slight emendations by Scotto of Venice in 1562, he appears to have neither composed nor published new madrigals during the succeeding years.

Hoste's *Il primo libro de madrigali a tre voci* of 1554 was succeeded at the Moscheni firm by two rather diverse musical collections – Hermann Matthias Werrecore's *Cantuum quinque vocum quas Motetta vocant . . . Liber primus* and Pietro Taglia's *Il primo libro de madrigali a quattro voci*. Werrecore's *Cantuum quinque vocum* appears to be a compendium of works composed for use at the Duomo of Milan, and contains motets to be sung at Mass and Vespers on various feasts of the liturgical year. The collection is discussed at some length in Chapter 3. Taglia's *Il primo libro de madrigali a quattro voci* contains twenty-nine madrigals, about half of which utilize the increasingly popular alla breve mensuration. Although it seems that Taglia spent most of his career in Milan, the archival sources yield little regarding his professional activities, aside from the fact that he served as the interim maestro di cappella at Santa Maria presso San Celso while Simon Boyleau was on leave from his duties there in 1565.[69] However, the preface to his *Il primo libro . . . a quattro*, which is dedicated to one Giovanni Bracelli, mentions singing of compositions such as those contained with the learned Gorla.[70] This is most assuredly a reference to Giovanni Petro Gorla, who served as the organist at the Duomo of Milan from 1551 to 1558.[71] Such intimate familiarity with the local musical scene suggests that Taglia had forged strong connections in Milan. His first book of five-voice madrigals, in fact, was also published by the Moscheni, who, eager to comply in the obligation of bringing honor to the city, favored local composers over foreign ones. Indeed, Taglia, who is identified in notarial document as a 'nobile domino' and a resident of the parish of Santo Sebastiano in the Porta Ticinese district of Milan, purchased property in the parish of San Pietro in Camminadella for 1000 lire on 30 August 1564.[72] Thus, it seems clear that Taglia resided and worked in Milan during the 1550s and 1560s, despite the fact that it is not currently possible to account for all his professional activities.

Jessie Ann Owens has observed that Taglia's *Il primo libro de madrigali a quattro voci* is tonally organized according to clef and signature, and further noted the rather unorthodox use of the natural sign to indicate the pitch B-mi.[73] These individual trademarks, however, are incorporated into a style that does not depart radically from Milanese traditions. Like Hoste da Reggio, Taglia appears to have preferred poetry on the order of that of Petrarch, Ariosto, and Cassola, but he often sets only the ottava of the sonnets he chooses, thereby relying upon the natural division into quattrains as a means of defining structural perimeters. Moreover, Taglia frequently presents the text chordally, but often with one or two voices offset by a beat or two in order to provide contrapuntal interest, a technique that lends natural clarity to the declamation while maintaining textural interest. Phrases are often repeated with harmonic and melodic variation for added emphasis, and are clearly articulated through the introduction of cadential figures and chromatic turns of phrase. Although madrigalisms are sometimes employed to musically illustrate specific words or phrases, meaning is conveyed largely through the introduction of colorful accidentals.

The multiple-impression volume that constitutes Taglia's *Il primo libro*, which Owens characterizes as 'unusually handsome,'[74] most likely was among those submitted to Cardinal Cristoforo Madruzzo for approval in 1556. In a lengthy letter addressed to Madruzzo dated 8 settembre 1556, Francesco Moscheni laments the recent demise of classical language skills and reminds the newly appointed governor of his firm's commitment to the local dissemination of Latin, Greek, and Italian classical texts. He further praises Milan's advancement in the sciences and letters, and, obviously desirous of a new commission, concludes by acclaiming the grandeur of the house of Madruzzo. Moscheni then offers a gift of several books produced by the firm, some of which contained music, for the Cardinal's perusal:

> And in order that Your Most Illustrious and Reverend Lord see these in part, we present you these copies thus of music, as well as of prose and verse. And because we are certain, due to your innate kindliness, that help does not lack where the need is seen, which you are able to discern of us through Mr. Nicolò Secco and through Mr. Giuliano Gosellini, who were those that brought us to live in this city . . .[75]

The circumstantial evidence suggests that the Moscheni firm's attempts to secure the patronage of Madruzzo were largely unsuccessful, at least from a musical point of view. Madruzzo is not connected to any music prints produced locally, perhaps because his Milanese tenure spanned only a brief two years. Madruzzo's vigorous efforts toward the cultivation of the arts, in fact, were focused upon the Madruzzo family palace in Trent, where he had a resident court chapel at his disposal.[76]

The Moscheni, evidently undaunted by Madruzzo's apparent disinterest, persisted in the publication of music, giving the bulk of their attention to locally recognized composers. Their next musical venture was the first book of five-voice motets by Pietro Taglia, which was dedicated to one Alessandro Cremona and published in 1557. Between 1562 and 1566, moreover, they issued between one and three volumes of hymns, motets, madrigals, and canzoni alla napolitana per year, focusing upon, but not restricting themselves to, local composers.[77] At least one of these prints, the *De diversi autori canzoni alla napolitana à tre voci novamente poste in luce* of 1562, appears to have been initiated at the Milanese court. On 7 June 1559, Massimo Troiano, a Neapolitan musician in the service of governor Cordova, was awarded a five-year privilege for the printing of idiomatic Neapolitan songs,[78] and the 1562 Moscheni print is the only extant volume issued in Milan between 1559 and 1564 that fits the description in the privilege.

The Moscheni also introduced the secular works of Giuseppe Caimo, a Milanese organist who appears to have spent his entire career in the city despite at least one opportunity to join the ducal retinue in Bavaria.[79] Conservative Milan did not initially embrace the likes of Caimo, who made a disastrous debut as organist at the Duomo of Milan in early 1560. The deputies of the Fabbrica of the Duomo, who historically had been comparatively casual in their management of the positions of organist and assistant organist, were especially eager to show off a new organ constructed by Antignate of Brescia on which they had spent the considerable sum of 15,000 scudi,[80] and the newly elected Archbishop Carlo Borromeo, overstepping his bounds in typical fashion, took it upon himself to expedite matters by appointing Caimo.[81] Unfortunately, however, Caimo was retained at the Duomo for a mere three months, during which, if the report of the deputies is to be at all believed, he created a rift among the ordinaries and scandalized the entire community with his impertinence, his idiosyncratic rhythmic style and registrations, and his destructive adjustments to the instrument. Whether Caimo's inauspicious beginning at the Duomo was entirely due to his inexperience and avant-garde approach to the instrument is unclear, for the deputies clearly had intended to lure Giovanni Battista Perotto away from his position at Sant'Ambrogio, and they may well have resented Borromeo's interference into matters commonly entrusted the officers of the Fabbrica. In any event, the deputies responded to the supposed furor over Caimo's audacious playing by temporarily appointing the assistant organist Giovanni Jacopo da Cremona in his stead, sending a letter of explanation to Borromeo after the fact.[82] Borromeo, undaunted, pressed Andrea Ruberto, the Archiepiscopal deputy, on Caimo's behalf, and, after pursuing the matter with little success, cast about on his own for another replacement.[83] By 1563, however, the deputies has succeeded in enlisting the services of Perotto as they had initially intended, thus closing the matter once and for all.[84] Caimo, meanwhile, remained in Milan, where he soon acquired the competing position of organist at Sant'Ambrogio.[85] There Caimo gradually achieved local recognition as a virtuoso performer and improviser of counterpoint, as is evidenced in a letter from Prospero Visconti to Duke Wilhelm V of Bavaria dated 1 October 1575.[86]

That Francesco Moscheni championed Caimo at a time when Milanese officials regarded the organist with some distaste seems rather remarkable unless the printer's own political problems are taken into account. In March 1563 Moscheni, his wife, and two sons were arrested by Borromeo's grand inquisitor for the possession of certain heretical books. After Moscheni had been imprisoned for eight days without examination, Archiepiscopal deputy Ruberto intervened, inquiring into the matter and demanding that, at the very least, he be permitted to witness the examination of Moscheni's wife. Ruberto's interference caused a minor furor, both because the inquisitor perceived his request as arrogant and because the office of the inquisition was already aggravated by its singular lack of success in finding a convent in which to temporarily hold Moscheni's spouse.[87] Upon his release, Moscheni may have consciously chosen to promote Caimo in a show of filial homage to Borromeo. Moscheni not only published Caimo's *Il primo libro de madrigali a quattro voci* of 1564, but also may have been responsible for the *Canzoni napoletane a tre* of 1566.[88]

Caimo's *Il primo libro de madrigali a quattro voci*, which was dedicated to Count Ludovico Galerate, features eighteen madrigals on texts by Sannazaro, Cassola, Tasso and Alfonso D'Avalos. Its content, which includes a madrigal dedicated to Princes Rudolf and Ernst of Austria and several *poesie per musica* acclaiming one Gratia, appears at least tangentially related to activities at the Milanese court. In 1563 Rudolf and Ernst, the two eldest sons of Maxmilian II of Austria, were entertained in Milan by governor Don Consalvo-Fernando di Cordova, Duca di Sessa,[89] and, thus, the madrigal devoted to them was likely composed for that occasion. The *poesie per musica* for Gratia, moreover, are quite typical of those slated for performance at court during the annual Milanese carnival in terms of their simple, declamatory style, their personification of female virtue, and their frequent references to figures from classical literature.

The madrigal for Rudolf and Ernst, *Eccelsa e generosa prole*, lauds the Austrian princes as the worthy progeny of the Holy Roman Emperor and encourages them to follow his example in demonstrating valor, virtue, and wisdom. The initial two quattrains that comprise the sonnet's prima parte are set in the declamatory chordal style typical of Milanese madrigals of the period, but the declamation itself is more rhythmically flexible and harmonically pungent than the works of Caimo's predecessors Hoste da Reggio and Pietro Taglia. At the outset of the closing sestina some imitation is introduced into the texture, perhaps to illustrate the concept of the princely pair blossoming 'under the shadow' of their illustrious father. The imitation eventually dissolves, however, into the homorhythmic style favored by Milanese composers.

Much has been made of a potential stylistic relationship between Caimo and Nicola Vicentino, and, indeed, the two composers must, at the very least, have been acquainted. In 1565 Vicentino took up residence in Milan as one of two rectors at San Tommaso in terra amara, a parish church which Borromeo elevated to collegiate status through the suppression and transfer of other local benefices during the 1570s.[90] Vicentino resided at San Tommaso for the remaining thirteen years of his career,[91] during which he published his fifth book of five-voice madrigals (1572) and his fourth book of five-voice motets (1571).[92] Like Vicentino's *Motecta cum quinque vocibus. Liber quartus*, Caimo's *Il primo libro de madrigali a quattro voci* is dedicated to Count Ludovico Galerate, thus suggesting that both composers moved in the same social circles. Like Vicentino, moreover, Caimo is thought to have been a member of the Facchini della Val di Blemio,[93] a literary academy immortalized in Giovanni Paolo Lomazzo's *Rabisch* (1589). In fact, both composers may have become acquainted with Ludovico Galerate through the academy. Finally, like Vicentino, Caimo received a remuneration from the Bavarian court via the agency of Gaspare Visconti in 1570.[94] It has been suggested that both composers were championed for potential positions there by none other than the meddlesome Carlo Borromeo. Yet neither appears to have actually entered the service of Duke Wilhelm. Instead, both remained in Milan, although for different personal reasons. Caimo for his own part, had a wife and four sons, and had wished to bring at least two of them to Bavaria.[95]

The Moscheni production of the 1560s of which Caimo's madrigals formed a part features a gradual transition from attempts to attract court composers to increased attention upon those associated with local ecclesiastical institutions, and thus reflects the expanding domination of the church in Milanese cultural life under Carlo Borromeo. During the 1560s and 1570s Borromeo sought to curb, with only limited success, the Milanese passion for carnival entertainments. Although his attempts to abolish carnival and other similar entertainments met with strong resistance among the Milanese nobility,[96] his strategy of substituting secular pastimes with public religious displays seems, in the end, to have been somewhat successful, for the eye-witness historical accounts of the 1570s and 1580s appear consumed by festal processions, rather than by civic celebrations. In addition, Borromeo began to press local musicians with ecclesiastical credentials into service, thus widening the sacred circle to include composers previously active primarily in the production of secular genres. Hoste da Reggio, for example, was employed at the Duomo between 1558 and 1563 and thereafter resumed his canonry at San Calimero, while Simon Boyleau and Pietro Taglia served as *maestri da cappella* at Santa Maria presso San Celso. Nicola Vicentino, as noted above, took up residence as a rector at San Tommaso in terra amara in 1565, while Gioseffo Caimo moved from Sant'Ambrogio to the Duomo in 1580. Despite the emphasis on spiritualization programs at many of the institutions that employed these and other such musicians, however, the production of madrigals did not wane. Vicentino's *Madrigali a cinque voci . . . Libro quinto*, for example, was printed by Paolo Gottardo Pontio of Milan in 1572, while Gioseffo Caimo's *Madrigali a cinque voci . . . libro quarto* was issued by Amandino of Venice under arrangement with Tini of Milan in 1584. In fact, the spiritualization programs, each of which was designed to target a specific aristocratic, merchant, or ecclesiastical population, seem to have strengthened the concept of audience. This is, perhaps, nowhere more evident than at Santa Maria presso San Celso, a pilgrimage church staffed with an eighteen-member choir that was founded by Gian Galeazzo Sforza in 1485. During the sixteenth century, Santa Maria presso San Celso sponsored a Vespers service in the evenings during the summer, on the first Sunday of the month, and on special feasts, as well as a Compline service during the lenten season and on Saturday evenings. According to Paolo Morigia, the Saturday Compline service was especially popular with the local nobility of the late sixteenth century. Morigia's comments, when considered in light of the archival evidence, suggest that the Compline service was part of a larger program that comprised a combination of Vespers and Compline services aimed at fostering collective Marian devotion among the nobility.[97] During his tenure as maestro di cappella at Santa Maria presso San Celso, Simon Boyleau composed not only a cycle of magnificats for use in the services there, but also a collection madrigals for four to eight voices. The latter collection, entitled *Madrigali a IIII, V, VI, VII, et VIII voci*, was published by the Moscheni in 1564.

Although this peculiar collection of madrigals is dedicated to Ferrante's son Cesare and contains several works expressly for him, it seems to have been intended as a sort of audition document for the Borromeo family. In August 1563, evidently unaware that Vicenzo Ruffo had already been appointed, Carlo Borromeo's sister Suor Corona Isabella enthusiastically endorsed Boyleau for the position of maestro di cappella at the Duomo. Eager to accommodate his sister's wishes, Carlo instructed his personal secretary Tullio Albanese to find something suitable for Boyleau.[98] In September of the same year, Albanese reported that he could do nothing for Boyleau, particularly since Ruffo was already holding the position at the Duomo. Boyleau must have been appointed at San Celso shortly thereafter.[99] He may have persisted in angling for a different appointment, however, and, if so, likely envisioned the 1564 madrigal book as a potential introduction to the Borromeo family via Carlo's sister Camilla, who had recently wed Cesare Gonzaga.[100] Although the individual texts of Boyleau's *Madrigali a IIII, V, VI, VII, et VIII voci* are devoted largely to members of various local aristocratic families, including the Lampugnavi, Latuati, Belgioiosi, Rho,

Biraghi, Cicogni, as well as distinguished Milanese ecclesiastics such as Monsignor Cesare Speciano and Francesco della Torre, wedding madrigals for Marc'Antonio and Isabella Latuati, Cesare and Camilla Gonzaga, and Antonio and Anna Cicogna complete the collection (see Table 6.2). The nuptial madrigal for Cesare and Camilla Gonzaga occupies the central position in the print, and the collection itself is framed by two other madrigals that also address Cesare. It, thus, seems probable that the composer viewed the Gonzaga – Borromea nuptials as an opportunity to curry the newfound favor of the Borromei while retaining his well-established connection to the Gonzaga. The madrigal for Cesare and Camilla focuses more strongly on the union of the families than it does on the immediate objects of the dedication, and the Borromei are afforded pride of place in the nominal order established by the somewhat amateur poetry (Example 6.3).

Table 6.2 Dedicatees of Simon Boyleau, *Madrigali a IIII, V, VI, VII, et VIII voci* (1564)

Madrigal	*Dedicatee(s)*
Signor che con misura	Cesare Gonzaga
Accendiamo cantando	Isabella Gonzaga, Princess of Molfetta
Lutia gentil	Lutia Lampugnava
Chi vol veder	Isabella Lampugnava
Ben fanno, ò Meraviglia	Margherita Maraviglia
Laccio dolc'e gentile	Marc'Antonio e Isabella Latuati (wedding)
Saggio signor	Mons. Cesare Speciano
Appollo, se giamai gl'occhi	Lodovico Belgioioso
Franca torre securo e docle	Francesco della Torre
Moderno e liberal buon Macenate	Francesco della Torre
Mentre canto do voi	Girolamo Cavenago
Rabbia che con pensier lodato	Luigi Rabbia
A me par ch'alla guerr'Amor	Giulio Centurione
O invidia nemica di virtude	Cesare Bosso
Prima che torni à voi	Agosto da Ró
Invito Henrico	Henry II of France
Ercol divin più del Thebano	Henry II of France
A così lieti	Cesare e Camilla Gonzaga (wedding)
Questa nova di ciel	Camilla Centuriona
Se si mira al crin d'or	None
2p. Ma poi si spiega	
Questa donna gentil	Faustina Nuvolona
Spargete o Nimphe	Antonio et Anna Cicogni (wedding)
Signor mio caro	Domenico Negruolo
Mentr'ameran i nudi	Mario Birago
Ardo per voi	Lelio Guidiciano
Non so tosto dal ciel	Cesare Gonzaga
Dialogo: Caron Caronte	None

The inclusion of three nuptial works in a volume otherwise concerned with the general acclamation of various noble dedicatees only serves to strengthen the volume's tentative association with Santa Maria presso San Celso. It, in fact, suggests that the popular nuptial custom of making a pilgrimage to Santa Maria presso San Celso for a special Marian blessing was frequently observed by the nobility as early as the sixteenth century, and, further, that the custom was one of the qualities that endeared the local aristocracy to the institution. In any case, Boyleau's *Madrigali a IIII, V, VI, VII et VIII voci* is clearly intended for members of an aristocratic audience of the type that reportedly attended the services at Santa Maria presso San Celso. It is both personalized and emblematic in its inclusion of madrigals devoted to individuals who possessed the economic means to purchase the book, the rudimentary musical training required to interpret its content, and the social conditioning necessary to appreciate its aesthetic value. The print, therefore, admittedly catered to an elite assembly that shared, at its very core, a relationship to Santa Maria presso San Celso. Yet Santa Maria presso San Celso's reputation rested not only in the nobility of its congregation, but also in its status as pilgrimage site. The intersection of dedicatory and nuptial themes in Boyleau's *Madrigali a IIII, V, VI, VII et VIII voci*, therefore, underscores both the church's dual character and the appeal of this character in aristocratic circles. Thus, the *Madrigali*'s idiosyncratic organization, whether a marketing strategy contrived by the printer or an obsequious tribute conceived by the composer, indicates that the aristocratic audience in Milan was increasingly drawn to ecclesiastical rather than courtly venues during the latter half of the sixteenth century.

Example 6.3   Boyleau, *A così lieti*, measures 16-30

Notes

1   'E io danno il gioco in tutto, ma non così le novelle; pur per non parere che vogliamo rubare, o imitare il Boccaccio, se vi governarete a modo mio cantaremo e novelleremo a un tempo; perché dove altri si passa cantando asciuttamente col dire solo; diciamolo un'altra volta, quest'è bello, e simili chiacchiere, noi ci diffonderemo un poco più nel parlare ragionando di poesia, di burle, di novelle e d'altre dolci fantasiette, come più a sesto ci verrà, e a proposito; e così cibando il corpo d'un dolce riposo, pasceremo l'anima ancora d'una soave dolcezza, anzi d'un cibo divino.' *L'opera musicale di Antonfrancesco Doni* in *Instituta et Monumenta* I, ed. Anna Maria Monterosso Vacchelli (Cremona, 1969), 102.

2   See *L'opera musicale*, 47-48.

3   See, for example, Merkley and Merkley, *Music and Patronage*, 125-154 and 370-405.

4   The canonicate and cantoria was vacated by the deceased Luchinus Curtus on 4 July 1530. *Sforzesco: Registri ducali* 73 (Benefizi 1523-1525), 138r, ASM. A pair of documents dated 8 and 14 December 1530 in *Sforzesco* 1429 (Milano città e ducato 1530 dicembre e 1530 senza data), Busta 1 (1530 dicembre), n.n., ASM, reveal that efforts were not made to replace him until early December 1530. *Sforzesco* 1430 (Milano città e ducato 1531 gennaio), n.n., ASM, contains a letter dated 6 January 1531 from Jacopo Picenardus, the episcopal officer in charge of economic matters, to Francesco II Sforza discussing the nomination of Giovanni Maria del Corte to the position. I have found no documents confirming his appointment to that post, but the benefice registers do contain a cancelled letter of appointment for Andrea de Germanis, another of the ducal singers, that is dated 1 December 1530. *Sforzesco: Registri ducali* 84 (Benefizi 1525-1535), 140r, ASM.

5   *Sforzesco: Registri ducali* 84 (Benefizi 1525-1535), 60r-v and 73v, ASM.

6   Ibid., 77v, ASM.

7   Ibid.,73v, ASM.

8   Ibid., 100r, ASM.
9   *Sforzesco: Registri ducali* 73 (Benefizi 1525-1535), 153r-v, ASM.
10   *Ordinazioni* VII (1519-1531), 188v-189r, AVFDM.
11   *Vacchette* 401 (1536-1537), 31v, AVFDM.
12   *Sforzesco: Registri ducali* 73 (Benefizi 1523-1525), 69r-70r, ASM. See Appendix I, Document 5, which is also discussed in Chapter 3 above. For a summary of the research regarding Werrecore's Flemish heritage, see Marco Brusa, 'Hermann Matthias Werrecore,' 176-179.
13   Guglielmus is first identified as a ducal singer in a property transaction of 9 September 1523. *Notarile* 7135 (Alessandro Zavettari q. Ambrogio 31/07/1523-11/10/1525), 9 septembris 1523. I am grateful to Professore Grazioso Sironi for this notarial reference. When Guglielmus passed on shortly before the death of Francesco II, a portion of his estate was promised to another courtier named Stephanus Vitulonus. However, some questions arose regarding the legal ramifications of disposal of an inheritance connected to the court treasury, and the chief magistrate of the chancery became involved. Vitulonus filed a formal supplication on 7 December 1536. Its outcome is unknown. *Potenze sovrane* 124 (Musicisti), f. 27, ASM.
14   *Sforzesco* 1471 (Potenze sovrani: Francesco II Sforza 1499-1535), 18 and 19, ASM.
15   *Ordinazioni* VIII (1532-1534), 97v-98v, ASM, and Registri 728 (1533-1536), AVFDM.
16   *Cancelleria dello Stato* 67 (1547 febbraio), f. 59, ASM. This document appears to be a continuation of folios 57 and 58, which comprise a list of items heard in the chancery on 9 February 1547.
17   Germanis is identified as a ducal singer as early as 20 August 1525 in a document regarding the payment of an annual pension of an unspecified amount. The pension was likely connected to his benefice at Santa Maria Adurni. *Sforzesco: Registri ducali* 84 (Benefizi 1525-1535), 16v, ASM.
18   *Sforzesco: Registri ducali* 73 (Benefizi 1523-1525), 11r-v and 19v, ASM
19   *Sforzesco: Registri ducali* 84 (Benefizi 1525-1535), 140r-v, ASM.
20   Ibid., 152r-v, ASM
21   *Ordinazioni* IX (1535-1544), 256v, AVFDM.
22   '. . . in casa sua, io udi cantare si leggiadramente da M. Sebastiano, e da suoi compagni una battaglia Francese, e certe altre canzonette scritte nella medesima lingua, come se fossero nati, et allevati in mezzo alla Francia:' Matthias Werrecore, *La bataglia tagliana*, dedication.
23   Alfred Einstein, *The Italian Madrigal* (Princeton: Princeton University Press, 1949), II, 743-749.
24   See Chapter 1.
25   On Vincentino's acquisition of benefices in Milan see Daolmi, *Don Nicola Vicentino*, 4-47.
26   Don Harrán, ed. *The Anthologies of Black-Note Madrigals*, 5 vols (Rome: American Institute of Musicology, 1980), III, xi.
27   See Wolfgang Wtorzyck, 'Die Madrigale Vincenzo Ruffos' (Ph.D. dissertation, Freien Universität Berlin, 1955), 80-82.
28   James Haar, 'Lassus: (1) Orlande de Lassus,' *The New Grove Dictionary of Music and Musicians*, 2nd edn. (London and New York., 2001), XIV, 295. Also see Orlando di Lasso, *Canzoni Villanesche and Villanelle*, x.
29   See Chapter 5 above.
30   'vestiti uscirono con la guida inanzi sonando il corno, et con bell'ordine à duoi à duoi, et passando per mezzo la Città cavalcorono à Corte; dove in una gran sala si trovava

l'Illustriss*ima* et Eccellentiss*ima* Sig*nora* Principessa . . .' Antonfrancesco Raineri, *Pompe de Messer Antonfrancesco*, n.p.

31 The *Pompe dei corrieri amorosi* and *Dei poeti amorosi* are described in detail in Raineri, *Pompe*, n.p., a prose text composed on 20 February 1553 in commemoration of the 1553 carnival entertaiments.

32 'Giunta la Mascarata superbissima nella detta Corte, con tanto bel ordine, e con silentio et stupore universale de circonstanti e giratala tre volte, passeggiando e sonando gli detti musici, con armonia dolcissima si fermar*ono* alfin'tutti al conspetto delle Signore e gentildonne, e fatto le muse ala, si fecer*ono* inanzi i poeti, presso ad Apollo; i tre più antichi da man destra, il moderni da man sinistra, ciascuno al suo loco, ed egli sonando la lira, col plettro d'oro, cantò soavemente le stanze infrascritte' Raineri, *Pompe*, n.p..

33 'Finite le quali, fu fatto un' cherchio da le Muse intorno ad Apollo, e lo raccolsero in mezzo; inginocchiandosi tutte d'intorno à lui, che stava ritto e con divina dignitate inanzi à quelle Sig*nore* e gentildonne; e dopoi una bella ricercata con gl'Instrumenti musicali, di concerto, cantor*ono* le dette Muse il seguente madrigale in canto. Amar' cari tacendo Occhi beati;// Et sofferir' tacendo;// Et non chieder morendo anco mercede;// E' più grave dolor, ch'altri non crede.// Amor' che'n tutti i lati// Mi vai serrando il cor, l'anima aprendo// Perche mi chiudi ancora// La labra algenti? E vuoi ch'io taccia e mora? Doppoi cantato il madrigale; e replicato un altra volta, si levar*ono* le Muse in piè; e tornar*ono* à girar la Corte di nuovo, con bel'ordine, sonando quegl'Instrumenti diversi, con armonia troppo dolce; e poco dopoi si partir*ono* con li Cupidini inanzi, che g*i*ravano saltellando e scherzando come di sopra.' Raineri, *Pompe*, n.p.

34 Raineri, *Pompe*, n.p.

35 The tenor partbook in housed in München, Universitätsbibliothek.

36 See Chapter 3 above.

37 Simon Boyleau, *Madrigali a IIII, V, VI, VII, et VIII voci*, dedication. A complete set of extant partbooks is housed in the British Museum, London.

38 Ascanio Certorio delgi Ortensi, *I grandi apparati e feste fatte in Melano dalli Illustr. et Eccell. S. il Duca di Sesso Governatore . . .in casa dell'Illust. S. Gio. Battista Castaldo Marchese di Cassano* (Milan: Giovann'Antonio degli Antonij, 1559), 3r-4v, notes that it was typical to hold such entertainments in the homes of the nobility during carnival, and further, that the city trumpeters publicized the 1559 event in advance of its performance. On 18 January 1559 court treasurer Paolo Emilio Gambaloyta was reimbursed 200 scudi for expenses incurred in preparing a 'torneo' at the home of Giovanni Battista Castaldo, thus confirming that the 1559 entertainment which is the subject of Certorio's chronicle enjoyed official gubernatorial sponsorship. *Registri della Cancelleria dello Stato* XXII-12 (Mandati 1558-1562), 59r.

39 Certorio degli Ortensi, *I grandi apparati*, 5v-7r.

40 ' . . .una excelle*n*tissima musica di viole d'arco, di tromboni, di cornetti, e di voci; i cui sonatori vestiti con veste lunghe di velo bianco stavano posti per ordine à sedere ne i gradi del tempio suonando i loro istromenti si soavemente che all'armonia . . .' Certorio degli Ortensi, *I grandi apparati*, 7v.

41 'un concerto d'una divinissima musica di varij istromenti.' Certorio degli Ortensi, *I grandi apparati*, 10v.

42 Certorio degli Ortensi, *I grandi apparati*, 11v-16v.

43 Ibid., 16v-18r.

44 Ibid., 29r-32v.

45 Ibid., 18r-20r.

46 Ibid., 20r-29r.

47   '. . .Cantava ancora Oratio Tuttavilla, in questo mezzo che cantavamo così bene si finì di giocare a primera, et il Marchese venne a sentire la nostra bella musica e per conciarla cantando Oratio volse cantare ancora lui, tal che la si finì in ridere perche mi bisognava tratto per tratto rimetterli. Il Marchese diceva che era Orazio che fallava, et Oratio diceva che era il Marchese, il Conte Manfre*dino* dette la sentenza e disse che tutti doi non ne sapevano strazzo,' Transcription reported in Iain Fenlon, *Giaches de Wert: Letters and Documents*, 81.

48   '. . .venne a basso in la camera de quadri con questi signori, et voleva cantare, ma non eramo in tanti.' Fenlon, *Giaches de Wert*, 87.

49   A modern edition is found in Giaches de Wert, *Collected Works III: Madrigals in Corpus mensurabilis musicae* 24, ed. Carol MacClintock (Rome: American Institute of Musicology, 1962).

50   Fenlon, *Giaches de Wert*, 50.

51   See Donà, *La stampa musicale*, 44.

52   *Studi parte antica* 97, fol. 4, ASM.

53   *Registri di Lettere Ducali* 1552-1562, 28v-29r, BTASCM.

54   'una stampa nova corretta e molto elegante.' *Registri di Lettere Ducali* 1553-1562, 29v-30r, BTASCM.

55   In late 1548 Hippolita married Fabrizio Colonna. Colonna apparently passed on in 1550, for the cartella Gonzaga di Guastalla 2 in ASP contains a number of documents dating from the years 1550 and 1551 regarding financial matters that were left unresolved after his death.

56   Alfonso Ulloa, *Vita del valorosissima e gran capitano Don Ferrante Gonzaga* (Venice: Nicolò Bevilacqua, 1563), 179r. Also see R.M. Ridolfi, 'Gonzaga, Ippolita,' *Dizionario biografico degli italiani* (Cantanzaro: Grafico Abramo S. r.l., 2001), LVII, 794-796.

57   Hoste da Reggio, *Il primo libro de madrigali a tre voci*, dedication. Also see Getz, 'New Light on the Milanese Career of Hoste da Reggio,' 292-293.

58   Hoste da Reggio, *Il primo libro de madrigali a tre voci*. Only the altus partbook, which is housed in the British Museum, is extant. The revised version, *Il primo libro de madrigali a tre voci novamente per Antonio Gardane ristampati* (Venice, 1562), is reorganized according to system, cleffing, and tone. Moreover, several works included in the original volume are omitted.

59   The others include *Il secondo libro delli madrigali a quattro voci* (Venice: Girolamo Scotto, 1554c); *Il terzo libro delli madrigali a quattro voci* (Venice: Giroamo Scotto, 1554d); and *Il primo libro delli madrigali a cinque voci* (Venice: Girolamo Scotto, 1554a). A modern edition of *Il secondo libro delli madrigali a quattro voci* is available as volume 9 of the *Sixteenth-Century Madrigal*, ed, by Jessie Ann Owens (New York and London: Garland Publishing, Inc., 1988). *Il terzo libro delli madrigali a quattro voci* was the subject of a degree thesis by Barbara Torre entitled 'Hoste da Reggio: il Terzo Libro di madrigali a 4 voci' (Università degli Studi di Milano, 1990/1991).

60   *Il secondo libro delli madrigali a quattro voci* is dedicated to Isabella de Capova Gonzaga, Principessa di Molfetta and wife of Ferrante Gonzaga, while *Il primo libro delli madrigali a cinque voci* is dedicated to the governor himself. *Il terzo libro delli madrigali a quattro voci* is dedicated to Cristoforo Fornari, treasurer of the Imperial army in Piedmont.

61   *Notarile* 13010 (Camillo Rho q. Giovanni Antonio 20/11/1553-9/10/1556), 4 septembris 1555, ASM, and *Santo Calimero* I-93 (Visite pastorali e documenti aggiunti 1567-1604), ASDM. The benefice included a share of all profits made on the premises and rights to a private room with two windows overlooking the garden in a house on the property.

62   On the biography of Hoste da Reggio, see Chapter 3 above.

63   *Primo libro de madrigali a quattro voci* (Venice, 1547), dedication. Erole Gonzaga was
      Ferrante's brother. For a modern edition of the *Primo libro*, see Jessie Ann Owens, ed.,
      Sixteenth-Century Madrigal 8 (New York and London: Garland Publishing, Inc., 1988).

64   Hoste da Reggio, *Il secondo libro delli madrigali a quattro voci*, dedication.

65   See Hoste da Reggio, *Il secondo libro delli madrigali a quattro voci* in *Sixteenth-
      Century Madrigal* 9, ed. Jessie Ann Owens, xii.

66   ' . . .sotto'l suo gloriosissimo nome sperando che se quelle non faranno l'Eccellen*za*
      vostra lodata del vitto che ella mi da, sodisfaranno almeno ad una certa ambitione, che io
      ho, che s'intenda per tutto, com'io mi ho saputo procacciare un Padrone di tanta
      grandezza, V*ostra* Eccellen*za* adunque degni di ricevere in grado il buon voler mio, che
      tuttavia quando ella bagnata di sudore e di sangue, si sara spogliate l'armi vittoriose, e da
      le cose gravi, et alte le sara lecito scendere a le basse e leggiere . . .' Hoste da Reggio, *Il
      primo libro delli madrigali a cinque voci*, dedication.   Bologna, Civico museo
      bibliografico musicale.

67   See C. Vianello, 'Feste, tornei, congiure nel cinquecento milanese,' *Archivio storico
      lombardo, nuova serie* I (1936), 370-381.

68   Hoste da Reggio, *Il primo libro delli madrigali a cinque voci*, XIIII-XV.

69   *Santa Maria presso San Celso: Libri giornalieri della cassa 1563-1569*, n.n., ASDM.
      On 5 September 1555, Taglia, identified as the maestro di cappella, was reimbursed L 21
      s7 d6 for the cost of a music book. Simon Boyleau served as the maestro di cappella in
      1563-1564 and 1566-1568. See Christine Getz, 'Simon Boyleau and the Church of the
      'Madonna of Miracles', 149-150.

70   The preface is translated by Jessie Ann Owens in Pietro Taglia, *Il primo libro de
      madrigali a quattro voci* in *Sixteenth-Century Madrigal* 27, xi.

71   See Appendix II.

72   *Notarile* 11224 (Celso Bologna q. Bernardino), 13/04/1562-20/02/1556, 30 agosto 1564,
      ASM.

73   Pietro Taglia, *Il primo libro de madrigali a quattro voci* in *Sixteenth-Century Madrigal*
      27, ed. Jessie Ann Owens, xii-xiii.

74   Taglia, *Il primo libro de madrigali a quattro voci*, xi.

75   'Et accio c*he* v*o*st*r*a Illu*st*ri*ssi*ma et Reverend*issi*ma Signo*r*a veda in parte de essi vi
      presentiamo queste copie, cosi di Musica, come di Prosa et Verso. Et p*er*che siamo certi,
      p*er* l'innata sua amorevolezza non manca dove conosce sia il bisogna d'aiuto, quella
      potra saper chi siamo dal Sig*n*or Nicolo Secco; et dal Sig*n*or Giuliano Gosellini, quali
      furono quelli che ne feccero venire ad habitare in questa Citta . . .' *Sforzesco* 1607
      (Potenze sovrane ed altre voci), n.p., ASM. This is a later copy of the original document,
      which itself appears to be missing.

76   On Madruzzo's patronage at Trent see Lunelli, 'Contributi trentini alle relazioni
      musicali,' 55-70.

77   For a summary of the prints issued by Francesco and Simone Moscheni during this
      period, see Donà, *La stampa musicale a Milano fino all'anno 1700*, 44-47.

78   *Studi parte antica* 97, fols. 16 and 17, ASM.

79   See Henry William Kaufmann, *Musicological Studies and Documents 11: The Life and
      Works of Nicola Vicentino* (Rome: American Institute of Musicology, 1966), 41-42, and
      Henry Simonsfeld, 'Mailänder Briefe zur bayerischen und allgemeinen Geschichte.'
      *Abhandlungen der historischen Classe der königlich bayerischen Akademie der
      Wissenschaften* XXII (1902), 290-291, 320-321, and 334. In July 1574 Caimo also
      forwarded several compositions to Wilhelm from Milan. See Simonsfeld, 'Mailänder

Briefe,' 335.

80   F. 36 inf .(Lettere a S. Carlo Borromeo) , 26r-27r, BAM. A letter from the deputies of the Duomo to Carlo Borromeo dated 26 March 1560. See Appendix I, Document 6. The Duomo registers also indicate that in 1558 work on the organ was drawing to a close, with payments being made approximately every two weeks to artisan Andrea de Meda and his assistants, who were responsible for ornamenting the exterior. *Vacchette* 412 (1558-1559), AVFDM.

81   F. 36 inf. (Lettere a S. Carlo Borromeo), 24r-25v, BAM. Excerpt of a letter from Guido Borromeo to Carlo Borromeo dated 27 March 1560.

82   F. 36 inf. (Lettere a S. Carlo Borromeo), 26r-27r, BAM.

83   F. 100 inf. (Lettere a S. Carlo Borromeo,. 268r and 315v, BAM. Letters to Carlo Borromeo from Andrea Ruberto, acting Vicario Archivescovile, and Giovanni Battista Reynaldo, President of the Senate.

84   On 30 December 1563 Perotto was paid L90 s13 d3 for services rendered between June and July 1563. Vacchette 414 (1562-1563), 119v, AVFDM. He thereafter appears in the registers as late as 1569, when he was receiving a salary of L110 for six months of service. *Registro* 748 (Uscite 1569-1570), 47r, AVFDM. By 1571 Perotto had been replaced by Octavio Bariola.

85   Caimo is first identified as the organist at Sant'Ambrogio on the frontispiece of his 1564 collection of four-voice madrigals. See Gioseppe Caimo, *Madrigali and Canzoni for Four and Five Voices in Recent Researches in Music of the Renaissance* LXXXIV and LXXXV, ed. Leta E. Miller (Madison: A-R Editions, 1990), viii.

86   ' . . .un raro virtuoso con la mano assai gagliarda e velocissima . . .sarebbe sonare alla sprovisa una fuga, che V. E. le darà, et ancora alla riversa et doppia et farla sentire molte volte con tutte le parti.' Reported in Simonsfeld, 'Mailänder Briefe,' 357.

87   F. 103-104 inf. (Lettere a S. Carlo Borromeo), 87r-89r, BAM.

88   Unfortunately, only the cantus of this collection survives, and it contains no printer's colophon.

89   P. 248 (Urbano Monti, *Delle cose più notabili successe a la città di Milano*, prima parte), 81r, BAM.

90   Daolmi, *Don Nicola Vicentino*, 58-59.

91   Ibid., 62.

92   Kaufmann, *Nicola Vicentino*, 41-42.

93   Daolmi, *Don Nicola Vicentino*, 93-94.

94   Each received ten kronos. Kaufmann, *Nicola Vicentino*, 41-42, and Simonsfeld, 'Mailänder Briefe,' 263-264.

95   Kaufmann, *Nicola Vicentino*, 41-42, and Simonsfeld, 'Mailänder Briefe,'290-291.

96   In February 1580, for example, a struggle between Borromeo and the patriciate ensued when Count Pietro Lonate reportedly applied directly to Rome for permission to retain the so-called Ambrosian carnival. See Chapter 7 below. In addition, Danilo Zardin, *Riforma cattolica e resistenza nobiliari nelle diocesi di Carlo Borromeo* (Milan: Jaca, 1983), 77-106, discusses similar local conflicts over pre-established social and religious customs, as well as the rebellions that accompanied them.

97   On the development of the post-Tridentine Vespers and Compline services at Santa Maria presso San Celso, see Getz, 'Simon Boyleau and the Church of the 'Madonna of Miracles,'' 145-168.

98   'Qui inclusa sarà una di suor Corona scrittami in rac*commandatio*ne di certo che vorebbe esser m*aestro* di cappella del Duomo. Però quando sia persona idonea, farete per lui quei buoni offitij che vi parrano conveniente.' Excerpt of a letter from Carlo Borromeo to

Tullio Albanese dated 2 agosto 1563. S.Q. + II.7 (Lettere da S. Carlo Borromeo), 71r, BAM. Unfortunately, Suor Corona Isabella's initial letter to Carlo is not extant, but Albanese's response to Carlo Borromeo clairfies its content.

99 'Non ho possuto far opera alcuna per Simone Boylau musico raccommandato a vostra singora Illustrissima dalla Reverendissima signora Sor' Corona Isabella essendo che gia il Duomo s'era provisto per Maestro de Cappella di Messer Vincenzo Ruffo contra il quale non ho voluto far' ufficio alcuno conoscendola meritendola di quel loco.' Excerpt of a letter from Tullio Albonese to Carlo Borromeo dated 1 September 1563 (excerpt). F. 103 inf. (Lettere a S. Carlo Borromeo), 359v, BAM.

100 The nuptials took place in 1560, and the preparations for them are mentioned in several letters written by Guido Borromeo to Carlo Borromeo during the spring of 1560. F. 36 inf. (Lettere a S. Carlo Borromeo), 24r-25v and 28r-29v, BAM.

Chapter 7

Public Devotion in Post-Tridentine Milan

For the urban dweller of the sixteenth century, identity within the civic space was intricately bound to local religious institutions. This aspect of Milanese life is reflected in such mundane details as the format of the legal document, which invariably identified the participating parties by patrimony and parochial residence. Yet the patrician and the artisan of sixteenth-century Milan sought a religious identity that extended beyond the mere issue of personal statistics to embrace a collective devotional experience. While the Duomo served as the physical and symbolic center of Milanese gubernatorial and ecclesiastical authority, the secondary churches served as repositories for citizens of similar patrimony, economic status, and devotional aims. Each church was as diverse as was its clientele. For example, the pilgrimage church of Santa Maria presso San Celso, which was supported by an administrative system designed largely by Gian Galeazzo and Ludovico Maria Sforza, was governed by and catered to the established nobility. Santa Maria della Scala, founded by the Visconti and subsequently crowned the official gubernatorial chapel, and San Francesco Grande, a patrician necropolis on the order of Santa Croce in Florence, similarly served those branches of the aristocracy which laid claim to a common legacy within the ecclesiastical hierarchy of the institution. Confraternities and monasteries also abounded, and these provided rich devotional programs aimed not only at patrician families, but also at the expanding bourgeois class. There was no shortage of opportunity for collective religious expression in sixteenth-century Milan, and this aspect of the urban experience rendered the post-Tridentine city ripe for theological experimentation. With the appointment of the imperious reformer Carlo Borromeo as Archbishop of Milan on 15 May 1560, [1] Milan was subjected to a substantive reorganization of its devotional institutions. This reconstruction, accompanied as it was by the proliferation of local printing presses that were prepared to produce music books, not only inexorably altered the face of public devotion itself, but also shaped the inextricable musical experience that formed a part of it.

Within a decade of his ascension, Borromeo seized control of the city to such a degree that the seat of the Archbishop of Milan effectively replaced that of the former Sforza dukes, a vantage point that would be enjoyed by Milanese archbishops for at least a half-century to come. Such a dominant role in civic government was not historically atypical to the Milanese episcopate, which had served as the principal force in local politics until the fourteenth century. Nonetheless, Borromeo's strategy was nothing short of brilliant. Firmly convinced that the successful implementation of post-Tridentine reform rested in the hands of the individual bishops, he initiated a series of pastoral visits, diocesan synods, and provincial councils intended for the purpose of rooting out abuses and regulating ecclesiastical practices in the diocese.[2] By regularly invoking his ecclesiastical authority and frequently exercising his extensive connections to both the Lombard aristocracy and the Vatican, Borromeo crippled the local government of the Hapsburg crown. Key to his success in this regard was the establishment of an independent clerical tribunal complete with its own squad of episcopal police in 1566. Although the Milanese senate initially filed a formal complaint against this blatant encroachment upon its jurisdiction, Borromeo eventually succeeded in convincing the Hapsburg crown of its legitimacy.[3] Thereafter, his reform projects proceeded virtually unopposed, and, even in the face of papal disapproval, gradually transformed Milan into his personal version of a modern City of God.

Borromeo and the Patriciate

Despite Borromeo's rather Machiavellian tactics, his spiritual and social legacy to Milan provided ample fodder for public discourse even during his own lifetime. No figure of the period was more beloved and yet more despised, and few were the subjects of as many rumors, speculations, and legends. Even the now well-worn tale of the failed assassination attempt conducted by the Humiliati, which Borromeo supposedly diverted through the singing of a motet on the text *Nolite timere*, is recorded in the chronicles of the period with a curious mixture of malicious delight and unbounded adoration.[4]   The Milanese patriciate chafed under certain of Borromeo's strictures, particularly those that either served to constrain innocent social pleasures or encroached upon the jurisdiction of established civic institutions. Even as the art of the dance was increasing in popularity under the tutelage of Cesare Negri and his associates, this innocuous pastime, along with such pleasures as playing cards and football, was publicly suppressed and, in some cases, even forbidden. Violation of episcopal bans carried monetary and religious penalties as mild as frequent confession, forced attendance at Christian Doctrine schools, or obligatory donations to confraternal initiatives, and as formidable as excommunication.[5] Yet such penalties generally failed to dissuade the patriciate from participating in censured activities, particularly when they were distinguished by long-standing local traditions. Such was the case of the Ambrosian carnival, which traditionally was observed in Milan during the week preceding Lent. In 1580 when Borromeo attempted to abolish the observance, Count Pietro Antonio Lonate circumvented Borromeo's authority and applied directly to Rome for permission to retain it. While the issue was still undergoing papal review, Governor Antonio de Guzman, who argued that such decisions were under his own purview, declared an official Ambrosian carnival for the Sunday preceding Quadregesima. The Milanese court, consequently, prepared and presented the traditional *mascherata a cavallo* featuring many of the nobility in prominent roles. Borromeo retaliated by excommunicating both the participants and the attendees, but because the activity had been initiated by a gubernatorial decree, he was forced to place a number of priests in the Duomo to absolve and assign penance to them the day following.[6]   The Ambrosian carnival remained a source of tension between Borromeo and the patriciate until his death in 1584; in both 1583 and 1584 several young noblemen sponsored a *mascherata a cavallo* at the Porta Romana despite Borromeo's vociferous objections, and even succeeded in drawing the gubernatorial court into the event by issuing a number of public challenges to which cavaliers from all over the city surreptitiously responded.[7] Borromeo's ecclesiastical powers were obviously of little effect in erasing such revered Milanese traditions as the Ambrosian carnival. Nonetheless, if Urbano Monti's personal account of daily life in post-Tridentine Milan at all reflects patrician habits of the period, then it can certainly be said that Borromeo's strategy of replacing secular pursuits with religious processions and confraternal activities largely succeeded in reshaping the public consciousness.[8]

Because Borromeo was temporarily occupied with administrative duties in Rome, he did not officially enter Milan until 23 September 1565. While in Rome, however, he immediately began initiating reforms via correspondence with the curial officials serving under him, including Nicolò Ormaneto, Ottaviano Forero, Cesare Speciano and Francesco della Torre. Most of his initial concerns, which embraced issues regarding clerical training and performance, were clearly shaped by his participation in the final meetings of the Council of Trent and his activity in the reform of the papal chapel and the Roman seminaries.[9] With the first Council of Milan in late 1565, however, it became clear that Borromeo's reform program would have both a direct and an indirect influence on Milanese musical practices. He clearly sought to abolish improprieties in clerical and monastic life, to purge the liturgy of secular musical influences, to inspire the listeners to piety, to enforce standards of text intelligibility, to ensure that as many ecclesiastical musicians as possible be clerically trained, and to limit the use of instruments in the church to the organ.[10]

As Robert Kendrick has ably demonstrated, many of Borromeo's policies regarding music were shaped largely as a response to non-musical issues. This is particularly evident in his interaction with Milanese convents, where the strict regulation of female musical activity that characterized his tenure stemmed from attempts to enforce Pius V's 1566 injunction that female monasteries adhere to the traditional practice of clausura. As Borromeo sought to bring Milanese monasteries, many of which were controlled by a patriciate that opposed such strictures, into conformity and to spiritualize their activities, he resorted, in part, to the legislation on nuns' liturgy that had been discussed and dropped at Trent. Still other policies were designed in response to violations of clausura and propriety.[11] In fact, Borromeo's legislation of music in monastic life might be described as both highly reactionary and overly restrictive, and contrasts distinctly with his general attitude toward music, particularly as it applied to the laity.

Foremost among Borromeo's attempts to shape the spiritual role of music for the lay listener was the purification and supervision of music used in public devotion. Borromeo's influence on the Mass and Offices held in the Duomo of Milan, where he initially marshaled most of his local authority, is well-known through the exhaustive scholarship of Federico Mompellio and Lewis Lockwood, both of whom document the improvements made in the management of the choir and discuss his relationship with composer Vincenzo Ruffo, maestro di cappella from 1563-1572.[12] These extremely valuable studies have shed considerable light upon Borromeo's views regarding plainchant and polyphony and their subsequent adoption by Milan's principal ecclesiastical institution. Yet they focus upon only one landscape of the vast panorama. Borromeo sought to spiritualize every aspect of Milanese life, and music was a utilitarian tool which his deft hands easily manipulated in pursuit of that goal. Polyphony sung by the Duomo choir was just one of the many means by which a civilian might be inspired to piety in Borromeo's Milan. Others included the Ambrosian services at the royal ducal chapel of Santa Maria della Scala in Milan, the Vespers services of the Madonna of Miracles at Santa Maria presso San Celso, the singing of the Ave Maria and other similar service music at the altar of Santa Maria del Pilone in the Duomo, the services of the Confraternity of the Rosary, and the singing of laude in the Schools of Christian Doctrine. Equally significant were Borromeo's attempts to establish Milanese centers for the musical and liturgical training of future clergy within pre-existing confraternal organizations.

Although Borromeo's ultimate success in many of these endeavors was directly dependent upon the support of the Milanese patriciate, he was sometimes rather oblivious to the sensitive matters of procedure and jurisdiction. This can be seen in the Gioseffo Caimo episode discussed above in which Borromeo unsuccessfully attempted to force the *Fabbrica* of the Duomo, a civic governing body exempt from direct archiepiscopal authority, to retain an organist that they had already deemed unfit for the position.[13] It is further evident in Borromeo's subsequent correspondence regarding the appointment of Vincenzo Ruffo as maestro di cappella at the Duomo, for even after sparring with the *Fabbrica* over Caimo, Borromeo still had not learned that the employment of musicians at the Duomo was not within his personal jurisdiction. When Hoste da Reggio was removed from the position of maestro di cappella at the Duomo after failing to return from the baths in June 1563, Borromeo apparently inquired about the procedure for selecting new maestri and then made it known abroad that he was accepting nominations for this and other positions.[14] Over the course of the next six months recommendations arrived from family and friends who sought vacancies and favors for their favorite musicians, including Simon Boyleau,[15] Nicola Vicentino,[16] and Vincenzo Ruffo. In the meantime, the officers of the *Fabbrica* had already retained Ruffo on their own, as a letter of nomination from Antonio Scarampo, Bishop of Nola, in fact, noted.[17] Although Borromeo had no control over the appointment, his interference was overlooked by the patriciate and his research may have proved fruitful in securing musicians for other posts that later became vacant, as well as in identifying composers who might experiment with the newly defined intelligible style. On 1 September 1563, Tullio Albanese, Borromeo's private secretary, reported that he was not able to do anything for Boyleau because Ruffo's services had already been secured at the Duomo,[18] but within weeks Boyleau appears on the rosters at Santa Maria presso San Celso. Nicola Vicentino, who was recommended by two different parties, was secured as a rector at San Tommaso in Terra Amara two years later.[19] Both Ruffo and Vicentino, moreover, were asked to provide intelligible masses for Borromeo in early 1565,[20] and Boyleau composed a set of austere Magnificats for the archbishop the following year.

The 'Madonna of Miracles' at Santa Maria presso San Celso

No Milanese church was more popular with the patriciate during the latter half of the sixteenth century than Boyleau's new place of employment, Santa Maria presso San Celso, also known as the church of the Madonna dei Miracoli. Founded in 1485 by Gian Galeazzo Sforza following a purported appearance of the Blessed Virgin on the site, Santa Maria presso San Celso was administered by a confraternity of eighteen noblemen.[21] Evidently, the combination of the reported miracle with the noble confraternity brought a unique mixture of foreign pilgrims and Milanese nobility to the site, rendering it especially fertile ground for Borromeo's spiritual education program.

As early as 1498, the church hosted a sung Vespers service daily during the summer and on high feasts throughout the year, as well as a Compline service during lent. In 1535, the practice was amended to include a High Mass and Vespers on the First Sunday of each month. These services were performed by a choir of eighteen chaplains, each of which held a benefice funded by either the Visconti or the Sforza family.[22]

The archival documents indicate that around 1563 Santa Maria presso San Celso, which boasted a recently completed interior space, became an important focal point for civic worship and, consequently, sacred music. During that year Boyleau, formerly maestro di cappella at the Duomo of Milan and a personal favorite of Borromeo's sister Suor Corona Isabella, was appointed maestro di cappella, a position that does not appear to have existed previously at Santa Maria presso San Celso. Boyleau, who appears to have been well-known in aristocratic circles as a madrigalist, held the post in 1563 and 1564 and again from 1566 to approximately December 1568. Pietro d'Italia, another madrigalist living in the city, temporarily took his place in 1565 for reasons that are unclear.[23] The year 1563 saw other alterations and innovations of a musical nature as well. During October 1563 the little-known organist Martan was replaced by Giovanni Antonio Brena, a well-respected keyboardist also experienced in instrument construction.[24] A flurry of preparatory activity ensued that included the construction of the choir, the repair of the organs (Table 7.1), and the purchase of psalters, laude collections, and other unspecified music books (Table 7.2) for use by the choir at the High Mass, Vespers, and Lenten Compline services. The physical alterations of the performance space and the purchase of polyphony for use in the choir accompanied construction on the facade, which was begun under Galeazzo Alessi in 1565. Funding for both the interior and exterior decoration projects, which were supervised by the eighteen deputies, was provided by the local patriciate.[25] As a result, attendance at the Vespers service, which comprised part of an already strong Marian tradition in the city, surged.

Table 7.1 Construction of choir and repairs on the organs at Santa Maria presso San Celso 1563-1570[26]

Date	Action	Payment
23 January 1563	To Giovanni Paolo, woodworker, for creating a model of the choir	L2 s 1
3 February 1563	To Francesco, wood carver, for engraving a model of the choir	L35 s 2
12 February 1563	To Mr Alessandro for providing wood used in the construction of 2 stands for the choirbooks used by the singers	s18
21 July 1565	For three curtains for the organ	s16
17 November 1565	To Baptista for constructing the bridge or scaffolding of the organs	L4
7 December 1566	For two sheepskins for work on the organ	L1 s11 d 6
11 January 1567	Expenses in carrying the five barrels of tinware for the organ	L1 s 1 d 6
1 February 1567	To Mr Alessandro for constructing the choir 'where those that sing the high mass stand'	L1 s 6
3 March 1567	For carrying the tinware to the organist	L1 s 5
19 April 1567	For the fitting together of an organ and the placing of a stall	L2 s 2
18 December 1568	For making a barrier for the organ	L2 s12 d 6
25 December 1568	To Giovanni Antonio, organist, for tuning the organ	L23 s12
5 September 1570	To Mr Paolo de Gaza for construction of choir	L177

Table 7.2 Music purchased for Santa Maria presso San Celso 1563-1570

Date	Item(s)	Payment
12 February 1564	2 'libri di canti'	L1 s15
16 April 1565	3 books for the singers	L3 s18
5 September 1565	2 'libri di canti' to Mr Pietro d'Italia, maestro di cappella	L21 s7 d6
4 May 1566	1 'libro da canto' given by Mr Simone [Boyleau]	L1 s5
10 August 1566	2 'libri de salterij' for use in the choir	L4 s14 d6
18 August 1566	1 book of 'laude della madonna' for use in the choir	L3
6 April 1567	Materials for copying 5 music books to Simone Boyleau	
	Lined paper	L4 s10
	Ruler? (ligatura)	L5 s1
	Binding (bindelli)	s10

At some point between 1563 and 1594 a Saturday evening Compline service was added to the observances.[27] The Saturday Compline service quickly captured the imagination of the patriciate, thus rendering it of continuing interest to visiting pilgrims as well.[28] As I have discussed elsewhere, historian Paolo Morigia indicates that the music performed there during Compline included the Marian antiphon 'Salve Regina,' certain versets with responsories, and other appropriate liturgical works in the form of plainchant, organ alternatim settings, and polyphony:

> Every Saturday evening at the hour of Compline one sings the Salve Regina, with certain versets and responsories and several ordinations to honor Saturday, the day dedicated by the Holy Church to the glorious mother of God: thus, at the appointed hour therein one finds music, the organist and the sacerdotes . . . the music begins, and the organ responds, and then the organ and the music [sound] together, with such sweetness and very beautiful harmony, which, because they seem an angelic choir, generates in the hearts of the listeners a whole-hearted composure and a holy devotion to the Mother of God.[29]

The service was, by all appearances, a combination of the 'Salve service' observed in the churches and confraternities of the Low Countries and the Compline service that was gaining ascendancy in northern Italy.[30]

Although only a few names of those who sang in the High Mass and Vespers services of the 1560s can be gleaned from the documents,[31] a fairly complete list of the choral chaplains survives from a pastoral visit of 1576:

D. pre. Francesco Bricum
D. pre. Antonio Brena
D. pre. Baptista Casale
D. pre. Hieronymo Baveno
D. pre. Joh*anne*s Angelo Porta Luppo
D. pre. Herculo Galbeso
D. pre. Iesapris 'la delphinono'
D. pre. Joh*anne*s Baptista Bugato, custodo Santo Joh*anne*s Laterano
D. pre. Joh*anne*s Riposso
D. pre. Ludovico, ognissan*t*i St Eufemia
D. pre. Stefano Benzano
D. pre. Paolo Fontana[32]

Even here, however, only fourteen of the eighteen chaplains are listed. This may be due to the fact that a plague swept the city during the same year, leaving many vacancies in the Milanese churches in its wake. Although Filiberto Nantermi does not appear on this roster, it has been postulated that he succeeded Boyleau as *maestro di cappella* in 1568 and remained until his death in 1605, and, further, that his son Orazio began singing at the church around 1570.[33] The surviving registers indicate that several additional singers were employed regularly to perform for various services beginning in 1565,[34] so Orazio was probably serving in this capacity. In any case, the number of choral chaplains available suggests a strong polyphonic tradition, and this is borne out in the extant data regarding the High Mass and Vespers from the early seventeenth century. On festal occasions, the musicians sang the Ingresso, Gloria, Credo, and Sanctus, and responses at the High Mass, which was intoned throughout, as well as the hymn, the choral response, the psalms and at least one motet at Vespers. When the eighteen deputies who governed the church were present at Vespers on solemn feasts, moreover, they sang two motets, one before and the other after the Magnificat.[35]

During the October 1576, Carlo Borromeo led four penitential processions from the Duomo to one of the main churches in the city with the intention of eradicating the aforementioned plague. The last of these is thought to have culminated at Santa Maria presso San Celso,[36] the very home of the miraculous Madonna who supposedly had liberated the city from the plague of 1485.[37] According to Gaspare Bugati, the processors, barefoot and clad in sackcloth, were drawn from all levels of Milanese society:

> Therefore, the Cardinal, the clergy, the Senate, and all of Milan, perceiving that the scourge came from the great hand of God, expected to placate his ire with mortifications, prayers, and penitence: and four general processions were made in which all the clergy, the majority of the disciplinati, and the people walked barefoot

with ashes on their heads and dressed in sackcloth – men and women, noble and base, boys and girls with crosses in their hands and cords around their necks – invoking all of the most high and most pious names of JESUS CHRIST our Lord, of the most Blessed Virgin, of all the saints, with the litanies and penitential psalms.[38]

The famous veil of the Madonna of Miracles was not, however, the central relic of this series of antidotes, for a reliquary supposedly containing one of the original nails from the cross had also been vested with healing powers. The reliquary was posted in the Duomo surrounded by lamps for much of the year, and carried at the head of each procession by the barefoot Borromeo himself.[39] When the processing body arrived at the destination church, 'the penitential psalms were sung in pious musical harmony, while all of the people, prostrate, meditated upon them.'[40] This shift of attention away from veneration of the veil to penitential prostration before the sacred nail arose from Borromeo's intention to infuse the populace with remorse for its frivolity through adoration of the suffering Christ. It later manifest itself in the institution of the Feast of the Holy Nail, which was celebrated in conjunction with the Invention of the Cross from 3 May 1577 onward.

A cycle of Magnificats by Simon Boyleau, maestro di cappella from 1563 to 1568, and a collection of motets and spiritual madrigals by Gasparo Costa, organist from 1577 to 1584, comprise the only polyphonic collections surviving from Santa Maria presso San Celso during Borromeo's lifetime. Boyleau's *Modulationes in Magnificat ad omnes tropos* was dedicated to Borromeo and issued by diocesan printer Pacifico Ponzio in 1566.[41] Like so many other Magnificat cycles of the period, the *Modulationes* features a Magnificat in each mode in which only the even-numbered verses are set polyphonically.[42] The plainsong intonations of each are elaborated either through decorative embellishment or by paraphrasing them within the fluctuating four to six-voice texture, as was also common during the era.[43] Two features, however, distinguish Boyleau's collection. The first is the obvious attention to textual clarity, which is evidenced in both the precision of the underlay found in the original print and the manner in which the natural declamation of the Latin text is reflected in the melodic contours (Example 7.1). The second is the inclusion of an alternate falsobordone setting for each mode, thus ensuring the availability of an even less adorned declamatory setting. The collection's dedication and style, when considered in light of the fact that it was issued within a year of Borromeo's first provincial Council, suggests that it had some connection to the proceedings.[44] Lewis Lockwood has postulated that Boyleau may have composed the cycle as a compositional challenge to Ruffo, with the intent of winning back his former position as maestro di cappella at the Duomo.[45] Although there is no archival documentation that explicitly indicates such, Lockwood's theory is certainly not without merit. Boyleau, who had been nominated for the position by Borromeo's sister in 1563, apparently was not the most dynamic director. As noted above, he was summarily dismissed from the Duomo in late 1557 after just six years of service in the position of maestro di cappella, literally having been run off by the

Example 7.1 Boyleau, *Magnificat second tone*, measures 12-22

members of the choir itself.[46] Moreover, he was temporarily replaced by Pietro Taglia at Santa Maria presso San Celso for reasons that remain unclear, and this occurred less than two years after he began serving in the position there. Whatever Boyleau's personal motivations, it is clear from the archival documents surviving from his tenure at Santa Maria presso San Celso that the works he composed there were intended to serve the practical needs of the church.[47] Thus, the *Modulationes* are indicative of the style of polyphony utilized in the Vespers services at Santa Maria presso San Celso during the 1560s – a style somewhat simple and austere in which the counterpoint is subservient to the declamation of the text.

Gasparo Costa's *Il primo libro de motetti et madrigali spirituali a cinque voci*, which was printed by Angelo Gardane of Venice in 1581, reflects the growing influence of the lauda and other similar devotional genres at Santa Maria presso San Celso during the decade preceding its publication. Two of the six motets included in the collection honor Duke Georgius Sluzco, the Polish prince to whom the print itself is dedicated.[48] The other four, however, which include a Pater Noster and two Marian hymn settings, feature texts and text types central to the teaching of Christian doctrine, an activity in which Borromeo engaged numerous confraternities and societies in Milan and for which the lauda, a genre also associated with Santa Maria presso San Celso's Vespers services, also came to be a useful didactic tool. Although there is no record of a Christian doctrine program at Santa Maria presso San Celso itself, participation in the institution's services was encouraged among the nobility, the social class for whom the church's services were primarily intended. Moreover, the texts and concepts taught in the schools were very basic to Christian education, and, thus, generally familiar to the upper classes.

As might be expected, the seven spiritual madrigals contained in Costa's collection are characterized by a somewhat didactic approach as well. Some refer to specific events recounted in the Bible, while others encourage penance and the adoration of the Savior. Of the penitential madrigals, *O sacro santo aventuroso chiodo*, has attracted the most scholarly interest because it may have been sung during the services attached to Borromeo's penitential processions during the pestilence of 1576. Even if the madrigal was not sung during the observances themselves, its text was clearly inspired by them, and reflects Borromeo's admonitions that the populace turn away from its relentless pursuit of secular entertainments toward contemplation of the divine, and, in particular, the crucifixion itself.[49]

Madrigals devoted to female biblical figures, including Susannah, Mary and Martha, and the Blessed Virgin, also figure prominently in Costa's collection, perhaps with the intent of making the works contained especially relevant to female users. In his *Historia* of Santa Maria presso San Celso, Paolo Morigia notes that the virtues of the Virgin were integral to spiritual education in post-Tridentine Milan, especially as they applied to women. Morigia further remarks that the emulation of the virtues of the Virgin was intimately bound with the city's Marian cults, and, in particular, with that of the Madonna of Miracles at Santa presso San Celso.[50] By identifying Marian virtues in other female characters and bringing them alive in affective settings of paraphrased versions of the original Bible texts, Costa underscored the application of Christian practice and its attendant virtues to the daily life of the women who frequented the services held in the church in which he performed. This is perhaps never more evident than in *Marta che debb'io fare*, a fanciful invention on Mary Magdalen's reply to her sister Martha upon being admonished for sitting idly at Christ's feet (Example 7.2). The attention afforded naturalness of declamation is obvious from the outset, for the Magdalen's frustrated opening rejoinder 'Marta, what would you have me do?' is spliced into short breathless segments in which the musical rhythms precisely mirror the cadence of spoken dialogue. Yet the homophonic texture so characteristic of the Milanese declamatory style is abandoned throughout in favor of closely spaced imitation in which clarity is achieved through rhythmic flexibility and balanced voicing. Text expression is further enhanced by sudden chromatic turns of phrase on significant words such as 'crying' ('piangendo') and 'disheartened' ('sconforto'). The text itself, a simple ottava rima, is divided asymmetrically so that the first seven lines are delivered without significant pause or repetition during the opening thirty-one measures, while the last is repeated incessantly for a full twenty-six measures. The introduction of this final line, which acknowledges the blessing of spending one's life in repentance, is further marked by a shift to triple meter that divides the work into two metrically distinct sections of relatively equal length. Costa is clearly no descendant of the Milanese tradition, for his approach to the text, relying as it does upon metrical invention, rhythmic flexibility, closely spaced imitation, carefully distributed voicing, and unsettling chromatic turns of phrase, has more in common with Vicentino than it does with Boyleau, Hoste da Reggio, and Pietro Taglia.

Example 7.2 Costa, *Marta che debb'io fare*, measures 1-18

The Society of the Ave Maria

The Madonna of Miracles was one of several local Marian cults that had its origins in vernacular culture, but during the sixteenth century it was rivaled in popularity only by the Society of the Ave Maria in the Duomo. According to the archival accounts, the Society itself was initiated during the 1490s by a mendicant friar known locally as the 'missionary from God.' Under his supervision, the Ave Maria and appropriate laude were sung at the Vespers hour before an image of the Madonna and child that had been affixed above a basin near the main doors of the Duomo.[51] All of the Milanese passing by were exhorted to enter the cathedral and participate,[52] and the resulting activity, which quickly evolved from a grassroots movement into a somewhat orderly devotional practice, was awarded official diocesan sanction in 1495.[53] Marco Burigozzi may well have been referring to this movement when he noted that by February 1532 the Milanese, heartened by the formal investiture and recent re-entry of Francesco II Sforza as Duke of Milan, performed the orations of the Ave Maria at the Duomo during the hour in which Christ expired. According to Burigozzi, on 25 February 1532 approximately one thousand were present for this activity, and a Carmelite preached in the Duomo afterwards. After praising the participants for the singing of the Ave Maria itself, the Carmelite launched into a diatribe against the Jewish synagogue facing Sant'Ambrogio, which he had identified as partially responsible for God's recent abandonment of the Milanese state.[54]

Like the Madonna of Miracles at Santa Maria presso San Celso, the Madonna of the Ave Maria was vested with various miraculous powers, thus rendering her a popular and well-tended devotional icon. By 1550 the practice of singing the Ave Maria before the image at the Vespers hour had garnered the support of a loosely organized school comprised of Milanese gentlemen and merchants. Intent upon the preservation of the tradition of singing the Ave Maria at the Vespers hour, the nascent school commissioned a marble statue of the Virgin and erected it at the altar 'in medio ecclesie' around the year 1550. For over a decade the Society of the Ave Maria sponsored a popular Vespers service at this newly created altar, which gradually became known among the Milanese as the altar of Santa Maria del Pilone.[55] Unfortunately, however, Carlo Borromeo found the altar of Santa Maria del Pilone and its trappings indecent for reasons that are not fully explained in the archival documents. Shortly after his arrival in Milan in 1565, he ordered it dismantled and the observances transferred first to the altar of Santa Maria dell'Albero, and then, following the plague of 1577, to the main altar itself. There he channeled the energies of the school and the attendant populace into a Vespers service that included the Litany of the Virgin and accompanying prayers, as well as the singing of the Ave Maria.[56]

The births of the madonnas at Santa Maria Presso San Celso and the Ave Maria in the Duomo have much in common with many of the so-called 'street corner virgins' of Venice, including popular or grassroots origins, the vesting of miraculous powers, a particular resonance with residents of the local neighborhood, and supervision by the local patriciate, but their subsequent history is less intertwined with secular themes such as urban image and the maintenance of public order.[57] Instead, the post-Tridentine lives of the Milanese madonnas was adopted into a city-wide ecclesiastical program aimed at promoting civic piety and religious education. This is especially true of Santa Maria del Pilone in the Duomo, for Borromeo clearly saw the reorganization of the Society of the Ave Maria as an unique opportunity to reach Milanese society at large. The Ave Maria itself was a part of the core curriculum taught in the burgeoning schools of Christian Doctrine, where, along with the Salve Regina, the Pater Nostre and the Credo, it functioned as a pillar text for Catholic devotions.[58] Moreover, the Ave Maria was the principal prayer used in reciting the

Rosary, an activity that was especially encouraged in post-Tridentine Milan.[59] In the second half of his aforementioned history of the church of Santa Maria presso San Celso, Morigia identifies the Ave Maria as the most important of the prayers to the Virgin, and states that every child should be taught how to recite it properly. Morigia even suggests that children be instructed to say the prayer at the table before and after every meal. Echoing concepts dating back to the fourth century, he notes that 'Ave Maria gratia plena' was the salutation with which the angel Gabriel greeted Mary and describes the Virgin as man's 'key to grace.'[60] He then invokes the writings of Anselmo,[61] and Bernard,[62] as support for his assertions. For Morigia, an ecclesiastic whose historical writings place him at the epicenter of societal discourse in post-Tridentine Milan, the Salve Regina and other Marian prayers had their virtues and their significance, but the Ave Maria was the quintessential Marian text.[63]

With the transfer of the Society of the Ave Maria from the altar of Santa Maria del Pilone, its activities were elevated to full public view. Following the transfer, the evening services were led by a canon from the Duomo. In addition, eight professional singers were provided for the performance of the Ave Maria itself.[64] Enrico Cattaneo, who appears to have seen one of the archival documents in the Diocesan relating to this matter but does not cite it, postulates that these singers were members of the Duomo choir.[65] However, the documents themselves consistently identify them only as the 'best singers in the city.'[66] The documents further note that the distribution of the Society's choir included two basses, two tenors, two altos, and two sopranos, and that a maestro di cappella was appointed to preside over the musical activities. The fact that independent salaries are specified for each indicates that the singers were not necessarily borrowed from the Duomo choir, but rather selected from among the best in the city as specified. The maestro di cappella received a remuneration of 100 lire per year, while the tenors, basses, and contraltos received 70 lire. Interestingly enough, the sopranos received only 50 lire per year.[67] This seeming anomaly is easily explained by the fact that adult sopranos were traditionally paid less at the Duomo, perhaps because their services were not as frequently required in the singing of polyphony.[68] The Society may well have been taking its cue from the *Fabbrica* of the Duomo, which has often been criticized for its niggardly treatment of musicians in the computation of salaries.

Although the archival documents reveal nothing regarding the matter, the introduction of the 'Ave' service at the main altar must have necessitated some supervision on the part of Duomo authorities. Without some coordination of the events unfolding at the main altar during the Vespers hour, sheer pandemonium would have ensued. It is likely that the 'Ave' service preceded Vespers itself, since the documents indicate that the participants were called to it at the sounding of the bell and the ordinaries of the Duomo assembled at that time as well.[69] Given its similarity to the 'Salve' services that had sprung up elsewhere, which often included the singing of motets and litanies, it is also possible that the 'Ave' service was held immediately following Vespers instead. In either case, the 'Ave' service, rooted as it was in popular tradition, was a fitting prelude of the sort characteristically employed by Carlo Borromeo to attract a large audience. Borromeo introduced lessons on the psalms, another popular vehicle in sixteenth-century devotional practices, in order to draw

Milanese society to the Duomo on holidays. That Borromeo's goal was the assimilation of a diverse, yet educated audience is made unabashedly clear in his letter of 10 May 1566 to Carlo Bonomi, Bishop of Vercelli:

> . . .I have taken part in the Canonical Hours in the cathedral church with great pleasure, attending on all holidays . . . I have begun the practice of having a lesson on the Psalms read here in public on holidays, and I try to attract all the noblemen of the city and the Chapters of the Collegiate churches and of the cathedral with their provosts and high officers, and for the first time there was an admirable audience; I hope that this will be a way of accomplishing much good.[70]

There appears no stronger social drawing card for the Vespers hour at the Duomo than the services sponsored by the Society of the Ave Maria, which evolved from a tradition that had been enthusiastically fostered in Milanese popular culture since the late fifteenth century.

The singing of the Ave Maria by the newly formed choir was clearly the principal event of the Society's daily service. Thus, it is rather perplexing that settings of the Ave Maria do not figure prominently among the works of Milanese composers who served as maestri at the Duomo during the introduction of the formal confraternity around 1550 and the gradual expansion of its observances under Borromeo. The motet books of Werrecore[71] and Ruffo[72], both of whom served as maestri at the Duomo between 1540 and 1570, do not include a setting of the text. Furthermore, two extant manuscripts from the late sixteenth and early seventeenth centuries found in the Duomo archives contain numerous polyphonic settings of hymns and Pater Nostres, but no Ave Marias.[73] A setting of the Ave Maria is found in Pietro Pontio's first book of five-voice motets,[74] which was published in 1582 at the close of the composer's five-year tenure as maestro di cappella at the Duomo.[75] Perhaps new polyphonic settings of the 'Ave' text were not required before 1580. The documents refer rather consistently to the singing of '*the* Ave,'[76] as if to indicate that a well-known and beloved setting functioned regularly as the centerpiece of the service. While a simple setting in the lauda tradition similar to that found in the widely disseminated *Modo per insegnar la Dottrina Christiana* of Diego Ledesma[77] might have been used (Example 7.3), it is not likely since a professional choir would not have been necessary to the successful performance of the work. In fact, documentary studies of other confraternities such as the Santissima Trinità dei Pelligrini in Rome have revealed that professional singers were typically hired for the performance of complex musical works rather than laude.[78] More importantly, a rather famous setting of the text featuring the plainchant melody that was probably sung in the earliest stages of the observance was available in *Librone* 3 of the Milan choirbooks.

Example 7.3 Ledesma, *Ave Maria*, measures 1-8

The setting is a four-voice litany motet by Loyset Compère,[79] a Flemish composer who served at the court of Galeazzo Maria Sforza in Milan from 1474 to 1477. It features an amalgamation of the Marian sequence Ave Maria, the Litany of the Saints, and the Marian *cantio* Virgo Galilaea. The sequence itself, which is transposed by a third, appears in the altus in measures 1-17, accompanied by recitation on the psalm tone in the tenor and a contrapuntal duet between the superius and the bassus voices. In measure 17 the sequence is aborted by the recitation of the litany, which is presented in short, syllabically-constructed imitative duets. The motet concludes with a declamatory tripla section in which the *cantio* Virgo Galilaea is embedded in the tenor voice. Ludwig Finscher has discussed the relationship of this motet to three other Marian motets from the same period that feature similar procedures, and, by virtue of its 'Italian style,' has dated it at approximately 1495 to 1500.[80] The text of the litany itself includes invocations to Mary, Sts Michael and Gabriel, the angels and archangels, St John the Baptist and all of the martyrs, and would have served any number of liturgical occasions celebrated at the Duomo.

Compère's *Ave Maria* was disseminated in numerous sources during the first thirty years of the sixteenth century, a fact, which, in part, attests to its continued popularity after the turn of the century.[81] Moreover, it was among eighteen works still being sung frequently in the papal chapel as late as 1568, as is indicated in a two-page memorandum drawn up by the Sistine singer Giovanni Antonio Merlo. Apparently the piece was sung in the papal chapel from a manuscript copied between 1495 and 1501, a time period roughly corresponding to the preparation of *Librone* 3.[82] While there is absolutely no evidence that Compère's motet was composed specifically for the singing of the Ave Maria in Milan, the coincidence of the dating of the piece, its appearance in *Librone* III and the evolution of the Ave Maria tradition is rather striking. More importantly, both the general popularity of the motet and its frequent use in the papal chapel during the second half of the sixteenth century provide compelling support for the possibility that it was still being sung in Milan from *Librone* III during Borromeo's tenure. Its four-voice texture was perfectly suited to the Society of the Ave Maria's choir of eight singers, and its text fulfilled the purposes of both acknowledging the Virgin in her perfect state of grace and calling upon her as divine intercessor.

By 1607 a substantial sum of 764 lire was budgeted for the maintenance of the Society's services, which were supported not only through contributions from Society members, but also by public donations. This impressive amount, which in itself attests to the success of the transformed Vespers service, was set aside to cover not only such expenses as linens, candles, and cleaning, but also music books.[83] Printed books containing more recent settings of the Ave Maria by such composers as Palestrina, whose third book of five-voice motets is among the Duomo's current holdings,[84] were undoubtedly purchased to replace those considered outdated. Furthermore, settings of other devotional texts such as the increasingly popular Song of Songs may have been adopted for use in the service as well.

The Schools of Christian Doctrine

Borromeo's interest in providing similar spiritual activities for women to those of the Society of the Ave Maria can be seen in the establishment of a sister organization known as the Congregation of the Assumption at a refurbished version of the altar of Santa Maria del Pilone in 1581.[85] The Congregation of the Assumption appears to have been intended as a prelude to the more ubiquitous Confraternity of the Rosary that was introduced in 1584, for it features both a similar approach to membership and a comparable purpose. Open to women of every social and marital status, the Congregation met for communion and meditation on every third Sunday of the month and the four principal feasts of the Blessed Virgin. Its members were further obligated to confess every fifteen days,[86] to say five Pater Nostres and five Ave Marias every day while meditating on the five sorrows of Jesus and the Blessed Virgin, and to recite the Little Office of the Virgin, the Corona, or the Rosary frequently, and to visit the sick.[87]

Although the Congregation does not appear to have held musical services, it likely did sponsor the school of Christian Doctrine that met in the Duomo.[88] The first school of Christian Doctrine in Milan was founded during the 1530s by Father Castellino de Castello, a Comascan who held a chaplaincy at Santa Maria Fulcorina in Milan, and Francesco Villanova, a local wool carder and member of the confraternity of Santi Giacomo e Filippo in Porta Nuova. Apparently, Villanova, who became known as 'the fisherman,' enticed the children playing on the streets to the porch behind the church of Santi Giacomo e Filippo with gifts of fruit. There, they were taught about Christianity and promised further gifts for attendance at subsequent lessons and correct recitation of the material learned.[89] Despite some initial opposition by Milanese citizens, Castellino and his associates succeeded in establishing several schools throughout the city. These were supervised by a lay confraternity that was founded in 1539 expressly for the administration of the schools.[90] As early as 1473, moreover, catechism had been introduced independently at the Latin grammar school of Tommaso Grassi. By 1544, however, any catechism taught there was derived directly from the texts sanctioned by Castellino for his doctrine schools.[91]

Although Borromeo did not found the doctrine schools, as is often supposed, he did see them as fundamental to combating heresy and spiritualizing all levels of society through both instruction and participation. He, therefore, encouraged their proliferation. Schools were founded in the Duomo,[92] Santa Maria Beltrade,[93] San Michele a Gallo,[94] San Dalmatio,[95] Santa Maria al Chercio,[96] San Satiro,[97] and San Giovanni Laterano,[98] to name a few. Moreover, the confraternities that ran the schools were given an official status within the diocese, and new rules of governance based upon the original ones penned by Castellino were drawn up, printed, and distributed.[99] Diocesan enthusiasm for the schools, in fact, appears to have been boundless. Between 1565 and 1567 alone, sixty-four neighborhood schools were established and papal sanction of the Confraternity of the Brothers (and Sisters) of Christian Doctrine that would run them was sought in Rome.[100] Following a pastoral visit to several of the Milanese schools in 1576, Bishop Ragazzoni observed 'that sainted and useful work, which is increasingly embraced and frequented, if not by the nobility, grows in the name of Christ and increases daily.'[101]

The schools themselves, which were run by a combination of clergy and laity, met on Sundays and religious feasts for approximately two hours. Children between the ages of five and fifteen were 'fished' from the streets of the city by members of the confraternities that sponsored the schools, sometimes with gifts of fruit or other similar enticements. Although girls and boys were educated separately, the same basic material was emphasized, and often included the rudimentary reading and writing skills necessary to the study of the catechism texts.[102] Students were typically taught via rote memorization of easily assimilated texts such as the *Tavola*[103] and Socratically organized catechisms such as the *Dialogo*[104] and *Interrogatorio*.[105] The topics covered included the 'Ave Maria,' 'Pater Nostre,' 'Salve Regina,' the sign of the cross, the ten commandments, the articles of faith, the seven sacraments, the three theological virtues, the four cardinal virtues, the seven gifts of the Holy Spirit, the twelve fruits of the Holy Spirit, the seven works of corporeal mercy, the seven works of spiritual mercy, the three principal counsels of Jesus Christ, the three enemies of man, and the mysteries of the Rosary. In addition, memorization of the Little Office of the Virgin, one of the most widely disseminated religious texts of the sixteenth century, was greatly encouraged, especially for girls.[106] Basic social manners and respect for religious authority were also incorporated into the lessons, and boys were often taught how to serve at Mass.

Music played a significant role in the schools, for laude that reinforced the primary texts and concepts taught were sung to five or six easily memorized monophonic songs that might appeal to the youngsters [107] In the preface to the 1576 diocesan edition of the *Lodi e Canzoni spirituali per cantar insieme con la Dottrina Christiana*, nine reasons are given for singing laude, and, in particular, laude in two choirs, during the doctrine classes:

1. The texts are more easily learned and memorized.
2. The lessons are more fun, and the children are invited to play, as if at a party.
3. Those that speak with difficulty might learn by singing.
4. It eases the teaching, as one must listen to them neither all together nor one at a time.
5. To replace the naughty songs that children learn because they know no others.
6. To help those who hear the children singing, but don't attend the classes, to learn doctrine.
7. It is easier to praise God in this manner.
8. To imitate the singing of the canonical hours.
9. To imitate the angels.[108]

The nine points of this preface echo several found in Diego de Ledesma's *Modo per insegnar la Dottrina Christiana*, a standard guide for teaching doctrine that was published in Rome in 1573. Ledesma maintains that children, particularly those who neither speak nor read well, learn more easily by singing. He further states that laude assist in memorization and serve to replace rustic and bawdy songs, and compares them to hymns that are sung both morning and evening in the church.[109] The Milanese practice of singing laude in two choirs may also have been derived from Ledesma, who suggests that 'two to four are able to sing that are first well supervised in that separately. And first only these sing it. And when one will see that the others have learned, all are able to respond.'[110] As Giancarlo Rostirolla has pointed out, the use of such responsorial and alternatim techniques were fundamental to the pedagogical process espoused by Ledesma, who maintained that all singing in the schools must be easy, simple, and manageable.[111] In fact, Ledesma recommends singing as much of the catechism as is possible, and, at the very least, the Ave Maria, Pater Nostre, Credo, and Salve Regina either word for word or in verses until it is mastered in full. He further provides a simple four-part setting of the Ave Maria for this purpose, and notes that all four prayers, as well as anything else desired, might be sung to the same music (Example 7.3).[112] The obvious differences in syllabic structure and scansion from text to text assume the instructor's ability to adapt the various texts to the music provided through variation, melodic alteration, or minor adjustments of the simple rhythms, and, thus, perhaps render Ledesma's advice more theoretical than practical.

Table 7.3 Content of the *Lodi e Canzoni spirituali per cantar insieme con la Dottrina Christiana* (1576)

Melody	Text	Didactic Purpose	Occasional Usage
Canto 1	1. Spirito santo amore	To pray to the Holy Spirit for illumination	Pentecost
Canto 1	2. Somma Signore, e Dio	To pray for grace from the Holy Spirit	None provided
Canto 1	3. O Madre del Signore	To pray to Mary for intercession	Feasts BVM, Sundays
Canto 1	4. Giesù clemente, e pio	To encourage frequent communion	Corpus Christi
Canto 1	5. Il Confessor sacrato	To say on days devoted to the Confessors	Confessors
Canto 2	6. Chiamiam' il buon Giesù	To encourage the soul to call on Jesus	Circumcision, Epiphany, Sundays
Canto 2	7. Lodiam tutti Giesù in suono	To exhort to honor the name of Jesus	Epiphany, Resurrection, Sundays
Canto 2	8. Risguarda anima mia	To consider the sorrows of Jesus	Forty Hours, Passion
Canto 2	9. Chi vuol gustar Giesù	To consider Jesus's sacrifice on the cross	Forty Hours, Passion, Trinity
Canto 2	10. Corona de beati alma Maria	To give thanks for the intercession of Mary	Feasts BVM, Sundays
Canto 2	11. Adore te Giesù clemente	To laud the sacrament of the Eucharist	Corpus Christi
Canto 3	12. Giesù, Giesù, Giesù	To honor the name of Jesus	Circumcision, Sundays
Canto 3	13. Seguir voglio Giesù	To encourage the soul to follow Jesus	Sundays
Canto 3	14. O Madre del Signore	To exhort to turn to Mary as an example of virtue	Feasts BVM, Sundays
Canto 3	15. Lodiam tutti Dio	To encourage to honor and thank God for blessings received	Trinity, Sundays
Canto 3	16. Lodiam Signor la sposa	For virgins and martyrs	Feasts BVM, Virgins, Sundays

---

[1]Index reads number 16.

Canto 6	28. Un conseglio vi vo dare	With which the soul is instructed to acquire paradise	None provided
Canto 6	29. O Regina alma Maria	To the Virgin Mary, in order that you pray for us	Feasts BVM, Sundays
Canto 6	30. O Giesù ver Redentore	To pray for the soul in purgatory	All souls in purgatory
Canto 6	31. Giesù mio, Giesù mio	With which one considers the life and virtue of Jesus Christ	Christmas, Sundays?[2]
Canto 6	32. Noi siam angeli viventi	To consider the nature and office of angels	Feasts of the Angels
Canto 6	33. O Giesù mio Redentore	With which one mourns the pain suffered by Our Lord on the Cross	Forty Hours, Passion, Sundays

---

[2] Index reads number 36.

The *Lodi e Canzoni spirituali* of 1576 contains thirty-three texts that are sung to one of six monophonic tunes (Table 7.3).[113] Rostirolla has demonstrated that at least eighteen of the thirty-three texts had already appeared in collections published between 1508 and 1573, with Animucccia's *Iesus Maria Canto. Il primo libro delle laudi* (1563), Razzi's *Libro primo delle laudi spirituali* (1563), and the 1572 Modena edition of laude comprising the most frequently accessed sources.[114] Each of the texts has a didactic and occasional usage that is clearly indicated. According to Rostirolla, the occasional designations, when considered in light of the preface's reference to the canonical hours, suggest use in the liturgy.[115] Although a para-liturgical usage of the songs cannot be ruled out, particularly since the schools participated frequently in processions, the overriding spirit of the collection is purely didactic. The carefully prepared index, which provides the occasional designations upon which Rostirolla's hypothesis is based, directed the teacher to the song most appropriate to the Sunday or feast day on which the school was convened.[116] Given an instructor who adhered to the directions in using the book, the attentive student would emerge from the doctrine classes with both a sanctioned repertoire of occasional prayer texts and a clear sense, however elementary, of the function and order of the liturgical calendar.

A second edition of laude for use in the Milanese schools was published by diocesan printer Pacifico Pontio in 1586. Interestingly enough, this 'newly collected' edition contains a number of texts that did not appear in the 1576 collection. Like its predecessor, however, the 1586 edition features rubrics that indicate the occasional usage or didactic purpose of each song included (Table 7.4). Although the melodies of the songs are not provided by the printer, an early owner of the book appended a modest manuscript containing five melodies to which the twenty-five songs contained might be performed. Four of these melodies are among the six provided in the 1576 edition, while the fifth, 'Felice e nobil,' likely was borrowed from another source.[117] Careful scrutiny of the four concordant melodies reveals, however, that none of them were copied directly from the 1576 edition, for the melodies appended to the 1586 edition feature substantial variation in content (Example 7.4). The scribe appears to have been relying on his memory, and, thus, the differing versions of the melodies demonstrate the role that oral transmission played in the dissemination and development of the songs used in teaching the doctrine.

In addition to singing of the laude in the schools, the Milanese documents emphasize the singing the Litany of Saints and the Litany of the Virgin, both of which are included at the close of the *Lodi e Canzoni spirituali* of 1576.[118] Teaching the children to sing the litanies, in fact, is among the duties enumerated in the earliest post-Tridentine archival documents devoted to the Milanese Confraternity of Christian Doctrine, and it is, indeed, the only musical activity typically mentioned specifically.[119] An *Interrogatorio* published in Milan in 1568 reveals that these litanies were taught in much the same manner as the musical items discussed by Ledesma. Two children, one of whom first announced verbally the textual incipit of each successive phrase, sang the lines alone, and the rest of the children responded by repeating the same line after them. According to the author, this method prepared the children for participation in processions, an activity in which the pupils reportedly participated often.[120]

Table 7.4 Content of *Lodi divote per cantarsi nelle scuole della Dottrina Christiana raccolta novamente* (1586)

Melody	Text	Didactic and/or Occasional Purpose
Canto 1	Giesù, Giesù, Giesù	To call upon the name of Jesus
Canto 1	Viva Giesù bambino	For the Nativity of the Lord
Canto 1	Degnati ò buon Giesù	For the Sacred Sacrament of the Altar (Corpus Christi)
Canto 1	Lodiam tutti Maria	To laud the Blessed Virgin
Canto 2	Dite ò lieti Pastori	For the Nativity of the Lord
Canto 2	Di nove luce adorna	Of the Ascension of Our Lord
Canto 2	Vieni Spirito Santo	To the Holy Spirit
Canto 2	Qual rapido torrente	To the Sinner who turns to God
Canto 3	Vergine degna d'ogni laude, e honore	To laud the Blessed Virgin
Canto 3	Dolce Giesù d'ogni Armonia più grato	To Jesus Our Lord
Canto 3	L'unico figlio del de l'eterno Padre	About the Nativity of Our Lord
Canto 3	A piè del duro sasso, ove sepolto	Of St Mary Magdelene at the sepulcher of Our Lord
Canto 3	Perder gli amici, e perder i favori	Of the dispirited of the world
Canto 3	Giunto che fù quel giorno	Of Christ's departure from the Blessed Virgin at the Passion
Canto 4	Disposto hò di seguirti	Of the Passion of Christ Our Lord
Canto 4	Giesù monarea eterno	To Jesus Our Lord
Canto 4	Santa Madre e Dio	To the Blessed Virgin
Canto 4	Facciam tutti allegrezza	On the feasts of most martyrs
Canto 4	Leviam i nostri cori	In honor of all saints
Canto 5	Felice, e nobil Pianta	On the feast of a saint
Canto 5	Anima mia che pensi	Dialogue between the body and the soul
Canto 5	Il velen non offende	On sin
Canto 5	Ecce il terribil nostro	On death
Canto 5	Dianzi al tribunale	On universal judgement
Canto 5	Anima che non ami	On hell

Example 7.4 A comparison of (a) the 1576 and (b) the 1586 canti for *Vergine degna d'ogni laude*

(a)

(b)

The School of St Michael in San Calimero

Borromeo's interest in providing similar, yet more intensive theological training for potential clergy can be seen as early as 1564 in his involvement with the Roman Seminary. His earliest efforts to duplicate in Milan the practices already in place in Rome appear to have occurred in connection with an unidentified seminary school in Milan where one Dom Camillo Perego was the maestro of plainchant.[121] Whether or not this school was already in operation when Borromeo ascended to the seat of archbishop is unclear. It is clear, however, that Borromeo wished to increase the number of seminar schools in the city. To this end, he enlisted the support of the School of St Michael in San Calimero, a parish church in which Hoste da Reggio held one of the three available benefices between 1555 and 1569.[122] At the time of Borromeo's first pastoral visit to the church in 1567, San Calimero sponsored several confraternities, including a recently organized School of St Michael. However, no Christian Doctrine was taught there. A substantial list of recommendations made by Borromeo survives from the visit, and these concern not only repairs of the church and the construction of a choir, but also the erection of a school for teaching boys 'the Christian life and singing.' The last was to be accomplished through the unification of the School of St Michael and the School of the Blessed Sacrament, another confraternity that also met in the church.[123] Although the spirit of Borromeo's original plan remained intact, the practical implementation of it apparently necessitated several minor alterations in order to secure confraternity sponsorship without violating existing constitutions. In point of fact, the School of the Blessed Sacrament was united with the School of St Joseph, while the School of St Michael retained its independent status and was transformed into an oratory. From the year 1570, this oratory, which was comprised of twenty-five scholars, sang the canonical hours daily and the Roman office BVM on Marian feasts at its own altar in San Calimero. In addition, the Oratory of St Michael sponsored a 'Christian school' for training boys to sing the liturgy in the manner originally intended by the Archbishop.[124]

The Confraternity of the Rosary and the Spiritual Madrigal

The documentation strongly suggests that although some members of the adult aristocracy participated in teaching and supervising in the Italian schools of Christian Doctrine, they very seldom enrolled their children in the programs. Paul Grendler even goes so far as to suggest that the majority of the schools' teachers hailed from the same social ranks as their pupils, despite the repeated efforts of clergy to recruit instructors from the patrician classes, and cites a letter addressed to the Milanese nobility by the priest Giovanni Petro Giussani in 1609 as a case in point. A patrician himself, Giussani notes the reluctance of the aristocracy to participate, and portrays the activity as a demonstration of noble virtue.[125] Thus, the schools were largely an instrument for the spiritual education and participation of the lower classes, and Borromeo was forced to concentrate his efforts to reach the patriciate on activities sponsored by Santa Maria presso San Celso and the Society of the Ave Maria in the Duomo .

The installation of Milanese branches of the Confraternity of the Rosary, was, perhaps, the only spiritual offensive aimed at the laity by Borromeo that cut entirely across class distinctions. The Confraternity of the Rosary was founded in approximately 1460 by a Dominican friar who, claiming to act upon the Virgin's command, inscribed Dutch citizens into a society formed for the express purpose of reciting the Rosary regularly. Similar companies subsequently were founded in Britain, France, Spain, and, finally, Italy.[126] Unlike many other religious companies of the period, admission to the Confraternity of the Rosary carried no restrictions with regard to religious training, gender, or social status.[127] There were neither admission fees nor membership dues. Participation in confraternity processions, which were held on the first Sunday of the month, and attendance at masses for the departed and special services on the feasts of the Nativity, Annunciation, Purification, and Assumption were encouraged, but were not required. Prospective members merely pledged to recite the Rosary while meditating its fifteen mysteries at least once per week.[128]

The first official Confraternity of the Rosary in Milan was founded by Carlo Borromeo on 25 March 1584.[129] It was assigned to the Madonna dell'Albero, the central altar in the Duomo that also hosted the Society of the Ave Maria following its transfer from Santa Maria del Pilone. The pseudonym Madonna del Rosario was added to the list of those already associated with the altar, and an official pastoral letter explaining the structure of the confraternity housed there was printed for distribution. The letter was issued with the order that it be read in all the Parish churches of the diocese for six months, and, in particular, on the first Sunday of the month, which marked the monthly processions of the Confraternity of the Rosary at the Duomo.[130]   Sometime between March and early November 1584, a second Confraternity of the Rosary was established for the Spanish-speaking segment of the Milanese population at the Castello of Porta Giovia.[131]

A document surviving from a pastoral visit made to the altar of the Madonna del Rosario in the Duomo by Federico Borromeo in 1595 reveals the importance placed upon the musical activities of the confraternity during the years succeeding Carlo's death, for a choir was appointed to sing the 'Ave Maris Stella,' antiphons of the Blessed Virgin, and the 'Magnificat' while the clergy led a candlelight procession through the church, as well as subsequently leading the congregants in the singing of laude and the litany of the Virgin.[132]   Whether or not the singers involved were members of the Duomo choir or one that was specially formed, as was found in the Society of the Ave Maria, unfortunately remains unclear. Nonetheless, the activities of this society clearly had an impact on music-making in both the public and the private sphere.

The singing of laude has long been associated with confraternal recitation of the Rosary. Laude for the Madonna del Rosario, for example, were used at San Filippo Neri, and a setting of Petrarch's 'Vergine bella' was performed in connection with the recitation of the rosary in Florence.[133]   Likewise, at least one lauda, *Al Rosario su venite*, was specifically associated with the Confraternity of the Rosary and circulated in Milan at some point after the founding of the organization at the Duomo. Although the music to which the lauda was sung is not extant, its text is preserved in a nineteenth-century print issued by Tamburini. The text invites Milanese of all classes and occupations, including merchants, artisans, professional soldiers, widows, mothers, and virgins, to come together for the purpose of reciting the Rosary.[134]

The potential introduction of motets and magnificats into the Confraternity's observances, which is noted in the aforementioned document of 1595, opened the door to the possibility of including a wide variety of polyphony in the services. Undoubtedly the spiritual madrigal, with its affinity for Marian texts, presented fertile ground for the cultivation of worship music associated with the Confraternity of the Rosary. In fact, the genre likely was already gaining ground with the aristocratic Milanese through its introduction at Santa Maria presso San Celso via organist and composer Gasparo Costa. Like Santa Maria presso San Celso, the Confraternity of the Rosary in the Duomo regularly sponsored large public functions. However, its primary activity was the daily recitation and meditation of the Rosary, an observance that was carried out in the private domestic sphere. It, therefore, is not surprising that the most important collection of music associated with the Confraternity of the Rosary was a cycle of spiritual madrigals intended for domestic use. The collection, *La Donna vestita di sole*, was composed in 1602 by Orfeo Vecchi, maestro di cappella at Santa Maria della Scala. It is dedicated to Hippolita Borromea Sanseverina Barbiana, the Countess of Belgioioso.[135] In the dedication, Vecchi compares Hippolita to the mother of Christ, and exhorts her to sing the madrigals contained often with her children as a means of contemplating the virtues of the Blessed Virgin.[136] The collection evidently was intended as a post-partum gift, for Hippolita died of complications from childbirth on the same day that the dedication was penned. Hippolita was thirty-six years old at the time of her death[137] and left behind a husband, a son aged 19, two younger daughters, and a newborn son.[138] The infant, Giovanni Baptista Belgioioso, died of an epileptic seizure a little over a month later.[139]

As I have discussed elsewhere, *La Donna vestita di sole* is a textually and tonally ordered cycle based upon the text of Revelation 12:1-2.[140] No source for the individual texts of the madrigals has yet been identified, but the cycle likely has its roots in one of the many collections of spiritual poems that circulated during the second half of the sixteenth century. The cycle itself is textually and tonally divided into three sections (Table 7.5). The first of these is comprised of twelve madrigals in G cantus durus, each of which explores a different 'star' or virtue of the Virgin's corona. The second features two madrigals in A cantus durus that function as an exegesis of the Revelation 12:1 text. The final section recounts seven events in the life of the Virgin that served as the basis for important Marian feasts of the Ambrosian calendar. The first four madrigals of this final section, which are dedicated to events preceding the birth of Jesus, are set in F cantus mollis, while the final three, which are devoted to post-partum celebrations, are cast in G cantus mollis. All seven of the madrigals in the final section are set in lower clefs, a characteristic that emphasizes the earthly realm in which the episodes occur. Moreover, the rather problematic A tonality of the second section, when considered in light of the Revelation texts, seems to illustrate its spiritual separation from the realms of the first and third sections. The upward modal shift from F to G in the third section is also significant, for it underscores the Virgin's passage to motherhood at the point of transition from the Visitation to the Birth of Jesus.

The frontispiece of Vecchi's collection features a depiction of the Revelation text in which the Blessed Virgin, bathed in the sun, standing on the moon, and crowned with twelve stars, holds the infant Jesus in her arms.[141] It is strikingly similar to the frontispiece found in the 1583 edition of Bartolomeo Scalvo's *Meditationi del*

Table 7.5 Cyclical ordering in Orfeo Vecchi: *La Donna vestita di sole*, 1602

Title	Topic		Cleffing	System	Final
Prima stella: Bellezza	Più bella donna	Beauty	$G_2G_2C_2C_3C_4$	0	G
Seconda stella: Sapienza	Più saggia donna	Wisdom	$G_2G_2C_2C_3C_4$	0	G
Terza stella: Fortezza	Più magnanima donna	Fortitude	$G_2G_2C_2C_3C_4$	0	G
Quarta stella: Purità	Più pura donna	Purity	$G_2G_2C_2C_3C_4$	0	G
Quinta stella: Liberalità	Più liberal, più pia	Generosity	$G_2G_2C_2C_3C_4$	0	G
Sesta stella: Tranquilità	Più pacifica in terra	Tranquility	$G_2G_2C_2C_3C_4$	0	G
Settima stella: Taciturnità	Più quieta donna il nostro	Taciturnity	$G_2G_2C_2C_3C_4$	0	G
Ottava stella: Humilità	Più grave donna, e mite	Humility	$G_2G_2C_2C_3C_4$	0	G
Nona stella: Santità	Più strettamente unita	Sanctity	$G_2G_2C_2C_3C_4$	0	G
Decima stella: Carità	Più fervorosa donna	Charity	$G_2G_2C_2C_3C_4$	0	G
Undecima stella: Perseveranza	Più stabil donna	Perseverance	$G_2G_2C_2C_3C_4$	0	G
Duodecima stella: Perfettione	Più preghiata non visse	Perfection	$G_2G_2C_2C_3C_4$	0	G
Vestita di sole	Non di porpora ò d'oro	Dressed in the Sun	$G_2C_2C_3C_3F_3$	0	A
Calcante la luna	Se fan coron'al crine	Treading on the Moon	$G_2C_2C_3C_3F_3$	0	A
Della Natività di Maria Vergine	Al vostro nascer nacque	Nativity of the Virgin	$C_1C_1C_3C_4F_4$	1 Flat	F
Della Presentatione	Allor ch'al sacro Tempio	Presentation	$C_1C_1C_3C_4F_4$	1 Flat	F
Dell'Annonciatione	Spiegò veloce il corso	Annunciation	$C_1C_1C_3C_4F_4$	1 Flat	F
Della Visitatione	Piena di Dio sen poggia	Visitation	$C_1C_1C_3C_4F_4$	1 Flat	F
Del Parto	Oggi dal Ciel un lampo	Nativity of Jesus	$C_1C_1C_3C_4F_4$	1 Flat	G
Della Purificatione	Qual gentil Colomba	Purification	$C_1C_1C_3C_4F_4$	1 Flat	G
Dell'Assontione	Questa che spiega il volo	Assumption	$C_1C_1C_3C_4F_4$	1 Flat	G

Rosario della Gloriosa Maria Vergine,[142] a collection of meditations on the Rosary that is thought to be associated with the Confraternity of the Rosary in Milan.[143] The *Meditationi*, which were first printed in Latin by Diocesan printer Pacifico Pontio in 1569,[144] elaborate upon the fifteen mysteries of the Rosary by providing an individual meditation to accompany each 'bead' or prayer. Like *La Donna vestita di sole*, the *Meditationi* are divided into three sections, and include fifty-five meditations on New Testament events from the Incarnation through the raising of Lazarus, fifty-five meditations on the Passion, and fifty-five meditations on the Resurrection. Each individual meditation draws upon related biblical and liturgical texts that are woven into a gloss or commentary on the designated subject. The Latin text and austere appearance of the 1569 diocesan edition suggests that the book was initially intended for use by ecclesiastics and scholars of Latin, perhaps in the Jesuit schools. However, the 1583 edition, with its Italian text and the added feature of an illustrative woodcut to accompany each meditation, smacks of a shift in marketing towards the general public. Its publication was perhaps intended as a prelude to the official founding of the Confraternity of the Rosary in the Duomo. In any case, the uncannily similar frontispieces and organization shared by Vecchi's madrigal collection and Scalvo's *Meditationi* underscores the common approach to spiritual meditation that permeates both texts.

Orfeo Vecchi, the most prominent composer of sacred music in Milan during the years immediately following the establishment and expansion of the Confraternity of the Rosary, apparently tried his hand at domestic devotional literature again the year following year. His second volume of 'spiritual madrigals,' the *Scielta de Madrigali* (1604), is even more anachronistic than *La Donna vestita di sole*. It contains secular madrigals by post-Tridentine composers that have been transformed into motets through the substitution of sacred Latin texts, a technique that Vecchi had used occasionally in his earlier motet collections. According to Vecchi's brother, who arranged the posthumous publication of the volume during the year following his death, the settings were chosen and arranged by Vecchi himself.[145] Each of the madrigals that provided the musical material is clearly identified in the print, and the final madrigal utilized is by the composer himself. Unlike *La Donna vestita di sole*, however, the *Scielta de Madrigali* is neither tonally nor thematically ordered. Instead, it features an abstractly arranged series of antiphons, psalms, and other biblical texts, only a few of which are Marian in nature. Nonetheless, the composer appears to have made a conscious effort to tailor the collection to the scholastic background and social milieu of its dedicatees Luca Francesco, Ambrogio, and Giovanni Battista Brivio. Of the three, Giovanni Battista, who served as both the Bishop of Cremona and an Apostolic Protonotary,[146] was the most prominent, and his ecclesiastical orientation may account for the use of Latin in the retexting process. The *Scielta de madrigali*, moreover, is not the first Milanese motet collection derived from secular madrigals. It was preceded by two sets of Latin contrafacta compiled by Simon Molinari in 1599[147] and one contrafacta collection prepared by Geronimo Cavaglieri in 1600.[148] The sudden emergence of this body of literature around the turn of the century, however, points towards a surge of interest in private devotions that evolved, at least in part, from the official institution of the Confraternity of the Rosary in 1584.

The death of Carlo Borromeo on 3 November 1584 marked the beginning of a new spiritual era in Milan, rather than the twilight of one. Girded by the order imposed by the statutes and reforms introduced through Carlo Borromeo's diocesan synods, provincial councils, and pastoral visits, his immediate successors, Gaspare Visconti and Federico Borromeo, were free to focus upon the development of Milanese spiritual life, and this spiritual dimension affected the collective musical experience markedly. Under their pastoral care, the royal ducal chapel at Santa Maria della Scala and the cappella musicale in the pilgrimage church of Santa Maria presso San Celso attained an international prominence that had previously eluded them. Musical life in the monasteries flourished. The musical activities of the Society of the Ave Maria in the Duomo and the Confraternity of the Rosary were expanded and provided increased financial support. The Schools of Christian Doctrine continued apace, and with them, spiritual music in the vernacular proliferated. In short, sacred music began to outpace secular genres in the proverbial competition for public attention. Yet Carlo Borromeo's death was, indeed, a culmination of sorts. For Milan, it heralded the close of the tumultuous sixteenth century, an era in which its citizens witnessed the colorful kaleidoscope of political dissension, economic upheaval, and religious reformation that shaped its modern civic identity. The emergence of that modern identity, however, need no longer elude us musically, for it is richly preserved in the surviving sacred and secular literature that formed a part of the collective civic discourse.

Notes

1   *Registri di Lettere Ducali* 1553-1562, 188v, BTASCM, notes that the ordination services were held in the Cathedral of Milan on 15 May 1560.

2   See John B. Tomaro, 'San Carlo Borromeo and the Implementation of the Council of Trent' in *San Carlo Borromeo: Catholic Reform and Ecclesiastical Politics in the Second Half of the Sixteenth Century*, ed. John M. Headley and John B. Tomaro (London and Toronto: Associated University Presses, 1988), 67-84.

3   Tomaro, 'San Carlo Borromeo and the Implementation of the Council of Trent,' 72-77, and Lewis Lockwood, *The Counter-Reformation and the Masses*, 102-103.

4   Consider, for example, P. 248 sup. (Urbano Monti: *Delle cose più notabili successe alla città de Milano*, prima parte), 86v-95r, BAM.

5   Zardin, *Riforma cattolica e resistenza nobiliari nelle diocesi di Carlo Borromeo*, 94-99.

6   P. 248 sup. (Urbano Monti: *Delle cose più notabili successe alla città de Milano*, seconda parte), 70v-71v, BAM.

7   P. 248 sup. (Urbano Monti: *Delle cose più notabili successe alla città de Milano*, seconda parte), 84r-86r and 87r-89v, BAM.

8   P. 248-251 sup. (Urbano Monti: *Delle cose più notabili successe alla città de Milano*), BAM.

9   See Domenico Sella, *Lo stato di Milano in età spagnola* (Turin: UTET Libreria, 1987), 86-95, and Hubert Jedin, *Carlo Borromeo* (Rome, 1971), 13-60.

10   Fabbri, 'La normativa istituzionale,' 19-20. Also see Lockwood, *The Counter-Reformation and the Masses*, 106-111.

11   See Robert Kendrick, *Celestial Sirens: Nuns and their Music in Early Modern Milan* (Oxford: Clarendon Press, 1996), 58-71.

12   Lockwood, *The Counter-Reformation and the Masses*, and Federico Mompellio, 'La cappella del Duomo da Matthias Hermann di Vercore,' 769-784. Also see Lewis Lockwood, 'The Counter-Reformation and the Sacred Music of Vincenzo Ruffo'.

13   See Chapter 6.

14   'Intendo che ne la Chiesa maggiore è vacato una Custoderia è [sic.] una Cantoria informatemi del valor loro, et se sono de quelle che i Can*cellerie* sogliono optare, ò pur toccano à me liberalmen*te*, et con le prime datene avviso.' An excerpt from a letter by Borromeo to his private secretary Tullio Albanese dated 19 June 1563. S.Q. + II.7 (Lettere da S. Carlo Borromeo), 61v, BAM.

15   'Qui inclusa sarà una di suor Corona scrittami in rac*commandatio*ne di certo che vorebbe esser m*aest*ro di cappella del Duomo. Però quando sia persona idonea, farete per lui quei buoni offitij che vi parrano conveniente.' A reference to Boyleau in a letter from Borromeo to his private secretary Tullio Albanese dated 2 August 1563. S.Q. + II.7 (Lettere da S. Carlo Borromeo), 71r, BAM.

16   Vicentino was recommended by both Ferdinand D'Avalos and one Senator Claro. F. 103 inf. (Lettere a S. Carlo Borromeo), 451r and 482r, BAM. The letter from Ferdinando D'Avalos is transcribed in Appendix I, Document 13.

17   F. 103 inf. (Lettere a S. Carlo Borromeo), 408r, BAM. See Appendix I, Document 15.

18   'Non ho possuto far opera alcuna per Simone Boylau musico rac*commanda*to a v*ostra* s*ingora* Illu*strissi*ma dalla R*everendissi*ma sig*nor*a Sor' Corona Isabella *e*ssendo che gia il Duomo s'era provisto per Maestro de Cap*pella* di M*esser* Vincenzo Ruffo contra il q*uale* non ho voluto far' ufficio alcuno conoscendola meritendola di quel loco.' Excerpt of a letter from Tullio Albanese to Borromeo dated 1 September 1563. F. 103 inf. (Lettere a S. Carlo Borromeo), 359v, BAM.

19   Daolmi, *Don Nicola Vicentino*, 58.

20   Lockwood, *The Counter-Reformation and the Masses*, 93-96.

21   Modern architectural histories of Santa Maria presso San Celso include Ferdinando Reggiori, *Il santuario di Santa Maria presso San Celso e i suoi tesori* (Milan: Banco Popolare di Milano, 1968) and Nicole Riegel, *Santa Maria presso San Celso in Mailand: Der Kirchenbau und seine Innendekoration 1430-1563* (Worms am Rhein 1998). A sixteenth-century history of the church and its administrative body is found in Paolo Morigia: *Historia dove si narra l'origine della famosa divotione della Chiesa della Madonna, posta vicina à quella di S. Celso di Milano* (Milan: Pacifico Pontio, 1594), and Paolo Morigia, *Origine miraculosa della celebre Madonna appresso a S. Celso in Milano riconosciuta ed illustrata da Giuseppi Girolamo Sememzi* (Milan: Ambrogio Ramellati, 1700.) Each noble member or 'deputy' held a specific office, the most important of which were the prior, subprior and treasurer. Morigia's history contains a full list of the deputies of 1594, and partial lists for the 1550s are found in *Santa Maria Presso San Celso: Amministratum 60 (Sedute Registri 1490 al 1582)*, ASDM.

22   Christine Getz, 'Simon Boyleau and the Church of the 'Madonna of Miracles': Educating and Cultivating the Aristocratic Audience in Post-Tridentine Milan,' *Journal of the Royal Music Association* 126/2 (2001), 148-149.

23   Getz, 'Simon Boyleau and the Church of the "Madonna of Miracles,"' 149-150.

24   *Santa Maria presso San Celso: Libri giornalieri della cassa 1563-1569,* 27 November 1563, ASDM. In 1569 Brena sought a controversial patent for a harpsichord that could be transposed by several tones. See Barbara Torre, 'Alcune note su uno sconosciuto ritratto di musicista del XVI secolo,', 15-16, and Christine Getz, 'New Light on the Milanese Career of Hoste da Reggio,' 301-302.

25   On the architectural history of Santa Maria presso San Celso, see Riegel, *Santa Maria*

presso San Celso in Mailand and Reggiori, *Il santuario di Santa Maria presso San Celso e i suoi tesori.*

26   Compiled from Santa Maria *presso San Celso: Libro giornalieri della cassa* 1563-1569 and *Santa Maria presso San Celso: Libri maestri* 1558-1576, ASDM.

27   Morigia, *Historia*, 17.

28   Morigia, *Historia*, 18 and 27.

29   '. . .ogni Sabbato la sera all'hora della Compieta s'habbi da Cantare la Salve Regina, con certi versetti e risponsori, con alquante oratione per venerar il Sabbato giorno dedicato da Santa Chiesa alla gloriosa madre di Dio: ilche all'hora deputata quivi si trova la Musica, e l'Organista, ed i Sacerdoti . . . la Musica comincia, e l'Organo risponde, e hora l'Organo e la Musica unite, con tanto dolcezza, e bellissima harmonia, che genera nei cuori de gli uditori una santa divotione verso la Madre di Dio, e compontione di cuore, perche sembrano un choro angelico.' Morigia, *Historia dove si narra l'originie della famosa divotione della Chiesa della Madonna*, 17. A nearly identical description is found in Morigia, *Origine miraculosa della celebre Madonna appresso S. Celso*, 13. For further discussion, see Getz, 'Simon Boyleau and the Church of the 'Madonna of Miracles,'' 148-161.

30   On the Salve service in the Low Countries, see Kristine K. Forney, 'Music, Ritual and Patronage at the Church of Our Lady, Antwerp,' *Early Music History* 7 (1987), 1-57. The evolution of North Italian Compline into a service that rivaled Vespers in social significance is documented in John Bettley, '"L'ultima hora canonica del giorno": Music for the Office of Compline in Northern Italy in the Second Half of the Sixteenth Century': *Music and Letters* 74 (1993), 163-214.

31   *Santa Maria presso San Celso: Chiesa* 10 (Musica e Cantori 1606-1800), Busta Boyleau, fasc. 5, ASDM. Those listed include Paolo Fontana, Cesare, Giovanni, Ferando, and Simon Boyleau.

32   *Sant'Eufemia* VI-125 (*Visite pastorali e documenti aggiunti: Santa Maria presso San Celso*), q. 3, ASDM.

33   Renata and Rosella Frigerio, 'Giovanni Paolo Cima organista nella Madonna di S. Celso in Milano: documenti inediti dell'Archivio diocesano di Milano, *Il flauto dolce* XVI (April 1987), 32-33.

34   The singers, who are not listed individually in any of the surviving documentation, were paid a total of 56 lire per quarter. *Santa Maria presso San Celso: Libri maestri 1558 al 1576*, 71r, 83r, 87v, 91v, 97r, 111r, ASDM. In addition, a bass named Giovanni Antonio received an occasional 15 lire. The documents suggest that this singer may have been the organist Giovanni Antonio Brenna. *Santa Maria presso San Celso: Libri maestri 1558 al 1576*, 87r, 102v, 148r, 220r, 223r, ASDM.

35   Giuseppe Riccucci, 'L'attività della cappella musicale di S. Maria presso S. Celso e la condizione dei musici a Milano tra il XVI e il XVII secolo' in *Intorno a Monteverdi*, ed. Maria Caraci Vela and Rodobaldo Tibaldi (Lucca: L.I.M.,1999), 295-296.

36   Reggiori, *Il santuario di Santa Maria presso San Celso*, 35-36. According to Urbano Monti, P. 248 (Urbano Monti: *Delle cose più notabili successe alla città di Milano, prima parte*), 104v, BAM, the other three processions were to Sant'Ambrogio, Santa Maria della Scala, and San Nazarro. The processional route of the fourth, which must have been the one that culminated at Santa Maria presso San Celso, covered the entire city.

37   Morigia, *Historia*, 13.

38   'Adunque il Cardinale, il clero, il Senato, e tutto Milano conoscendo che'l flagello veniva dalla gran mano d'Iddio: s'attese à placare l'ira sua con le humilationi, orationi, e

penitenze: e furono fatte quattro generali processioni caminando tutto il clero, tutta la massa de disciplinati, e'l popolo scalzo con le cenere in capo, vestito di sacco, huomini, e donne, nobil, ignobili, fanciulli, e fanciulle con le croci in mano, e funi al collo, invocando tutti l'altissimo e pietosissimo nome di GIESU CHRISTO nostro signor, della Beatissima Virgine, di tutti i Santi, e Sante, con le Litanie, e Salmi penitientiali.' Gaspare Bugati, *L'aggiunti dell'Historia universale et delle cose di Milano . . .dall 1566 fin'al 1581*, 154.

39 Bugati, *L'aggiunti dell'Historia universale*, 154-155.

40 '. . .cantati i Salmi penetentiali con pietosa musical armonia, meditandogli tutte le gente prostrate.' Bugati, *L'aggiunti dell'Historia universale*, 155.

41 Simon Boyleau, *Modulationes in Magnificat ad omnes tropos . . .quatuor, quinque, ac sex vocibus distinctae* (Milano: Pacifico Ponzio, 1566), dedication.

42 On the rise of the modally ordered magnificat cycle during the sixteenth century, see David Crook, *Orlando di Lasso's Imitation Magnificats for Counter-Reformation Munich* (Princeton, 11-13).

43 Gustave Reese 'The Polyphonic Magnificat of the Renaissance as a Design in Tonal Centers,' *Journal of the American Musicological Society* 13 (1960), 68-78 remains one of the best general studies of tonal ordering procedures in the Magnificat cycle.

44 For further discussion, see Getz, 'Simon Boyleau and the Church of the "Madonna of Miracles,"' 155-159.

45 Lockwood, *The Counter-Reformation and the Masses*, 48.

46 See Getz, 'Simon Boyleau and the Church of the "Madonna of Miracles,"' 150-151, and Mompellio, 'La cappella del Duomo da Matthias Hermann di Vercore,' 763.

47 Getz, 'Simon Boyleau and the Church of the "Madonna of Miracles,"' 153-155.

48 See Gasparo Costa, *Il primo libro de motetti et madrigali spirituali a cinque voci* (Venice: Angelo Gardano, 1581).

49 Lothar Schmidt, 'Beobachtungen zur Passionsthematik im italienischen geistlichen Madrigal,' *Schütz-Jahrbuch* 13 (1994), 70-77. Also see Robert Kendrick, *The Sounds of Milan, 1585-1650* (Oxford and New York, 2002), 139.

50 Morigia, *Historia*, 27-44.

51 *Metropolitana* LXXXII-456 (Visite pastorali e documenti aggiunti), fasc. 20, ASDM, and *Metropolitana* XIII-86 (Visite pastorali e documenti aggiunti), fasc. 86, ASDM. These documents date from the early seventeenth century and 1596, respectively. The pertinent section of the former is transcribed as Appendix I, Document 15. Also see Cattaneo, *Maria santissima nella storia della spiritualità Milanese*, 105. Although Cattaneo provides no citations for his source material on this matter, the accuracy of his reporting suggests that he was familiar with at least one of these documents.

52 *Metropolitana* LXXXII-456 (Visite pastorali e documenti aggiunti), fasc. 20, ASDM, and *Metropolitana* XIII-86 (Visite pastorali e documenti aggiunti), fasc. 86, ASDM.

53 Maria Cecelia Visentin, *La pietà mariana nella Milano del Rinascimento* (Milan: NED, 1995), 31, reported that Archbishop Guido Antonio Archimboldo approved a Congregation of the Ave Maria in the Duomo in 1495. Her source is a document catalogued by her as Archivio storico milanese, Panigarola, reg. 20, n. 21, ff. 73-86. The other archival documents relating the history of the confraternity make no reference to this document.

54 Gianmarco Burigozzi, *Cronaca Milanese*, 509-510.

55 *Metropolitana* LXXXII-456 (Visite pastorali e documenti aggiunti), fasc. 20, ASDM, Also see Giovanni Battista Sannazzaro, 'Altari,' 21.

56 *Metropolitana* LXXXII-456 (Visite pastorali e documenti aggiunti), fasc. 20, ASDM,

and *Metropolitana* XIII-86 (Visite pastorali e documenti aggiunti), fasc. 86, ASDM. Also see Sannazzaro, 'Altari,' 21 and 23. Although the archival documents regarding the Society of the Ave Maria are unclear on the dating of the transfer, historians of the Duomo altars date it to 1566. On 24 August 1604 the society was officially renamed the School of the Holy Cross and a new constitution and set of orders were issued. The documents reveal that the essential function of the confraternity remained the same. *Metropolitana* XXXIII-406 (Visite pastorali e documenti aggiunti), q. 26, ASDM.

57   See Edward Muir, 'The Virgin on the Street Corner: The Place of the Sacred in Italian Cities' in *Religion and Culture in Renaissance and Reformation*, ed. Steven Ozment (Kirksville: Sixteenth Century Journal Publishers, 1989), 25-40.

58   Niccolò Ormaneto, *Interrogatorio della Dottrina Christiana* (Milan: Pacifico Pontio ad instanza di Matteo Besozzi, 1575; Milano, Biblioteca Nazionale Braidense ZY.I. 46/2); Diego di Ledesma, *Giesu Maria. Dottrina Christiana, a modo di dialogo del Maestro et Discepolo per insegnare alli Fanciulli* (Milan: Pacifico Pontio, 1576; Milano, Biblioteca Nazionale Braidense, Musica B 39/2); and Dottore Ledesma della Compagnia di Gesù, *Modo per insegnar la Dottrina Christiana* (Rome, 1573; Milano, Biblioteca Nazionale Braidense, Musica B 39/1.). On the organization of the schools of Christian Doctrine see Paul F. Grendler, *Schooling in Renaissance Italy* (Baltimore and London: The Johns Hopkins University Press, 1989), 333-362; Miriam Turrini, '"Riformare il mondo a vera vita christiana": le scuole di catechismo nell'Italia del Cinquecento, *'Annali dell'Istituto storico italo-germanico in Trento* VII (1981), 419-447; Giambattista Castiglione, *Istoria delle scuole della dottrina cristiana fondata a Milano* (Milan: Cesare Orena nella Stamperia Malatesta, 1800), I, 12-26; and Angelo Bianchi, 'Le scuole della dottrina cristiana: linguaggio e strumenti per una azione educativa "di massa,"' in *Carlo Borromeo e l'opera della 'grande riforma'* (Milan: Silvana Editoriale, 1997), 145-158.

59   The first branch of the Confraternity of the Rosary in Milan was founded on 25 March 1584. *Metropolitana* LXXX-454 (Visite pastorali e documenti aggiunti), q. 24, ASDM, and *Metropolitana* XLVI-419 (Visite pastorali e documenti aggiunti), q. 28, ASDM, The original confraternity, however, was founded in the Netherlands in 1460, and, as a result of its expansion across Europe, rosary recitation was already being encouraged in a number of other local confraternities.

60   Morigia, *Historia*, 37-38.

61   'Consideri l'alto misterio dell'incarnatione del figliolo di Dio, accioche ráempiuta di stupore tu saluti la dolcissima Maria tua Signora insieme con l'Angelo che la salutò dicendo, Ave Maria et cetera. Et ac? accioche tu possa far cosa grata à Maria Vergine salutela spesso col dolce verso angelico, e procura con basci di divota salutatione di basciargli almeno i piedi dicendo, Ave Maria.' Morigia, *Historia*, 39.

62   'A te, ò Maria, è quasi basciarti il sentir questo verso angelico Ave Maria: percioche tante volte ò beatissima, tu sei basciati, quante volte sei salvata. Adunque fratelli carissimi appressatevi all'imagine sua, ed inginocchiatevi divotamente, e daregli divoti basci, e dite, Ave Maria. Et in un altro luogo dice, I Cieli respondono, gli Angeli giubilano, il Mondo essulta, e i demonii tremano, quando io dica Ave Maria; Cosa dice San Bernardo.' Morigia, *Historia*, 39.

63   Morigia, *Historia*, 37-40.

64   *Metropolitana* LXXXII-456 (Visite pastorali e documenti aggiunti), fasc. 20, ASDM,

65   Cattaneo, *Maria santissima nella storia della spiritualità Milanese*, 105. Cattaneo appears to have derived his information from *Metropolitana* LXXXII-456 (Visite pastorali e documenti aggiunti), fasc. 20, ASDM.

66   *Metropolitana* LXXX-454 (Visite pastorali e documenti aggiunti), q. 24, ASDM. See

Appendix I, Document 16.

67   *Metropolitana* LXXX-454 (Visite pastorali e documenti aggiunti), q. 24, ASDM.

68   See Christine Getz, 'The Milanese Cathedral Choir,' 212-221. Laurentio Putheo, an adult soprano who served in the Milanese cathedral choir from 1534-1550 typically received a salary that was one-third that of his contemporaries for reasons that are not explained in the documents.

69   *Metropolitana* LXXXII-456 (Visite pastorali e documenti aggiunti), fasc. 20, ASDM, and *Metropolitana* XIII-86 (Visite pastorali e documenti aggiunti), fasc. 86, ASDM.

70   Lewis Lockwood, *The Counter-Reformation and the Masses*, 109.

71   Matthias Verecorensis, *Cantuum quinque vocum* (Milan, 1555). Although he stepped down in 1550 after serving as maestro for 28 years, Werrecore was present at the Duomo until at least 1574. He is customarily identified as the retired or 'other' maestro di cappella in the documents.

72   Vincenzo Ruffo, *Sacrae modulationes vulgo motecta. Liber secundus.* (Brixoniae: Petrus Maria Marchettum, 1586). Although this collection was published after Ruffo left the Duomo, it may contain some works composed for use there. Ruffo's motet books of 1542 and 1555 cannot be linked to musical activity at the Duomo, but they do not contain settings of the Ave Maria text either. However, *Pistoia, Biblioteca Capitolare Ms. B. 38 n. 7* contains the bassus part of a six-voice Ave Maria attributed to Ruffo. It was likely composed for use there.

73   For an inventory of these manuscripts, which are catalogued as *Libroni 25* and *26*, see Claudio Sartori, *La cappella musicale del Duomo di Milano: Catalogo delle musiche dell'Archivio della Veneranda Fabbrica del Duomo* (Milan: Istituto Editoriale Milano, 1957b), 54-56.

74   Pietro Pontio, *Motectorum quinque vocibus liber primus* (Mediolani: Francesco ed eredi Simonis Tini, 1587). Only the tenor, altus, and quintus partbooks survive.

75   On Pontio's career, see Russell E. Murray, 'Pontio, Pietro,' *The New Grove Dictionary of Music and Musicians*, 2nd edn. (London and New York: Macmillan Publishers, Ltd., 2001), vol. 20, 97-98, and Murray, 'The Voice of the Composer'.

76   Italics mine.

77   *Modo per insegnar*, 11r-v and 52r-57r.

78   Noel O'Regan, *Institutional Patronage in Post-Tridentine Rome: Music at Santissima Trinità dei Pelligrini 1550-1650* (London: Royal Music Association, 1995), 8-57.

79   For a facsimile reproduction, see Milan, *Archivio della Veneranda Fabbrica del Duomo, Sezione Musicale, Librone 3* (olim 2267), 187v-189r.

80   Ludwig Finscher, *Loyset Compère (c. 1450-1518): Life and Works* (Rome: American Institute of Musicology, 1964), 161-166.

81   Finscher, *Loyset Compère*, 161 and Ludwig Finscher, *Loyset Compère: Opera Omnia* IV (Motets) in *Corpus mensurabilis musicae* 15 (Rome: American Institute of Musicology, 1961), II.

82   Jeffrey Dean, 'The Evolution of a Canon at the Papal Chapel: The Importance of Old Music in the Fifteenth and Sixteenth Centuries,' in *Papal Music and Musicians in Late Medieval and Renaissance Rome*, ed. Richard Sherr (Oxford: Clarendon Press, 1998), 151-153.

83   *Metropolitana* LXXX-454 (Visite pastorali e documenti aggiunti), q. 24, ASDM.

84   Giovanni Pierluigi da Palestrina, *Liber III. Motectorum quinque vocum.* Milan: Francesco ed eredi Simonis Tini, 1587.

85   *Metropolitana* XXVI-399 (Visite pastorali e documenti aggiunti), q. 19, ASDM. This document is undated, but others devoted to the Congregation that are cited below confirm

that it was founded in 1581. The refurbished altar of Santa Maria del Pilone was renamed the altar of the Assumption.

86   Frequent confession figures prominently in the requirements of most of the confraternities active in Milan during this period, including those devoted to the teaching of Christian Doctrine. On the role of confession in Borromeo's reform program, see Wietse de Boer, *The Conquest of the Soul: Confession, Discipline, and Public Order in Counter-Reformation Milan*. Boston: Brill, 2001.

87   *Metropolitana* XCIV-467 (Visite pastorali e documenti aggiunti), q. 2, q. 4, and q.8, ASDM, and *Regole appartenenti alle Donne della Congregatione della Gloriosssima Vergine Madre Maria nella Chiesa Metropolitana* (Milan: Michele Tini, 1582.) Milano, Biblioteca Nazionale Braidense H.VIII.190.

88   *Metropolitana* XCIV-467 (Visite pastorali e documenti aggiunti), q.8, ASDM, notes that officer elections, which occurred several times throughout the year, were held after the school of Christian Doctrine.

89   Giambatista Castiglione, *Istoria delle scuole della dottrina* christiana, I, 12-15.

90   The confraternity was originally known as the Company of the Christian Reformation, but later took the name of the Company of the Servants of Children in Charity. Paul F. Grendler, *Schooling in Renaissance Italy*, 335-336.

91   Castiglione, *Istoria delle scuole della dottrina christiana*, I, 18 and 26. These texts included the *Libretto, Tavola, Interrogatorio*, and *Office of the Blessed Virgin*. Also see Grendler, *Schooling in Renaissance Italy*, 334. The Latin school apparently was that known as the Scuola delle quattro Marie in San Michele ad Gallo.

92   At the altar of Santa Maria del Pilone, as discussed above. Giovanni Battista Sannazzaro, 'Altari,' 21-22.

93   *San Sepolcro* III (Santa Maria Beltrade: Visite pastorali e documenti aggiunti), q. 15, ASDM. This 1567 list of the *operai* of the school indicates that it was for boys.

94   *Santa Maria Segreta* VI-289 (Visite pastorali e documenti aggiunti), q. 18, ASDM contains a list of the operai of this boy's school dated 1596. The school probably was connected to the Latin school founded there by Tommaso Grassi in 1473. *Santa Maria Segreta* VI-289 (Visite pastorali e documenti aggiunti), q. 20, ASDM.

95   *Metropolitana* VII-380 (San Protasio: Visite pastorali e documenti aggiunti), q. 8, ASDM, contains a 1592 supplication from the parish at Varedo questioning certain payments that supported the school at San Dalmatio.

96   *San Giorgio* IX-227 (S. Maria ad Circulum e S. Quirico: Visite pastorali e documenti aggiunti). q. 8, ASDM. Documents from the pastoral visits of 1567, 1575, and 1581 to Santa Maria al Cerchio record the presence of a school for girls only.

97   *San Satiro* IV-304 (Visite pastorali e documenti aggiunti), q. 10, ASDM. A notary document recording the convocation of the confraternity that administered this school for boys on 20 April 1592.

98   *Metropolitana* LXXXV-459 (Visite pastorali e documenti aggiunti), q. 22, ASDM, contains a 1592 list of the officers that administered the schools for girls and boys held in S. Giovanni Laterano.

99   See, for example, the *Interrogatorio del maestro al discepolo per istruir li fanciulli* (Milan: Vincenzo Girardoni ad instanza di M. Matteo de Sesozzo, al segno della stella, 1568), which contains a printed copy of the statutes at its close, and the *Constitutioni et Regole della Compagnia, et scuole della dottrina cristiana* (Milan: Pacifico Pontio, 1585). Milano, Biblioteca Nazionale Braidense 24.19.A.9/1 and H.II.138, respectively.

100   *Metropolitana* XXXIII-406 (Visite pastorali e documenti aggiunti), q. 34, ASDM.

101   'Cresca nel nome del Signore et s'augumenti ogni giorno più quella Santa et util opera, la

quale sij più abbracciata, et frequentata che non è da persone nobili:' *Miscellanea città e pievi* XVI-513 (Visite pastorali e documenti aggiunti), f. 81v, ASDM.

102 See Grendler, *Schooling in Renaissance Italy*, 333-362; Turrini, '"Riformare il mondo a vera vita Christiana": le scuole di catechismo nell'Italia del Cinquecento,' 419-447; Castiglione, *Istoria delle scuole della dottrina cristiana*, I, 12-26; and Bianchi, 'Le scuole della dottrina cristiana,' 145-158.

103 *Tavola della Dottrina Christiana* (Parma, 1563). Milano, Biblioteca Nazionale Braidense R. MIN. 22.

104 Ledesma, *Giesu Maria. Dottrina Christiana*.

105 Ornamento, *Interrogatorio della Dottrina Christiana*.

106 Castiglione, *Istoria delle scuole della dottrina cristiana*, 26; Turrini, 'Riformare il mondo,' 431-432; and Grendler, *Schooling in Renaissance Italy*, 96.

107 Six melodies were used to sing the thirty-three laude of Societas Nominis Jesù, *Lodi, e Canzoni Spirituali per cantare insieme con la Dottrina Christiana* (Milan, 1576). Milano, Biblioteca Nazionale Braidense, Musica B 39/3. Five melodies, which are inserted in manuscript at the close of the book, were used to sing the 25 laude of Compagnia di Gesù, *Lodi devote per cantarsi nelle scole della Dottrina Christiana raccolta novamente* (Milan, 1586). Milano, Biblioteca Nazionale Braidense Z.Y.I.41. In addition to music appended in manuscript, this latter collection featured appended texts, including Petrarch's 'Vergine bella,' several other spiritual sonnets by Petrarch, some anonymous spiritual poems and laude, a 'Triumph of the Divine,' and instructions for teaching the seven deadly sins.

108 Societas Nominis Jesù, *Lodi e canzoni spirituali*, 3r-v. This preface is also reproduced in Giancarlo Rostirolla, 'Laudi e canti sprituali nelle edizioni della prima "controriforma" Milanese' in *Carlo Borromeo e l'opera della 'grande riforma'*, 161-162.

109 Ledesma, *Modo per insegnar*, 9v.

110 ' . . .potranno cantare due ò quattro, che siano prima bene amaestrati in quella separatamente. Et prima questi soli la cantino. Et quandro vedrà che gli altri l'habbiano imparata, potranno rispondere tutti.' Ledesma, *Modo per insegnar*, 16v.

111 Rostirolla, 'Laudi e canti spirituali,' 162-163. Also see Ledesma, *Modo per insegnar*, 11r-13v.

112 Ledesma, *Modo per insegnar*, 11r-v and 52r-57r.

113 Societas Nominis Jesù, *Lodi e canzoni spirituali*, 3v-36v.

114 Rostirolla, 'Laudi e canti sprituali,' 163. Also see the Table on page 167.

115 Ibid.,' 163-166.

116 Societas Nominis Jesù, *Lodi e canzoni spirituali*, 44-46.

117 Compagni du Gesù, *Lodi devote per cantarsi nelle scuole della Dottrina Christiana*. Milan: Pacifico Pontio, 1586. Biblioteca Nazionale Braidense ZY.I.41.

118 Societas Nominis Jesù, *Lodi e canzoni spirituali*, 37-43.

119 *Metropolitana* XXXIII-406 (Visite pastorali e documenti aggiunti), q. 34, ASDM.

120 *Interrogatorio del maestro al discepolo per istruir li fanciulli*, n.p. Milano, Biblioteca Nazionale Braidense 24.19.A.9/1. This compilation actually includes two editions, only one of which bears the publication information. Attached to the dated version is a list of rules for those working in the doctrine schools in Milan. These discuss the teaching of the litanies.

121 Lockwood, *The Counter-Reformation and the Masses*, 90-91. Camillo Perego is credited with two treatises on singing Ambrosian plainchant, as well as a collection of four-voice madrigals. Apparently, only the bassus part of the madrigal collection is extant. See Luigi Werner, 'Una rarità musicale della Biblioteca Vescovile di Izombathely,' *Note*

d'Archivio VIII/2 (1931), 99-101.

122   Getz, 'New Light on the Milanese Career of Hoste da Reggio,' 296-301.

123   *San Calimero* I-93 (Visite pastorali e documenti aggiunti), q. 1, fasc. 12v-24v, ASDM.

124   *San Calimero* I-93 (Visite pastorali e documenti aggiunti), q. 2, fasc. 72v-77v, ASDM. This quire contains historical notes from a pastoral visit made by Federico Borromeo in 1604.

125   Grendler, *Schooling in Renaissance Italy*, 356-359. For a discussion of Giussani's letter, see page 358.

126   Francesco Fontana, *Rosario della Gloriosa Vergine Raccolto dal R.P.F. Francesco Fontana Comasco* (Como: appresso G. Trova, 1587), 3r-4r. Milano, Biblioteca Nazionale Braidense Gerli 2321. A book of orders and statutes governing the operation of the Confraternity of the Rosary.

127   Fontana, *Rosario della Gloriosa Vergine*, 9v-10r.

128   Ibid., 10r-11r. A number of the exercises, including those held for inscription and special feasts, are subsequently described on 14r-22v.

129   *Metropolitana* LXXX-454 (Visite pastorali e documenti aggiunti), q. 24, ASDM. Both this official erection notice and the summary of indulgences found in *Metropolitana* XLVI-419 (Visite pastorali e documenti aggiunti), q. 28, ASDM, reinforce a number of the concepts found in the statutes compiled by Fontana.

130   *Metropolitana* XXXIII-406 (Visite pastorali e documenti aggiunti), q. 33, ASDM.

131   A supplication for candles to be used by this branch survives as *Miscellanea Città* IX-498 (Visite pastorali e documenti aggiunti), Q. 19, ASDM. Although the document itself is undated, it is addressed to Carlo Borromeo and clearly was composed prior to his death.

132   *Metropolitana* XXXV-408 (Visite pastorali e documenti aggiunti), q. 9, fols. 66r-67v, ASDM. 'Primo dominio die cuius*que* mensis . . .ante hoc altare conveniunt, ubi sacra imagine, pannis, sericis detecta cantores musici incipiunt, ac prosequientur hymnum sancti Bernardi, Ave Maris Stella; quo finit trino*que* thuribuli ductu imagine incensata, Clerus, processionaliter dirigintur, cereos accensos manibus gestans et prolato eiusdem Virginis Vexillo, in platea huius Templi processio agitur, in qua antiphonae de B. Virgine per choro officiales, tum Magnificat, alaique cantica per cantores musicos decantantu*m*. Populo partim prosequente, partim verò spectante, Inde ad locum ande discesserunt eus' ordine redeunt ubi per cantores B. Virginis laudes et litanie canuntur . . .'

133   Katherine Powers, *Vergine bella* 'as Devotional Song in the Cinquecento', paper presented at the annual national meeting of the South-Central Renaissance Conference, April 2001.

134   *Lode bellissima alla Beata Vergine Maria del SS. Rosario* (Milan, n.d.). Milano, Biblioteca Nazionale Braidense, Misc. Stampe pop. R2.

135   In Orfeo Vecchi, *La Donna vestita di sole* (Milano: erede di Simone Tini e Giovanni Francesco Besozzi, 1602), the composer implies that he had actually been in the employ of Hippolita's husband, Count Alberigo Barbiano di Belgioioso. However, I currently am unable to connect Belgioioso to any other publication or significant event in Vecchi's life. According to McGinnis, *Moving in High Circles*, 436, Hippolita was also the dedicatee of one of the dances of Cesare Negri's *Le gratie d'amore* (1602).

136   Vecchi, *La donna vestita di sole*, dedication.

137   *Porta Nuova Parocchia San* Martino in Nuxigia. Il*lustrissi*ma Co*ntessa* Hippolita Borromea Belzoiosa anni 36 post partu*m* corepta vehementib*us* dolorib*us* ventris cu*m* febre . . .' *Popolazione* p.a. 107 (Registri mortuari 1602-1604), 1 February 1602, ASM.

138   Fausto Bagatti-Valsecchi, Felice Calvi, Luigi Agostino Casati, Damiano Muoni and Leopoldo Pullé, *Famiglie Notabili Milanesi* (Milan, 1875), I, Barbiano e Belgioioso

Tavola IV.

139 *Popolazione* p.a. 107 (Registri mortuari 1602-1604), 13 March 1602, ASM.

140 Christine Getz, 'L'altare mariano nella Milano della Controriforma e La donna vestita di sole (1602),' *Barocco Padano 3. Atti dell'XI Convegno internazionale sulla musica italiana nei secoli XVII-XVIII* (Como: Antiquae Musicae Italicae Studiosi, 2004), 83-101.

141 Vecchi, *La donna vestita di sole*, frontispiece.

142 Bartolomeo Scalvo, *Meditationi del Rosario della Gloriosa Maria Vergine* (Venice: Domenico e Giovanni Battista fratelli della Guerra, 1583). Milan, Biblioteca Nazionale Braidense, Gerli 2313.

143 Maria Luisa Gatti Perer, 'Per la definizione dell'iconografia della Vergine del Rosario' in *Carlo Borromeo e l'opera della 'grande riforma'*, 185-216.

144 Bartolomeo Scalvo, *Le Meditationi del Rosario della gloriosissima Maria Vergine* (Milan: Pacifico Pontio, 1569). Milano, Biblioteca Nazionale Braidense, H.IV.21.

145 Orfeo Vecchi, *Scielta de madrigali à cinque voci . . . accomodati in motetti* (Milan, 1604), dedication. Ferrara, Biblioteca Communale Ariostea. A modern edition of the motets with introductory and analytical remarks is found in Penny Kaye Pekrul Draper, 'A Comprehensive Study and Critical Edition of Orfeo Vecchi's' *Scielta de Madrigali a Cinque Voci* (Ph.D. dissertation: Michigan State University, 1997).

146 Paolo Morigia, *La nobiltà di Milano* (Milan: Giovanni Battista Bidelli, 1615; reprinted 1619), 190 and 543, and Morigia, *Il supplimento della nobiltà di Milano*, 24-25.

147 These include Simon Molinari, *Fattiche spirituali ossia Motetti, libro primo* (Milan, 1599; reprinted Venezia: R. Amadino, 1610), and Simon Molinari, *Fattiche spirituali ossia Motetti, libro secundo* (Milan, 1599; reprinted Venice, R. Amadino, 1610).

148 Geronimo Cavaglieri, *Della nova Metamorfosi dell'infrascritti autori. Libro primo.* (Milano: Agostino Tradate, 1600.)

Appendix I

Documents

Document 1

[*Sforzesco* 1431 (Milano città e ducato 1531 febbraio), n.n., ASM]
Illustrissimo et Excellentissimo Signor Suo e patron' mio Collatorissimo. Eri ebbi de vostra Excellenza per la qual mi comette chio paga al Monzino suo muxicho scuti centodeceotto a conto de sua provixione et de li altri muxici, et Per che non sono Informati di questo particolar e la littera de vostra Excellenza non haver il contrassigno et hanche per non ritrovarmi il modo, per che il Reverendissimo Carraciolo ogniora mi mette in croce, per il suo resto non ho voluto ne potuto satisfar' al predetto Monzino, Del che ne ho voluto pero dar' havixo a vostra Excellenza la qual si dignara commandarmi quanto la vole chio facia et in sua bona gratia humilmente me li ricommando. In Millano alli 25 febraio 1531. Da vostra Illustrissima et Excellentissima signoria vostro humilissimo servitore Hieronymo Brebbia.

Most Illustrious and Excellent Sir My Patron. Yesterday Your Excellency ordered that I pay Monzino your musician the 180 scudi that comprise his salary and that of the other musicians. Because I was not informed of the necessity that the letter of Your Excellency carry the appropriate counter-signature and had no method of obtaining it, and because the Most Reverend Carraciolo is crucifying me every hour, I neither wished nor have been able to satisfy the salary of the aformentioned Monzino. Of this I wished to inform Your Excellency in order that you will deign to command me of what you wish that I do. And in your gracious mercy I humbly recommend myself to you. In Milan on 25 February 1531. From Your Most Illustrious and Excellent Lordship's most humble servant Hieronymo Brebbia.

Document 2

[*Cancelleria dello Stato* 91 (1548 dicembre), 18, ASM]
Eccellentissimo Principe
Il Capitano Melchior di Sayavedra ottene li anni passati dal Marchese del Vasto bone memoria gratia d'uno homicidio commesso in persona d'uno soldato nominato Osuna. Et perche si trova esser'passato il tempo dell'interinatione del Senato, supplica vostra Eccellenza esser'servita commandar' che non obstan' che sij passato detto tempo li sij interinata, il che come cosa iusta spera d'ottener' dall'Eccellenza vostra et cetera.

Most Excellent Prince

In the years past Captain Melchior Sayavedra obtained pardon from the Marchese del Vasto of blessed memory for a homicide of a soldier named Osuna committed personally. And because he finds the time of the internment of the Senate to have passed, he petitions Your Excellency to be used to command that (not withstanding that said time has passed) it will be interned for him, which as a just thing he hopes to obtain from your Excellency, et cetera.

Document 3

[*San Fedele* XXII (Santa Maria della Scala: Visite Pastorali e documenti aggiunti), q. O., ASDM]

1562. Millessimo quingentessimo sexagessimo secundo indictione quinta die-------
---.

Coram vobis Ill*ustre* et R*everendo* iuris u*triusque* d*octore* Domi*no* Paulo pallavicino pr*otonotario* apostolico regi*sque* et duc*alis* M*ediolani* senatore et in esta parte dellegato p*er litte*ras sue R*eale* M*aesta.*

Comparuit ven*erabilis* d*ominus* pr*esbite*r Brumanensius de Manzonibus cappellanus Duc*alis* in ecc*les*ia S*anc*te Marie della Scalla M*ediolani* suo no*mine* proprio et tam*enque* procu*ram* et eo nomine ven*erabilium* d*ominorum* pr*esbite*r*orum* Bartolomei de herba et paoli de mozate amboru*m* Mansionarioru*m* ac d*ominorum* pr*esbite*r*orum* Francisci de pagani Caroli de castilliono et Jo. Petri de cantono o*mn*ium capellano*rum*, et Ludovico de Leynate levite respective reffere*ntur* in dicta ecc*les*ia Sancte Marie della Scala Mediolani Iuri*s*patronatus sue R*eale* M*aesta* ratione status et dominij m*ediolan*i semper cu*m* reservatione Iur*e* suoru*m* et Inherendo comparitioni et requisitioni ac Iur*em* productioni p*er* eos pr*o*vidie factas et licet stante errectione et creatione auc*tori*te apostolica facta eti*am* ad supplicati*ones* et Instan*tiam* felicis recordationis Illustri et Ecc*ellentissi*mi D*o*mini D*omi*ni Francisci Sfortie olim Ducis M*ediolan*i ex quibus l*itte*ris apostolicis cave*tur* q*uod* singuli ex pr*aeposi*to Archidiacono Archipresbitero et Canonicis pr*efa*tis que*cunque*, quodcunqu*e*, et qualiacunqu*e* alia benefitia ecclesiastica sive cura dumtaxat se invice*m* cum propositum archidiaconatu*m* archi*presbite*ratum et canonicatubus ac canonicalibus portionibus c*on*patentia cuiusquoqu*e* qualitatis existentia alias sibi Canonice conferenda retinere et recipere possint et prout latius in eis l*itte*ris apostolicis concessis p*er* felicis recordationis Clementu*m* papa*m* decimu*m* sub data Roma Apud Sanctum Petrum anno incarnati*onis* Dominice 1531 octavo Ca*lendas* settembras pontificatur anno oct*obris*que ibidem si opus fuerit exhibet ipsi d*omi*ni Capp*ellani*j Mansionarij et Levite nullatenus teneantur nec cogi possint aut debeant ad notifficandum alia beneficia ecc*les*iastica que ipsi obtinent sibi Canonice collata et dicit suo et dicto nomine pr*opterea* in concessionibus et constitutioni*bus* dicte ecc*les*ie nullibi prohibitum reperit*ur* ipsas Cappelanias Mansionarias et Levitas no*n* posse obtinere alia beneficia ecc*les*iastica invicem se compacientia sibi Canonice collata vel conferenda initiusque cavetur in nominationibus et presentationibus sue R*eale* M*aesta* pr*opterea* no*n* possint obtinere alia benefitia preter huiusmo*di* beneficia

Jurispatronatus sue R*eale* M*aesta* quibus stant*is* nullatenus ipsi Cappellanij Mansionarij et Levite tenen*tur* nec cogi possint ad nominandum et specificandum alia benefitia ecclesiastica que p*er* eos tenen*tur* quoniam si sua R*eale* M*aesta* id nollisset in euis privilegijs et concessionibus seu nominationibus et presentationibus ita mandasset et si talis c*on*dictio adiecta fuisset forsan ipsi comparentes illa no*n* acceptassent ob tenuitatem reddituu*m* et s*er*vitutem contiuam qua*m* impendere tenentur dicte ecclesie et nisi aliqua alia benefitia obtinerent no*n* possunt vacare dicte ecclesie et divinis offitijs ac horis continuis que in ea celebrant interesse et propterea prefatus d*omi*nus comparem suo et dictis nominibus petit att*enta* continua s*er*vitute et honore celebrandi eos ulterius non esse molestan*tur* quia alia beneficia que per eos obtninent obtinere possint et valeant iuxta forma pre*f*actar*um* litte*r*arum Apostolicar*um* et et*iam* voluntatis bone memorie Ducis Francisi secundi primafundatoris et ita et*iam* firmiter credunt suam Reale Maesta observari debere maxime att*enta* reddituu*m* tenuitate ut supra et continua servitute interessendi in divinis dicte ecclesie ali*ter* et c*etera.*

Document 4

[*Fondo di Religione* 364 (Capitolo Milano: S. Maria della Scala, Visite Arcivescovile), Busta Armario Primo: 1574, ASM]
Alla salve quale p*er* antico c*on*sueto si vuole cantar' ogni sera dalli beneficiati in chiesa gli inc*on*venghi semp*re* ordinamente il canonico ebdemodario a far officio con la cotta et almutia. . .Niuno canonico ne cappellano ò altro beneficiato dil choro vada in tempo della messa, at altri divini officij di questa collegiata a s*er*vir in altra chiesa, sotto pena di uno scudo p*er* vuolta oltra la p*re*deta della distributione di q*u*ello officio, in che haveva mancato concediamo p*er*o facolta al p*re*vosto di puoter'dar licenza ad alcuno in qualche accidentale occorr*en*za rara di andar' a celebrar' o far' altro officio in altra chiesa, mentre per questa occassione in quale si voglia modo quello tale no*n* riceva mercede ne elimosine alcuna, non vogliamo p*er*o che nella presente ordinatione, si comp*re*hendino il Canonico Danioto curato do Santo Carpoforo, ne il capellano Rippa curato do Santo Giovanni quattro facie p*er* il s*er*vicio di dette loro cure . . .Per obviar' alli errori quali ò p*er* ignoranza overo p*er* transcuragine no*n* senza scandalo si possano cometter' da alcuni ò canonici ò officiali di questa chiesa nel leger' le lettioni cantar' epistole, et evanglij ò simili altre cose, ordeniamo che q*u*elli a che tochera leger' ò cantar' le dette cose le prevedino ò cantino prima q*u*ella mattina ò il giorno ivanti alla p*re*senza di q*u*ello canonico che sera deputato dal p*re*vosto, possa p*er*o esso prevosto tralasciar' l'essecutione di questo n*os*tro ordine in q*u*elli che vedera manifestamente sicuri in modo che no*n* vi sia bisogno alc*un*o di questa diligenza . . .
Li canti fermi si cantino semp*re* sop*ra* il libro p*er* oviar' alli errori quali non senza scandalo et devotione dil cap*i*tolo alla p*re*senza dil popolo nascendo dal cantarli a memoria . . .

Document 5

[*Sforzesco: Registri ducali* 73 (Benefizi1523-1525), 69r-70r (nuovo 137-139, ASM]

Franciscus et c*etera*: Providere volentes q*u* a*liter* curata ecclesia S*anti* Michaelis Busti magni et Canonicatus in ecclesiae Collegiata Galerati dio*cesis* M*edio*lan*ensis* quam et quem p*resbyte*r Cesar de Crispis possidebat, et nunc propter absentiam eius, qui a nobis ad hostes n*o*st*r*os transfuga factus est rectore carent, solita debita obsequia in divinis et circa curam animarum habeant ac eor*um* reditus, et fructus in sinistrum non transeant, Confisi de virtute industria, et integr*i*t*a*te dilecti cantoris n*o*st*r*i Ma*gni*f*i*ci Mathie Flandrensis clerici: Tenore pr*e*s*e*ntium Constituimus et Deputamus eum in Rector*e*m, et Administrator*e*m dicte ecclesiae, et can*o*nica*t*us cum auctoritate, arbitrio, et plena potestate illam et illum regendi nomine camere n*o*st*r*e, ac illor*um* reditus fructus, et census percipiendi ad illor*um* fictabilibus, Massarijs, Censuarijs, et colonis, et de receptis quietantias faciendi, Cetera*qu*e alia agendi ad legitimum administrator*e*m et rectorem pertinientia absqu*e* eo q*u*od de perceptis teneat*ur* ullam reddere rationem Proviso tamen Imprimis q*u*od circa Divina obsequia et curam animar*um* dict*u*s ecclesia et Can*o*nica*t*us solitis non careant securitijs: Iniungenter R*e*ver*e*nd*o* Iconomo g*e*n*e*rali n*o*st*r*o et alijs ad quos spectat, ut ponant eum in poss*e*ssion*e*m dicte administrationis, ac in illa manuteneant atque conseruent, prestan*do* eidem omne auxilium et favorem necessarium ad consequen*dum* reditus fructus et census antedictos quia in ea n*o*st*r*am exeque*tur* voluntatem: Datem Mediolani sub nostri fide sigilli xxij martij M.D.xxiiij. Fran*ciscu*s. Visa Moronus. Ge. Gadius

Francesco [Sforza] et cetera. Wishing to provide that the curated church of St. Michael of Great Busto and the canonry in the collegiate church in Gallerate, in the diocese of Milan, both of which were possessed by the presbyter Cesare de' Caspi, and now owing to his absence, since he has deserted to Our enemies, shall have the accustomed due services in divine worship and the cure of souls, and that their income and profits shall not go to waste, trusting in the virtue, hard work, and integrity of Our well-beloved singer Matthias of Flanders, clerk, We by the tenor of these presents appoint and depute him rector and administrator of the said church and canonry with authority, discretion, and full power over both of ruling them in the name of Our chamber, and of receiving their income, profits, and wealth from their leaseholders, mass-tenants, rent-payers, and serfs, and making quittances for the receipts, and doing all other things pertaining to a lawful administrator and rector, without being required to render account for his receipts, provided above all that in divine worship and cure of souls the said church and canonry shall not lack the customary services, enjoining on Our Reverend Bursar-General and others to whom it pertains that they put him in possession of the said administration and maintain and preserve him therein, according him their honesty, every assistance and favour necessary for obtaining the income, fruits and wealth aforementioned because in it he will execute Our will. Dated in Milan under the faith of Our seal on 22 March 1524.

Document 6

[F. 36 inf .(Lettere a San Carlo Borromeo), 26r-27r, BAM]
Illustrissimo et Reverendissimo signor signor Patrono nostro osservissimo

Ringratiamo quanto potemo vostro signor Illustrissima et Reverdissima dell'honorata gratia dell'Indulgentia, che per mezzo d'essa habbiamo havuto da Sua Santita non solo d'esser' perpetua à questa ammiranda fabrica, et al venerando Hospidale ma anchora con l'aggionta della dispense oltra il solito, La Gloriosa Madre del summo Iddio sia quella, che remuneri vostra signora Reverendissima d'un tanto dono, Et benche l'inimico dell'humana natura l'havesse seminato un'pocho di zinzania, nodimeno mediante la gratia d'esso Iddio se li é provisto, et accio vostra Reverendissima signora sia dil tutto requaliata, ha sapere, che havendo noi Deputati d'essa fabrica fatto far' un'organo novo, et mirabilissimo per honor' della singular' Machina d'essa Giesa, et de tutta la Citta nostra, et gia spesi in esso circa scuti 15,000 recercassimo di haver un'organista Eccellentissimo, et Intendendo, che Messer prete Egidio, che sonava à Santo Ambrosio era il meliore organista, usassimo diligentia d'haverlo, et havuta la mala sorte fra alcuni mesi lo condusse à morte, et per modo di provisione noi deputatissimo un'Joseph Caymo giovene sbarbato con ordine, che ciascuno di noi usasse diligentia in cercar' persona Eccellente et degna di tal organo, et che noi deputati sopra esso organo usassimo ogni arte per haver' Messer Giovanni Battista Perotto, che sonava à Santo Ambrosio, et primo organista di Milano, et musico perfettissimo, le cui compositioni lo dimonstrano, un d'accio piu facilmente se Inducesse alla volunta, et desidero nostro gustando egli tal' Eccelente et Immenso organo, fur pregato contento fusse di sonar' le due feste d'Indugentia sapendo noi che in tali giorni 'Illustrissimo signor Duca di Sessa con tutta la corte, l'Eccellentissimo Senato, il Magnifico Magistrato, et [crossed out: forastieri sariano] tutta la Citta, et forastiero sariano concorsi, et havendo havuto bona risposta ordinassimo che in essa doi giorni non se intromettesse, ma come giovene, et inobediente insiema con il padre rispose molto scortesamente, et conferto il tutto con il Reverendo signor vicario di vostra Reverendissima signora laudo quanto fatto havevamo, et se bene à tal' effetto presente et consentiente fusse il Reverendo Giussano ordinario collegha nostro, nondimeno intendendo noi, che molti d'essi signoriordinarij murmuraveno de non voler', che detto Messer Giovanni Battista sonasse, ne parse per tor via ogni obietto, parlarni all'Illustro signor Presidente del Eccellentissimo Senato, qual' vedendo cio redondar' ad'honor' della Giesa, et di tutta la Citta mando un' secretario à far' intender' ad'essi signori ordinarij non volessero interrumper'la nostra ordine, ma essi alquanto retrogredi inviorono il signor Rozza, et signor Dechano d'esso signor Presidente, et trovandosi lui alchuni di noi, et trutinana? la cossa, et conosciuto chella ellettione delli Cantori, et organiste spettava al nostro Capitolo disseli appertamente che torto havevano, et se ben'anchora da poi tal cossa fusse discursa nante all'Illustro signor Giovanni Battista Raynaldo senator, et Sua Santita havendo il tutto conferto con esso signor Presidente, et commisso ad essi signori ordinarij, che se aquietasserono, et che torto havevano, et benche parimente il signor vicario di vostra Reverendissima signora ditto havesse et essi dopo l'havere raggionato assai promesso havesserono di eseguire l'ordine nostro,

nondimeno domenicha che fu alli 24 dil presente alchuni gioveni ordinarii, et
quelli della mutia fecerono tanto rumor' nella secrestia che detteno da murmurar'à
tutta la Citta, et non volserono venir' in giesa, et benche li signori ordinarij maturi
venesserono à cantar' in giesa, nondimeno et essi usorono stratagema, che
continuamente volserono cantar', per non lassar' sonar' esso Messer Giovanni
Battista, che non pocho scandalo dette al popolo, et alli Audienti et intendendo noi,
che una parte de detti ordinarij non voleva andar' alla processione, che congregar'
si doveva nella scala secondo il consueto, et che ivi se doveva ritrovarsi il predetto
signor Duca con tutto la corte, esso Eccellentissimo senato, il Magnifico
Magistrato, et dir' si puo, mezzo Mellano per sedar' tal scandalo per il mezzo dil
Magnifico signor Alessandro Archinto in loco del Magnifico singor vicario di
provisione ordenassemo che Messer Giovanni Jacopo maestro del organo sonasse
sino che poi si mettese sesto à tal' loro novita, In vero contra ogni giustitia,
raggione, et equitate, perche come apar' per molti ordinarij passate non solo la
ellettione di organisti, ma anchora delli cantori spetta al Capitolo della veneranda
fabrica nel qual tre singnori ordinarij hanno intervenir', et intervengono, et quanto
si fa per noi deputati ha tenir', vostra Reverendissima signora farsi tutto ad' honor'
del summo Iddio, della Beata Virgine, della giesa, et in conseguentia delli
Reverendissimi Archiepiscopi, et de tutta la Citta, come ad ogni uno è notissimo, et
tanto piu in questo caso retrovandosi esso Josepho inesperto, et sonar'senza
misura, et haver' disordinato ess'organo, che gia sono 8. giorni che in esso detto
Messer Giovanni Jacopo ha lavorato, et nondimeno anchora non è ridduto alla
perfettione, era di prima, et detto Messer Giovanni Battista sia unico organista et
ottimo musicho in queste parti, ne forsi trovarsi altrove par' alchuno ad'esso, perho
con bona satisfattione di vostra Reverendissima signora non si manchara di
haverlo, et condurlo per sonar' ess'organo, che sara honor' à tutti et alla veneranda
fabrica honor', et utile, che sonando esso, non havra far'spesa in reconzarlo, come
ad hora ha fatto, per esser'lui in tal arte espertissime et eccellente.

     Et perche s'Inteso che alchun' d'essi signorij ordinari volevano scriver' à
vostra Reverendissima signora et forsi fingevano cosse non vere,ò, in gener', ò, in
particolare perho pregamo vostra signora Reverendissima prudentissima, si degna
avante li dia cardenza farmi dar' aviso, che senza dubio justificaremo il tutto et
restara ben satisfatta di noi tutti affetionatissimi, et bon servitori di quella, alla cui
bona gratia se raccommando et basamoli le sacratissime mani, pregando il summo
Iddio che la conservi, et felicita in ogni suo desiderio. Da Milano alli 26 di Marzo
dal 1560. Da vostra Illusstrissima et Reverentissima signor
Affetionatissimi servitori Deputati della Veneranda Fabrica.

Document 7

[*Famiglie* 205 (Visconti 1500-1550), ASM]
     Illustrissime signor patrono mio observantissimo
Trovandome a polesino ho trovato il presente lator Giovanni Petro dil notaio da
polesino il qual me a fato uno apiacer singular che Io non lo potrai remunerare e
parlando lui de vostra Illustre signoria li domandai sel cononsceva quela e dise che

si et che haveva da venir in breve da quella per havere licentia di una puocha quantitade di grana per conducere in suo paese. Suplico a vostra Illustre signoria sia cometta di farli tal gratia metendo questo obligo presso li altri et la supplico ad non manchare acioche non possendo lo remunere il presente lator al mancho sia remunerato da uno mio patrone al qual humilmente li baso la mane. In polesino adi 12 aprile 1543.
Da vostra Illustre signoria servitore,
Ludovico Vesconte deto Moscatello

Most Illustrious sir and my most observant patron
Finding myself in Polesino I found the present bearer Giovanni Pietro of the notary of Polesino who paid me a singular favor that I am not able to remunerate. And speaking with him of your illustrious signory I asked him if he was familiar with that and he said yes and that he had to come there shortly in order to obtain permission to conduct a small quantity of grain to his country. I entreat your Illustrious signory to commit yourself to grant him that privilege, sending this obligation with the others and I entreat you not to fail in order that, since I do not possess the means to compensate the present bearer, at least he be remunerated by my only patron, whose hands I humbly kiss. In Polesino on 12 April 1543.
From your Illustrious signory's servant,
Ludovico Vesconte, called Moscatello.

Document 8

[*Potenze estere* 2 (Austria), n.p., ASM]
Illustrissimo signore
Havendo sua santita fatto'gratia di certi benefitij di non molta valuta à messer Gabbriello casato gentil'homo et doctore milanese et à messer Francesco da milano musico, de quali havendo secondo dicono trovato impedito el possesso da uno che vi pretende ragione sopra, desidererieno che vostra signoria Illustrissima fussi contenta commettere al commissario appostolico (al quale portano un Breve di sua santita per pigliarne el possesso), che conosca summariamente chi di loro a ragione, et a quello si lassino godere, et poi che dalli detti non si domanda senon il dovere, et complimento della iustitia, non ho possuto mancare raccomandargli à vostra signoria Illustrissima alla quale mi raccomando et offerisco che nostro signor Dio La prosperi, et preservi come desidera. Da Roma el di xxiiij di Giugno M. D. XXXXIJ al comando di vostra signoria Illustrissima,
Margarite d'Austria
(al signor Marchese del Vasto)

Most Illustrious Sir
His holiness having made a gift to Mr Gabriele Casato, Milanese gentleman and doctor, and Francesco da Milano, musician, of certain benefices of little value, of which, according to them, they have been hindered from taking possession by one who there pretends authority over [them], they desire that your most Illustrious

signory be willing to make the apostolic commission (to which they carry a breve from his holiness in order to take possession of it), know who of them has the right so that they will be allowed to enjoy it. And then the aforementioned ones do not expect anything except the right and courtesy of justice, I could not avoid recommending them to your most Illustrious signory, to which I recommend myself and pray God our father favor and preserve you as you desire. From Rome on 24 June 1542 at the command of your most Illustrious signory.
Margarite of Austria
(to the signor Marchese del Vasto)

Document 9

[*Registri della Cancelleria dello Stato* IV-7 (Grazie, donazioni, privilegi 1548-1549). 223r-224v, ASM]
Ferdinandus et cetera. Nomine Francesci Brugore e Jo. Domenici Cytharedorum de loco Basilij accepimus preces, huiusmodi, ut supra. Illustrissimo et Eccellentissimo signor Nel anno 1547 à di XV de giulio fu formata una inquisitione contra li fidelissimi servitori di Vostra Eccellenza Francesco da Brugora et Gio. Domenico sonatori de viola et habitatori nel loco de Basilio per il di decimo di tenore che essendo loro sopra una festa nel loco di Rozzano dove sonarono et essendo venuto à contentione Hieronymo e Gio. Domenico de la Isabetina, et essendo Marco Veronese con una ronca sopra detta festa restato ferito nella fronte, et che essendo Francesco Vercellese interrogato dal detto Marco se lui l'haveva ferito non gli diede risposta ma fugite verso la chiesa di Rozzano et che'l detto Marco con aiuto et favore de detti supplicanti quali alhora haviano lasciato stare di sonare, et con le spade sfodrate habbiano insieme con detto Marco seguitato detto Francesco qual' restò ferito da quattro ferite ciò è due nella schena de ponta, et una sopra la testa presso l'orechia sinistra di taglio, l'altra nel fianco con grande effusione di sangue, de le quali incontestamente ne morse et che tutte queste cose siano fatto col favore, et aiutto di detti supplicanti et più che detti supplicanti habbiano havuto ardire di sonare nel detto luoco di Rozzano et nel loco di Bissono sopra la strata di Pavia mentre ditto Marco stasesse sopra essa festa con dette roncha, et pugna le arme prohibite per la forma de le cride, et ordini di questo stato per le quali pare se commandi che li sonatori subito vederanno sopra le feste arme d'hasta ò altre arme prohibite debbiano cessare di sonare altrimente incorrano nella pena di scudi XXV da esser applicati alla Cesarea camera ò vero de tratti tre de corda al arbitrio del Capitano de Iustitia, et come più ampliamente si contiene si in detta inquisitione quanto in dette cride, quali si esshibiscono, et essendo detti supplicanti citati, et inthimata loro detta inquisitione sono in contumacia messi in bando per non haver' loro havuto il modo di comparere, et difendersi . . .

Ferrante et cetera. On behalf of Francesco Brugore and Giovanni Dominco, citharist, of Basil we extend praise of the sort above. Most illustrious and excellent Sir: In the year 1547 on the fifteenth day of July an inquisition was formed with the most trustworthy servants of Your Excellency Francesco of Brugora and Giovanni

Domenico, players of the viola and residents of Basil, regarding the tenth day to the effect that they, being at a festival in Rozzano where they play, and having come into contention with Hieronymo and Giovanni Domenico de la Isabetina, and Marco Veronese being wounded on the forehead with a pruning knife during that said party, and Francesco Vercellese, being questioned by the aforementioned Marco whether he had injured him, did not give him a response but fled towards the church of Rozzano. And that the aforementioned Marco, with the help and cover of the aforementioned supplicants, who then had ceased to play, and with their swords drawn together with the aforementioned Marco followed the aforementioned Francesco, who was wounded by four blows, that is two punctures in the back, and one cut over the head near the left ear, [and] the other in the flank with grand effusion of blood, from which he incontestably died. And that all of these things occurred with the cover and help of the aforementioned supplicants. And, moreover, that the aforementioned supplicants had the audacity to play in the aforementioned location of Rozzano and in the place of Bissono above the street of Pavia while the aforementioned Marco was near this party with the aforementioned pruning knife and dagger, arms prohibited by the form of the decrees and ordinances of this state, which seems to command that the musicians, if they see lances or other prohibited arms near the entertainment, must immediately cease playing or otherwise incur a penalty of 25 scudi to be applied to the Imperial chamber or three lashes of the whip at the liberty of the Captain of Justice. And how, moreover, the extension is contained in the aforementioned inquisition, just as in the aforementioned decrees, which are displayed. And the aforementioned supplicants, being cited and intimated by the aforementioned inquisition, were banished from the state by default for not having had a manner to appear before the court and defend themselves . . .

Document 10

[*Sforzesco* 1607 (Potenze sovrane ed altre voci), n.p., ASM]
Narratio del facto
Nel anno 1552 Petro paulo borrono quale era introducto in casa del Il*lu*strissimo si*gnor* Don Ferra*n*do per pratica de havere uno che tra bandito dal stato e stava in Parma et offeriva da fare s*er*vitio ogni volta che si volesse tentare da havere Parma stando esso drento con molti compagni ho*mini* valorosi et cogescenti vene dal gran can*celliere* quale era molto bene instructo del negotio e gli disse da per del si*gnor* Don Ferrando che facesse uno salvoco*n*ducto p*er* quelli che esse borrono nominava p*er* che importava al s*er*vitio de sua M*ae*sta esso gran cancelliere gli fece dare una forma de salvoco*n*ducto per iustificare a cio no*n* venesse in notitia de alcuno la causa et gli disse q*ue*sta e la forma fa lo fare in et me*n*titi q*ue*lli voi che io poi la signava fa cosi fara al volere da sua *Eccellentia* e cosi esso fece scrivere il salvoco*n*dutto e posto li nomi quali no*n* mi ricordo salvo de fantono de fantoni principale ben*eficij* mi ricordo che passavano de doi et io disse il tutto al si*gnor* Don Ferrando quello mi haveva dicto il borrono da parte de sua *Eccellenti*a e che mi haveva portato una nota de molti e quello voleva chio facesse e sua *Eccellentia*

me risposte che io dovesse expedir tutti quella me haveva data il borrono e cosi io li expedir a sua *Eccellentia* signo il salvoconducto dopo fra dui o tre giorni vene il dicto borrono e me disse che haveva fallato e che gli mancava uno o doi nominando , ma io non mi ricordo il nome danendo che quello inmesava pui che altri per grandi effetti quali sa havemo a fare et non meno che quelli da Parma pero che io *similmente* lo facesse agiongere. Et io gli disse che non si poteva fare non lo volevo senza ordine de sua *Eccellentia* e cosi esso ritorna da me e da parte da sua *Eccellentia* me lo replico glielo insendomi consento che *Vostra Signor* gli voleva *servire* de costui tra gli altri mi fare amazare il Cardinale farenzie e volendomi dire il modo io gli disse non voglio sapere queste cose fa pure in gli fatti soi ma narasse tutto al che Io resposte che facto voleva cosi lo facia ma prima io disse di questo una parola a esso *signor* direndo il borrono mi haveva dicto esser stato commesso nil salvocondutto uno et che *nostra* Eccellentia vole che *prima* gli agionga et esso risposta da si et Credo vi fosse possessor esso borrono o almeno in la camera cose posse questo vene il et in mia *presenza* Instando in casa mia messer agnostino da monte semetava chi gli agiongassi costui doi che il signor me lo haveva ordinato e messer agnostino havendomi risposta che facesse che io lo dicesse venendo lui *similmente* lo disse et poi che il resto fu scritto per mano di uno procuratore del borrono quale credo sia de suigo *similmente* lo facesse metter da quello istesso et cosi fu facto 'cora poi me rifesse il predicto agnostino da monte e a queste instantie et parole del borrono. Credo gli fossero presente altre persone di quali non mi ricordo.

Narration of the fact(s)

In the year 1552 Petro Paolo Borrono, who was admitted into the house of the Illustrious signor Don Ferrante for practically being one that was among the banished of the state, was in Parma and offered to render service every time that he wished to take Parma. Standing ready with many companies of valorous men and acquaintances, he came to the Grand Chancellor, who was very well informed of the matter, and told him, on behalf of signor Don Ferrando, to issue a safe-conduct for those that this Borrono named. Because it was important to the service of His Majesty, the aforementioned Grand Chancellor prepared him a style of safe-conduct to make it legal so that nobody would know the motivation. And he told him this and the form in which to put it and you put those you wish and then I will sign it. To do it thus will be according to the wish of His Excellency. And thus he had the aforementioned orders and the safe-conduct written with the names which I don't remember except that of Fantono de Fantoni, principal of the beneficiaries that I remember passed by of the two. And I told Sir Don Ferrando all that Borrono had told me about His Excellency and that he had brought me a notice containing much that he wished me to do and His Excellency responded to me that I should have expedited all that which Borrono had given me. And thus I expedited them on behalf of His Excellency up until the safe-conduct. Between two and three days later comes the aforementioned Borrono and told me that he had erred and that he lacked the names of one or two nominated, but I don't remember the name given which he mentioned, and, moreover which others, and that because of the great events that were coming, and not in the least for those from Parma similarly have added it. And I told him that it was not possible and I did not want to do it without an order of His Excellency. And thus he returns to me and on the part of His Excellency repeats it, indicating to me consent that Your Lordship consented and wished this fellow to serve him [and], among other things, to make me assassinate Cardinal Farnese and wishing to tell me the manner. I told him that I do not wish to know these things [and] please take care of your own business, but he told all to which I responded that if he wished it done in that way, he could do it, but before I said a word to this gentleman saying Borrono had told me of having been commissioned in one safe-conduct and that our Excellency wishes that first he add them. And he responded to me "yes." And I believe this Borrono possessed it or at least influence in the chancery. This occurred in my presence and in my house before Mr Agostino da Monte who wanted me to add the two fellows that the gentleman had ordered me. And Mr Agostino, having responded to me that he did that which I told him, comes likewise to tell it and further that the rest was written by the hand of an attorney of Borrono who I believe is from Zurich who similarly attested to this himself and this did still. Further, I refer anew to the aforementioned Agostino da Monte and to these importunities and words of Borrono. I believe there were others persons present, but do not recall their names.

Document 11

[*Studi parte antica* 97, fol. 16, ASM]
Singnore Petranigra mio Ca*rissi*mo ho veduto certi libri di canto dil *prese*nte latore Massimo Troiano napol*itano* Musico dell'ecc*ellenz*a del *Signor* Duca, Et gli ho dato licenza ch*e* si stampino, Et più ne ho parlato con il molto Ill*ustre Signor* Presidente *no*str*o* il quale si contenta co*n*cedergli uno privilegio ch*e* niuno possi stampare ne venderle tali libri nel termino de cinque anni senza licenza del detto Troiano. Et cosi in esseguntione delle premisse cose V*ostra Signor* sara contenta fare quanto si appartene et a q*ue*lla mi racc*omando* Da casa alli sei di Giugno 1559 Vostro quanto Fratello,
Marc'Antonio Caimo

To my dearest Mr Petranigra. I have seen certain books of song of the bearer of this letter, Mr Massimo Troiano, excellent musician of the Duke. And I have given him license to print them. And, moreover, I have spoken with our very Illustrious Signor President, who is pleased to concede to him a privilege that no-one may print or sell such books for a term of five years without permission from the aforementioned Troiano. And so in execution of the above mentioned things Your Lordship will be content to do that which is fitting. And to that end I recommend myself. From home on 6 June 1559. As much as your brother, Marc'Antonio Caimo.

Document 12

[*Studi parte antica* 97, fol. 17, ASM]

Philippus Rex et *cetera* Mediolani Dux

Maximus Troianus neapolitanus musicus in aula Ill. Ducis Suessae in provincia Mediolanensi Gubernatoris multum acceptus, cum quasdam cantiones neapolitano idiomate, et concentu scriptas in artem musicam redegisset, et edere vellet, ne suis laboribus, et sumptibus fraudaretur, petijt, à nostro Senatu Mediolanensi facultatem, et privilegium sibi concedi, ne quis eo inconsulto ipsas cantiones imprimiere, aus imprimi facere audeat. Nos autem cum ex iudicio peritorum intellexerimus eas esse secundum artem elucrubratas, et nihil in se continere, quod sit contra religionem Christianam, aut Remp., censuimus eius petitioni annuendum esse. Atque ita harum serie edicimus et prohibemus, ne quis excusor, librarius, bibliopola vel quispiam alius sit, qui velit audeat, vel presumat ipsas cantiones, vel earum partem imprimiere, aut imprimi facere in provincia nostra Mediolanensi, vel alibi impressas, in eam importare, et venalis exponere contra voluntatem, et sine licentia ipsius Troiani per annos quinque proximos. Sub poena amissionis omnium librorum, et ulterius scutatorum aureorum trium pro quolibet volumine, cuius tertia pars adiudicetur ipsi Troiano, Tertia accusatori, seu denuntiatori, et tertia fisco nostro, irremissibiliter exigenda. Mandantes et *cetera* in quoquam et *cetera*. Arrigonus

Massimiliano Troiano, a Neapolitan musician in the chamber of the Duke of Sessa, Governor in the province of Milan, having had composed according to the art of music, certain songs written in the Neapolitan idiom and harmony, and wishing to publish them, lest he should be cheated of his labors and his expenses, has petitioned Our Senate of Milan to be granted the opportunity and the privilege that none shall venture to print these songs or cause them to be printed without consulting him. We, having understood from the judgment of experts that they have been devised in accordance with the art, and to contain nothing in them that is hostile to to the Christian religion or State, have judged that his petitions should be granted. And therefore by the tenor of these presents we proclaim and enjoin that no printer, bookscribe, bookseller, anyone else whoever he be that so wishes shall venture to print or cause to be printed the said songs or any part thereof in our province of Milan, or importing into it [copies] printed in another location and displaying [them] for sale against the wishes and without the permission of the said Troiano for the next five years under penalty of loss of all the books, and further of three gold scudi for each volume, of which a third shall be awarded to the said Troiano, a third to the accusor or informer, and a third to our treasury, to be exacted without possibility of remission. Ordering et cetera in whatsoever manner et cetera. Arrigono.

Document 13

[F. 103 inf. (Lettere a San Carlo Borromeo), 451r, BAM]
Io so che V*ostra* Ill*ustrissi*ma è tanto desiderosa d'honorar de vertuosi questa sua patria, che qualunche occasione che si appresenti di cio, le fia gratiss*ima*. Don Nicola Musico chromatico è suggetto tale, che merita, che si ponghi particolar pensiero in ridurlo ad habitar quà. Io dal canto mio m'adoprerò volentieri in ciò. Ma desidero che anco V*ostra Signor* Ill*ustrissi*ma dal suo canto mi ce aiuti con cento scudi d'entrata de benefici semplici che tutto di vengono à vacare in questa sua diocesi, et s'hanno à dare altrui, Il che sarà esca opportuna ad disegno mio. Io la su*pplic*o che per far gratia particolare à me, scrivi qui à m*esser* Tullio suo, che ci concede con tal entrata sopra le prime vacanze; et sia per ella certa, che questa picciola so*mm*a m'obligherà assai, come cosa dà mè so*mm*amente desiederata et che dignamente sarà impiegata. Bacio le mani a V*ostra* Ill*ustrissi*ma. Di Milano a 14. di Nov*em*bre 1563. [Il Marchese di Pescara.]

I know that Your Most Ilustriousness is so desirous to honor the virtuosi of this your country, that any occasion which presents itself will be appreciated by you. Don Nicola, chromatic musician, is one such subject who deserves to be given particular thought in convincing him to live here. I, for my part, will dedicate myself gladly to this. But I desire that also You Most Illustrious Sir, for his part, assist me in this with an income of 100 scudi from simple benefices that are becoming vacant in this your diocese and have to be given to others, which will be opportune allurement for my plan. I supplicate you that as a particular favor to me, you write to your Mr Tullio here that he grant him such income above the first vacancies, and it is for you certain that this small sum will oblige me greatly as a thing extremely desired by me, and that it will be employed appropriately.]I kiss You Most Illustriousness's hands. From Milano on 14 November 1563. [The Marchese di Pescara]

Document 14

[F. 103 inf. (Lettere a San Carlo Borromeo), 408r, BAM]
Ill*ustrissi*mo sig*no*r mio oss*ervatiss*imo
La virtu rara di m*esser* Vincenzo Ruffo, qual è assai consciuta dove se n'è fatto prova, m'hai indutto à supplicar' v*ostra* sin*gora* Ill*ustrissi*ma d'haverlo per ra*ccommanda*to nella co*m*petentia, qual da alcuni emuli gl'è fatta nella Cantoria di Milano. Et con quanto le buone parti di detto m*esser* Vincenzo, lo possono far' raccommandato, io haverle obligo infinito, s'intenderò li preghi di q*ue*sta haverli giovato, come m'assicuro per la protettione che vuol tener' delle p*er*sone singulari. È con questo fine le baccio le mani, et in g*ra*tia sua me raccommando p*re*gando Iddio che l'acresca, come desia. Di Carneghi il 18 d'ottobre 1563. D*a* v*ostra* sin*gora* Ill*ustrissi*ma s*ervito*r Antonio Scarampo.

The rare virtue of Mr Vincenzo Ruffo, which is well known where it has been tested, has induced me to ask your Most Illustrious Signor to have him by a recommendation regarding his qualification, which earned him the Cantoria of Milan from several imitators. And given the many good voices of Mr Vincenzo that are able to recommend him, I will have infinite obligation to you, if I will intend prayers to have assisted this, as I assure myself by the protection that you wish to hold of particular persons. And for this I kiss your hands, and commend myself to your grace asking God that it grows as your desire. From Your Most Excellent Signor's servant Antonio Scarampo in Carneghi on 18 October 1563.

Document 15

[*Metropolitana* LXXXII-456 (Visite pastorali e documenti aggiunti), fasc. 20, ASDM]
La Devotione dell'Ave Maria, qual si canta ogni sera nella Chiesa Maggiore del Duomo di Milano, hebbe principio circa l'anno 1495 et fu un Heremita forastiero, il quale dal Popolo era chiamato, Missus à Deo. Trovavasi quest'Hermita la sera al tardi nella Piazza del Duomo, et publicamente predicando, esortava à vivere christianamente, con lasciare li peccati, et servare li Divini prezzetti, et come sentiva la campana dell'Ave Maria invitava l'Audienti ad'entrare seco in Duomo à fare orationi et dire l'Ave Maria. Esortò in particolare alcuni à voler convenirsi insieme, et far cantare ogni sera in Duomo l'Ave Maria con qualche Laude in honore della Glorioso sempre Vergine Maria ringraziandola delli ricevuti benefitij, et supplicandola ad'impetrare dal suo diletto figliolo misericordia aggiutto per l'avenire. A quest'esortazione si unirono alcuni Gentilhuomini e Mercanti sotto il nome del Santissimo Chrucifisso et diedero principio a far cantare l'Ave Maria al Terzo Pilone, entrando nel Duomo, à mano sinistra Il quale Pilone verrà ad esser il sesto, quando la chiesa sarà finita hanvendogli per questo effetto posta un'immagine dipinta della Gloriosa Vergine; di poi vi fecero fare una statua di Marmo dell'istessa Gloriosa Vergine, et in detto luogo Iddio per li meriti di essa Gloriosa Vergine dimonstrò molti miracoli, per il che era tanto il concorso del Popolo a quella Divotione, che apportava qualche impedimento all'entrare della Porta ivi vicina, e per questo l'anno 1550 memoria si transportò detta immagine all'Altare dove hora si trova che è dentro la Scuola della Dottrina Christiana delle Pute, vicina all'Altare di Santo Benedetto, et la spesa di essa Trasportatione fu fatta da un Alessio Albanese, come si vede ancora da alcuni versi, che sono scritti in una tavola di Pietro vicina ad esso Altare. Di poi l'anno 1578 memoria il Reverendo Carlo Borromeo Cardinale del titolo di Santa Prassede all'hora nostro Vigilantissimo Arcivescovo, transportò detta Divotione all'altare dov'era la Madonna dell'Arbore qual all presente è di Santa Tecla, et ivi alcune volte esso Reverendo Carlo interveniva a detta Divotione, all'Altare Maggiore di detta Chiesa per più decoro et Commodità, stando che li Hostarij erano soliti Doppo la liberatione della Città della prossima passata Peste dell'anno 1577 ogni sera dire le lettanie con alcune orationi al detto Altare Maggiore, per ringraciare Nostro Signore di tanto benefitio per detta liberatione, pregarlo ad'haverci misericordia, et

preservarci p*er* l'avenire per ciò ordinò, che al suono dell'Ave Maria, si trovassero avanti ad Altare M*aggio*re, et detta prima la salutatione Angelica, secondo il Costume, mentre si sona susseguentem*ente* dicessero le d*ette* litanie et orationi solite, et subito si cantasse l'Ave Maria, et che sempre si intervenisse uno de li S*ingo*ri Canonici Ord*inar*ii, a dire tutte le d*ette* orationi, et così, si è sempre perseverato, accendendovi li Cerei avanti la prima Balaustrata del Choro, mentre si dice la d*etta* oratione, et Ave Maria . . .

Document 16

[*Metropolitana* LXXX-454 (Visite pastorali e documenti aggiunti), q. 24, ASDM]

L'anno 1604. Vedendo li S*igno*ri Deputati della divotione dell'Ave Maria che si canta ogni sera nella Metropolit*ana* Chiesa di Milano . . .La dove si vede che l'entrate della sudetta divotione sono in tutto L 370 l'anno et solevano li S*igno*ri Deputati mandare ogni giorno una bussola per la Città et un altra bussola ogni mese dalli Si*gno*ri quali herano al men'di dodeci; con l'elemosina delle quale due bussole comprerano a pagare li salarij ordinarij d'essa divotione che è un M*aest*ro di Capella con otto cantori, et si dava al M*aest*ro di Capella solo L100 l'anno, a Duo Bassi, a Duo Tenori, a Duo Contralti L 70 p*er* ciascuno l'anno. Et a Duo Soprani L 50 per ciascuno l'anno. Procurando sempre havere de migliori cantori di questa Città . . .

Appendix II*

Maestri, Singers, and Organists of the Cappella Musicale of the Duomo 1522-1563

Maestri di cappella

Hermann Matthias Werrecore, 1522-1550
Olivero de Phalanis, 1550-1551
Simon Boyleau, 1551-1557
Hoste da Reggio, 1558-1563

Tenors

Laurentio de la Strata, 1522-1534; 1538-1548; at half pay 1549
Francesco da Marliano, 1522-1563
Jo. Augustino Montiono, 1534-1540
Andrea de Germanis, 1542-1553
Ambrosio Francesco Lodo, 1549
Galeazzo de Relonibus (=Galeazzo Novo), 1549-1551
Francesco Antonio Menino, 1550-1561
Ludovico Aijroldo, 1551-1558
Jo. Jacobo Zimatoribus (=da Regio), 1558-1560
Cristoforo de Verona, 1558
Paolo de Verona, 1559
Hermann Matthias Werrecore, 1559
Pietro de Nigris (=de Carera), 1560-1563
Bernardino de Vicomerate, 1560-1563
Hieronymo de Dateris, 1562-1563

Contraltos

Bernardino Galassino, 1522-1552
Augustino Sodarino, 1523-1562
Bartolomeo de Molteno, 1531-1542
Virgilio Cingullo, 1536-1549
Jo. Antonio de Rapis de Busti, 1541-1562
Nicolai Galareijs (=Galassino), 1547-1562
Ludovico Aijroldo, at half pay 1550-1551
Fabritio de Baretis, 1560-1562
Giovanni Angelo de Pirovamo, 1563

Contrabasses

Jo. Jacobo de Canibus, 1522-1554.
Rocho Soldino, 1524-1549
Conte de Merate, 1531-1551; at half pay 1552-1558
Ottaviano Bosisio, 1534-1549
Gabriele Aliardus de Trivultio (=Gabriele de Castello), 1540-1544; 1549-1563
Jacobo de Ferraria, 1549
Philippo, for three months of 1550
Stephano de Corugate (=de Noxetis), 1551-1563
Gaspare de Galino, 1551-1557
Francesco de Lusigano,1558
Gaspare de Bonorius, 1558-1560
Alvisio de Cumis, 1559-1562
Andrea de Ruschis, 1560-1563
Francesco de Castoldo, 1562-1563

Sopranos

Battista da Bussero, puero 1522; adult 1534-1549
Laurentio de Putheo, adult designated as 'falsettist,' 1534 -1561
Baptiste de Lande, puero 1522
Francisco de Lande, puero 1522
Paulo de Oltrona, puero 1522
Jo. Petro de Biffis, puero 1522-1524
Alexandro de Capris, puero 1522-1524
Camillo de Brippo, puero 1522-1524
Cesare Morono, puero 1523-1524
Jo. Ambrosio Valle, puero 1523-1524
Melchiore de Padrinis, puero 1524-1525
Laurentio de Vertua, puero 1524-1525
Baptiste de Balletis, puero 1524-1530?
Jacobo de Confanonierijs, puero 1524-1530?
Petropaulo de Serono, puero 1524-1530?
Jo. Ambrosio de Porris, puero 1526-1530?
Gaspare de Bossis, puero 1527
Baldesare Caymo, puero 1527-1531
Hieronymo de Castellano, puero 1531-1533
Hieronymo de Grassis, puero 1531-1535
Petrofrancesco Pontremolo, puero 1531-1535
Baptiste de Regibus, puero 1531-1539
Battista della Chiesa, puero 1533-1535
Fabritio Beretta, puero 1534-1542
Francesco de Mantiganijs, puero 1536-1537
Battista Rechalcatis, puero 1536-1539
Jo. Antonio Casalino, puero 1536-1541

Antonio Maria Dolzago, puero 1537-1543
Hieronymo Crispo, puero 1539-1540
Benedicto da Brixia, puero 1539-1541
Gaspare de Melianachis, puero 1540-1542
Alvisio Casalino, puero 1542-1543
Jo. Ambrosio de Bosisio, puero 1542-1546
Baldesare de Rapis, puero 1542-1546
Battista Dolzago, puero 1543
Jo. Ambrosio Calstellanio, puero 1543-1544
Jo. Petro de Gorla, puero 1543-1546
Defenderti de Borsano, puero 1544-1546
Ludovico de Airoldis, puero 1545-1549
Francesco de Alexis Brixiano, puero 1546-1548
Ferrando de Santa Anna, puero 1546-1549
Fabritio de M^{ci} Mathie, puero 1546-1549
Sisto Michis, puero 1547-1548
Jo. Petro Forninio, puero at half pay in 1548
Hieronymo Mamo, puero at half pay 1548-1549
Andrea de Castello (=Andrea de Castoldo), puero, at half pay in 1548; 1549-1550
Jo. Jacobo de Piravamo, puero 1548-1550
Jo. Paulo de Blanchis, puero at half pay 1548-1551
Petropaulo de Aiyroldo, puero 1548-1552
Baptiste Todeschino, puero, at half pay in 1549
Alvisio de Gatis, puero ,at half pay 1549-1550;1550-1551
Jo. Petro de Bossijs (=Petroni de Bostijs), puero at half pay 1549-1550; 1550-1552
Baptiste de Rachino detto 'lo dophinio,' puero at half pay in 1550; 1552
Baldessare de Varexio dicto 'Lande,' puero at half pay 1550-1551
Baptiste de Dianis, 1550-1552
Jo. Baptiste de Ruchinis (=Baptiste de Porta Romana?), puero, 1551 and 1553
Fabritio de Pessina, puero, at half pay 1551; 1552-1553
Francesco de Oxio (=della Corsia), puero, 1552-1554
Dionysio Monzino, puero, 1552-1555
Baptiste de Draperio, puero, 1553-1554
Jo. Antonio de Bilio, puero, 1553-1557
Francesco da Ripa, puero,1554
Hieronymo de Bossijs, puero, 1554-1555
Francesco de Baldizono, puero, 1554-1555
Jo. Maria de Nigris, puero, 1554-1555
Hieronymo de Ripa, puero 1555-1556
Hieronymo de Remenulfis (=Hieronymo de Penagijs?), puero, 1555-1558
Cesarine de Sodarinis, puero, 1556
Messer Jo. Antonio Paijrava, adult, 1556-1557
Joseph de Cribellis, puero, 1556-1557
Francesco de Iuxola, puero, 1556-1560
Vialbo de penatia (=Appelato Vialbo), puero, 1557-1558
Jo. Antonio Gorla, puero, 1558

Francesco Segazono (=de Gambis), puero, 1558-1561
Annibale Sodarino, puero, 1558-1561
Julio 'Clarino' de Gattis, puero, 1558-1560; 1563
Caesare appellato clarino, puero, 1559
Darius de Gluxiano, puero, 1559
Jo: Paolo de Candianis, puero.1558-1560
Onorio de Tornellis, puero, 1560
Danielle de Gluxiano, 1561-1562
Jo. Battista de Radicijs, puero, 1560-1563
Jo. Paulino de Busti, puero, 1560-1561
Battista (=Nicolao) de Brochis, puero, 1561-1563
Ludovico de Colijs, puero, 1561-1562
Altobello de Galenijs de Pizzighitone, puero, 1561
Jo. Jacobo de Bassis, puero, 1562-1563
Andrea de Fontana, puero,1562
Joseph de Toscanis, puero, 1563

Unspecified Adult Voices

Petropaulo de Comite, 1522
Nicolai de Niguarda, 1522
Stephano de Romagnano, 1522
Jo. Petro de Organis, 1522-1524
Leonardo de Birago, 1522-1524
Jo. Jacobo Parpaliano, 1522-1524
Theodoro de Beluscho, 1523-1524
Petro de Vulpinus, 1523-1524
Francesco de Modoctia, 1524
Jo. Ambrosio de Bonis, 1524-1530?
Coradino Cremonensi, 1524-1530?
Gaspare da Ello, 1524-1533; returned temporarily in 1535
Jo. Petro de Galletis, 1525-1530?
Jo. Petro de Scotis, 1526-1527
Johannes Bregnio, 1531-1533
Hieronymo Organista, 1531-1533
Bernardino de Pivis, 1532-1534
Jo. Antonio de Vergiate, 1522-1533; at reduced pay 1534-1549
Jo. Petro de Gabbianus, 1522-1533; at reduced pay 1534-1551

Organists

Jo. Stephano de Putheobonello, 1522-1551
Jo. Petro de Gorla, 1551-1558
Vincenzo de Braschis, 1558
Prete Egidio Marliano, 1559
Gioseffo Caimo, 1560

Giovanni Battista Perotto, 1563

Assistant Organists

Bertino de Gravedola, 1522-1524
Alvisio de Cumis, 1525-1531?
Baptiste de Melegnano, 1532-1558
Jo. Jacobo de Cremona, 1558-1562

---

* Annual lists of the singers employed at the Duomo from 1522-1529 and 1531-1549 with their respective salaries can be found in Getz "The Milanese Cathedral Choir," 208-221.

Bibliography

Alberigo, G. 'Aragona, Maria d',' *Dizionario biografico degli italiani*. Rome: Società Grafica Romana, 1961, III, 701-702.

Albicante, Giovanni Alberto Furibondo. *Trattato del'intrar in Milano di Carlo V.* Milan: A. Caluus, 1541.

_____. *Al gran Maximiliano d'Austria archiduca. Intrada di Milano di Don Philippo d'Austria, Re di Spagna*. Venice: Marcolini, 1549.

Alvarez-Ossorio Alvariño, Antonio. *Milán y el legado de Felipe II: Gobernadores y corte provincial en la Lombardía del los Austrias*. Madrid: Sociedad estatal per la Commemoracíon de los centenarios de Felipe II y Carlos V, 2001.

Anglés, Higinio. *La Musica en la corte de Carlos V* in *Monumentos de la Música Española* II. Barcelona: Casa Provincial de Caridad Imprenta-Escuela, 1944.

Annali della Veneranda Fabbrica del Duomo di Milano, 7 vols. Milan: Gaetano Brigola, 1883.

Ansani, Michele. 'Da chiesa della communitá a chiesa del Duca. Il vescovado sfortiana.' in *Metamorfosi di un borgo. Vigevano in etá visconteo-sforzesco*. Milan: FrancoAngeli, 1992, 117-144.

Appian. *Roman History*, trans. Horace White, New York: Macmillan Company, 1912.

Asor-Rosa, A. 'Albicante, Alberto,' *Dizionario biografico degli italiani*. Rome: Società Grafica Romana, 1960, II, 1-2.

Bagatti-Valsecchi, Fausto, with Felice Calvi, Luigi Agostino Casati, Damiano Muoni, and Leopoldo Pullé, *Famiglie Notabili Milanesi*, 4 vols. Milan: Antonio Vallardi, editore, 1875.

Bailey, Terrence. *The Ambrosian Cantus*. Ottawa: The Institute of Medieval Music, 1987.

_____. *Antiphon and Psalm in the Ambrosian Office*. Ottawa: The Institute of Medieval Music, 1994.

Bailey, Terrence and Paul Merkley. *The Antiphons of the Ambrosian Office*. Ottawa, Canada: The Institute of Medieval Music, 1989.

Barblan, Guglielmo. 'La vita musicale in Milan nella prima metà del cinquecento,' *Storia di Milano*, 16 vols. Milan: Giovanni Treccani degli Alfieri, 1961, IX, 853-895.

Bendiscioli, Mario. 'Carlo Borromeo cardinal nipote arcivescovo di Milano e la riforma della Chiesa Milanese,' *Storia di Milano, primo edizione* 16 vols. Milan: Giovanni Treccani degli Alfieri, 1957a, X, 119-199.

_____. 'I conflitti giurisdizionali tra l'arcivescovo card. Borromeo e le autorità pubbliche,' *Storia di Milano, primo edizione*, 16 vols. Milan: Giovanni Treccani degli Alfieri, 1957b, X, 200-255.

_____. 'Vita sociale e cultura,' *Storia di Milano, prima edizione*, 16 vols. Milan: Giovanni Treccani degli Alfieri, 1957c, 352-495.

Benrath, Karl. *Bernardino Ochino of Siena*, trans. Helen Zimmern. New York: Robert Carter and Brothers, 1977.

Bernstein, Jane A. 'The Burning Salamander: Assigning a Printer to Some Sixteenth-Century Music Prints,' *Music Library Association Notes* XLII/3 (1986), 483-501.

_____. *Music Printing in Renaissance Venice: The Scotto Press (1539-1572)*. New York: Oxford University Press, 1999.

Bernstein, Lawrence. 'The Bibliography of Music in Conrad Gesner's *Pandectae* (1548),' *Acta*

Musicologica XLV (1973), 119-164.

Bertolotti, A. *Musici alla Corte di Mantova dal secolo XV al XVIII*. Milan: G. Ricordi, 1890; reprinted Genève: Minkoff, 1978.

Besozzi, Cerbonio. *Cronaca milanese*, ed. Cesare Malfatti. Trent: Società per gli Studi Trentini, 1967.

Bettley, John. "'L'ultima hora canonica del giorno": Music for the Office of Compline in Northern Italy in the Second Half of the Sixteenth Century,' *Music and Letters* 74 (1993), 163-214.

Bianchi, Angelo. 'Congregazioni religiose e impegno educativo nello stato di Milano tra '500 e '600', *Lombardia borromaica. Lombardia spagnola*, ed. Paolo Pissavino and Gianvittorio Signorotto. Rome: Bulzoni editore, 1995, 765-809.

_____. 'Le scuole della dottrina cristiana: linguaggio e strumenti per una azione educativa "di massa,"' in *Carlo Borromeo e l'opera della 'grande riforma.'* Milan: Silvana Editoriale, 1997, 145-158.

Bollini, Alessandra. 'L'attività liutistica a Milano dal 1450 al 1550: nuovi documenti,' *Rivista italiana di musicologia* XXI/1 (1986), 31-60.

Borrono, Pietro Paolo. *Intavolatura di lauto*. Venice: Girolamo Scotto, 1548.

Boyleau, Simon. *Madrigali a IIII, V, VI, VII, et VIII voci*. Milan: Francesco e Simone Moscheni, 1564.

_____. *Modulationes in Magnificat ad omnes tropos . . .quatuor, quinque, ac sex vocibus distinctae*. Milan: Pacifico Ponzio, 1566.

Brauner, Patricia B. 'Giuseppe Caimo, "nobile milanese."' Ph.D. dissertation, Yale University, 1969.

Brenet, Michel. *Musique et musiciens del la vieille France*. Paris: Librairie Félix Alcan, 1911.

Breviarium ambrosianum. Milan: Matthaeus Besutius, 1574.

_____. Milan, 1582; reprinted haeredum Pacificij Pontij, 1649.

Breviarium iuxta istitutionem Sancti Ambrosij. Venice: Hieronymo Scotto, 1539.

Breviarium mediolanense. Milan: Nicolai Landriani et Andrea Opicini, 1549.

Breviarium romanum. Lugduni: apud Theobaldum Paganum et haeredes Iacopo Iunctae, 1556.

Breviarium romanum nuper impressum. Venice: haeredes Luce Antonius Iuncte, 1567.

Bridgman, Nanie. 'La participation musicale a l'entrée de Charles Quint a Cambrai,' *Fêtes et Cérémonies au temps de Charles Quint* in *Les fêtes de la Renaissance*, 3 vols., ed. Jean Jacquot. Paris: Editions du Centre National de la Recherche Scientifique, 1960, II, 235-254.

Brivio, Ernesto. 'Fabbrica del Duomo,'in *Il Duomo di Milano: Dizionario storico artistico e religioso*, 2nd edn, ed. Guilia Benati and Anna Maria Roda. Milan: NED, 2001, 244-247.

Brown, Howard Mayer. *Instrumental Music Printed before 1600*. Cambridge: Harvard University Press, 1965.

_____., ed. *Milan, Archivio della Veneranda Fabbrica del Duomo, Sezione Musicale, Librone 3 (olim 2267)*, fascimile edition. New York and London: Garland, 1987.

Brusa, Marco. 'Hermann Matthias Werrecoren 'maestro di cappella del Domo di Milano' 1522-1550, Biografia. Bibliografia. Elenco delle opere,' *Rivista internazionale di musica sacra* XV/3-4 (1994), 173-229.

Bourne, M. 'Gonzaga, Cesare,' *Dizionario biografico degli italiani*. Cantanzaro: Grafiche Abramo S. r. l., 2001, LVII, 699-701.

Bugati, Gaspare. *L'aggiunta dell'Historia universale et delle cose di Milano . . .dall 1566 fin'al 1581*. Milan: Francesco ed Heredi di Simon Tini, 1587.

_____. *Histoire universale di M. Gaspare Bugati milanese*. Venetia: Gabriele Gioliti de Ferrari, 1571.

Burigozzi, Marco. *Cronaca milanese di Gianmarco Burigozzi merzaro dal 1500 al 1544*.

Milan: Francesco e Simone Tini, 1587; reprinted in *Archivio storico italiano* III (1842), 421ff.

Calusco, Bernardino, ed. *Mutetarum divinitatis liber primus*. Milan: Giovanni Antonio Castiglione, 1543.

Calvete de Estrella, Juan Cristóbal. *El felicísimo viaje del muy alto y muy poderoso Príncipe Don Felipe*. Anvers: Martin Nucio, 1552; reprinted Madrid: Sociedad de Bibliófilos Españoles, 1930.

Cardamone, Donna G. 'Orlando di Lasso and Pro-French Factions in Rome,' *Orlandus Lassus and his Time*. Peer: Alamire Foundation, 1995, 23-47.

Cardanus, Hieronymus. *Writings on Music* in *Musicological Studies and Documents* 32, trans. and ed. Clement A. Miller. Rome: American Institute of Musicology, 1973.

Casimiri, Raffaele. 'Un accenno poetico a Giosquino e Finoto di Francesco Spinola' (1520?-1567), *Note d'Archivio* VIII/1 (1931), 143-145.

_____. '"Disciplina Musicae" e "Maestri di Capella" dopo il Concilio di Trento nei Maggiori Istituti Ecclesiastici di Roma,' *Note d'Archivio* XII (1935), 1-26.

Castiglione, Giambattista. *Istoria delle scuole della dottrina cristiana fondata a Milano*, 2 vols. Milan: Cesare Orena nella Stamperia Malatesta, 1800.

Cattaneo, Enrico. *Maria santissima nella storia della spiritualità Milanese* in *Archvio Ambrosiano* VIII. Milan, 1955.

_____. 'Elezione degli arcivescovi' *Storia di Milano*, 16 vols. Milan: Giovanni Treccani degli Alfieri, 1961a, IX, 509-542.

_____. 'La tradizione ambrosiana,' *Storia di Milano*, 16 vols. Milan: Giovanni Treccani degli Alfieri, 1961b, IX, 543-573.

Certorio delgi Ortensi, Ascanio. *I grandi apparati e feste fatte in Melano dalli Illustr. et Eccell. S. il Duca di Sesso Governatore . . .in casa dell'Illust. S. Gio. Battista Castaldo Marchese di Cassano*. Milan: Giovann'Antonio degli Antonij, 1559.

Cesariano, Cesare. *Di Lucio Vitruvio Pollione de architectura libri dece*. Como: Gotardus da Ponte, 1521.

Chiappelli, Alberto. 'Il maestro Vincenzo Ruffo a Pistoia,' *Bulletino Storico Pistoiese* I (1899), 3-10.

Chittolini, Giorgio. 'Di alcuni aspetti della crisi dello stato Sforzesco' in *Milano e Borgogna. Due stati principeschi tra Medioevo e Rinascimento*, ed. Jean-Marie Cauchies and Giorgio Chittolini. Rome: Bulzoni Editore, 1990, 21-34.

_____. 'La crisi dello stato milanese alla fine del Quattrocento' in *Città, communità e feudi negli stati dell'Italia centro-settentrionale XIV-XVI secolo*. Milan: Edizioni Unicopli, 1996, 167-180.

Ciceri, Angelo and Eugenio Migliavacca, eds. *Liber Cappelle Ecclesiae Maioris: Quarto Codice di Gaffurio* in *Archivium musices metropolitanum mediolanense 16*. Milan: La musica Moderna S.p.A., 1968.

Compagnia di Gesù, *Lodi devote per cantarsi nelle scole della Dottrina Christiana raccolta novamente*. Milan: Pacifico Pontio, 1586.

Compère, Loyset. *Opera Omnia* IV (Motets), in *Corpus mensurabilis musicae* 15, 2 vols, ed. Ludwig Finscher. Rome: American Institute of Musicology, 1961.

Constitutioni et Regole della Compagnia, et scuole della dottrina cristiana. Milan: Pacifico Pontio, 1585.

Cordero di Pamparato, S. 'Emanuele Filiberto di Savoia protettore dei musici,' *Rivista musicale italiana* 35 (1928), 29-49.

Costa, Gasparo. *Il primo libro de motetti et madrigali spirituali a cinque voci*. Venice: Angelo Gardano, 1581.

Crook, David. *Orlando di Lasso's Imitation Magnificats for Counter-Reformation Munich*.

Princeton: Princeton University Press, 1996.

Cuyler, Louise. *The Emperor Maximilian I and Music*. London: Oxford University Press, 1973.

D'Accone, Frank A. *The Civic Muse: Music and Musicians in Siena during the Middle Ages and the Renaissance*. Chicago and London: The University of Chicago Press, 1997.

D'Alessi, Giovanni. 'Una stampa musicale del 1566 dedicata a S. Carlo Borromeo,' *Note d'archivio* IX (1932), 255-259.

Dal Prà, Laura. *I Madruzzo e l'Europa 1539-1658*. Milano: Charta, 1993.

Daolmi, Davide. *Don Nicola Vicentino: Arcimusico a Milano*. Lucca: Liberia Musicale Italiana, 1999.

Dean, Jeffrey. 'The Evolution of a Canon at the Papal Chapel: The Importance of Old Music in the Fifteenth and Sixteenth Centuries,' in *Papal Music and Musicians in Late Medieval and Renaissance Rome*, ed. Richard Sherr. Oxford: Clarendon Press, 1998, 138-166.

De Boer, Wietse. *The Conquest of the Soul: Confession, Discipline, and Public Order in Counter-Reformation Milan*. Boston: Brill, 2001.

De Caro, Gasparo. 'Avalos, Alfonso D'. *Dizionario biografico degli italiani*. Rome: Società Grafica Romana, 1962a, IV, 612-616.

_____. 'Avalos, Carlo D',' *Dizionario biografico degli italiani*. Rome: Società Grafica Romana, 1962b, IV, 619.

_____. 'Caracciolo, Marino Ascanio,' *Dizionario biografico degli Italiani*. Rome: Società Grafica Romana, 1976, XIX, 414-425.

Degrada, Francesco. 'Musica e musicisti nell'età di Ludovico il Moro,' *Milano nell'età di Ludovico il Moro: atti del Convegno internazionale, 28 febbraio-4 marzo 1983*, 2 vols. (Milan: Commune di Milano, Archivio storico civico e Biblioteca Trivulziana, 1983), II, 409-415.

De Luca, Giuseppe. ''Traiettorie' ecclesiatiche e strategie socio-economiche nella Milano di fine Cinquecento. Il capitolo di S. Maria della Scala dal 1570 al 1600,' *Nuova rivista storica* LXXVII/3 (1993), 505-569

Dentice, Fabritio. *Da Napoli a Parma: itinerari di un musicista aristocratico. Opere vocali di Fabritio Dentice*, ed Dinko Fabris. Milan: Skira Editore, 1998.

Des Prez, Josquin. *Masses Based on Solmisation Themes* in *New Josquin Edition* 11, ed. James Haar and Lewis Lockwood. Utrecht: Koninklijke Vereniging voor Nederlandse Muziekgeschiedenis, 2002.

Dobbins, Frank. *Music in Renaissance Lyons*. Oxford: Clarendon Press, 1992.

Donà, Mariangela. *La stampa musicale a Milano fino all'anno 1700*. Florence: Leo S. Olschki, 1961.

Doni, Antonfrancesco. *L'opera musicale di Antonfrancesco Doni* in *Instituta et Monumenta* I, ed. Anna Maria Monterosso Vacchelli. Cremona: Athenaeum Cremonese, 1969.

Draper, Penny Kaye Pekrul. 'A Comprehensive Study and Critical Edition of Orfeo Vecchi's Scielta de Madrigali a Cinque Voci.' Ph.D. dissertation: Michigan State University, 1997.

Dunning, Albert. *Die Staatsmotette, 1480-1555*. Utrecht: A. Oostoek's Uitgeversmaatschappij N. V., 1970.

Einstein, Alfred. *The Italian Madrigal*, 3 vols. trans. Alexander H. Krappe, Roger H. Sessions, and Oliver Strunk. Princeton: Princeton University Press, 1949.

Eisler, William. 'Celestial Harmonies and Hapsburg Rule: Levels of Meaning in a Triumphal Arch for Philip II in Antwerp,' *Triumphal Celebrations and the Rituals of Statecraft* in *Papers in Art History from the Pennsylvania State University* VI/1. University Park: The Pennsylvania State University Press, 1990, 332-356.

Essequie celebrate nella chiesa del Domo di Milano per Carlo Quinto et per la regina Maria d'Inghilterra. Milan: Giovanbattista da Ponte e fratelli, 1559.

Fabbri, Paolo. 'Lanormativa istituzionale,' *La cappella musicale nell'Italian della Controriforma: Atti del Convegno Internazionale di Studi nel IV Centenario di Fondazione della Cappella Musicale di S. Biago di Cento*, ed. Oscar Mischiati and Paolo Russo. Florence: Leo S. Olschki, 1993.

Fenlon, Iain. 'Music, liturgy, and identity in Renaissance Venice,' *Revista de musicologia* 16/1 (1993), 603-606.

_____. 'Music, ceremony, and self-identity in Renaissance Venice' in *La cappella di San Marco nell'eta moderna* (Venice, Fondazione Ugo e Olga Levi, 1998), 7-21.

_____. *Giaches de Wert: Letters and Documents*. Abbeville: Éditions Klincksieck, 1999.

Ferrari da Passano, Carlo. *Il Duomo di Milano: Storia della Veneranda Fabbrica*. Milan: Nuove Edizioni Duomo, 1998.

Finscher, Ludwig. *Loyset Compère (c. 1450-1518): Life and Works*. Rome: American Institute of Musicology, 1964.

Fiorentino, F. 'Donna Maria d'Aragona, Marchesa del Vasto,' *Nuova Antologia* 43 (1884), 212-229.

Fiorentino, Lessandro Verini. *La entrata che ha fatto il sacro Carlo Quinto Imperadore Romano nella inclita citta di Milano et la festa fatta*. Milan: Gottardo da Ponte, 1533.

Fontana, Francesco. *Rosario della Gloriosa Vergine Raccolto dal R.P.F. Francesco Fontana Comasco* (Como: appresso G. Trova, 1587.

Forney, Kristine K. 'Music, Ritual and Patronage at the Church of Our Lady, Antwerp,' *Early Music History* 7 (1987), 1-57.

Franceschini, Gino. 'La dominazioni francese e le resaurazioni Sforzesche,' *Storia di Milano*. Milan: Giovanni Treccani degli Alfieri, 1957a, VIII, 83-132.

_____. 'Milano nell'ultima difesa della libertà italiana,' *Storia di Milano*. Milan: Giovanni Treccani degli Alfieri, 1957b, VIII, 241-276.

_____. 'Gli ultimi anni del ducato indipendente,' *Storia di Milano*. Milan: Giovanni Treccani degli Alfieri, 1961), VIII, 308-333.

Frigerio, Renata and Frigerio, Rosella. 'Giovanni Paolo Cima organista nella Madonna d S. Celso a Milano: documenti inediti dell'Archivio diocesano di Milano,' *Il flauto dolce* XVI (April 1987), 32-37.

Ganda, Arnaldo. 'Giovanni Antonio Castiglione e la stampa musicale a Milano,' *La Bibliofilía* C/2-3 (1998), 301-324.

Gatti Perer, Maria Luisa. '"In medio civitatis" Il centro di Milano tra Cinque e Seicento e il ruolo di Alessandro Bisnati nella sua definizione civile e religiosa,' *Arte Lombarda* 72/1 (1985), 18-54.

_____. 'Per la definizione dell'iconografia della Vergine del Rosario' in *Carlo Borromeo e l'opera della 'grande riforma.'* Milan: Silvana Editoriale, 1997, 185-216.

Geisberg, Max. *The German Single-Leaf Woodcut 1500-1550*, rev. and ed. Walter L. Strauss. New York: Hacker Art Books, 1974.

Getz, Christine. 'The Milanese Cathedral Choir under Hermann Matthias Werrecore, maestro di cappella 1522-1550,' *Musica Disciplina* XLVI (1992), 169-222.

_____. 'New Light on the Milanese Career of Hoste da Reggio,' *Studi musicali* XXVII/2 1998a), 287-309.

_____. 'The Sforza Restoration and the Founding of the Ducal Chapels at Santa Maria della Scala in Milan and Sant'Ambrogio in Vigevano,' *Early Music History* 17 (1998b), 109-159.

_____. 'Simon Boyleau and the Church of the 'Madonna of Miracles': Educating and Cultivating the Aristocratic Audience in Post-Tridentine Milan,' *Journal of the Royal Music Association* 126/2 (2001), 145-168.

Gillet, Joseph E. 'Was Secchi's *Gl'Inganni* performed before Philip of Spain?' *Modern*

Language Notes XXXV (1920), 395-401.

Gorse, George. 'Between Empire and Republic,' *Triumphal Celebrations and the Rituals of Statecraft* in *Papers in Art History from the Pennsylvania State University* IV/1. University Park: The Pennsylvania State University Press, 1990, 188-256.

Grendler, Paul. F. *Schooling in Renaissance Italy.* Baltimore and London: The Johns Hopkins University Press, 1989.

Haar, James. 'The 'madrigal arioso": a mid-century development in the cinquecento madrigal,' *Studi musicali* 12 (1983), 203-219.

_____. 'Lassus: (1) Orlande de Lassus,' *The New Grove Dictionary of Music and Musicians*, 2nd edn. London and New York: Macmillan Publishers, Ltd., 2001, XIV, 295-322.

Haberl, F.X. 'Matthais Hermann Werrecorensis. Eine bibliographisch-kritische Studie,' *Monatschefte für Musikgeschichte* III (1871), 197-212.

Harrán, Don, ed. *The Anthologies of Black-Note Madrigals*, 5 vols. Rome: American Institute of Musicology, 1980.

Hoste da Reggio. *Il primo libro delli madrigali a cinque voci.* Venice: Hieronymo Scotto, 1554a.

_____. *Il primo libro de madrigali a tre voci.* Milan: Francesco et Simone Moscheni, 1554 b.

_____. *Il secondo libro delli madrigali a quattro voci.* Venice: Hieronymo Scotto, 1554c.

_____. *Il terzo libro delli madrigali a quattro voci,* Venice: Hieronymo Scotto, 1554d.

_____. *Il primo libro de madrigali a tre voci novamente per Antonio Gardane ristampati* Venice: Gardane, 1562.

_____. *Primo libro de madrigali a quattro voci* in *Sixteenth-Century Madrigal* 8 New York and London: Garland Publishing, Inc., 1988a.

_____. *Il secondo libro delli madrigali a quattro voci* in *Sixteenth-Century Madrigal* 9, ed Jessie Ann Owens. New York and London: Garland Publishing, Inc., 1988b.

Ianziti, Gary. 'Patronage and the Production of History: The Case of Quattrocento Milan,' *Patronage, Art and Society in Renaissance Italy.* Oxford: Clarendon Press, 1987, 299-311.

Intabolatura de leuto de diversi autori. Milan: Giovanni Antonio Casteliono, 1536; reprinted Florence: Studio per Edizioni Scelte, 1979.

Interrogatorio del maestro al discepolo per istruir li fanciulli. Milan: Vincenzo Girardoni ad instanza de M. Matteo de Besozzo , al segno della stella, 1568.

Jacquot, Jean. 'Panorama des Fêtes et Cérémonies du Règne,' *Fêtes et Cérémonies au temps de Charles Quint*, 3 vols. Paris: Editions du Centre National de la Recherche Scientifique, 1960, II, 413-491.

Janequin, Clément. *Chansons polyphoniques*, ed. A. Tilman Meritt et François Lesure. Le Remparts, Monaco: Éditions de L'oiseau-Lyre, 1971.

Jedin, Hubert. *Carlo Borromeo.* Rome, 1971.

Kastner, Marcario Santiago. 'Il soggiorno italiano di Antonio e Juan de Cabezòn,' *L'Organo* I (January 1960), 49-69.

Kaufmann, Henry William. *Musicological Studies and Documents 11: The Life and Works of Nicola Vicentino.* Rome: American Institute of Musicology, 1966.

Kendrick, Robert. *Celestial Sirens: Nuns and their Music in Early Modern Milan.* Oxford: Clarendon Press, 1996.

_____. *The Sounds of Milan, 1585-1650.* Oxford and New York: Oxford University Press, 2002.

Kroyer, Theodor. *Die Anfänge der Chromatik im italischen Madrigal des XVI Jahrhunderts.* Leipzig: Breitkopf und Härtel, 1902.

Kurtzman, Jeffrey. 'Tones, modes, clefs and pitch in Roman cyclic Magnificats of the 16th century,' *Early Music* 22/4 (1994), 641-664.

Lambrecht, Jutta. *Das 'Heidelberger Kapellinventar' von 1544 (Codex Pal. Germ. 318): Edition und Kommentar,* 2 vols. Heidelberg: Heidelberger Bibliothekschriften, 1987.

_____. 'Peschin, Gregor,' *The New Grove Dictionary of Music and Musicians,* 2nd edn. London: Macmillan Publishers Ltd., 2001, XIX, 482.

Lasso, Orlando di. *Canzoni villanesche and villanelle,* ed. Donna G. Cardamone, in *Recent Researches in Music of the Renaissance* 82-83. Madison: A-R Editions, 1991.

Ledesma, Diego di. *Giesu Maria. Dottrina Christiana, a modo di dialogo del Maestro et Discepolo per insegnare alli Fanciulli.* Milan: Pacifico Pontio, 1576.

Ledesma, Dottore della Compagnia di Gesù, *Modo per insegnar la Dottrina Christiana.* Rome: per gli heredi d'Antonio Blado, 1573.

Lewalski, Kenneth A. 'Sigismund I of Poland: Renaissance King and Patron,' *Studies in the Renaissance* XIV (1967), 49-72.

Leydi, Silvio. *Sub umbra imperialis aquilae: Immagine del potere e consenso politico nella Milano di Carlo V.* Florence: Leo S. Olschki, 1999.

Libro delle litanie secondo l'ordine Sant'Ambrogio per la città di Milano. Milan: al segno della Croce d'Oro, 1546.

Lightbown, Ronald. *Mantegna.* Berkeley and Los Angeles: University of California Press, 1986.

Liva, Giovanni. 'Il controllo e la repressione degli «ozioso e vagabondi»: la legislazione in età spagnola,' *La città e i poveri,* ed. Danilo Zardin. Milano: Jaca, 1995.

Lockwood, Lewis. *The Counter-Reformation and the Masses of Vincenzo Ruffo.* Venice: Fondazione Giorgio Cini, 1967.

_____. 'The Counter-Reformation and the Sacred Music of Vincenzo Ruffo.' Ph.D. dissertation, Princeton University, 1960.

_____. *Music in Renaissance Ferrara 1400-1505.* Oxford: Clarendon Press, 1984.

_____. 'Adrian Willaert and Cardinal Ippolito I d'Este: New Light on Willaert's Early Career in Italy, 1515-1521,' *Early Music History* 5 (1985), 85-112.

_____ and Amati-Camperi, Alexandra, 'Ruffo, Vincenzo' in *The New Grove Dictionary of Music and Musicians,* 2nd ed. New York and London: Macmillan Publishers, Ltd., 2001a, XXI, 874-875.

_____ with Giulio Ongaro, Michele Fromson, and Jessie Ann Owens 'Willaert, Adrian,' *The New Grove Dictionary of Music and Musicians,* 2nd edition. London: Macmillan Publishers, Ltd., 2001b, XXVII, 389-400.

Lomazzo, Giovanni Paolo. *Libro terzo dei grotteschi* in *Rime di Giovannni Paolo Lomazzo Milanese pittore divise in sette libri.* Milan: Paolo Gottardo Pontio, 1587.

_____ *Rabisch (1589),* ed. Dante Isella. Turin: Einaudi, 1993.

Lunelli, Renato. 'Contribuiti trentini alle relazioni musicali fra l'Italia e la Germania nel Rinascimento,' *Acta musicologica* XXI (1949), 41-71.

Lynch, John. *Spain 1516-1598: From Nation State to World Empire.* Oxford and Cambridge: Basil Blackwell, 1991.

Manchicourt, Pierre de. *Opera Omnia* VI in *Corpus mensurabilis musicae* 55, ed. Laverne J. Wagner. Rome: American Institute of Musicology, 1984.

Marchi, Lucia. 'Simon Boyleau: studio biografico ed edizione critica dei Madrigali a quattro voci (1546).' Tesì di laurea discussed at the Università degli Studi di Pavia, Scuola di Paleografia e Filologia Musicale, 1995-1996.

_____. 'La cappella musicale del Duomo di Torino nel tardo Cinquecento e la reggenza di Simon Boyleau' in *Barocco padano 2: Atti del X Convegno internazionale sulla musica sacra nei secoli XVII-XVIII* (Como: A.M.I.S., 2002), 387-407.

Maselli, Domenico. 'I concilii provinciali nella prassi di S. Carlo e i loro rapporto con il

Concilio di Trento,' *Storica borromaica* 7 (1993), 71-81.

Massetto, Gian Paolo. 'Monarchia spagnola, senato e governatori: la questione delle grazie nel Ducato di Milano. Secoli XVI-XVII,' *Archivio Storico lombardo*, Serie 11, VII (1990), 75-112.

McGinnis, Katherine Tucker. 'At Home in the 'casa del trombone': a Social-Historical View of Sixteenth-Century Milanese Dancing Masters,' Proceedings of the Society of Dance History Scholars XX (1997), 203-216.

_____. 'Moving in High Circles: Courts, Dances, and Dancing Masters in Italy in the Long Sixteenth Century.' Ph.D. dissertation, University of North Carolina at Chapel Hill, 2001.

Merkley, Paul A. and Merkley, Lora L.M. *Music and Patronage in the Sforza Court.* Amsterdam-Cremona: Brepols, 1999.

Meroni, Paola. 'Santa Maria della Scala: un aspetto della politica ecclesiatica dei duchi di Milano,'*Archivio Storico Lombardo* 115/6 (1989), 37-89.

Miller, Clement A. 'Jerome Cardan on Gombert, Phinot, and Carpentras,' *Musical Quarterly* LVIII/3 (1972), 412-419.

Mischiati, Oscar. 'Recensione di *Sei secoli di musica nel Duomo di Milano* a cura di Graziella De Florentiis [e] Gian Nicola Vessia,' *L'organo* XXVII (1991-1992), 178-184.

Missale secundum morem . . . S. Ambrosij. Milan: Jo. Angelo Schinzenzeller, 1522.

Mitchell, Bonner. *The Majesty of State: Triumphal Progressions of Foreign Sovereigns in Renaissance Italy 1494-1600.* Florence: Leo S. Olschki, 1986.

Mompellio, Federico. 'La capella del Duomo da Matthias Hermann di Vercore a Vincenzo Ruffo,' *Storia di Milano*. Milan: Giovanni Treccani degli Alfieri, 1957, IX, 749-785.

_____. 'La cappella del Duomo dal 1573 al 1714,' *Storia di Milano* (Milan: Giovanni Treccani degli Alfieri, 1957), XVI, 506-554.

Monti, Urbano. Delle cose piu notabili successe alla città de Milano. Bilioteca Ambrosiana P.248-251bis.

Morigia, Paolo. *Historia dove si narra l'origine della famosa divotione della Chiesa della Madonna, posta vicina à quella di S. Celso di Milano.* Milano: Pacifico Pontio, 1594.

_____. *La nobiltà di Milano.* Milan: Pacifico Pontio, 1595.

_____. *La nobiltà di Milano.* Milan: Giovanni Battista Bidelli, 1615; reprinted 1619.

_____. *Il supplimento della nobiltà di Milano.* Milan: Giovanni Battista Bidelli, 1619.

_____. *Origine miraculosa della celebre Madonna appresso a S. Celso in Milano riconosciuta ed illustrata da Giuseppi Girolamo Sememzi.* Milan: Ambrogio Ramellati, 1700.

Motetti del Fiore IV. Lyons: Jacques Moderne, 1539.

Motta, Emilio. 'Musici alla corte degli Sforza,' *Archivio storico lombardo* XIV (1887), 29-64.

Mozzarelli, Cesare. 'Patrizi governatori nello stato di Milano a mezzo il cinquecento. Il caso di Ferrante Gonzaga,' in *L'Italia degli Austrias. Monarchia cattolica e domini italiani nei secoli XVI e XVII*, ed. Gianvittorio Signorotto. Mantua: Edizioni Centro Federico Odorici, 1993, 119-134.

Murray, Russell. 'The Voice of the Composer: Theory and Practice in the Works of Pietro Pontio.' Ph.D. dissertation, University of North Texas, 1989.

_____. 'Pontio, Pietro,' *The New Grove Dictionary of Music and Musicians*, 2nd edn. London and New York: Macmillan Publishers, Ltd., 2001, vol. 20, 97-98.

Mutini, C. 'Contile, Luca,' *Dizionario biografico degli italiani*. Rome: Società Grafica Romana, 1983, XXVIII, 497-498.

Nobili Volterano, Alberto de. *La triomphale entrata del serenissimo prence di Spagna nell'inclitta città di Melano.* Milan: Antonio Borgo, 1548.

Noblitt, Thomas L. 'The Ambrosian Motetti Missales Repertory,' *Musica Disciplina* XXII (1968), 77-103.

Nugent, George. 'Berchem, Jachet de,' *The New Grove Dictionary of Music and Musicians*, 2nd edn. London and New York: Macmillan Publishers, Ltd., 2001, III, 304-306.

Ordo oficij divini. Rome: In aedibus Populi Romani, 1584.

O'Regan, Noel. *Institutional Patronage in Post-Tridentine Rome: Music at Santissima Trinità dei Pelligrini 1550-1650.* London: Royal Music Association, 1995.

Ormaneto, Niccolò. *Interrogatorio della Dottrina Christiana.* Milan: Pacifico Pontio ad instanza di Matteo Besozzo, 1575.

Palestrina, Giovanni Pierluigi da. *Liber III. Motectorum quinque vocum.* Milan: Francesco ed eredi Simonis Tini, 1587.

Paschini, Pio. 'Un umanista disgraziato nel Cinquecento. Publio Francesco Spinola,' *Nuovo archivio veneto, serie II*, XXXVII (1919), 65-186.

Pastore, Alessandro. *Marcantonio Flaminio, Fortune e sfortune di un chierico nell'Italia del cinquecento.* Milan: Franco Angeli, 1981.

Pavan, Franco. 'Francesco Canova and his Family in Milan: New Documents,' *Journal of the Lute Society of America* XXIV (1991), 1-13.

Payne, Robert. *The Roman Triumph.* London, New York, and Toronto: Abelard-Schuman, Ltd., 1962.

Pedrocchi, Anna Maria. 'Il coro della chiesa di San Fedele in Milano,' *Arte Lombarda* 65 (1983), 89-92.

Phinot, Dominici. *Opera Omnia I: Motets* in *Corpus mensurabilis musicae* 59, ed. Janez Höfler. Rome: American Institute of Musicology, 1972.

_____. *Opera Omnia II: Motets* in *Corpus mensurabilis musicae* 59, ed. Janez Höfler. Rome: American Institute of Musicology, 1974.

Pirotta, Nino. *Music and Theatre from Poliziano to Monteverdi*, trans. Karen Eales. Cambridge: Cambridge University Press, 1982.

Pissavino, Paolo. 'Per un'immagine sistemica del milanese spagnolo. Lo stato di Milano come arena di potere,' *Lombardia borromaica. Lombardia spagnola*, ed. Paolo Pissavino and Gianvittorio Signorotto. Rome: Bulzoni editore, 1995, 163-231.

Pistarino, Geo. 'Un episodio della vita di Pietro Paolo Borrono,' *Rivista musicale italiana* 51 (1949), 299-305.

Plutarch, *Lives of Dion and Brutus, Timoleon and Aemilius Paulus*, trans. Bernadotte Perrin. Cambridge: Harvard University Press, 1943.

Porro, G. *Catalogo dei Codici Manoscritti della Trivulziana.* Turin, 1884.

Powers, Katherine 'Vergine bella as Devotional Song in the Cinquecento,' paper presented at the annual national meeting of the South-Central Renaissance Conference, April 2001.

Prizer, William F. 'Music at the Court of the Sforza: The Birth and Death of a Musical Center,' *Musica Disciplina* XLIII (1989), 141-193.

_____. 'Secular Music at Milan during the Early Cinquecento: Florence, Biblioteca del Conservatorio, MS Basevi 2441,' *Musica Disciplina* L (1996), 9-57.

Psalmista secundum more curie Romane. Milan: frati di Legnano, 1569.

Raineri, Antonfrancesco. *Pompe di Messer Atonfrancesco Raineri.* Milan: Giovanni Antonio Borgia, 1553.

Reese, Gustave. 'The Polyphonic Magnificat of the Renaissance as a Design in Tonal Centers,' *Journal of the American Musicological Society* 13 (1960), 68-78.

Reggiori, Ferdinando. *Il santuario di Santa Maria presso San Celso e i suoi tesori* (Milano: Banco popolare di Milano, 1968.

Regole appartenenti alle Donne della Congregatione della Gloriosssima Vergine Madre Maria nella Chiesa Metropolitana. Milan: Michel Tini, 1582.

Riccucci, Giuseppe. 'L'attività della cappella musicale di S. Maria presso S. Celso e la condizione dei musici a Milano tra il XVI e il XVII secolo' in *Intorno a Monteverdi*, ed.

Maria Caraci Vela and Rodobaldo Tibaldi. Lucca: L.I.M., 1999, 289-312.

Ridolfi, R.M. 'Gonzaga, Ippolita,' *Dizionario biografico degli italiani*. Cantanzaro: Grafiche Abramo S. r. l., 2001, LVII, 794-796.

Riegel, Nicole. *Santa Maria presso San Celso in Mailand: Der Kirchenbau und seine Innendekoration 1430-1563*. Worms am Rhein, 1998.

Roncaglia, G. *La cappella musicale del Duomo di Modena*. Florence: Leo S. Olschki, 1957.

Rostirolla, Giancarlo. 'Laudi e canti sprituali nelle edizioni della prima "controriforma" Milanese' in *Carlo Borromeo e l'opera della 'grande riforma.'* Milan: Silvana Editore, 1997.

Ruff, Julius R. *Violence in Early Modern Europe*. Cambridge: Cambridge University Press, 2001.

Ruffo, Vincenzo. *Il primo libro de motetti a cinque voci*. Milan: Giovanni Antonio Castiglione, 1542.

_____. *Seven Masses* in *Recent Researches in Renaissance Music* XXII and XXIII, ed. Lewis Lockwood. Madison: A-R Editions, 1979.

_____. *Il primo libro de motetti a cinque voci* (Milan, 1542) in *Sixteenth Century Motet* 19, ed. Richard Sherr. New York and London: Garland, 1988.

_____. *Salmi suavissimi et devotissimi a cinque voci,* ed. Mauro Casadei Turroni Monti and Carlo Berlese. Lucca: Libreria Musicale Italiana, 1999.

Ruggiero, Guido. Violence in Early Modern Venice. New Brunswick: Rutgers University Press, 1980.

Sandàl, Ennio. *Editori e tipograpfi a Milano nel cinquecento*. Baden-Baden: Valentin Koerner, 1977.

_____. *L'arte della stampa a Milano nell'èta di Carlo V* (1526-1556) in *Bibliotheca Bibliographica Aureliana* CXIV. Baden-Baden: Valentin Koerner, 1988.

Santa Cruz, Alonso de. *Crónica del Emperador Carlos V* , 1551. Printed in Madrid: Caracas, Patronato de Húerfanos de Intendencia é Intervención Militare, 1925.

Sannazzaro, Giovanni Battista. 'Altari,' *Il Duomo di Milano: Dizionario storico*, 2nd edn, ed. Giulia Benati and Anna Maria Roda. Milan: NED, 2001, 14-25.

Santoro, Caterina. *Gli Sforza: La cassata nobilare che resse il ducato di Milano dal 1450 al 1535*. Milano: TEA Storica, 1994.

Sartori, Claudio. 'Matteo da Perugia e Bertrand Ferragut, i due primi maestri di cappella del Duomo di Milano,' *Acta Musicologica* XXVIII/1 (1956), 12-27.

_____. 'La cappella del Duomo dalle origini a Franchino Gaffurio,' *Storia di Milano*. Milan: Giovanni Treccani degli Alfieri, 1957a, IX, 725-734.

_____. *La cappella musicale del Duomo di Milano: Catalogo delle musiche dell'Archivio della Veneranda Fabbrica del Duomo*. Milan: Istituto Editoriale Italiano, 1957b.

_____. 'La musica nel Duomo di Savona dal XVI al XVII secolo,' *Nuova rivista musicale italiana* XVI (1981), 259-270.

Scalvo, Bartolomeo. *Le Meditationi del Rosario della gloriosissima Maria Vergine*. Milan: Pacifico Pontio, 1569.

_____. *Meditationi del Rosario della Gloriosa Maria Vergine.*Venice: Domenico e Giovanni Battista fratelli Guerra, 1583.

Scattolin, Pier Paolo. 'Werrecore, Matthias Hermann,' *The New Grove Dictionary of Music and Musicians*, 2nd edn. London: Macmillan Publishers Ltd., 2001, XXVII, 296.

Schmidt, Lothar. 'Beobachtungen zur Passionsthematik im italienischen geistlichen Madrigal,' Schütz-Jahrbuch 13 (1994), 67-84.

Scogna, Flavio Emilio. 'La musica nel Duomo di Savona dal XVI al XVII secolo,' *Nuova rivista musicale Italiana* XVI (1981), 261-262.

_____. *Vita musicale a Savona dal XVI al XVII secolo*. Savona: Cassa di Risparmio di Savona, 1982.

Sella, Domenico. *Lo stato di Milano in età spagnola*. Turin: UTET Libreria, 1987.

Sherr, Richard. 'Competence and incompetence in the papal choir in the age of Palestrina,' *Early Music* XXII/4 (November 1994), 607-629.

Signorotto, Gianvittorio. *Milano spagnola: Guerra, istituzioni, uomini di governo (1635-1660)*. Milan: Sansoni, 1996.

Simonsfeld, Henry. 'Mailänder Briefe zur bayerischen und allgemeinen Geschichte.' *Abhandlungen der historischen Classe der königlich bayerischen Akademie der Wissenschaften* XXII (1902), 233-480.

Societas Nominis Jesù, *Lodi, e Canzoni Spirituali per cantare insieme con la Dottrina Christiana*. Milan: Pacifico Pontio, 1576.

Spinola, Publio Francesco. *Epigrammi Liber* III in *P. Francisci Spinulae Mediolanensis Opera omnia*. Venice: I. Zileti, 1563.

Stras, Laurie. ''Onde havrà'l mond'esempio et vera historia:' Musical Echoes of Henry III's Progress through Italy,' *Acta Musicologica* 72/1 (2000), 7-41.

Strohm, Reinhard. *Music in Late Medieval Bruges*. Oxford: Clarendon Press, 1990.

Strong, Roy. *Art and Power: Renaissance Festivals 1450-1650*. Berkeley and Los Angeles: University of California Press, 1984.

Taglia, Pietro. *Il primo libro de madrigali a quattro voci (Milan, 1555)* in *Sixteenth-Century Madrigal* 27, ed. Jessie Ann Owens. New York and London: Garland Publishing, Inc., 1995.

Taricani, Jo Ann. 'The Early Works of Jacquet de Berchem: Emulation and Parody,' *Revue Belge de Musicologie* 46 (1992), 53-79.

Tarrini, Maurizio. 'Contribuito alla biografia di Vincenzo Ruffo: l'attività a Savona e Genova (1542-1546, 1562),' *Note d'archivio per la storia musicale, nuova serie* IV (1986), 105-118.

Tavola della Dottrina Christiana. Parma: appresso Sebastiano Viotti, 1563.

Toffetti, Marina. 'Nuovi documenti su Orfeo Vecchi,' *Nuova Rivista Musicale Italiana* 30/3-4 (1996), 445-465.

Tomaro, John B. 'San Carlo Borromeo and the Implementation of the Council of Trent' in *San Carlo Borromeo: Catholic Reform and Ecclesiastical Politics in the Second Half of the Sixteenth Century*, ed. John M. Headley and John B. Tomaro. London and Toronto: Associated University Presses, 1988, 67-84.

Torre, Barbara. 'Alcune note su uno sconosciuto ritratto di musicista del XVI secolo,' *Rivista italiana di musicologia* XIX/1 (1994), 7-26.

Torri, Luigi. 'Vincenzo Ruffo, madrigalista e compositore di musica sacra del sec. XVI,' *Rivista Musicale Italiana* III (1896), 635-683.

Turrini, Miriam. ''Riformare il mondo a vera vita christiana': le scuole di catechismo nell'Italia del Cinquecento,' *Annali dell'Istituto storico italo-germanico in Trento* VII (1981), 419-447.

Turrini, Mons. Giuseppe. 'Il maestro fiammingo Giovanni Nasco a Verona (1547-1551),' *Note d'Archivio* XIV/4-6 (July-December 1937), 419-447.

Ulloa, Alfonso. *Vita e fatti dell'invitissimo Imperator Carlo Quinto*. Venice: Vincenzo Valgrese, 1562.

———. *Vita del valorosissima e gran capitano Don Ferrante Gonzaga*. Venice: Nicolò Bevilacqua, 1563.

Vale, Giuseppe. 'Gli ultimi anni di Vincenzo Ruffo,' *Note d'Archivio* I/1 (March 1924), 78-81.

Vecchi, Orfeo. *La Donna vestita di sole*. Milan: erede di Simone Tini e Giovanni Francesco Besozzi, 1602.

_____. *Scielta de madrigali à cinque voci . . .accomodati in motetti.* Milan: per l'erede di Simon Tini e Filippo Lomazzo, 1604.

_____. *Missarum quatuor vocibus: Liber primus,* ed. Ottavio Beretta. Lucca: Libreria musicale italiana, 1991.

Verecorensis, Matthias. *Cantuum quinque vocum quos motetta vocant . . . liber primus.* Milan: Francesco et Simone Moscheni, 1555.

Verità, Landolfo. *L'entrata in Milano di Don Ferrante Gonzaga.* Milan: Antonio Borgo, 1546.

Vianello, C. 'Feste, tornei, congiure nel cinquecento milanese,' *Archivio storico lombardo, nuova serie* I (1936), 370-381.

Vigevani, Laura Mauri. 'Orfeo Vecchi, maestro di cappella at Santa Maria della Scala,' *Rivista internazionale di Musica Sacra* VII/4 (1986), 347-369; 399-448.

Visentin, Maria Cecelia. *La pietà mariana nella Milano del Rinascimento,* Milan, NED, 1995.

Vogel, Emil, with Alfred Einstein, Francois Lesure and Claudio Sartori. *Bibliografia della Musica Italiana Profana pubblicata dal 1500 al 1700,* 3 vols. Pomezia: Staderini, 1977.

Ward, Lynn Halpern. 'The *Motetti Missales* Repertory Reconsidered,' *Journal of the American Musicological Society* XXXIX/3 (1986), 491-523.

Weil, Mark S. 'Devotion of the Forty Hours and Roman Baroque Allusions,' *Journal of the Warburg and Courtauld Institutes* XXXVII (1974), 218-238.

Welch, Evelyn. 'Sight, sound and ceremony in the chapel of Galeazzo Maria Sforza,' *Early Music History* 4 (1993), 151-190.

Welch, Evelyn. *Art and Authority in Renaissance Milan.* New Haven and London: Yale University Press, 1995.

Werner, Luigi. 'Una rarità musicale della Biblioteca Vescovile di Izombathely,' *Note d'Archivio* VIII/2 (1931), 99-101.

Werrecore, Matthias. *La bataglia tagliana.* Venice: Antonio Gardane, 1549; reprinted in facsimile by Peer: Alamire, 1987.

Wert, Giaches de. *Collected Works III: Madrigals* in *Corpus mensurabilis musicae* 24, ed. Carol MacClintock. Rome: American Institute of Musicology, 1962.

Willaert, Adrian. *Opera Omnia 3: Motetti V Vocum* in *Corpus Mensurabilis Musicae* III, ed. Hermann Zenck. Rome: American Institute of Musicology, 1950.

Wytorzck, Wolfgang. 'Die Madrigale Vincenzo Ruffos.' Ph.D. dissertation, Freie Universität Berlin, 1955.

Zardin, Danilo. *Riforma cattolica e resistenze nobiliari nella diocesi di Carlo Borromeo.* Milan: Jaca, 1983.

_____. 'Nobili e ricchi nella Milano del '500: i dati di un'inchiesta vescovile del 1586,' *L'Italia degli Austrias. Monarchia cattolica e domini italiani nei secoli XVI e XVII,* ed. Gianvittorio Signorotto. Mantua: Edizioni Centro Federico Odorici, 1993, 307-357.

Index